DEDICATION

This book is dedicated first to my wife Jan and sons David and Brian for their patience and understanding, and then to my colleagues at DePaul University College of Law for their advice and support.

Jerold Friedland

D1302575

Understanding
International Business and
Financial Transactions

Jerold A. Friedland
Professor of Law
DePaul University College of Law

LexisNexis™

Library of Congress Cataloging-in-Publication Data

Friedland, Jerold A.
　　Understanding international business and financial transactions/Jerold A. Friedland.--
2nd ed.
　　　p.　cm. — (Understanding series)
　　Includes index.
　　ISBN 0–8205–6339–0 (softbound)
　　　1. Business Law—United States. 2. Foreign trade regulation—United States 3.
　　Export sales contracts. 4. Foreign exchange—Law and legislation. I. Title II.
　　Understanding series (New York, N.Y.)
　　KF390.B8 F75 2005
　　346.7307—dc22   2005013865

Editorial Offices
744 Broad Street, Newark, NJ 07102 (973) 820-2000
201 Mission St., San Francisco, CA 94105-1831 (415) 908-3200
701 East Water Street, Charlottesville, VA 22902-7587 (804) 972-7600
www.lexis.com

PREFACE TO THE SECOND EDITION

This second edition reflects recent developments relating to international business and finance and expands the discussion about issues and geographic areas that have become increasingly important. As with the first edition, this book is designed to provide an overview of many topics relating to international business and finance, and serve as a guide to the basic issues that confront attorneys and businesspeople in international transactions. My thanks to Greg Ealick and the editorial staff at Lexis for their patience and assistance.

Jerold A. Friedland
Wilmette, Illinois
June, 2005

TABLE OF CONTENTS

Page

Page

Chapter 1

MONEY, CURRENCY AND FINANCE IN INTERNATIONAL TRADE

SYNOPSIS

§ 1.01   Foreign Exchange Transactions

[1]   Money and Currency

Throughout much of human history, trade did not involve money or currency but occurred through barter; the direct exchange of goods and services. Even today, international barter, called *countertrade*, is an important segment of global commerce, particularly for countries that lack a widely acceptable currency. But barter and countertrade create two serious economic inefficiencies: (1) trade is limited to partners who both want and have specific commodities, and; (2) production cannot be specialized because many items that cannot be acquired by trade must be made locally.

Money, of course, has replaced barter in the vast majority of domestic and international transactions. Money performs three basic functions: it is a medium of exchange that may be used to acquire goods and services from anyone who is willing to accept it; it is a store of wealth that may be accumulated for future transactions; and it serves as a unit of account for determining the relative value of different commodities and services. For example, the relative values of a book and a haircut is established by the fact that the book costs twenty dollars and the haircut thirty.

Until relatively recently, most of the money used in international trade consisted of metal coins — typically gold or silver — that had a measurable intrinsic value. However, growing commerce involving larger transactions at longer distances required governments and banks to substitute paper bills for heavy coins that were difficult to transport and protect. Over time, national governments assumed sole responsibility for issuing money, and the paper bills and coins circulated by a country's government constitutes its *currency*.

Initially, paper money was acceptable as medium of exchange only if people were confident that the issuer would eventually convert it to gold or silver. Indeed, until 1933, the U.S. Treasury would exchange gold coins for paper dollars upon demand. The convertibility of paper dollars into gold ended, however, with the economic reforms enacted during the Great Depression. Since that time, creditors in the U.S. must accept paper currency in settlement of debts (*i.e.*, it is legal tender), without the ability to convert it to gold. This is true for most of the world's monetary systems; the value of a nation's currency is determined by government actions and policies rather than by reference to gold or silver.

The institution with the sole authority to issue a nation's currency is referred to as its *central bank*. Central banks also regulate the supply of credit in a country's economy. Examples of central banks are the U.S. Federal Reserve, the Bank of England, the Bank of Japan and the German Bundesbank. The European Central Bank, located in Frankfurt, acts as the central bank for the European Monetary System.

The central bank of the United States is the Federal Reserve System (the Fed), consisting of a seven-member Board of Governors in Washington, D.C., 12 regional Reserve Banks, and national and state chartered member depository institutions. The Fed controls the nation's monetary policy by managing the supply of money, setting interest rates and supervising the banking system. It also manages international monetary affairs by establishing and maintaining the value of the U.S. dollar in global markets.

The Federal Reserve usually increases or decreases the domestic money supply through *open market operations* that are directed by the Federal Open Market Committee (FOMC). The FOMC directs the New York Federal Reserve Bank to buy or sell securities (government and other kinds) to control the amount of money and credit in the economy. When the FOMC purchases securities, new money and credit are introduced into the banking system, and economic expansion is fostered. Conversely, if the FOMC sells securities, money and credit are taken out of the system and economic activity is slowed.

[2] Foreign Exchange

International transactions are often complex because they involve the currencies of more than one nation. Ordinarily, this means that the transaction will require one party to convert its nation's currency into the national currency used by the other party. For example, if a U.S. importer of Chilean wine must pay for the goods in Pesos, the importer must use its dollars to buy Pesos from a currency dealer or bank. If payment is made in dollars, the Chilean exporter must convert the dollars to Pesos if he is to spend the money in Chile.

Another country's currency is called *foreign exchange* and the price of one currency in terms of another currency is called the *foreign exchange rate*. In the U.S., the exchange rate usually is stated as how many units of a specified foreign currency will be received for a dollar. Thus, if the wine importer must pay one dollar to receive five pesos, the foreign exchange rate is 5.00. It is important to know foreign exchange rates in order to compare the international prices of goods and services. For example, if the wine importer wants to compare the prices in dollars of Chilean and Italian products quoted in their home currencies, he must know the exchange rate for Chilean pesos and Italian Euros.

Foreign exchange may consist of cash, credit and debit card funds, traveler's checks, bank deposits, and other short-term rights to funds. For larger transactions, such as those conducted by banks and foreign exchange dealers, the transactions usually are conducted by trading bank deposits denominated in different national currencies. For example, a dealer-to-dealer sale of dollars for pesos is conducted by exchanging a dollar bank deposit for a peso bank deposit.

As discussed in § 1.01[4][c] *below*, world trade now operates under a system that does not permanently fix exchange rates between currencies, but allows most currencies to fluctuate (*float*) in accordance with market conditions. In a floating rate system, many factors affect the exchange rate of a nation's currency, including the relative value of imports to exports, the amount of investment capital attracted, government monetary policies, domestic political and economic stability, and inflation and interest rates. Ultimately, the value of a nation's currency is determined by private traders in the global *foreign exchange market*.

The most important factor affecting the value of a nation's currency is the international demand for the goods and services it produces. One nation's currency is simply a commodity in other countries, so that its price (exchange rate) depends upon the demand and supply of the currency on the foreign exchange market. If Americans buy more items from foreign countries (imports) than they sell abroad (exports), eventually the supply of U.S. dollars will exceed the international demand and the exchange rate for the dollar will go down.

Changes in currency exchange rates directly affect the relative prices of foreign goods and services. Continuing the wine importer example, a decrease in the exchange rate of the peso from 5.00 to 4.00 per dollar results in a 25 percent increase in the cost to import Chilean wine. A bottle of wine priced at 20 pesos previously cost four dollars (20 ÷ 5), but now costs five dollars (20 ÷ 4). When the dollar price of a foreign currency increases, the dollar is said to *depreciate* and the other currency is deemed to *appreciate*.

In theory, an efficient, free market should restore the exchange rates between currencies to their equilibrium point. Depreciation of the dollar with respect to another currency means the dollar price of that currency (*e.g.*, peso) rises; it takes more dollars to buy a peso. Conversely, the peso price of the dollar falls; it takes fewer pesos to buy a dollar. As a result, Chilean goods become more expensive in the U.S. and U.S. products become cheaper in Chile. Absent other factors affecting prices, the lower cost for U.S. goods should increase demand for them in Chile, increasing the demand for dollars, which in turn will cause the dollar to again appreciate against the Peso.

[3] Foreign Exchange Markets

Currencies are traded in a number of financial markets centers around the world, including New York, Chicago, Los Angeles, London, Tokyo, Singapore, Frankfurt, Paris, Zurich, and Milan. Most market participants are commercial and investment banks throughout the world that are linked to each other by electronic means such as computers and telephones. The basic transaction between these participants is the purchase of a bank deposit denominated in a specific currency. Thus, a Japanese Bank that buys dollars is really buying a dollar denominated bank deposit in the U.S. or a foreign bank's claim to dollar deposits in a U.S. bank.

Because the foreign exchange market operates in different time zones, a *twenty-four hour market* has developed in which financial institutions are trading currencies every hour of every day and night. Exchange rates fluctuate all day long in response to global developments, so that market participants must carefully monitor exchange rate changes. Market information is simultaneously received by dealers around the world, resulting in an exchange rate for the key currencies that usually is the same in all financial markets. Any differences between the rates would allow for *arbitrage*, which is the buying and selling of identical securities in two markets to take advantage of price differences. Discrepancies that arise between exchange rates in different markets are quickly eliminated by arbitrage transactions that use fast technologies and communications to find rate inequalities and instantly buy and sell the currencies in two different locations. This fast, low risk profit source ensures that currency rate discrepancies do not exist for long.

Although hundreds of currencies are in use around the world, most exchange transactions involve only a few key currencies — the dollar, yen, pound sterling, and euro. By far, the dollar is the most widely traded currency, accounting for nearly 90 percent of foreign exchange transactions. Much of this dollar trading arises from transactions in which it is used as a vehicle for trading other currencies. For example, parties wishing to exchange Brazilian reals for Hungarian forints are likely to sell the reals for dollars and then sell the dollars for forints. This is because an active market and ready price are available between dollars and reals and dollars and forints, while a direct market and accurate price between reals and forints would be difficult to find. Although the dollar is the most used vehicle, other currencies such as they yen and euro also are used for this purpose.

[4] Eurodollars

Eurodollars are bank deposits denominated in dollars held in banks outside the U.S.[1] This type of deposit originally developed in Europe but is now found in major financial centers around the world, including many Asian and Caribbean nations. The deposits, which may be owned by individuals, corporations, or governments, are called Eurodollars regardless of the country where held.

Eurodollars do not represent actual U.S. dollars deposited abroad, but merely change the ownership of dollar deposits located in the U.S. For example, a U.S corporation that writes a $10 million check on its U.S. bank to deposit in a foreign bank changes ownership of the U.S. deposit from itself to the foreign bank. The foreign bank treats the transaction as if it acquired the $10 million deposit in the U.S. bank as a new asset and a new liability of $10 million to the U.S. corporation. The U.S. bank records the transaction as a shift in its $10 million liability from the corporation to the foreign bank.

The Eurodollar market has grown rapidly because it is generally free of government regulation. Eurodollar deposits are simply obligations of the banks that accept them and are not guaranteed by any government. The lack of regulation makes Eurodollar deposits more profitable for banks than deposits subject to U.S. banking requirements (such as minimum reserves and Federal Deposit Insurance premiums) and interest rates on Eurodollars generally exceed the yields of other money markets.

A major portion of global financial transactions is conducted in Eurodollars. The market is huge, consisting of many trillions of dollars deposited by large corporations, central banks, supranational institutions such as the Bank for International Settlements, and wealthy individuals. The maturity on deposits is generally short term, often less than six months. Most Eurodollar loans are quite large, going to corporations funding foreign operations, and foreign governments funding national projects or balance-of-payment deficits.

Eurobonds. Eurobonds are bonds denominated in a different currency than used by the country in which they are issued. Most Eurobonds are issued by international syndicates and are classified by reference to the currency of denomination. For example, a Japanese company may issue a eurodollar bond (i.e., a bond denominated in U.S. dollars) in any country other than the U.S. and a Euroyen bond (denominated in yen) in any country other than Japan.

Eurobonds are attractive financing instruments for several reasons. A Eurobond allows the issue to denominate its obligation in a preferred currency. The instruments also allow an issuer to offer bonds in a country without regard to many of the regulations applicable to bonds denominated

---

[1] Non-U.S. residents also may conduct Eurodollar transactions at International Banking Facilities (IBFs) in the United States. *See* Goodfriend, *Eurodollars*, Federal Reserve Bank of Richmond (1998).

in the local currency. Generally, Eurobonds have low par values that make them highly liquid.

Global Bonds. Unlike Eurobonds, Global Bonds can be issued in the same currency used by the country of issuance. For example, a global bond denominated in U.S. dollars can be issued in all countries, including the U.S. Thus, Global bonds can be issued in several markets simultaneously. However, the offering must satisfy the financial regulations of the currency denomination country, so that such offerings may be quite complex. Accordingly, Global bonds usually are issued by very large organizations with high credit ratings.

[5] Regulating Foreign Exchange Rates

National and international policies and agreements that regulate the exchange rate between different national currencies are referred to as exchange rate systems. Although many systems have been adopted over the centuries, most fall into one of two categories: fixed or floating exchange rates systems. In a *fixed exchange rate* system, a nation's currency is set at a predetermined exchange rate that does not change in response to supply and demand for the currency. Usually, a country's central bank accomplishes this by fixing the exchange rate between its currency and a commodity (such as gold), or a specific foreign currency (such as the dollar). In a *floating exchange rate* system, the central bank allows its currency exchange rate to be determined by supply and demand through trading in the foreign exchange market.

In either system, a nation's currency will appreciate or depreciate when its value changes relative to another currency. A currency appreciates when one of its units can buy more units of another currency and depreciates when one of its unit can buy fewer units of another currency. In a floating rate system, these value changes are determined by market forces. In a fixed rate system, a nation may deliberately *devalue* its currency through a downward adjustment to its official exchange rate set or "pegged" to a standard such a gold or the U.S. dollar. Conversely, a government can *revalue* its currency by an upward adjustment of the pegged exchange rate.

Freely convertible currencies that are not expected to depreciate greatly in the near future are referred to as *hard currencies.* These include key currencies such as the dollar, yen, pound and euro. A currency is convertible if it can be readily exchanged for other currencies without excessive government controls or restrictions. By contrast a currency that cannot be readily exchanged is a *soft currency.* A number of governments impose foreign exchange controls that restrict the purchase and sale of foreign currencies by residents or the purchase and sale of domestic currency by foreigners.

Advocates of fixed exchange rates (like the gold standard described *below*) argue that history shows that they provided a long period of exchange rate stability for most trading nations. Under this view, the fixed rate standard provides a simple, automatic mechanism for adjusting trade imbalances without government interference. Supporters believe that a fixed exchange rate system:

- prevents governments from adopting inflationary monetary policies;

- promotes international coordination of monetary policies by removing the ability to adopt independent monetary policies, and;

- enhances international trade and investment by eliminating exchange-rate risk.

Although a dedicated band of "gold bugs" continues to argue for restoration of the gold standard, that seems unlikely to occur anytime soon.

Many disagree that the fixed rate gold standard enhanced economic well-being. They argue that during the Great Depression the fixed rate system prevented governments from taking economic measures to restore beleaguered economies, decrease unemployment and enhance domestic living standards. Proponents of floating exchange rates hold that these systems:

- enhance optimal resource allocation in the world economy;

- allow for policies that help internal economic conditions without disrupting the balance of payments, and;

- reduce the need for unproductive foreign exchange reserves to support the fixed rate.

As described in the following sections, most of the exchange rate systems used today combine elements of fixed and floating rates.

[a] The Gold Standard

From the mid-1800s through the start of the First World War in 1914, most of the world's major trading countries used the *gold standard* of fixed currency exchange rates. The United States began to apply the gold standard in 1879, and formally adopted it by legislation in 1900. Under the gold standard, each participating country defined the price of gold in terms of its domestic currency, and promised to convert its paper currency to gold on demand at the central bank of the issuing country. Under this system, a U.S. exporter of goods to Chile could take payment in pesos, exchange the pesos for dollars at his U.S. bank, which would then exchange the pesos for dollars at a U.S. Federal Reserve bank. The Federal Reserve would ship the pesos to Chile in exchange for gold, thus increasing the U.S. gold supply and decreasing Chile's gold supply.

Because each unit of currency was backed by a specific amount of gold, a nation's money supply increased or decreased directly with the gain or loss of gold. A country that spent more for imports than it earned from exports (*i.e.*, a balance of payments deficit) had to ship gold abroad to cover the deficit. The decrease in the nation's gold stock required a reduction in its money supply, resulting in lower domestic prices and wages (deflation). A nation that exported more than it imported (*i.e.*, a positive balance of payments) received additional gold and expanded its money supply, resulting in higher domestic prices and wages (inflation). Theoretically, these wage and price increases or decreases would create shifts in trade that would automatically adjust the imbalance of payments to equilibrium and restore each country's gold and money supply. In practice, however, these automatic adjustments frequently did not occur because countries adopted policies inconsistent with a gold standard to avoid domestic unemployment or inflation.

During the First World War, many European counties stopped exchanging gold for currency and adopted floating exchange rates. After the war, the exchange rate of many European currencies fluctuated widely and steeply lost value against the U.S. dollar. Because of their weakened economies and large war debt burdens, returning to the gold standard was infeasible. The dollar became an attractive currency for international transactions because it was still convertible to gold and backed by a strong U.S. economy. Although Great Britain and other European nations reverted to the gold standard for a brief period in the 1920s, the financial strains of the Great Depression forced them to abandon it again during the early 1930s.

The Great Depression upset foreign exchange markets and devastated the international monetary system, which depended upon international cooperation. Many nations adopted unrealistic measures to restrict imports and enhance exports. These included high tariffs, trade restrictions, foreign exchange controls and steep currency devaluations. A breakdown of confidence in paper currency incited a demand for gold that central banks could not meet, requiring many nations to abandon the gold standard. As a result, trade became increasingly difficult between the many nations that abandoned the gold standard and the few, like the U.S. that continued to use it. Indeed, some governments encouraged barter arrangements as a means of avoiding international exchange transactions altogether. The resulting chaos in exchange rates contributed to a precipitous decline in international trade, which dropped by almost 65 percent between 1929 and 1932. The economic rivalries of the 1930s provided the stimulus for the economic reforms and monetary cooperation that would be implemented after the Second World War.

[b] The Bretton Woods Agreement

Toward the end of Second World War, the U.S. and Great Britain organized an international conference at Bretton Woods, New Hampshire, to plan the political and economic arrangements that would govern the post-war era. The participating nations generally agreed that chaotic international monetary conditions were causative factors in the Great Depression that subsequently led to the war. As a remedy, the U.S. and Great Britain proposed a new global system of international monetary policy cooperation that would stabilize exchange rates. The goal was to promote the free convertibility of currencies at clearly established exchange rates and to discourage the competitive monetary policies that inhibited international trade and investment during the Depression era. In July, 1944, the 44 nations convened at Bretton Woods accepted the proposed system and established the International Monetary Fund (IMF) to administer it.[2]

The Bretton Woods agreement established a foreign exchange rate system based upon gold and the U.S. dollar. In this system, participating nations "pegged" their currencies to a stated exchange rate — called "par value"— to the dollar and allowed their currencies to be converted into dollars. Dollars, in turn, could be converted into gold at the U.S. Federal Reserve if presented by other central banks. Initially, the Federal Reserve was obligated to buy or sell gold for dollars to central banks at $35 per ounce.

The IMF participants pledged to maintain stable exchanges rates for the dollar, that could be adjusted, with IMF permission, only if a "fundamental disequilibrium" arose. Their central banks would keep their currency-dollar exchange rate stable by buying or selling dollars in the exchange markets. This gold exchange system, it was believed, would impose monetary discipline on IMF members because any country that excessively expanded its money supply could not maintain its currency's par value to the dollar. A key part of the IMF agreement provided that the Fund would make loans to its members whose balance of payments problems made it difficult to stabilize their currencies.

The strong post-war economic recoveries in Europe and Japan upset the basic assumption of the Bretton Woods arrangement — that the dollar would indefinitely retain its strength and convertibility to gold. Although the initial weakness of most European economies postponed implementation of Bretton Woods, these difficulties were addressed by a massive infusion of capital through the Marshall Plan. When the IMF plan eventually was put into effect in the late 1950's, strong European and Japanese economies had improved their balance of payments, while the U.S. position had deteriorated. Foreign nations that acquired more dollars than they needed began to convert them to gold, causing the U.S. gold stock to decline. In turn, the exchange of dollars for gold accelerated as nations began to question whether the U.S. could continue the $35 per ounce convertibility standard.

Although the IMF instituted a number of measures to relieve the strains created by the dollar-gold standard, the pressure on the dollar continued and worsened. Some of this pressure arose from U.S. domestic deficits related to the Vietnam War and the social programs of the Great Society, but most was attributable to the competitiveness of the European and Japanese economies. In response to increasing demands for its gold, in 1971 the U.S. ceased converting dollars to gold and terminated the Bretton Woods system.

---

[2] The IMF began operations in Washington, D.C. in May 1946, with 39 members.

[c] The Contemporary Floating Rate System

Despite two devaluations of the dollar and several attempts to restore it, the gold standard period was over.[3] In March, 1973, the *Group of Ten* major industrial nations formally abandoned the Bretton Woods standard and allowed their currencies to float. After extensive consideration and debate, the international community accepted that a floating rate regime would be beneficial if nations were discouraged from adopting the destructive exchange rate policies of the 1930s. Accordingly, the IMF changed its Articles of Agreement in 1978 to allow member nations to select an appropriate exchange rate regime, subject to "firm surveillance" of their policies by the IMF. These policies must encourage exchange rate stability, and preclude adjusting exchange rates to obtain an unfair trade advantage or to prevent effective adjustment to an imbalance of payments.

This system, which is in effect today, permits an IMF member nation to choose the exchange rate system that best suits its economy. Most economically developed countries, like the U.S., allow their currencies to float, with limited management or intervention by central banks. For the most part, their currency exchange rates are determined in the world market. However, exchange rates are frequently influenced, or managed, through actions of governments and international monetary institutions. Generally, floating exchange rates are managed by central banks that buy or sell their currency, or another country's currency, in the foreign exchange market to influence market conditions or exchange rate movements. Many other countries peg their exchange rates to another currency such as the dollar, yen or euro.

[6] Managing Foreign Exchange Risk

Fluctuations in foreign exchange rates can create significant risks in international transactions where payment is to occur at some future date. The possibility that the value of a transaction will change because of changes in currency exchange rates is referred to as *exchange rate risk*. If, for example, our wine importer contracted to purchase wine from next year's vintage at 20 pesos per bottle (equal to four dollars), a depreciation of the dollar from 5.00 to 4.00 pesos per dollar results in a 25 percent higher cost for the wine even though its price in pesos is unchanged. The importer now needs five dollars to purchase 20 pesos instead of the four dollars required when the contract was signed. Of course, the importer will not suffer a loss if he contracted to pay for the wine in dollars instead of pesos. In that case, the exporter bears and suffers the exchange rate risk; he can exchange the four dollars per bottle for only 16 pesos rather than the 20 pesos obtainable when the contract was signed.

Foreign currencies are available in a several different markets. The *spot market* allows for immediate exchange of currencies, requiring settlement (payment) within one day (North America) or two days (other markets) after

---

[3] *See, e.g.*, Smithsonian Agreement, December 1971.

commitment. In this market, which accounts for 50 percent of foreign exchange activity, the participants agree to exchange specified amounts of currencies at the current spot exchange prices. Although frequently used by traders requiring currencies for immediate use, it does not reduce exchange rate risk with respect to future payments. Typically, businesses and investors insure or *hedge* against future adverse changes in exchange rates by purchasing derivatives — forward or futures contracts — in expectation of a later need for a foreign currency.

[a] Derivatives in General

A number of strategies exist for minimizing the exchange rate risk that can create a loss in an otherwise profitable transaction. Most of these strategies involve *derivatives*, which are financial instruments having a price that depends upon (*i.e.*, is derived from) an underlying asset such as a security or another nation's currency. Derivatives involve trading rights or obligations based on the underlying asset, but do not directly transfer interests in that property. Examples of derivatives include futures contracts, which are derivatives of commodities such as currencies, and options, which are derivatives of futures contracts. Many derivatives are traded on regulated exchange markets, while others are sold over-the-counter.

Derivatives have become somewhat notorious as a result of a number of highly-publicized profile cases involving substantial losses on derivative investments. For example, a major British Bank, Barings PLC, was bankrupted by losses one of its traders sustained on Nikkei index futures and options, while Orange County, California, one of the richest counties in the U.S., went bankrupt in 1994 due to a $1 billion loss on structured note investments. These transactions reflect the overuse of derivatives as a means of speculation, rather their more appropriate role as a hedge against the risks inherent in many transactions.

[b] Forward Contracts

A *forward* contract is an agreement between two parties to buy or sell an asset at a specified future time for a specified price. In a *forward exchange contract*, one party agrees to buy a specified amount of foreign currency from another at a stated exchange rate on a fixed, future date. For example, a U.S. company that will purchase and pay for goods from a Japanese firm in six months may contract to buy the necessary amount of yen from a bank in six months at the current dollar exchange rate. The U.S. corporation has the *long position* in this forward contract while the bank has the *short position*.

The contract requires the corporation to buy the underlying asset (yen) from the bank on the specified date and the bank must then deliver the yen to the buyer for the agreed price in dollars. Payment on the contract does not occur when the forward contract is signed, but when the foreign currency is delivered. The forward contract currently fixes the future sales price of the underlying asset, thereby reducing the buyer's risk of loss from an adverse change in the exchange rate for yen. The purchase date may be days, months or years in the future, as required to protect against adverse exchange rate change during the period of risk exposure. Because the exchange rate is fixed when the contract is signed, subsequent exchange rate fluctuations do not affect the agreed contract rate.

The value of a forward contract at inception is zero because both parties are initially obligated to provide money or commodities that are equal in value. However, the contract value will change as the value of the underlying asset increases or decreases. For example, if the value of the yen appreciates against the dollar (*i.e.*, it takes fewer yen to purchase a dollar), the value of the corporation's long position is positive and the value of the banks short position is negative. At the end of the contract term, the contract value is the difference between the contract price and the spot price for the underlying asset, and that will determine each party's gain or loss in the transaction.

The *forward exchange rate* is the rate fixed on a particular day for exchanging currency at a specified future date. If that rate is lower than the price on the spot market, the currency trades at a *forward discount*. If the rate is higher than the spot market price, the currency trades at a *forward premium*. The annualized difference between the spot market price and the forward rate is called the *forward differential*. Whether a currency trades at a premium or discount on a particular day depends upon the market's expectation, based upon current information, about its future strength or weakness.

What Determines the Forward Exchange Rate?

The difference between the spot and forward exchange rates between two currencies reflects the different interest rates in effect for risk free assets (*e.g.*, government securities) denominated in each currency. This relationship between the forward and spot exchange rates, *interest rate parity*, precludes an investor from converting assets into another currency in order to obtain a higher interest rate. If this were not the case, an investor could easily obtain the highest risk-free interest rate available in any country and then convert the investment proceeds back into his domestic currency without bearing any exchange rate risk. Too good to be true!

To illustrate, assume that a one year U.S. Treasury note pays an interest rate of 6 percent and a one year U.K. note denominated in pounds pays 7 percent. Currently, the spot exchange rate is $1.5 for £1. A $1,000 investment in the U.S. note would result in a total interest and principal payment of $1,060 at maturity. To obtain the higher U.K. rate, an investor must sell $1,000 to obtain £666, invest that amount in the bond, and then convert the investment proceeds back into dollars. The investment at 7 percent would yield a total payment of £712.62 (£666 principal plus £46.62 interest). An investor that wished to insure his investment against an adverse change in

> currency exchange rates could do so through a one year forward contract for dollars. He will find that the one year forward exchange rate is $1.487 for £1, resulting in a total sum of $1,060 from the investment (712.62 × 1.1487 = 1,060) — the same amount that he would receive from the dollar denominated investment.

Forward contracts are not traded on exchanges, but often involve banks that tailor the contracts to their client's needs. The contract terms are not standardized and vary with the purchaser's needs. Typically, forward contracts involve very large amounts, often many millions of dollars.

Because no payments are made with respect to a forward contract until maturity, a significant *credit risk* exists that one of the parties will not be able to perform. In practice, this credit risk limits the use of forward contracts to larger corporations and financial institutions that have substantial lines of credit available. For example, a manufacturer may use forward contracts in connection with its foreign currency requirements to pay for imported raw materials. Forward (and spot) contracts are marketed through a worldwide network of financial institution and banks. Forward contracts are not federally regulated, but are governed by state contract law.

[c] Currency Futures Contracts

Foreign currency futures are similar in effect to forwards; they are contracts for the future delivery of a foreign currency on a fixed future date at a specified exchange rate. Futures differ from forwards, however, in their standardization and trading venue. Unlike the individualized, tailor-made forward contract, futures are written in fixed amounts and maturity dates and regularly traded on regulated exchanges (*e.g.,* Chicago Mercantile Exchange, London International Financial Futures Exchange, Paris Marche a Terme d'Instrument Financiers). Most standard futures contracts are set at about $100,000 or less. In addition to foreign currencies, futures contracts are written on many kinds of commodities and financial assets, including agricultural products, precious metals and natural resources, and financial instruments such as fixed-income obligations and stock indices.

To ensure a readily available, liquid market for trading of futures, each futures exchange has established a *clearinghouse,* owned by the members of the exchange, that acts on behalf of the parties on both sides of a futures contract. The clearinghouse guarantees that a contract party will not sustain a loss if the other party fails to perform its financial obligations. All trades are cleared through clearinghouse members, who contribute the funds required for the clearinghouse's guarantee.

Unlike a forward contract, which does not require any payment until maturity, futures contracts are *marked to market* at the end each trading day. This means that the value of the contract is adjusted daily to reflect the changes in the underlying currency's exchange rate. These adjustments result in a daily profit or loss on the contract that is *settled* through a cash payment each day. In effect, this daily revaluation and settlement of a futures contract is equivalent to having a new futures contract written each day at the new market price. Because of this daily settlement, a futures contract entails far less credit risk of nonpayment by a contract party than a forward contract that is not settled until the end of the contract when a substantial loss may have accrued.

To ensure that all participants are able to meet the claims arising from the continuous settlement process, the purchaser of a futures contract must deposit a percentage of the contract value — called *margin* — with its broker. In effect, the margin requirement serves as security for the purchaser's obligations. The amount of the margin is adjusted daily as settlement is made to reflect changes in the value of the contract. If the purchaser has a gain, its margin account increases and it may withdraw the profit from the account. In the case of a loss, the margin account decreases. The purchaser may be required to make additional margin deposits if the daily settlements reduce the margin account below a specified level. Failure to pay the additional margin may result in liquidation of the margin account.

The vast majority of futures contracts do not actually result in a party taking delivery of the currency underlying the contract. Ordinarily, a party cancels the futures contract by buying a second contract that reverses the first, resulting in a net position of zero. Because futures contracts can be terminated so easily, they often are used by parties engaged in financial hedging or speculation, rather than to obtain foreign currency for a specific transaction. In this respect, futures differ greatly from forward contracts which are generally used by parties that intend to take delivery.

Generally, the *Commodity Futures Trading Commission* (CFTC) regulates futures contracts, including currency futures, that are traded on exchanges. The CFTC does not regulate non-exchange traded contracts such as forward contracts.[4] This limitation means that the CFTC's jurisdiction does not extend to the huge interbank market in which foreign exchange forward contracts and many other financial instruments are traded.[5] These instruments are regulated by the various Treasury Department agencies responsible for banking activities.

[d] Options

A currency option contract creates a right, but not an obligation, to buy or sell a specified amount of a currency at a specified rate on or before the contract's expiration date. Unlike futures and forward contracts, the option does not bind the participant to perform a transaction; it creates a right, not an obligation, to exercise the option. The option buyer pays a fee (premium) to the seller that depends on: (1) option's maturity; (2) the relationship between the option price and the currency spot market price, and; (3) the volatility of the currency price.

---

[4] 7 U.S.C. § 2-2a (1994).

[5] *See* 7 U.S.C. § 2(a)(1)(A)(ii) (1994).

An option purchaser need not exercise its right to buy or sell the underlying currency and obviously will not do so if a loss would be incurred. The option seller (writer), however, is obligated to perform under the contract if the option is exercised. To account for these different obligations, the option purchaser makes a *premium* payment to the option writer at the start of the contract.

The contract price is called the *strike price*. If the strike price would produce a profit for the holder if the option were exercised when the contract is made, the option is *in the money*. If a loss would result, the option is *out of the money*. Generally, the premium paid for the option reflects how much it is in the money when obtained. The value of an out of the money option usually depends upon its duration and the possible change in value over time.

An option that grants the right to buy a currency at a specified price and date is a *call option*. The seller of a call option is obligated to sell the currency at the strike price if the option is exercised. Usually, call options are bought if the currency is expected to increase in price. The option holder will exercise the option if the strike price is lower than the market price of the option. If the market price is lower, the option will not be exercised and the buyer loses the fee paid for it.

An option that grants the right to sell a currency is a *put option*. A seller of a put option must buy the currency at the strike price if the option is exercised. Typically, put options are purchased by holders of a currency who seek protection against a fall in its price. The option will be exercised if the put price is greater than the market price of the currency.

Like futures, currency options are traded on organized exchanges. These include the Philadelphia Stock Exchange and the Chicago Mercantile Exchange in the U.S. and a number of exchanges abroad such as in Singapore, Amsterdam, Paris, and Brussels. Exchange-traded options are traded in contracts that are standardized for the amount of currency, exercise price, and expiration date. Each exchange operates a clearinghouse which guarantees that a contract party will not sustain a loss if the other party fails to perform its financial obligations. No margin requirement is imposed on the option buyer, who must only pay a premium for the contract. However, the option writer does bear a financial risk on the contract and is subject to the exchange's margin account requirements.

In addition to foreign currencies, exchange-traded option contracts are written on many of the same kinds of commodities and financial assets involved in the futures markets. Options are also traded over-the-counter by banks and other financial institutions. The two basic forms of options are the *European* style option that may only be exercised on the expiration date, and the *American* style option that may be exercised at any time before or on the expiration date. Most over the counter options are European style, while most options traded on exchanges are American style.

The regulatory agency responsible for a currency option depend upon the exchange on which the option is traded. Foreign currency options traded on national securities exchanges are regulated by the Securities and Exchange Commission (SEC). Foreign currency options traded on other exchanges are regulated by the Commodity Futures Trading Commission (CFTC). The regulatory agency responsible for other types of options depends on the underlying asset. Stock options and options on securities are governed by the SEC, while commodity options are regulated by the CFTC.

[e] Swaps

Swaps are derivatives that are frequently used by large companies to lower borrowing costs and to hedge risks associated with changing interest rates or foreign exchange rates. Most swap transactions are arranged through commercial banks, utilizing customized contracts that are not traded on exchanges. A standard form contract has been developed by the *International Swaps and Derivatives Association* (ISDA), that establishes the parties' responsibilities upon default or premature termination. The key contract terms, such as price, duration, and quantity are not standardized, but are written for each transaction. Generally a swap contract is not tradable or assignable without both parties' consent. The transaction is not guaranteed by a clearinghouse so that each party bears a credit risk that the other party will not perform it financial obligations.

Generally, a swap is a contract between two parties, called *counterparties*, to exchange specified cashflows at predetermined future times. The amount of cashflow each counterparty will exchange usually is determined by reference to a hypothetical amount, called the *notional* amount, and an underlying market (*e.g.* foreign exchange, securities, or commodities) or financial index (*e.g.,* LIBOR or the Consumer Price Index). Although these transactions are tailor made to fit the specific needs of the counterparties, there are two basic categories of swaps: *interest rate swaps* (the most frequently used type), and *currency swaps*. A transaction that combines both of these variants is referred to as a *cross currency swap*.

Because most swap transactions are conducted through banks, the swap market is regulated by banking authorities rather than by securities agencies such as the SEC or CFTC. The rights of the parties under the swap contracts are governed by contract law of the relevant jurisdiction. Quite often, a swap contract specifies that the law of New York or the United Kingdom will apply because the major swap dealers are located in these places.

In regulating activities of banks with respect to swaps and other derivatives, bank examiners must assess whether these activities result in unsound banking practices. Factors considered in this assessment include:

- Whether senior managers must approve and monitor derivative transactions.

- Whether decisions about risk exposure to derivatives are made by parties that are independent of the bank's derivative transactions.

- The amount of risk the bank is exposed to on its derivative transactions.

To ensure that a bank is not exposed to excessive risk, banks are required to maintain adequate reserves of capital. The *Basel Accord*, discussed at 1.02[1][a] *below*, requires banks involved in international activities to maintain capital reserves that are determined from an analysis of the credit risk of their transactions, including their exposure to loss on derivatives.

[i] Interest Rate Swaps

Interest rate swap transactions generally involve one party that can advantageously borrow funds at a fixed interest rate and another party that can more advantageously borrow at a variable or floating rate. For example, one company may have fixed revenues and a credit rating that limits it to borrowing at variable interest rates. Another may have revenues that fluctuate with prevailing interest rates, but can borrow at long term fixed rates. In a swap, each party borrows in the market in which it has an advantage and agrees to exchange or swap its interest payments for the other party's.

In a typical interest rate swap (sometimes called a *plain vanilla* swap) contract, the *counterparties* exchange payments on a floating interest rate for payments on a fixed-interest rate for a set period. Under the contract, one counterparty agrees to exchange a series of payments calculated by applying a fixed rate of interest (the *long* position) to a *notional* principal amount for a stream of payments from the other counterparty calculated by applying a floating interest rate (the *short* position) to the notional principal amount. The principal amount is notional because each party's obligation to its lender for the underlying debt is not affected.

The floating interest rate usually is based upon a commercial index, such as LIBOR (London Interbank Offered Rate) rate, commercial paper, or Treasury bill rates. The LIBOR rate applies to loans of *Eurodollars*, which are dollars that are deposited in institutions outside the U.S. Interest rates for Eurodollar loans usually are lower than domestic rates because the loans are not subject to many U.S. banking regulations. The fixed rate usually matches the rate on a Treasury Note of comparable maturity. Ordinarily, only the difference between the cashflow obligations of the counterparties actually is paid. Accordingly, if the fixed-rate payment is $1.2 million and the floating-rate payment $1 million, the fixed-rate counterparty pays $200,000 to the floating-rate counterparty.

Example: Americo wants to borrow $100 million at a 7 percent interest rate. Euroco wants to borrow $120 million at a floating rate that tracks the 10 Year Treasury Bill. Because of their credit ratings and location, each company can borrow more advantageously at the rate the other company wants. The companies enter a swap contract, agreeing that Americo will borrow at the floating rate, and Euroco will borrow at the fixed rate and each party will make a stream of payments to the other equal to that party's interest payment obligation on a notional $100 million loan.

Because swaps are customized for each transaction, many variations of the plain vanilla swap have been created.[6] For example, the amount of each counterparty's swap payments may change over time to reflect the repayment of an amortized loan. In some swaps, both counterparties use a floating interest rate, but a different rate index (*e.g.*, LIBOR and commercial paper). In a *callable* swap, one of the counterparties has the right to prematurely terminate the contract. Quite often, an interest rate swap is linked to an interest rate option that sets a maximum (cap) or minimum (floor) for the floating rate involved in the contract. If both a cap and a floor are used, the contract is referred to as a *collar*. A *swaption* is an option on a swap that allows the swaption holder to enter or terminate a specific swap at a future time.

Pricing a swap. In a swap contract, one counterparty is exchanging a future steam of payments based upon a fixed interest rate for a future stream of payments based upon a floating rate. Accordingly, at the beginning of the contract, the fixed rate counterparty must determine that the current value of the future payments based upon the floating rate is equal to the current value of the fixed rate payments. This determination is based upon economic models that track the relationship between interest rates and future time periods, usually based upon the projected yield of risk free government securities. Once the current value of the floating rate payments under the swap is calculated as explained, the fixed rate payments are set at the amount that the provides an equal current value, so that the present value of the swap is zero.

---

[6] *See* Romano, *A Thumbnail Sketch of Derivative Securities and Their Regulation*, 55 Md. L. Rev. 1 (1996).

Interest rate swap

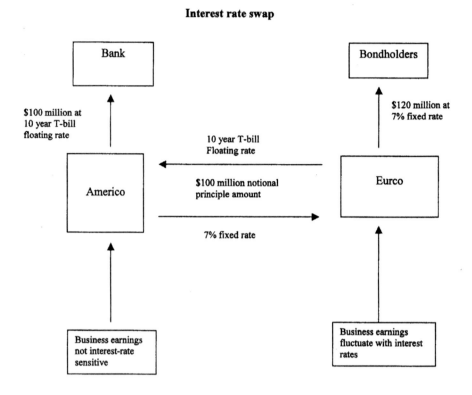

[ii] Currency Swaps

In a typical currency swap, one party agrees to make a series of payments in one currency in exchange for the other party's series of payments in another currency. A company may wish to engage in a currency swap transaction for a variety of reasons, including:

- to benefit from its better credit rating in a foreign market;
- to change a loan from one currency to another;
- to change cash flow into or out of a foreign currency;
- to hedge against exchange rate changes affecting a loan;
- to use proceeds of a loan denominated in one country's currency to meet currency needs in another country, or;
- to avoid capital or currency exchange controls in a particular country.

A currency swap contract usually requires the counterparties to —

(1) Make an initial exchange of equal principal amounts of two currencies at the spot market rate. (In some transactions this initial principal exchange does not actually occur.)

(2)   Exchange a stream of interest rate payments (or pay the net difference between them) in the swapped currencies for an agreed time period, and;

(3)   at the end of that period, re-exchange the principal amount at the initial spot market rate.

It is important to note that, unlike an interest rate swap, a currency swap involves an actual exchange of principal amounts. The requirement for a principal payment at the end of the swap creates a credit risk in a currency swap that does not exist in an interest rate swap.

Cross currency swaps. Ordinarily, in a currency swap, the interest rates that determine each party's swap payment are fixed. In a cross-currency swap, however, the interest rates may vary in the same manner as interest rate swaps. Thus, one or both interest payments may be floating. For example, a U.S. company can use a swap to convert a fixed rate dollar loan to a payment stream based upon a yen loan at a floating interest rate. The reverse also is possible and any number of cross currency swap arrangements can be structured.

Example: Americo needs to obtain $100 million worth of Yen to pay for a new plant in Japan. Americo determines that it can get the lowest borrowing rate by issuing fixed interest rate bonds in dollars and converting the borrowed dollars to Yen. Japanco wishes to borrow the same amount of dollars for its U.S. operations, but can borrow more cheaply in Japan at the LIBOR floating rate. Under their cross currency swap agreement, each party will borrow the money in its home country and swap its interest and principal payments for the other party's.

Americo sends its borrowed dollars to Japanco and Japanco sends its borrowed Yen to Americo. Americo has borrowed dollars at its lowest rate but will pay the principal and interest in Yen. Japanco has borrowed Yen at its lowest rate and will pay the principal and interest in dollars.

Cross Currency Swap

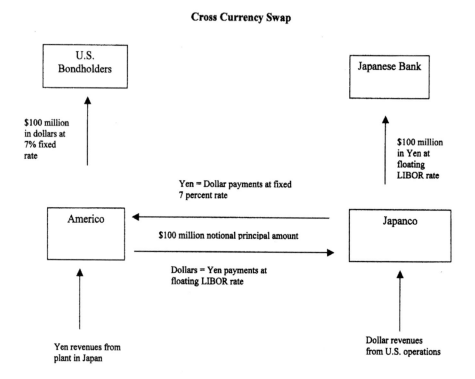

[f] Asset Securitization

Securitization is a method a company use to raise capital by selling its rights in financial assets, typically its right to receive payments on a future date (receivables), to a new specially created entity that issues securities to investors and uses the proceeds from the issue to pay for the financial assets.[7] By isolating these liquid assets from its general business risks, the company can use the assets to obtain capital at a lower cost than would be possible by issuing securities subject to these risks. The investors, typically large institutions, accept a lower rate of return, because they can rely upon the cashflow from the securitized assets, even if the originating company becomes bankrupt.

Usually, the financial assets are sold to a specially created corporation or trust called the *special purpose vehicle* (SPV). The SPV obtains the funds to pay for these assets by selling debt or equity securities to investors through private placements or public markets. As a result of these transactions, the originating company has acquired new capital relatively efficiently and inexpensively by selling its assets in a large, predictable market, and the investors hold interests in the securitized assets through the SPV that are insulated from the originating company's financial risks.

---

[7] *See* Schwarcz, *The Alchemy of Asset Securitization*, 1 Stan. J. L. Bus. & Fin. 133 (1994).

Securitization has been an important financing method in the U.S. for over thirty years. One of the earliest and most familiar forms of securitization is the mortgage backed security (MBS), that represents the right to receive income from a pool of home mortgages. Essentially, the MBS is an ownership interest in an entity that has purchased the right to receive the mortgage payments (receivables) from the bank or other financial institution that provided the mortgage loan and owns the underlying debt instrument. The transaction allows an investor to purchase the MBS based upon its judgment about the value of the underlying mortgages without regard to the financial condition of the originating bank. By pooling the mortgages into standardized financial instruments traded in a huge public market, the bank can convert the future income from these assets into current capital at a relatively low cost.

Securitization has expanded to include interests in a wide variety of receivables and similar financial assets, including receivables arising from oil and gas sales, auto loans, credit card transactions, equipment leases, franchise and licensing fees, litigation settlements, and even lottery winnings and record sales.[8] Indeed, virtually any asset may be securitized if it generates a predictable cash flow that is sufficient to make the required payments to the investors who purchase the security. The wide variety of securitization opportunities has made this an attractive method for domestic and foreign companies to obtain capital that would not otherwise be available, or which would be appreciably more expensive.

> **Note:** Until its recent revision, Article 9 of the Uniform Commercial Code applied to the sale of accounts and chattel paper that are short term financial assets that are frequently securitized.[9] Revised Article 9 expands the scope of the statute to include many more kinds of securitized financial assets, including accounts such as credit card, health care insurance, license, and franchise fee receivables, chattel paper, and promissory notes. Revised Article 9 also covers payment intangibles, which are intangibles for which the debtor's principal obligation is monetary even if not set out in a separate instrument.

International securitization transactions have become increasingly attractive for companies in lesser developed countries that must obtain funds in other countries that have established capital markets. For certain businesses in developing countries, securitization may provide a method for converting expected future revenues from natural resources and local industries into current capital at the lowest possible financing cost. Companies interested in securitizing their assets must structure the *cross border* arrangement in a manner that appeals to sophisticated investors in the

---

[8] *See* Dvorak, *Transplanting Asset Securitization: Is The Grass Green Enough On The Other Side?* 38 Houston L. R. 541 (Summer 2001).

[9] Schwarcz, *The Impact On Securitization Of Revised UCC, Article 9*, 74 Chi.-Kent L. Rev. 947 (1999).

capital markets, particularly in the U.S. — the world's largest securitization market. These transactions also require due diligence in examining the laws of the various countries that may have jurisdiction, and how these laws interact.

The basic cross-border securitization transaction involves some or all of the following steps:[10]

1. The company obtaining the finance (originator) identifies or acquires the underlying financial asset. Typically, these assets are receivables arising from loans or sales that the company has made. The amount of receivables should be large enough to represent a secure, predictable cash flow.

2. The originator sells the receivables to a specially created corporation or trust called the *special purpose vehicle* (SPV). The purpose for the sale is to isolate the receivables from the originator's general business risks, including the risk of its bankruptcy. Generally, the originator continues to service the receivables by making collections and enforcing delinquencies.

3. The SPV issues securities through private placements or public capital markets to raise the funds needed to buy the receivables. These funds can be obtained at a relatively low cost if the SPV is *bankruptcy remote* from the originator, meaning that the SPV's assets are not at risk if the originator becomes bankrupt.

4. In many cases, the SPV will obtain a favorable rating for its securities from a commercial rating agency such as Standard and Poor or Moody's. The rating will ensure that the securities can be issued at a lower cost than the originator could obtain by issuing its own debt or equity.

In a cross-border securitization, these transactions must be carefully constructed to ensure that each step will be respected under the laws of the countries involved. Note that the originator is likely to be organized in a different country than the SPV that purchases its receivables. Additional complexity may arise if the obligors for the receivables are not in the same country as the originator or SPV. To avoid currency risks, the receivables should be payable in the same currency as the securities issued by the SPV.

---

[10] *See* Schwarcz, *The Universal Language Of Cross-Border Finance*, Duke J. Comp. & Int'l L. (Spring 1998).

Structure of an Asset Securitization Transaction

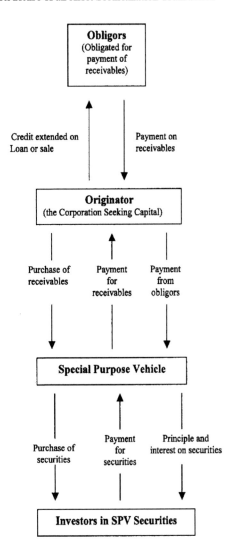

§ 1.02   Regulation of International Financial Transactions

[1]   Overview

The growing interdependence and internationalization of financial markets around the world has required increasing cooperation, coordination and communication between national banking and securities regulators. These linkages have created an expanding framework of national, regional and international rules and enforcement mechanisms to regulate cross-border financial transactions and institutions. In turn, these international developments are compelling domestic lawmakers and regulators to adopt laws and rules that are gradually integrating and converging local financial markets into an international regulatory system for financial institutions and services.

The convergence of international regulation must account for the increasing integration of different financial functions into large, comprehensive, financial services firms. Until recently, financial market regulators generally prohibited companies from offering integrated banking, securities and insurance services. Competition and other market forces, however, required relaxation of these rules and most countries now permit firms to offer comprehensive financial services that include banking, securities and insurance components.

The diversification of the financial industry means that many banks now engage in financial transactions and incur risks that are not subject to supervision by regulators and that non-banking firms, including securities and insurance companies, now conduct transactions formerly limited to regulated banks. Although large, financial companies can efficiently provide comprehensive financial services and products, they also can sustain enormous losses that upset international capital markets and endanger the global financial system. In light of these changes, the key international financial regulatory bodies are now cooperating to establish international standards for regulating all types of financial activities and markets. These regulatory bodies include the Basel Committee on Banking Supervision (Basel Committee), the International Organization of Securities Commissions (IOSCO), the International Association of Insurance Supervisors (IAIS), and the International Accounting Standards Committee (IASC). The cooperation between the Basel Committee and IOSCO has been particularly important because of the extensive and increasing integration of banking and securities firms.

[2] International Banking Regulation

The international nature of the banking industry is evident from the numerous U.S. banks that operate branches and subsidiaries in foreign countries and the many foreign banks that have offices in the U.S. Through this global system, banks located in one country commonly obtain deposits from parties in another country that are loaned to governments and businesses in a third nation. Generally, these international transactions allow for efficient and inexpensive movements of capital throughout the world. However, they also create a substantial *systemic risk* that the collapse of a bank in one country will cause banks in other countries to fail.

Because banks are so important to a nation's economic well-being they are subject to a significant amount of government regulation. Generally, these regulations are designed to ensure that banks maintain sufficient assets to satisfy their obligations to repay their liabilities. For the most part, a bank's assets equals the value of the loans that have been made to its customers and its liabilities equals the amount that is owed to its depositors. The bank has *capital* to the extent that the value of its assets (loans) exceeds its liabilities (deposits) and it is *insolvent* the extent that the actual value of its outstanding loans is less than the amount needed to repay its depositors. Thus, banking regulations focus upon preventing insolvencies by requiring banks to maintain adequate capital at all times.[11] International capital adequacy regulation is particularly important because of the global systemic risk associated with the modern banking system.

[a] The Basel Accords

The primary source of international banking regulation is the *Basel Committee on Banking Supervision* (Basel Committee), which was created in 1974 by the governors of the central banks of the *Group of Ten* (G-10) major industrialized countries.[12] The Basel Committee convenes at the Bank for International Settlements (BIS) in Switzerland and is staffed by the BIS secretariat. Although the proposals of the Basel Committee lack international legal force, the fact that its members are the central bankers for the world's largest economies gives its recommendations great authority. These recommendations provide broad supervisory standards and guidelines that may be implemented by each country's regulatory authorities in the manner best suited to its own national system.

The Basel Committee's most important regulatory pronouncement was issued in 1988 as the *Basel Capital Accord* (Basel Accord). This agreement reflected the Basel Committee's conclusion that regulations in many countries did not require banks to hold sufficient capital in reserve to meet the risks associated with global transactions. Thus, well-regulated banks were at a competitive disadvantage with respect to unregulated institutions that could take ill-advised risks. The Basel Accord principles have been adopted and implemented by the bank regulators of the G-10 as well as most other regulators that have banks involved in international transactions.

Basically, the 1988 Basel Accord promulgated standards for measuring and regulating bank risk. These standards include rules for assessing the risk associated with particular loans and a method for weighting the value of bank assets subject to these risks. To ensure capital adequacy, the Accord requires banks involved in international banking transactions to maintain minimum capital reserves equal to 8 percent of their risk-weighted assets. Generally, these requirements were fully implemented by the end of 1992.

By 1999, the numerous changes in banking practices, as well as the flaws in the 1988 Accord's rules, convinced the Basel Committee that the original

---

[11] Tarbert, *Rethinking Capital Adequacy: The Basel Accord And The New Framework*, 56 Bus. Law. 767 (2001).

[12] The Committee is made up of the leaders of the central bank of Belgium, Canada, Chile, Germany, Italy, Japan, Luxembourg, the Netherlands, Spain, Sweden, Switzerland, United Kingdom and United States.

capital maintenance requirements were no longer adequate. Of particular importance were the many new derivative and similar financial instruments that were being utilized to separate the actual risk associated with a transaction from the underlying assets. Accordingly, a *New Capital Adequacy Framework* was issued to form the basis for a subsequent accord.[13] The Accord also addresses issues regarding the need for home and host country supervisors to coordinate and cooperate to and to employ supervisory resources efficiently and effectively.

[b] Basel II

The new Accord, called *Basel II*, was adopted in 2002 and, after several postponements, is scheduled for implementation at the start of 2007. Basel II consists of three basic principles called *pillars*. These regulatory pillars are:

1. *Minimum Capital Requirements.* Although the 8 percent risk-weighted capital requirement is maintained, the methods for assessing risk are greatly changed. Banks may determine *credit risk* either by a standardized approach that is similar to the 1988 Accord or by an *internal rating based* approach (IRB). Larger banks are likely to use the IRB approach that bases capital requirements on each bank's own assessment of its borrower's creditworthiness. Banks using this system must meet high standards that show the accuracy of their internal measures. Banks also must measure operational risk and market risk related to their assets.

2. *Supervisory review.* This pillar requires increased supervisory review of an institution's capital adequacy and internal assessment process. Thus, regulators must ensure that a bank's capital is sufficient for its risk profile. Regulators are asked to examine each bank's risk management strategy and asset diversification in determining its capital requirements, and to coordinate their examinations of international banks with authorities in other countries.

3. *Market discipline.* This pillar would impose market discipline through economic rewards and punishments for banks that meet, or fail to meet, adequate capital standards. This will be accomplished through disclosures about a bank's capital and risk position that will affect the public's perceptions about the safety of their deposits. Accordingly, new regulations will require banks to make swift public disclosures about the key features of their capital adequacy and risk exposure. These disclosure rules, however, are unlikely to affect depositors in countries that have effective deposit insurance policies.

---

[13] *See* Basel Committee on Banking Supervision, A New Capital Adequacy Framework (June 1999).

[3] International Securities Regulation

The basic objectives of securities regulation are to protect investors, ensure that securities markets operate in a fair, efficient and transparent manner and reduce the risks to the financial system from the failure of any market participants.[14] In most countries, these objectives are pursued by requiring companies that offer their securities to the public to disclose important information about their financial condition. Generally, a country's financial disclosure standards and rules apply to foreign companies that wish to trade their securities in local capital markets.

Because the scope of disclosure and level of enforcement varies greatly among nations, it is often difficult and expensive for a company seeking access to foreign capital to comply with different regulatory regimes. The globalization of securities markets and increasing competition between national exchanges has compelled regulators to achieve their basic objectives by means that allow investors to readily buy and sell securities all over the world. Increasingly, regulators are adopting rules that enable investors to trade foreign securities and foreign companies to issue their securities in local capital markets. Although progress has been made in harmonizing international securities regulation, a number of important national differences persist.

[a] U.S. Securities Regulation

In the U.S., the distribution of domestic and foreign securities is regulated by the Securities and Exchange Commission (SEC). The key statute enforced by the SEC is the Securities Act of 1933 (Securities Act), which requires registration of any security offered or sold in the U.S. unless a specific exemption applies. A second important law is the Securities Exchange Act of 1934 (Exchange Act), which requires all publicly traded companies to file annual audited financial statements and other periodic reports with the SEC.

[i] Public Offerings

Public offerings, meaning securities offered to the public on established exchanges or informal over-the-counter markets, are subject to extensive disclosure requirements under the Securities Act.[15] Generally, an issuer must register a proposed public offering with the SEC and obtain approval of the registration statement before the securities may be offered or sold. The registration statement must disclose comprehensive information about the company's financial condition and business prospects. Pursuant to the Exchange Act, additional financial disclosure statements must be filed annually.

---

[14] International Organization of Securities Commissions (IOSCO), Objectives and Principles of Securities Regulation (May 2003).

[15] Securities Act of 1933, Section 5.

A foreign company that raises capital from the public or lists its shares on a U.S. securities exchange must satisfy the registration requirements of the Securities Act. The initial registration statement for a securities offering is made on Form F-1, which must include the prospectus that will be used to market the securities to investors. The financial disclosure requirements that apply to foreign companies are similar to the rules for domestic firms, although disclosure of non-financial information is somewhat different.

A company that will list its shares on a major stock exchange such as the New York, American or Nasdaq exchanges, must file an initial registration statement and subsequent annual reports pursuant to the Exchange Act. Generally, a foreign company provides this information to the SEC on Form 20-F, which requires comprehensive disclosure of the company's business operations and financial statements A foreign company also must notify the SEC about any information that has been made public pursuant to the regulations of its home country or of a non-U.S. stock exchange. [16]

Canadian Multi-jurisdictional Disclosure System. In 1991, the SEC adopted the Multi-jurisdictional Disclosure System (MJDS) which coordinates securities regulation with Canada. This was made possible by the similarity of the Canadian and U.S. systems. Under MJDS, Canadian foreign private issuers that qualify as large, established companies can satisfy most SEC registration and reporting requirements by providing disclosure documents that meet the requirements of the Canadian securities authorities. Correspondingly, the Canadian Securities Administrators adopted a multi-jurisdictional disclosure system that allows U.S. issuers to satisfy most Canadian registration and reporting requirements with documents that meet SEC requirements.

International Disclosure Standards. The SEC has adopted non-financial disclosure requirements for many foreign issuers that conform to the international standards endorsed by the International Organization of Securities Commissions (IOSCO). The SEC noted that adoption of the international standards would reduce barriers to cross-border securities offerings and capital by promoting a single disclosure document that is accepted in multiple jurisdictions. The international disclosure standards replace most of the previous disclosure requirements for foreign private issuers under the Exchange Act.

The basic disclosures required by the international standards include information about:

- The identity of directors, senior management and advisors;
- Specific statistics and expected timetable;
- Reasons for the offer, expected use of proceeds, and risk factors;
- Company information, including description of the issuer's business and properties;

---

[16] Form 6-K.

- Operating and financial reviews and prospects (corresponding to the U.S. requirement for management discussions and analysis of financial condition and operational results);

- Directors, senior management and employees, including compensation and shareholdings;

- Major shareholders and related party transactions;

- Financial information, statements and legal proceedings;

- Offer and listing including the plan of distribution, trading markets, selling shareholders, dilution and expenses; and

- Additional information, including a description of the issuer's share capital, significant provisions of its articles of incorporation and bylaws, its material contracts, and applicable taxes.

[ii] American Depository Receipts (ADRs)

Most foreign company stocks traded on U.S. markets are exchanged in the form of American Depositary Receipts (ADRs). An ADR is a negotiable certificate, issued by a U.S. bank, that represents a specified number of shares of a foreign corporation that trade on a foreign equity market. Typically, the underlying foreign shares are kept in the custody of a bank in the companies home jurisdiction. Although the owner of an ADR may obtain the foreign stock it represents, it is generally more convenient for a U.S. investor to hold the ADR.

An ADR is priced in dollars and trades on a U.S. stock market in the same manner as other securities. The depositary bank converts dividends or other cash payments to U.S. dollars before remitting them to U. S. owners. However, the depositary banks do charge fees for their services that are deducted from dividends and other distributions to ADR holders. ADRs reduce administrative and transaction costs by eliminating the difficulties of trading shares in different currencies and avoid foreign taxes on each sale.

Foreign companies often utilize ADRs to gain access to the U.S. equity markets. The information about these companies that is available to U.S. investors depends upon the market where its ADR trades. For companies that trade on the New York, American, NASDAQ or Regional exchanges, annual reports are available from filings with the SEC. These reports provide financial statements audited by independent accountants applying U.S. audit standards. Financial statements must conform to U.S. accounting principles or show how the key results would differ under U.S. principles. Companies traded on over-the-counter markets (OTC) generally are not registered with the SEC and only provide information that meets a foreign country's auditing and disclosure requirements.

Although ADRs are most widespread, other types of depository receipts are traded in non-U.S. securities markets. *Global Depository Receipts* (GDR) are priced in dollars and are traded in European markets such as London and Luxembourg. *European Depository Receipts* (EDR) are denominated and trade in Euros.

[iii] Private Placements

The most burdensome and expensive disclosure requirement for a public offering is a financial statement that satisfies U.S. accounting standards. This is true even though the SEC rules accommodate foreign issuers by accepting certain financial practices and standards used in other jurisdictions. Preparation of the statement usually requires expert legal and accounting services and an intensive *due diligence* process, and the statement must be examined and signed by many corporate officers, directors, and authorized U.S. representatives. False or misleading statements can result in substantial liability for the company and the individual signatories.[17]

Private placements, meaning transactions that do not involve a public offering, are exempt from the registration requirements if certain criteria are satisfied.[18] Generally, the private offer cannot be publicly advertised, must extend to a limited number of offerees, provide access to relevant information, and restrict resale of the securities. Under a "safe harbor" rule, a company qualifies for the private placement exemption if it:[19]

- cannot solicit or advertise to market the securities;
- sells its securities to
  - no more than 35 U.S. non-accredited investors, defined as persons having substantial knowledge and experience in financial and business matters, and
  - an unlimited number of accredited investors, defined as institutions, company officers and directors, and certain minimum net worth individuals;
- provides non-fraudulent information to accredited investors;
- provides non-accredited investors information that is equivalent to the requirements for registered offerings as well as any information given to accredited investors;
- is available to answer questions by prospective purchasers;
- provides specified financial statements; and
- issues restricted securities that cannot be sold for at least a year without registration.

Although companies that satisfy the safe harbor need not register or file reports, they must file a Form D after the first sale of their securities which provides the names and addresses of the company's owners and stock promoters.

---

[17] Securities Act of 1933, Sections 11(a), 18(a), 10b-5.

[18] Securities Act of 1933, Section 4(2); Regulation D.

[19] Rule 506 of Regulation D.

Rule 144A securities. The restriction on resale of securities issued in private placements often makes these issues illiquid and unattractive to investors. The illiquidity of privately placed securities particularly affects foreign companies that wish to enter the U.S. capital market. These companies often avoid public offerings because of the stringent disclosure requirements and expense and effort associated with the SEC registration and reporting process. As a result, many companies have listed their securities on less restrictive European markets.

To improve the liquidity and investor appeal of private placements in the U.S., particularly of foreign securities, the SEC adopted a new registration exemption in 1990 under Rule 144A.[20] That rule requires only limited disclosure and permits unrestricted resale of private placement securities to *qualified institutional buyers* (QIB), who are generally large financial institutions that own and manage $100 million or more in qualifying securities.[21] As a result of this rule, a *114A market* exists for foreign securities that can be readily traded to institutional investors.

Regulation S. Regulation S, issued in 1990, provides registration requirements regarding securities offerings and sales made outside the U.S. to foreign residents. The regulation permits domestic and foreign issuers to make such offers and sales without registration at the SEC if specified procedures are followed that prevent redistribution of the securities to the U.S. In some circumstances, it permits securites issued in a 144A private placement to be immediately resold outside the U.S. thereby creating a liquid market for foreign issuers seeking multiple markets.

[iv] Hedge Funds

Generally, the term *hedge fund* is applied to privately-held investment ventures that compensate their managers and advisors based upon a percentage of the fund's gains and appreciation. Many hedge funds use large amounts of borrowed money to *leverage* the return on their investments. Hedge fund advisors often invest substantial amounts of their own money in the funds they manage. Outside investors are invited to participate in private offerings, through word of mouth and personal relationships with hedge funds managers.

Hedge funds mangers frequently obtain very high returns through extensively researched, speculative trades of various types of securities. To provide liquidity, many funds periodically repurchase their own interests from investors. This usually occurs after a *lock-up* period when investors cannot liquidate their positions.

Generally, hedge fund managers obtain high yields by using complex, flexible investment strategies that are not available through traditional mutual funds, brokerage firms and banks. Some hedge funds speculate on

---

[20] 17 C.F.R. 230.144A.

[21] Only $10 million is required for a registered broker-dealer and a banking institution must satisfy a $25 million minimum net worth test.

the occurrence of future financial events such as currency exchange and interest-rate fluctuation. The large profits arise from highly leveraged, well-researched, but speculative investments.

Many ventures are *arbitrage funds* that use sophisticated economic models to find opportunities for arbitrage transactions in different financial markets around the world. Arbitrage opportunities arise when equivalent financial securities can be purchased at different prices in different markets together with options and other derivatives to hedge against future price changes. Theoretically, such transactions should result in riskless profits.

Many hedge funds are organized abroad, typically in offshore financial centers such as the Cayman Islands, Bahamas, British Virgin Islands, Panama, Netherlands Antilles, or Bermuda, that impose few regulatory constraints. Offshore hedge funds often provide significant tax benefits that are not available to domestic funds. These tax advantages may be particularly helpful to tax-exempt entities such as pension funds, charitable trusts, foundations and endowments that might be taxable on income earned from a domestic fund.[22] U.S. sales of offshore hedge fund interests are governed by Federal securities law registration and antifraud rules.

Hedge Fund Regulation. Until recently, most hedge funds were not required to register their offerings under the Securities Act because their ownership was limited and not open to the public. In December, 2004, however, the SEC adopted new rules under the Investment Advisors Act of 1940 (Advisors Act) requiring many hedge fund advisors and sponsors to register under the Act. Generally, the Advisors Act requires investment advisers that manage at least $25 million to register with the SEC. Under the new rules, offshore fund advisers must include their onshore (in U.S.) business in determining the funds they manage. An offshore fund advisor also must register if more than fourteen U.S. residents invest in each private fund it advises and investments by the U.S. residents exceed $25 million. An exception applies to funds having a principal place of business outside of the U.S. that are regulated as public investment companies under another country's law.

The new registration rules apply to traditional hedge funds and other private trading and investment funds that permit investors to redeem their interests within two years. The rules require hedge funds sponsors to either restrict the use of incentive compensation, the prevailing method for compensating advisors, or heighten the suitability requirements for fund investors. Fund Advisers are required to maintain substantial books and records, including performance records, and prepare and distribute specified disclosure documents to clients at the beginning of the advisory relationship.

---

[22] Under IRC § 511 such entities may be taxable on unrelated business income derived from a domestic partnership or LLC that uses borrowed money to acquire its investments.

[v] Accounting Standards

At present, the accounting principles securities regulators apply to determine the financial condition of a company differ from country to country. In the U.S., the Financial Accounting Standards Board (FASB) establishes the accounting standards publicly-traded companies must use in preparing financial statements for the SEC. The standards applied by FASB are called the U.S. Generally Accepted Accounting Principles (U.S. GAAP). A foreign company that files with the SEC may use U.S. GAAP, its home country GAAP, or certain international standards. However, a company that does not use U.S. GAAP generally must provide a reconciliation showing how its results would differ under the U.S. GAAP.

The integration of global capital markets has induced many countries to converge their accounting standards by adopting recently issued International Financial Reporting Standards (IFRS). Beginning in 2005, the European Union (EU) will require all EU based companies that are publicly traded in Europe to prepare their financial statements under IFRS and non-EU companies that trade their shares in Europe must apply these standards by 2006. It is expected that the vast majority of nations will converge their financial disclosure rules to accord with the IFRS.

The interaction of the U.S. GAAP rules with the IFRS rules has raised some important concerns. Although most U.S. companies currently use U.S. GAAP when issuing securities in the EU, this will be permitted after 2005 only if the EU Commission determines that the U.S. standards are equivalent to IFRS. The EU may refuse to make that determination in light of the fact that the SEC refuses to permit EU companies that issue securities in the U.S. to issue financial statements using IFRS. Instead, the SEC requires EU companies to either use U.S. GAAP initially or reconcile their IFRS accounting to U.S. GAAP. The stated rationale for the SEC position is that U.S. GAAP provides better investor protection. Because failure to resolve this issue will increase costs for both U.S. and EU companies and hinder the development of global capital markets, it is likely that resolution will be forthcoming before the end of 2006.

[b] The Sarbanes-Oxley Act

As noted above, the SEC's response to the globalization of capital markets has been a number of accommodations and exemptions that facilitate the listing and trading of foreign company securities in the U.S. These actions were necessary to meet the increasing competition from foreign capital markets and to provide opportunities for U.S. investors to diversify their portfolios through acquisition of foreign securities. The trend toward accommodating foreign companies, however, has been impeded by enactment of the Sarbanes-Oxley Act in 2002. That law, enacted in response to U.S. corporate scandals such as the Enron and Worldcom bankruptcies, requires foreign companies to follow the same stringent corporate governance and disclosure rules that apply to U.S. firms.

A major concern of foreign companies is that the extraterritorial effects of the Act require them to adopt corporate governance and audit rules that are burdensome and incompatible with the corporate culture and legal concepts of their home jurisdictions. In many areas of the world, particularly Europe, corporate ownership is not widespread and most companies are dominated by major shareholders and banks who can and do closely supervise management. In the U.S., by contrast, the wide dispersal of corporate ownership requires regulators to protect minority shareholders by imposing supervisory and fiduciary duties on directors and management. Although it is likely that the SEC eventually will accommodate foreign companies by providing significant exemptions from Sarbanes-Oxley, excessive exemptions may have the undesirable effect of encouraging U.S. companies to move abroad.

The Sarbanes-Oxley Act applies to all U.S. and foreign issuers of securities that have registered or filed reports under the Exchange Act or that have filed a registration statement for a securities offering under the Securities Act. The Act imposes significant new responsibilities on the companies, directors, attorneys, and auditors and expands the information that must be provided to U.S. regulators. Key provisions that affect foreign companies include:

- *Certification Requirements.* The Chief Executive Officer (CEO) and Chief Financial Officer (CFO) of a reporting company must certify that:

  - each periodic report containing financial statements *fully complies* with the requirements of the Exchange Act and that the information in the report *fairly presents* the company's financial condition and operating results;[23]

  - their office actually reviewed the report and that it does not contain any untrue statements of material facts;[24] and

  - internal controls have been established to ensure that all material information is available to the officer making the certification.[25]

The SEC currently lacks authority to exempt foreign companies from these requirements. Severe civil and criminal penalties may be imposed for violations.

- *Audit* Committee *Requirements.* The audit committee rules bar the listing of a company's securities on any major U.S. stock exchange unless the company has established an audit committee of independent board members that is responsible for appointing, compensating and overseeing its auditors.[26] Also, the company

---

[23] Sarbanes-Oxley Act, Section 906.

[24] Sarbanes-Oxley Act, Section 302.

[25] *Id.*

[26] Sarbanes-Oxley Act, Section 301.

must identify at least one member of the audit committee as a *financial expert* having U.S. GAAP expertise or explain why the committee lacks a financial expert.[27]

This rule raises serious governance problems for foreign firms whose home jurisdiction mandates different composition and responsibilities for corporate boards and committees. Although the SEC has not exempted foreign companies from these provisions of the Act, it has issued rules that address their concerns. Generally, these rules defer to the home country's law if that law provides a different independent means for control of management.

- *Non-GAAP Financial Information.* Although the Act restricts the use of non-GAAP financial information,[28] the SEC has provided a limited exemption for securities of a company that is listed on a non-U.S. exchange. The exemption, provided in Regulation G, applies if the relevant disclosure is made outside of the U.S.

- *Insider Trading Blackout Periods.* The Act bars insider trading during specified blackout periods.[29] This rule is designed to equalize the trading positions of employees and management, avoiding the Enron situations where management sold stock during periods that employees could not. Under SEC Regulation BTR, the trading bar applies only if fifty percent of the participants or beneficiaries under all pension accounts are affected. For a foreign company the SEC will apply the rule only if at least fifteen percent, or 50,000, of its employees are U.S. staff affected by a blackout.

- *Executives Loans.* The Act prohibits companies from providing or arranging credit or loans to directors and executive officers.[30] No exception is made for foreign companies even though such loans are rare outside the U.S.

[c] Enforcement

In the global market, the activities of companies and investors in one nation often affect or are affected by the laws and regulations of another. Accordingly, effective enforcement of national securities rules often requires regulators to investigate and prosecute activities that occur in another jurisdiction. To effectively deal with cross-border issues, various cooperative methods have been established, including Mutual Legal Assistance Treaties (MLATs) between governments and informal bilateral and multilateral Memoranda of Understanding (MOUs) between securities regulators.

Most international arrangements focus on sharing of information and evidence that will help each jurisdiction to enforce its own securities laws.

---

[27] Sarbanes-Oxley Act, Section 407.

[28] Sarbanes-Oxley Act, Section 401(b).

[29] Sarbanes-Oxley Act, Sections 306(a), 401(k).

[30] Sarbanes-Oxley Act, Section 402 (adding Section 13(k) to the Exchange Act).

Generally, the authority of a domestic regulator to obtain evidence in another country is set forth in an MOU with that country. In many cases, the agreements authorize domestic regulators to use their government powers on behalf of a foreign authority even though the information or evidence sought relates to a matter that does not violate local law.

The basic information that is desired and shared by regulators is illustrated by the *Resolution on Principles for Record Keeping, Collection of Information, Enforcement Powers and Mutual Cooperation to Improve the Enforcement of Securities and Futures Laws*, that was adopted by IOSCO in 1998. The Resolution notes that cooperating nations should require creation of contemporaneous records for all securities transactions, including information about funds and assets, beneficial ownership, price and quantity and brokers. It also notes that a regulator in each jurisdiction should be empowered to identify persons who own or control public companies, bank accounts and brokerage accounts. Where local law does not allow a regulator to provide such assistance, another government authority such as a criminal prosecutor should be empowered to share information.

A recent MOU with IOSCO establishes a framework for cooperation between IOSCO members. When adopted by a member nation, the MOU would authorize regulators to obtain and share a wide variety of information and evidence. This would include compelled, sworn testimony. Each authority must make reasonable efforts to provide unsolicited assistance to the other authorities such as information likely to help these other authorities to secure compliance with its laws and regulations.

[4] Electronic Systems

Given the distances, strange currencies, unfamiliar banking systems and other uncertainties involved in international transactions, it is not surprising that the timing and method of payment are of great concern. Generally, international payments are made and collected through the international banking system, facilitated by a variety of services provided by national central banks, wire payment organizations, and financial clearing houses. In recent years, the great volume of transactions, the very large sums and the attendant time value of money issues, have resulted in increased use of electronic payment technologies, a trend that will surely accelerate in the near future.

The U.S. utilizes a variety of systems for payment, clearance, and settlement of national and international accounts. Certain systems, referred to as *wholesale systems*, are only used for major financial transactions by banks and large corporations. These systems, such as *Fedwire* and the *Clearing House Interbank Payment System* (CHIPS) discussed *below*, can transfer and settle large dollar amounts for business transactions or financial products, such as securities, futures, and options.

Systems used for smaller dollar transactions, referred to as *retail systems*, are used in small business, consumer, and personal transactions, such as checks, credit cards, and debit card payments. Another form of retail electronic funds transfer is the *Automated Clearing House* (ACH), which business and governments often use for small-value, high volume transactions such as direct deposit paychecks or social security payments.

Many new retail payment products are being introduced, including *stored-value cards,* that use dollar amounts implanted on computer chips to make cash-like payments, and *electronic money* that holds funds in an online account that can be transferred between parties over the Internet. Although only in limited use now, these and similar electronic funds transfer methods are likely to represent a large percentage of retail transactions in the near future. Obviously, these emerging products raise significant issues about how the use, clearance, and settlement of these financial transactions should be regulated. These issues will be particularly complex with respect international transactions, many of which are likely to occur completely electronically by parties dealing over the Internet using electronic contracts, signatures, and payments.

[a]   Wholesale Electronic Funds Transfer (EFT)

Most transactions involving international payments are made through the large-value electronic funds transfer systems, such as Fedwire or CHIPS. Financial institutions use these payment systems to make time-critical transfers for customers as well as for their own accounts. Fedwire transfers are used for payments related to interbank overnight loans, interbank settlement transactions (*e.g.,* settlement payments between check clearing association members), payments between corporations, and settlement of securities transactions. The scale of these transactions is illustrated by the fact that check and credit card transactions account for over 90% of the total *number* of non-cash payments in the U.S., but only 10% of the total *value* of non-cash payments. Large-value payments, such as those that occur in international and financial markets account for less than 1% of the total *number* of non-cash payments, but 87% of the total value of such payments.

[b]   Herstatt Risk

These wholesale systems raise important issues about the risks that major financial institutions incur, as well as the national economies that depend on them, when large scale electronic transfers are made by parties that may not be able to settle their obligations. These risks are of particular concern with respect to the enormous and rapidly growing volume of transactions in international financial and foreign exchange markets. Because these markets rely upon fast-paced commitments to transfer enormous sums, their operations depend upon timely completion of payment obligations.

A large scale payment obligation that is not satisfied is likely to affect many financial institutions and may create a domino effect that severely damages an entire economic sector. This is referred to as *systemic risk,* which is the risk that the failure of one participant in a transfer system or financial market to meet its obligations will cause other participants or financial institutions to be unable to meet their obligations. Accordingly, a great deal of attention and concern focuses on the risks involved in these systems, and upon the regulatory measures used to control and mitigate these risks.

The basic risk involves the time gap between the clearance and settlement of financial transactions. A simple example involves the use of a check as payment for goods. The checkwriter bears the risk that the check may be altered or forged or that the goods will not be delivered or are defective. The merchant that takes the check bears the risk that it is forged, that payment will be stopped, or that there are insufficient funds in the payor's account. The payor's bank also risks mistakenly paying on a check which is not good for some reason. Although many things can be done to mitigate these risks, such as a check identification or verification system, the simplest and most effective method is to eliminate the time gap between when a check is issued and when payment actually occurs.

A frequently cited example of uncovered risk in an international transaction involved a small bank in Cologne, Germany, called the Bankhaus Herstatt. Indeed, time-associated risk in a large scale transaction, often referred to as a *Herstatt risk,* derives its name from this case. German banking authorities had withdrawn the license of the Herstatt and ordered it to be liquidated after the close of business that day. The bank had been active in foreign exchange markets and had entered into a number of large foreign currency trades with American banks in which it had agreed to exchange dollars for Deutsche marks. Before Herstatt's closure was announced, the bank received all the Deutsche marks, but had not paid the dollars, resulting in substantial losses for the Americans. Other banks sustained losses on forward contracts with Herstatt that were not due for settlement and still others lost the money that Herstatt owed for prior transactions that were left on deposit. The closure of the Herstatt bank created significant problems throughout foreign exchange markets and resulted in many changes to the foreign exchange payment system designed to reduce market risk.

[c] SWIFT Payment Instructions

Many international payments are facilitated by the *Society for Worldwide Interbank Financial Telecommunications* (SWIFT), an international cooperative organization incorporated in Belgium that is owned by over 2,800 banks from around the world. These owners include more than 150 U.S. banks that hold nearly 15 percent of its shares. The system processes about 2.5 million messages each day, having an estimated total value of $2 trillion per day.

SWIFT operates a network that processes and transmits financial messages to its members and other *financial* institutions. *The system transmits messages but does not make payments.* The messages convey information or instructions between financial institutions, but actual payment for a transaction described in a message must be made through a separate electronic payment system, such as Fedwire or CHIPS.

SWIFT messages are transmitted quickly and inexpensively through dedicated computer terminals maintained by participating institutions. The messages are computer encrypted and use a standard format to convey information about the transaction involved, including the originator, purpose, destination, terms, and recipient. Most of these messages provide instructions for one institution to make a payment to another institution. For example, many electronic letters of credit are drafted in SWIFT format and sent to the issuing bank for transmission through that system. SWIFT messages also are used to confirm the details of financial contracts, such as a foreign exchange trades, interbank deposits, and orders to buy, sell or deliver securities.

[d] Fedwire

The Federal Reserve System operates an electronic funds transfer system called *Fedwire* that allows financial institutions to make fast and secure transfers throughout the U.S. All Federal Reserve Banks, the Treasury Department, and over 9,000 depository institutions are connected through Fedwire. The depository institutions use Fedwire to make large, time-sensitive funds transfers on behalf of their customers, and the Treasury and other federal agencies use the system extensively to disburse and collect funds.

Nearly all Fedwire funds transfers are made by users that are directly connected to the system through dedicated computer terminals. Typically, these involve large transfers averaging over $3.5 million per transaction for a total amount of about $400 *trillion* each year. More than half the dollar value of Fedwire transfers originate in banks served by the New York Federal Reserve Bank.

The Fedwire funds transfer system is a fully automated system in which the sender of the funds initiates the transfer by instructing its bank to transmit funds to another party's account at another bank. It operates as a *real-time gross batch settlement* system (RTGS). Real time means that each transaction is processed when it is initiated and gross batch means that the system settles each transfer individually.

Generally, the funds are transferred between depository institutions that are required to maintain accounts in the Federal Reserve Bank of their district. If the payee and payor's banks are in the same Fed district, the transfer is quite simple; the Federal Reserve Bank transfers the designated funds from the one bank's account to the other bank's account. If the parties' banks are in different Fed districts, the sending bank debits its client's account and its Fed Bank sends a transfer order to the Fed Bank that serves the recipient's bank. The two Fed Banks then settle between themselves through the Interdistrict Settlement Fund, a bookkeeping system that records transactions between different Federal Reserve Banks. The banks make the appropriate debits and credits to their clients' accounts and the transaction is complete, usually within minutes. Once the credit is received, it is final and the funds may be used immediately.

The Fedwire system accommodates international transactions through the relationships that foreign banks have established with the large U.S. banks that are members of the New York Fed. A foreign buyer or seller can make or receive a Fedwire payment through its local national bank that either has an account in a New York Bank or has an account in a larger national bank that maintains an account in New York. This can be illustrated by assuming that a French buyer in Lyon wishes to Fedwire a payment to a seller with an account in a New York Bank. The Lyon Bank is likely to have an account in a Paris Bank which, in turn has an account in New York. The Fedwire system accomplishes the payment by crediting the funds to the seller's bank and debiting the Paris bank's account in New York. The debits and credits would be reversed if the payment was being made by a New York buyer to a French seller.

International Fedwire Transaction

FRENCH BUYER IN LYON FEDWIRES $1 MILLION PAYMENT TO SELLER
WITH ACCOUNT IN NEW YORK BANK.

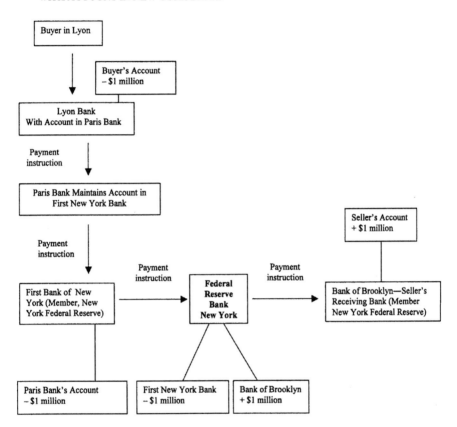

[e]   Clearing House Interbank Payment System (CHIPS)

The *Clearing House Interbank Payments System* (CHIPS) is the largest private sector payments network in the world. The CHIPS system was organized by a group of large New York City commercial banks in 1970, and has since expanded its membership to many more depository institutions, including foreign banks, that maintain offices in New York. The system operates a computerized network for transferring domestic and international payments which handles about 90 percent of all international interbank transfers relating to dollars. Each day, the system processes over 200,000 interbank transfers worth nearly $1.2 trillion.

CHIPS enables banks to transfer and settle international payments quickly by replacing paper bank checks with electronic bookkeeping entries.

These entries are quickly settled by wire payments at the end of each business day. To facilitate this fast settlement, the Federal Reserve Bank of New York maintains a special Fedwire escrow account for CHIPS participants. Each day, the participants use Fedwires to send debit settlements to, and receive credit settlements from, the settlement account.

In 2001, CHIPS introduced a number of changes to control risk and reduce operating costs. Before these changes were implemented, only 20 banks actually participated in the daily settlements. These *settling participants* settled accounts for themselves and for non-settling participants who designated one of the settling banks to act for them. Each day's settlement was completed when all settling participants that owed funds made their payments to the special escrow account and all settling participants that were due funds received disbursements from the account. The settling participants then settled their net positions with their corresponding non-settling participants.

This system involved substantial risk for the participants, because the accounts were cleared (*i.e.*, the instructions received from the non-settling participants) throughout the day, but only settled (*i.e.*, actually debited or credited to the relevant accounts) at the end of the day. The delay between clearance and settlement created a risk that a bank obligated to make a payment would fail to do so at settlement time. The system used a number of combined methods to decrease risk, including bilateral limits between the settling banks and their corresponding non-settling participants, caps on the net debit amount a participant could incur, loss-sharing agreements, and minimum collateral requirements in the form of Treasury securities. The loss sharing arrangement required each participant to provide a portion of the funds necessary to complete settlement if one or more CHIPS participants failed to meet their settlement obligations.

CHIPS operations were changed in 2001 by adopting a system under which final settlement occurs periodically throughout the day, instead of once at the close of the day. These settlements are controlled by a computer program *balance release algorithm* that determines the amount and timing of payments to and from the participants. Such *intraday finality* is designed to eliminate much of the risk inherent in a single large settlement failure at closing.

The former treasury securities collateral requirement has been replaced with a pre-funded balance account that each participant must maintain in the New York Federal Reserve. The amount of the balance is determined from the participants past activity. The balance must be deposited in the account each morning and will vary during the day as payment messages are sent to and received from other participants.

At the end of the day, a final net balance is computed for each participant and any debit balance must be funded with 30 minutes. The special class of settling participants has been eliminated, so all participants must settle their final balances at this time. Because most transactions have been settled intraday, the effect of a participant's failure to pay its final balance is likely to be limited to that participant.

Banks that are not CHIPS participants may utilize the system through a participating bank either by maintaining an account with the participating bank or arranging for separate payment or reimbursement. Thus, a client of a non-CHIPS bank seeking a fast, reliable dollar-denominated transaction governed by the CHIPS rules may instruct the bank to conduct the transaction through a participating bank

To illustrate CHIPS operations, assume that a French company wishes to buy computer software from a California producer for $1 million. If both parties maintain accounts at New York participating banks, the buyer may simply send a payment instruction to its bank, probably using a telex or SWIFT electronic message for this purpose. *See* 1.02[2][c]. The Buyer's bank will enter and then verify the transaction through a CHIPS computer. The message will state the account that will receive the funds, and the amount of the transaction as a payment message, with the identifying codes for the sending and receiving banks, instructing a transfer of $1 million to the Seller's Bank. The CHIPS computer verifies that the transaction is permissible under its risk and collateral rules, and then makes the appropriate debit and credit entries, and notifies both banks. The Seller's bank will notify the seller that payment has been received.

If the French buyer's account is with a Paris bank, it is likely that the Paris bank or an affiliate has an account at a participating New York bank. In that case, the participating bank will conduct the transaction through CHIPS and then debit the Paris bank's account. If the Paris bank does not have an account in New York, it must arrange another way to pay the $1 million to a participating bank. Usually, this can be accomplished through another bank in which both the Paris and participating banks have accounts.

Note that these funds transfers can occur quite reliably in just a few minutes, meaning that neither party loses the time value of its money. Because the process is so computerized, there is little chance of clerical error. Of course, as always, the major risk is that somewhere in the chain of funds transfer instructions lurks a party who is unable to actually make the required payment. Thus, settlement risk remains a focus of attention in regulation of payment system operations.

CHIPS Transaction

FRENCH BUYER WITH ACCOUNT IN PARIS BANK MAKES $50 MILLION PAYMENT TO SELLER WITH ACCOUNT IN NEW YORK BANK SETTLED THROUGH CHIPS SYSTEM.

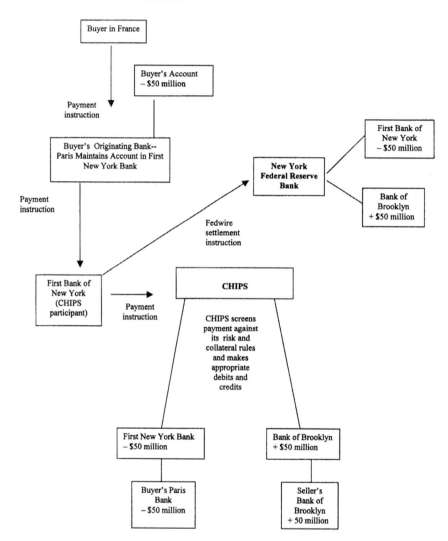

[f]   Foreign Funds Transfer Systems

Similar systems exist in other countries for making large inter-bank transfers. For example, the pound sterling portion of a foreign exchange transaction involving the United Kingdom is often settled through the *Clearing House Association Payments System* (CHAPS). This system is similar to Fedwire, in that member banks settle with each other through accounts at the Bank of England. Foreign transactions in Germany may be settled through the EAF system that operates through the Deutsche Bundesbank, which is the German central bank. The EU utilizes a system called Target to handle Euro transactions. Nevertheless, the U.S. system holds a dominating position in foreign exchange transactions because more than 80 percent of such transactions have a dollar denominated component. Thus, more than $1 trillion dollars a day is settled through the U.S., most of it through CHIPS.

[5] Countertrade

In a *countertrade* transaction, one party accepts goods or services as payment for its products instead of currency. Typically, a countertrade transaction involves commercial parties from two different countries. Countertrade is often used in transactions where credit or convertible currency is unavailable. It may be a resourceful way to arrange the sale of a product into a country that cannot provide payment in hard currency. The lack of foreign exchange may be specific to the buyer or may stem from the country's limited reserves.

Countertrade transactions are often facilitated by trading through an intermediary, such as an international broker, international bank, or export management company. These facilitators, however, can increase the transaction costs. A countertrade transaction also may involve additional risks regarding delivery and performance because of the time difference between each party's obligation to perform. It may be wise to draft separate contracts for each part of the contract, rather than have one contract that makes the two parts interdependent. The separate contracts can be linked by a separate countertrade document.

The U.S. Department of Commerce (DOC) maintains that "the U.S. Government views countertrade as generally contrary to an open, free trading system but will not oppose participation by U.S. businesses in countertrade transactions unless such activity could have a negative impact on national security. All normal import and export regulations must be observed, as there are no special exemptions for countertrade. transactions." Despite this negative opinion of countertrade, the DOC's export support program offers assistance to parties involved in or seeking countertrade transactions.

UNCITRAL has published a *Legal Guide on International Countertrade Transactions*.

[a] Barter

An ancient form of countertrade is barter, in which no money is used but the parties simply exchange merchandise directly for other merchandise or services. This may occur through a swap of one product for another or by switching products through a chain of merchants in different markets. Barter is infrequently used in contemporary trade because of the difficulties in matching the goods each party needs and in determining the values of the goods.

[b] Counterpurchase

A more common form of contemporary countertrade is referred to as *counterpurchase*. In this transaction, an exporter purchases goods from a country in exchange for that country's purchase of an equivalent valued amount of the exporter's product. Counterpurchase also may be conducted through separate parallel trade transactions that are contractually linked. For example, a contract may agree to pay the U.S. exporter in a convertible currency if the exporter (or another designated party) agrees to subsequently purchase an equivalent value of goods from the importing country using that currency.

A counterpurchase contract separates the timing of each party's contract performance so that one transaction can be completed even though the second transaction requires additional time. The participating parties sign two separate contracts that specify the goods and services to be exchanged. Thus, counterpurchases can be useful if performance depends on a future event, such as a harvest.

As an example of a counterpurchase, assume that Country X has abundant rice but needs computers from the U.S. It is unlikely that a computer manufacturer will need rice, so a barter transaction is not feasible. However, if a U.S. cereal producer can be involved, the transaction may be structured to have the computer manufacturer ship the computers to Country X which in turn ships the rice to the cereal producer. The cereal producer then pays the computer manufacturer.

[c] Buyback, Offset and Swap Transactions

In a *buy-back* arrangement, a seller of capital equipment or technology may accept partial payment in products manufactured with their equipment. Typically, the seller receives some currency in addition to the products. For example, a steelmaker may sell steel to a foreign auto parts maker and then buy the parts at a reduced price. The effect is to partially pay for the auto parts with steel. A *production sharing* arrangement is similar to a buyback, but used in mining and energy projects in which a developer will be paid a share of the mine or well output.

An *offset* transaction is often used between countries that are involved in high value industrial contracts, such as aerospace or military industries. It is quite common in civilian and military aircraft contracts. The contract involves reciprocal trade agreements in which the seller of a product made in one country agrees to purchase a specified amount of goods from the other country. For example, Country X agrees to pay $1 billion for airplanes made by a company in Country Y if that company buys an equivalent amount of telecommunications equipment from Country X. These contracts are designed to offset the adverse effects of large foreign purchases on a country's balance of trade. The arrangements often require certain portions of the product to be manufactured or assembled in the purchasing country.

The contract may be an *indirect offset*, meaning that the goods and services purchased are unrelated to the products being sold. In a direct offset contract, the goods on both sides are related, usually involving a form of co-production, license or joint venture. Developing countries often use offset contracts to facilitate technology transfers, providing goods or services in exchange for research and development, technical assistance, or patent agreements.

Swaps are relatively new arrangements that are used in countries that carry large debt burdens. The debt may be swapped for other items such as equity interests in local industry or local products. In some cases, the debt may be exchanged for a country's agreement to undertake environmental protection initiatives such as forest preservation of establishment of nature preserves.

§ 1.03   The International Monetary Fund

[1]   Organization

The central purposes of the *International Monetary Fund* (IMF) are to help expand and balance international trade, to promote international monetary cooperation, and to make loans that allow member nations to finance temporary international payment imbalances.[31] The Fund is a special agency of the United Nations that derives its legal authority from an international treaty called the Articles of Agreement that became effective in December, 1945. IMF policies are directed by Board of Governors comprising one member from each of its 182 member nations and an equal number of Alternate Governors. The Governors and Alternates usually are finance ministers or central bank chiefs who meet only once a year.

Daily IMF operations are conducted by the *Executive Board*, made up of 24 Executive Directors who meet regularly. About one-third of the Executive Directors represent individual countries with major economies and the rest represent regional groupings of other states. Executive Board decisions are arrived at through consensus among members, rather than formal votes.

The IMF has a large staff of economists, statisticians, and other experts and support personnel at its Washington, D.C. headquarters. The staff is led by a Managing Director appointed by the Executive Board. The Managing Director, customarily a European, also serves as Chairman of the Executive Board. Staff members do not represent individual countries, but are international civil servants.

---

[31] IMF Charter Article I.

[2] Contributions and Quotas

When a country joints the IMF, it must make a contribution, mostly in its own currency, called a *quota* subscription. The amount of a member's quota relates to the size of its economy — richer countries have larger quotas. The quota amounts are reviewed every five years and can increase or decrease in relation to each member's economic prosperity and the needs of the IMF.

A country's quota determines its voting power in the IMF, meaning that wealthier nations exert significant control over IMF decisions. For example, the United States contributes about 18 percent of total quotas and may cast about 18 percent of the total IMF votes. Although decisions are arrived at through consensus rather than formal votes, the actual voting power is always understood.

A member nation generally pays 75 percent of its quota in its own currency, usually as nonnegotiable, non-interest-bearing promissory notes. The remaining 25 percent portion of its contribution is paid in hard currencies of other nations or in the form of *special drawing rights* (SDR), a unique international reserve asset created and issued by the IMF. The SDR is a stable unit of account that is assigned a value based upon an average of the world's major currencies. It can be used for transactions with the IMF, to settle international balances between central banks, and to meet IMF membership subscription obligations.

In many cases, the IMF cannot effectively use the 75 percent of quota paid in a member's domestic currency because that currency is not readily acceptable in international transactions. Generally, the IMF uses only 20 currencies during a year, most of that in the form of major convertible currencies such as the dollar, yen and euro. It is estimated that one half of the money contributed to the IMF cannot be utilized in its operations. When the quota contributions are insufficient to its needs, the IMF may draw on a line of credit called the *General Arrangements to Borrow*, that it established with a number of governments and banks.

[3] Loans and Exchange Transactions

The IMF charter requires the Fund to provide temporary financial resources to members having economic difficulties related to trade imbalances. These imbalances arise in nations that do not receive enough foreign currency from exports of goods and services and from tourism to pay for their purchases from other countries. IMF help is needed by such nations to maintain a stable exchange rate for their currencies without incurring severe domestic unemployment or inflation or requiring significant reductions in imports.

Quota contributions are the primary source of currencies for IMF loans. The quota contributions form a pool of currencies that can be borrowed by members who need foreign exchange to fund their international obligations and restore their balance of payments. The amount a member nation may borrow from the IMF is based upon the quota it has contributed. If the member needs more funds, the IMF has discretion to provide additional loans totaling up to three times its quota over a three-year period.

Most loans are extended through IMF *arrangements*, which specify the amount of SDRs or foreign currency to be provided and the terms and duration of the loan. The IMF also provides concessional loans that are not related to a member's quota that support low income members efforts to deal with long-term balance of payment issues. These low interest loans and grants are provided through an Enhanced Structural Adjustment Facility (ESAF) and a heavily indebted poor countries (HIPC) debt initiative. In recent years, the IMF has established new discretionary loans that may exceed these limitations for member nations facing a sudden, disruptive loss of market confidence.

When the IMF allows a member to draw on resources related to its quota subscription, the transaction is not cast in the form of a loan. Instead, a member "purchases" another member's currency or SDRs from the IMF with its own currency, thereby obtaining needed foreign currencies, and agrees to later repurchase its own currency within a specified time. Because a fee is charged by the IMF and the member whose currency is borrowed, the transaction resembles a loan of the SDRs and usually is referred to as such.

[a] Lending Criteria

Many IMF loans are provided through longer term *standby* extended credit arrangements. These arrangements allow members to draw upon IMF resources up to a stated amount within a specified period. Typically, the standby credit is established at the beginning of the loan period through a letter of intent that commits the member to specific performance criteria regarding exchange rates, public debt, privatization and the like. In effect, the standby arrangement links IMF financial assistance to a nation's economic policies.[32] Stand-By Arrangements usually extend over 12 to 18 months and repayment is expected within 3 to 5 years of each drawing. The IMF's Extended Fund Facility (EFF) provides longer term assistance and larger amounts than standby arrangements. These loans are extended to remedy balance of payments problems arising from structural problems that require a longer period to resolve. These loans are disbursed over 4 to 5 years and repaid within 4 to 10 years of each drawing.

The IMF applies a range of lending criteria to different loan segments called *tranches,* that equal one quarter of the borrowing member's quota. Since one quarter of each nation's quota is contributed in SDRs or hard currencies, members may freely draw upon the first tranche, referred to as the *reserve* tranche. At any time, a member's reserve tranche is the amount by which its quota exceeds the amount of its own currency held by the IMF. A member may draw the full amount of its reserve tranche

---

[32] *See* Sidell, *The IMF and Third-World Political Instability: Is There a Connection?* (1988).

(by paying an equivalent amount of its own currency) at any time simply by stating that it is required for balance of payments purposes. Drawing on the reserve tranche is not considered an IMF loan, and is not subject to fees or repurchase obligations.

Borrowed amounts above the reserve tranche come out of IMF resources and are called *credit tranches*. These loans are subject to the *conditionality* requirements discussed *below*. To draw the first credit tranche, a member must show that it is making reasonable efforts to overcome its balance of payments problem. Borrowing against upper credit tranches usually is subject to more restrictive conditions and loan disbursements occur only as specified criteria are satisfied.

[b] Conditionality

When the IMF allows a member to draw upon the upper credit tranches, it usually imposes stringent conditions based upon two standards. First, the member must return the borrowed currencies as soon as its payment difficulty is resolved. This ensures that sufficient currencies are available to meet the needs of all members. Second, and most important, the member must describe the economic reforms it will introduce to solve its trade imbalance problem and demonstrate how the reforms will enable it to repay the loan within the agreed time period. In effect, most IMF loans are made only upon condition that the member use the borrowed funds to meet specific economic criteria established by the Fund.

This link between an IMF loan and the borrowers commitment to specific economic reforms is called *conditionality*. The required reforms usually relate to changed policies regarding government expenditures, interest and exchange rates, price deregulation, consumer subsidies, trade barriers, money supply, and similar matters. In recent years, however, the IMF has insisted upon more comprehensive and long range structural transformations, such as privatization of state owned enterprises, increased funding for social safety nets, health care, and education, strengthening banks and banking supervision, and undertaking effective measures to reduce corruption. The IMF is considering trade-related conditionality that would link financial aid to trade liberalization. A member's trade policies would be reported on an index of trade restrictiveness and, presumably, performance criteria would include adoption of specific free trade measures.

IMF Loans and Balance of Payments. A nation's balance of payments (BOP) account records its economic transactions during a year between its residents, including government, business and individuals, and the rest of the world. The BOP consists of the following elements:

    (1) The *current account*, which measures the country's net exports of goods and services.[33] A nation that exports more than

---

[33] Other elements of the BOP are the nation's capital account and foreign currency reserves.

it imports generates a surplus current account while a nation that imports more than it exports generates a deficit current account. A country with a deficit current account does not earn enough foreign currency from its exports to pay for what it buys from other nations. In that case, the deficit is financed either by spending the reserves of foreign currency the nation has accumulated in the past, or by borrowing from other countries.

(2) The *capital account,* which is the amount a country has borrowed from other countries. For example, when a U.S. Treasury bond is sold to a resident of Japan, the payment received from Japan is a capital inflow that creates a credit in the U.S. capital account. The reverse is true, so that a purchase of a Japanese bond by a U.S. resident is a capital outflow that is a debit to the U.S. capital account. A BOP deficit arises when a country's total payments to foreign countries (imports plus capital outflows) exceed its total receipts from abroad (exports plus capital inflows). In that case, the nation must use its foreign currency reserves to satisfy the unpaid amount.

(3) The nation's reserves of foreign currency.

To illustrate how an IMF arrangement may deal with a BOP imbalance, assume that Country X has a has a BOP deficit because the amount of dollars it receives from exports to the U.S. is less than the dollars it pays for imports from the U.S. If X has reserves of dollars in its central bank, it can use these to meet the deficit until the reserves are exhausted. If the BOP deficit is persistent, the foreign currency reserves are likely to be expended fairly quickly. Instead, X can borrow dollars from the IMF by exchanging its own currency for the dollars. The IMF will extend the loan, however, only on condition that X adopts specified policies that will increase its exports and reduce imports to the point that its BOP deficit is eliminated. Policies to reduce imports may include reductions in total domestic demand induced by tax increases, reduced government spending and credit limits. Policies to encourage exports may include elimination of export barriers and currency devaluations that make foreign goods much more expensive in the domestic market.

The IMF's guidelines on conditionality require the Fund to respect its members' domestic social and political objectives and their economic priorities and circumstances. Under these guidelines, conditionality is to be flexibly applied and provide for on-going review and consultation. Generally, performance criteria in standby or extended arrangement should be limited to economic variables related to satisfying IMF supported programs. The required policy changes are set forth in a "letter of intent," along with the performance criteria the member must meet to receive periodic loan disbursements. The IMF Executive Board regularly reviews the member's progress toward achieving the stated objectives.

Officially, a member's assurances about economic reforms, even if expressed in a letter of intent to a standby arrangement, is not a contractual obligation. Accordingly, no legal action may be taken to enforce these assurances or commitments. However, the IMF can indirectly enforce these agreements by withholding funds to countries that do not satisfy the loan conditions and restricting their access to future loans. Usually, the IMF will attempt to persuade or pressure a wayward nation into compliance, and in extreme case, it can expel a nation. In numerous situations, however, breaches of agreement have been overlooked.

[c] Criticisms of Conditionality

IMF lending policies have been the object of increasingly harsh criticism.[34] Some of the more common complaints about the IMF are summarized as follows:

- IMF secrecy about its activities makes it difficult for outsiders to evaluate its policies. The Fund does not report the details of its standby agreements with member nations nor the status of its loans.

- The IMF voting system based upon monetary contributions does not sufficiently account for the concerns of poor countries.

- Many of the conditions and performance criteria the IMF imposes do not foster economic growth and therefore, do not improve long-term economic conditions. Moreover, otherwise beneficial conditions often are ineffective because other national policies are not coordinated or work at cross-purposes.

- IMF conditions are not really enforced. In many cases, members that violate their agreements are granted waivers, modified conditions or newly negotiated loans. Thus, large sums have been provided to nations that misspent prior loans which they are unable or unwilling to repay.

- The IMF does not monitor its performance criteria uniformly, so that great variations exist between programs.

- Free-market solutions such as high interest rates to retain capital, and currency devaluations and austerity programs to discourage imports are overemphasized. These measures often result in high unemployment and dramatic declines in living standards that weaken the nation's political structure and prevent meaningful reform.

- The entire IMF lending program creates long-term dependency rather than short-term assistance.[35] Less-developed countries increasingly rely on IMF loans for longer periods.

---

[34] See "The IMF: A Record of Addiction and Failure," published in *Perpetuating Poverty: The World Bank, the IMF, and the Developing World*, edited by Doug Bandow and Ian Vasquez (1994).

[35] See Johnson and Schaefer, *The International Monetary Fund: Outdated, Ineffective, and Unnecessary* (Heritage Foundation 1997).

- IMF loans cannot be shown to improve the borrowers' economic conditions. Most borrowers of conditional loans are economically worse off than before the loan. It is unclear whether the decline is attributable to the conditions themselves or to lack of adherence to them. It may be both; most countries that meet IMF conditions outperform countries that do not, but borrowers as a whole exhibit low economic growth rates.

- Many criticisms are ideological, maintaining that the Fund provides too little or too much support to non-market or socialist economic systems.

- The IMF (and World Bank) is a tool of capitalism that operates to maximize profits for big multinationals and maintain U.S. domination over the world economy.

- The IMF conditions harm poorer people of lesser developed nations by requiring governments to privatize public assets and reduce expenditures for social services such as health care, education, and pensions. The poor bear a disproportionate burden of these policies. Of course, the issue is whether the short term distress created by the economic adjustments is necessary to achieve sustainable long term growth. In this view, the groups most affected by the economic reforms ultimately will obtain the most benefit from them. In response to this criticism, however, the IMF has begun to focus on "safety net" programs that moderate the impact of economic reform on a country's lower economic classes.

- Foreign multi-national corporations benefit more than the local population from conditions that require a country to de-regulate its economy by eliminating tariffs, trade barriers and subsidies to local industries. Most profits of the multinationals are taken out of the country.

- Removal of restrictions on foreign investment allows multinationals to destroy the environment and take advantage of cheap, sweatshop labor conditions.

- IMF programs result in lower wages and poorer working conditions in developing nations, which indirectly decreases workers' living standards in the industrialized countries.

[4] Other IMF Functions

[a] Currency Exchange Rate Surveillance

As noted above, the IMF abandoned the gold exchange standard in 1978 and has since allowed each member to choose its own system for determining its currency exchange value. Most of the major industrial countries have adopted floating systems that allow the value of their currencies to be determined, with little intervention, in the global market. A number of nations have floating rate systems that they more actively manage by having their central banks buy or sell their currencies in the exchange market. Still others have fixed rate systems that peg the value of their currency to another major currency such as the dollar.

Because of the variety of systems in use, the IMF has been given a *surveillance* and supervisory role regarding the currency exchange policies of its members. The surveillance is designed to ensure that IMF members'

- implement economic policies that are consistent with their exchange rate systems;

- maintain adequate capital inflows;

- have a strong banking and financial sector;

- pursue sound economic policies, and;

- provide the data needed for effective IMF surveillance.

In this role, the IMF may examine and monitor all aspects of a member's economy that affect the exchange rate of its currency and report its findings to the membership. Generally, this bilateral surveillance occurs through annual consultations between the Executive Board and staff with individual member countries.[36] By making each member's economic policies and conditions transparent, the IMF hopes to avoid the kind of sudden loss of confidence in a nation's currency that led to economic crises in Mexico and Asia in recent years.

Effective surveillance requires that members provide their macroeconomic and financial data to the Fund in a timely fashion. The IMF has developed standards for providing such information to the Fund and to the public. The *Special Data Dissemination Standard* (SDDS) sets forth the statistical information and standards to be provided by members desiring access to international capital markets. This information is posted on the IMF's Internet Dissemination Standards Bulletin Board (DSBB). The Fund has also established the *General Data Dissemination System,* which is a general standard for all IMF members in providing statistics and economic and financial indicators.

The IMF consults with each of its members at least annually to ensure that their currency policies are prudent and transparent and to obtain information about their economic condition. The consultation is conducted by a team of IMF staff that first collects extensive economic data about a member, and then meets with its government officials to discuss the effectiveness of its economic and currency policies during the past year and any new policies it intends to implement in the next year. These policy discussions also may include social, environmental, industrial, labor, and governance issues that affect the country's economic condition. A recent focus of the consultative discussions has been the economic consequences of highly unequal income distributions. The staff prepares a report for

---

[36] *See* IMF Charter Article IV.

discussion by the Executive Board and the Board forwards a summary of the discussion, with suggestions, to the member's government.

Special consultations are held with governments of members whose economic policies greatly impact the world economy. These special consultations are held to assess the global economy and forecast developments in the forthcoming year. The IMF publishes these reviews twice a year in the *World Economic Outlook,* which members can rely upon in setting their economic policies.

[b] Technical Training and Assistance

The IMF provides training and technical assistance to its members in the following areas:

- fiscal and monetary policies;

- institution building, such as central banks, treasuries, tax and customs departments, and statistical services, and;

- economic and financial legislation.

Specific areas of development have included financial analysis and policy, balance of payments methodology, public finance, government finance statistics, economic management, tax reform and administration, and central bank development. The Fund also provides advice about money and capital markets, banking interest rates, and how financial instruments are used in monetary management. These technical assistance projects are becoming larger and more complex, involving longer time periods and multiple sources of financing.

The IMF also provides numerous training courses for government officials at its Washington headquarters, and at regional locations. IMF missions and experts also are assigned to foreign posts to provide advice and support regarding monetary, fiscal, and statistical problems that contribute to trade imbalances.

§ 1.04 The World Bank

[1] General Structure and Operation

The World Bank is the commonly used name for the *International Bank for Reconstruction and Development* that was established at the Bretton Woods Conference in 1944. The Bank was created at the same time as the International Monetary Fund and both institutions work together in many areas. However, the institutions have different roles: the World Bank acts principally to foster economic development among its members, while the IMF acts primarily to maintain an orderly system of international payments between nations.

Bank policy is controlled by a board of governors comprising one governor from each member nation. Daily operations are conducted by the Bank's twenty-two executive directors, headed by the World Bank president elected by the board for a five year term. The President is neither a governor nor director. Five executive directors are appointed by the five countries holding the most capital shares in the bank. The remaining directors are elected by the governors from the other members.

The Bank comprises the International Bank for Reconstruction and Development (IBRD) and the International Development Association (IDA) and is associated with a number of other agencies including the International Finance Corporation. The institutions are legally and financially separate, but share staff and administrative services. The Bank employs more than 7,000 staff members and maintains 40 offices throughout the world. Its headquarters are in Washington, D.C.

The World Bank's initial task was to provide loans to Western European countries to finance reconstruction of industries that were destroyed in the Second World War. After completing that job, the Bank shifted its focus to poorer, economically developing countries in Africa, Asia, and Latin America. The Bank also provides a substantial amount of technical assistance to its members, both in relation to a loan or as a separate undertaking.

[2] Lending Activities

The World Bank is owned by the governments of its member nations, all of which also belong to the IMF. Members subscribe to, or purchase a minimum number of shares determined by reference to the relative size of their economies. The seven largest industrial countries together own about 45 percent of the World Bank and are therefore, very influential in determining bank policies. The U.S. is the largest shareholder at 17 percent. Because an 85 percent vote is needed to change the Bank's capital structure and Charter, the U.S. maintains an important veto power. Most other Bank decisions, including loans, are decided by majority vote.

A portion of each government's subscription amount is paid immediately and the rest may be called upon if required to meet the Bank's obligations. Most of the operating funds the Bank lends to members are obtained by issuing bonds through world capital markets and directly to governments, agencies, central banks, private institutions, and individuals around the world. The bonds are highly rated (AAA) because the Bank's member governments guarantee their repayment. The IDA part of the Bank makes concessional, low interest loans, that are financed by grants from donor nations. The bank's lending activities are generally profitable.

The bank's main activity is to provide low interest loans to its member nations that will finance specific projects. Loans are extended after the Bank's advisers and experts determine that the borrower can meet specified conditions ensuring productive use of the funds and ultimate repayment. The project must be feasible and economically sensible and the borrower must be unable to obtain the loan from other sources. Periodic reports to the Bank are made by the borrower and the Bank's observers regarding the use of the funds.

Under the Bank's charter, a loan can only be made for productive purposes with due regard to the prospects for repayment. However, the Bank must ascertain that the funds cannot be obtained elsewhere on reasonable terms. Each loan must be for a specific project and guaranteed by the Government involved. The loan terms cannot restrict use of the funds to purchases in a particular country.

World Bank loans are made to governments of developing nations, their agencies or to private businesses in their territories, with repayment arrangements that are most favorable to the poorest countries. A developing country with a per capita gross national product [37] (GNP) of about $1,300 or more may borrow from the IBRD at an interest rate slightly above the market rate for a 12 to 15 year period. These loans are funded by bonds sales. A poorer country with a lower per capital GNP, currently around $900, may borrow from the IDA interest free for a 35 to 40 year period. Essentially, these loans constitute outright grants that are financed by credits contributed by a number of wealthier member nations. Although the terms of IBRD and IDA loans differ, both institutions apply the same standards in assessing a project's viability.

During the first years of the Bank's operations, most of its loans were provided to fund infrastructure projects relating to electric power and transportation for large cities. More recently, Bank support has focused on projects that provide more direct benefits to poor people in developing countries. For example, many transportation projects now concentrate on bringing goods from farms to market and power projects on lighting for villages and small communities. Many recent World Bank loans relate to agriculture, rural and urban development, water safety, waste management, health care, family-planning, nutrition, education, housing and small enterprises.

[3] Criticisms of World Bank Activities

Like the IMF, the World Bank has been subject to harsh criticism. Some of the more common complaints about the Bank are summarized as follows:

- Bank funded agricultural projects often harm small farmers and favor larger producers. This occurs when projects encourage growing cash crops that require fertilizers, pesticides and contribute to soil erosion. Large irrigation projects, such as dams, usually benefit the large growers that have political power.

- The Bank has funded projects that harm the environment including dams, mines, and logging ventures. Pollution control agreements often are ineffective because developing nations resent

---

[37] Per capita GNP is determined by dividing the value of goods and services a nation produces in a year by the number of people in the country.

restrictions on the use of their resources that did not apply to the richer nations during their early periods of economic expansion.

- Bank policies favor the interests of the richest industrialized nations. These countries require poorer nations to deplete their natural resources, such as oil and lumber, in order to repay massive debt loads. Environmentally harmful projects are shifted from richer nations with substantial regulations to developing countries with less restrictive standards. Unemployment and low domestic wages make these activities attractive to poor countries despite the environmental hazards.

- Loans to governments that violate human rights help maintain these regimes in power. In such cases, a loan to a repressive government to build a school releases other funds for the army and weapons purchases. Some critics contend that the Bank has denied loans to countries, but later approved funding for the same project when a more authoritarian regime took power.

- The Bank funds projects that require forced resettlement of native inhabitants. This occurs when local populations are removed from the land required for projects such as dams or roads and when urban projects force residents to relocate. Often, the financial promises made to induce a population to resettle are not kept. A number of dam projects funded by the Bank have been harshly criticized because of the large scale forced migrations involved.

- Bank projects disproportionately impact indigenous populations tribal land rights, ethnic identities, and cultural autonomy. Although the Bank has adopted guidelines that allow tribal people a right to veto projects that affect these matters, critics contend that there has been little compliance.

- Bank funded projects do not proportionately benefit women. This may be true even for projects that have overall positive economic outcomes. For example, a project that provides employment for women does not account for the increased burden on a typical woman who must continue to perform all her homemaking duties in addition to the new job.

- Bank projects support state sponsored development rather than private initiatives. This often results in support for corrupt and ineffective regimes. By sponsoring large projects that are controlled by governments, the Bank encourages economic development that is highly centralized and regulated.

- Many projects the Bank and IMF supports create "moral hazard." This means that governments may undertake speculative and risky economic projects because they know that the Bank or IMF will provide financing to bail them out.

- Low interest loans to failing economies do not provide incentive to establish a good credit rating. Indeed, nations with good credit can obtain commercial loans at competitive rates, thereby making them ineligible for loans from the World Bank.

Chapter 2

THE RULES OF INTERNATIONAL TRADE

§ 2.01 General Considerations

[1] Free Trade and Comparative Advantage

National and International policies to encourage international trade are based upon the prevailing notion that free trade enhances economic growth. This idea is based upon the theory of *comparative advantage* which asserts that a nation will prosper if it concentrates on producing the goods and services that its natural and human resources allow it to produce best, and trading these for goods and services best produced by other countries. Under this theory, first enunciated by the economist David Ricardo (1772–1823), free trade policies that allow an unrestricted flow of goods and services provide greater prosperity for all trading nations.

This remains true even though a nation's comparative advantages in particular areas are likely to change over time. For example, a country can lose the comparative advantage of its natural resources because of technological change (*e.g.,* oil replacing coal, or plastic replacing metal) and it can lose its advantage in labor costs as its economy develops. In a free trade environment, however, the nation's businesses and entrepreneurs will gradually adapt to these changes by shifting production to areas where a comparative advantage currently exists.

It is important to distinguish comparative advantage from absolute advantage. A country has absolute advantage if it produces a product more efficiently than its trading partner. In that case, it is obvious that it will benefit by concentrating on producing and exporting that product. Comparative advantage exists when a nation can produce one product more efficiently than it can produce other products. To illustrate, assume that Country X is a highly competitive producer of computers and a good producer of steel and that Country Y produces steel well, but not as competitively as Country X. In that case, both countries will benefit by concentrating on producing and exporting the product they make best and importing the other product. Country X should concentrate on making its best product, computers, and import its steel. Country Y should concentrate on making its best product, steel, and import its computers. Both countries will benefit from trade because it will allow each to concentrate on producing the products it makes best and most efficiently.

Many nations and leaders learned the ruinous consequences of restrictive trade policies from the period between the two great World Wars. During this period of the Great Depression, many countries adopted *protectionist* trade policies that attempted to protect their industry, agriculture and labor from foreign competition by imposing high tariffs on imports. The result was higher costs for lower quality products and extensive government subsidies to keep inefficient producers in business. As more and more countries closed their borders to imports, economic activity around the world declined and the depression deepened. Although free trade policies often create hardships for workers and businesses that must adapt to economic change, economists believe that these problems tend to be temporary and less severe than the pervasive harm that results from restrictive trade policies.

[2]　Tariffs

A *tariff* is a tax on imported goods that raises the price of the goods in the importing country. The effect of a tariff is to allow domestic producers of the same or similar goods to receive a higher price for their products than they could in a free trade situation. Although the producers benefit from the tariff, as does the government that receives tariff revenues, this benefit is usually outweighed by the detriment to the consumer. Overall, tariffs are more likely to harm rather than help a country's economy.

A tariff expressed as a fixed charge per unit of the imported item is called a *specific tariff*. Although this kind of tariff is simple and inexpensive to administer, it is not an effective barrier to imports in inflationary times of rising prices. Most tariffs are *ad valorem* duties that require the importer to pay a stated percentage of the value of the imported goods. Because valuations may vary greatly over time and from country to country, ad valorem tariffs can be difficult to administer.

Notwithstanding the economic arguments against tariffs and other trade restrictions, many countries, including the U.S., find ample reasons to inhibit many kinds of imports. The most frequently cited reasons include:

- *Avoiding unemployment.* When domestic consumers purchase low-priced imported goods domestic production of those products declines, resulting in increased unemployment. The political consequences of unemployment often compels governments to impose tariffs or other trade restrictions.

- *Protection of nascent domestic industries.* Tariff protection allows budding national industries to develop and grow. Industries in developing countries whose workers are inexperienced and lack technological expertise require protection in order to compete with larger industrial nations. Once these new industries are established, they achieve the comparative advantage that eventually enhances the world economy.

- *Improving Trade Terms.* Because a tariff reduces the domestic consumption of an imported good, the foreign producer may be forced to decrease the price. Thus, the importing country benefits from the better terms of trade.

- *Preventing Dumping.* Dumping occurs when a foreign producer exports goods at a price that is lower than its cost of production in order to harm or destroy a domestic producer or prevent unemployment in its home country. Anti-dumping tariffs protect domestic producers against such unfair trade practices.

- *Enhancing National Security.* This noneconomic argument asserts that certain industries that are essential to national defense must be preserved through protectionism even if higher costs result.

Although any one or all of these arguments may be persuasive in a particular case, the economic evidence is quite clear that long-term, substantial trade restrictions inhibit economic growth and well-being. The fact that so many governments still impose such restrictions is explained by the fact that groups and interests that benefit from protectionist policies usually are highly focused and organized to influence government policies. The beneficiaries of tariffs include domestic business owners and unions that are quite effective in promoting their interests, while the adversely affected consumers are a diverse unfocused constituency.

§ 2.02 The World Trade Organization (WTO)

[1] History — GATT to WTO

The *World Trade Organization* was formed in 1995, replacing the prior international trade agreement and organization called the *General Agreement on Tariffs and Trade* (GATT). The GATT was created in 1947 to foster international cooperation in reducing tariffs and other barriers to international trade. It was originally intended to operate as part of a comprehensive International Trade Organization (ITO) that would work in conjunction with the International Monetary Fund and World Bank to regulate international economic affairs. Although the U.S. Congress rejected the entire ITO treaty as being too broad in scope, it did agree to provisional acceptance of a number of trade and tariff rules in the treaty. These rules, initially accepted by 23 nations, formed the GATT that became effective in January, 1948. From that time until the WTO was created in 1995, the "provisional" GATT was the principal international trade pact.

The GATT was expanded and modified by member nations at periodic lengthy conferences called *rounds* that are referred to by their locale or key participants. Altogether, eight GATT rounds were held between 1947 and 1994. The earliest five rounds in Switzerland, France, and the U.K focused on tariff reduction; the sixth Kennedy Round, from 1964 to 1967, resulted in an Anti-Dumping Agreement. At the seventh Tokyo Round, from 1973 to 1979, the members agreed to a number of measures to reduce non-tariff trade barriers.

At the eighth GATT conference, the Uruguay Round, from 1986–94, the participants adopted extensive new trade rules governing goods, services, and ideas, terminated the GATT, and incorporated most of its provisions into the new WTO that began operating in 1995. The Uruguay Round agreement, signed by 125 countries, consists of a Final Act that establishes the WTO and amends the GATT rules to dramatically lower tariffs and other trade barriers. An annex to the Final Act contains thousands of agreements that fix schedules for reducing national barriers to market access for specific goods and services.

Although the WTO incorporates many of the GATT trade rules, it has a far wider scope. The GATT was formed after the Second World War to govern trade in goods — the most important component of world trade at that time. Since then, other areas of economic activity have become increasingly important, including trade in services, such as banking, insurance, and telecommunications, and trade in intellectual property, such as inventions, trademarks, and copyrights. Accordingly, the WTO addresses these areas in a *General Agreement on Trade in Services* (GATS) and an *Agreement on Trade-Related Aspects of Intellectual Property Rights* (TRIPS). In addition to these uniform rules to govern new global trade relationships, the WTO provides a more effective dispute settlement system to resolve trade conflicts, and a *Trade Policy Review Mechanism* for monitoring and harmonizing its members' trade practices. A few WTO agreements are plurilateral (rather than multilateral) and apply only to signatory states with larger industrial economies.

During its first years of operation, the WTO has completed trade negotiations and resulting agreements in a number of areas. These agreements include the *Information Technology Agreement* (ITA) that commits 43 WTO members to eliminate tariffs on numerous information technology products such as computers and semiconductors and the *Agreement on Basic Telecommunications Services* that commits 69 WTO members to open their markets in this area.

[2] Membership and Organization

[a] Membership

More the 140 countries, including China and Taiwan, which became members in 2001, are currently members of the WTO. More than 30 nations are seeking membership, including Russia and other constituents of the former Soviet Union. To become a member, a nation must have full autonomy over its trade policies. A WTO committee will be formed to examine all aspects of the applicants trade and economic policies that may affect its WTO agreements. The applicant also must participate in bilateral negotiations with appropriate member nations to establish specific commitments and concessions on goods and services. After the committee presents its report on the application to the WTO Ministerial Conference, a two-thirds vote of the membership is required for acceptance of the new member. At its inception the WTO included all of the 128 GATT participants.

[b]   Joining the WTO — The Accession of China

The process by which a country becomes a member of the WTO is called *accession*. This process begins when the WTO establishes a *Working Party* to approve the terms of accession and recommend that the General Council invite the applicant to become a member.[1] All WTO members may participate in the Working Party which operates by consensus, meaning that any WTO member can block a favorable recommendation until its specific concerns are addressed. Once a favorable recommendation reaches the General Council, a two-thirds vote is required for accession, although in practice all accessions have been by consensus without a vote taken.

The accession recommendation is based upon specific bilateral agreements between the applicant and other WTO members regarding market access for their goods and services. These agreements, which are independently negotiated between the applicant and each member, are included in a schedule of specific commitments incorporated into the accession agreement (protocol), and are enforceable through the WTO dispute settlement mechanism. In addition to these bilateral agreements, the Working Party negotiates the applicant's specific commitments, rights, and obligations to conform to the WTO rules and deal with WTO members in accordance with these rules.

After the terms of accession are approved, the General Council formally invites the applicant to join at a specific future date. This date allows the applicant sufficient time to revise its domestic laws and regulations and prepare its business and economic community for the new trade regime. The accession process is finalized thirty days after the applicant accepts the invitation by reply to the Director General of the WTO.

The recent accession of China to the WTO in January, 2002, is an important event in itself, as well as an excellent illustration of the issues involved in the accession process. China's attempt to join the global trading community goes back to 1986 when it applied for membership in the GATT, the precursor of the WTO.[2] The GATT Council established a Working Party in 1987, beginning a 15-year long accession process for China. The process was completed at the 2001 WTO Ministerial Conference in Qatar, which finally approved China's accession agreement.

China's began its accession process by providing the Working Party with detailed and updated information about its trade laws, regulations and

---

[1] *See generally*, Field, *Status Of The Negotiations on China's Accession to the World Trade Organization*, 817 PLI/Comm 7 (February 2001).

[2] China had been an original member of GATT but withdrew in 1950 after the Communist regime took over.

procedures. This information was the basis for the multilateral negotiations between China and the Working Party regarding the rules that will govern trade between China and all WTO members. At the same time, China negotiated bilateral agreements with each interested WTO member establishing specific market access commitments and concessions.

A summary of the bilateral agreement between the U.S. and China regarding accession illustrates the substantial commitments that WTO membership may entail.

- **Industry.** China will phase out or significantly reduce quotas and tariffs on a wide range of industrial goods. Industrial tariffs will decline from an average of 25 percent in 1997 to 8.9 percent. Most reductions will be implemented by January 1, 2005, although reductions for some products will not be completed until 2010. China will participate in the Information Technology Agreement (ITA), which requires elimination of tariffs on most IT products by January 1, 2003 and elimination of all such tariffs by January 1, 2005.

- **Services.** China has committed to substantial liberalization of access in all major service sectors by eliminating most restrictions on foreign ownership and geographic locations. This access applies to important U.S. service industries such as banking, insurance, telecommunications, and professional services, such as accounting, legal, and management consultancy. China will accede to the WTO's Basic Telecommunications and Financial Services agreements.

- **Agriculture.** China will reduce its agricultural tariffs by more than half on U.S. priority products, from an average of 31% to 14% by January 2004, and it will eliminate certain trade-distorting export subsidies. U.S. producers may export and distribute directly inside China for most agricultural product without going through state-trading enterprises or middlemen. Sanitary and phytosanitary barriers that are not based on scientific evidence will be eliminated.

- **Trading and distribution rights.** China will phase in trading rights and distribution services over three years. US firms will be allowed to trade, distribute, and sell goods and engage in auxiliary services such as leasing, air-courier, warehousing, advertising, and packaging. These trading and distribution services agreements will permit U.S. businesses to export directly to China, using their own distribution networks in China. This differs from the pre-WTO situation that often required U.S. producers to establish factories in China to sell products through Chinese partners.

The U.S.-China bilateral negotiations also resulted in new *safeguard* provisions designed to protect specific sectors of the U.S. economy from surges in imports from China as well as from unfair trading practices such as dumping. These provisions include:

- **China-specific safeguards.** For a period of 12 years, safeguards that are specific to China will provide targeted relief to protect against surges of imports from China. These safeguards are in addition to the U.S. rules under Section 201,[3] and to the global safeguard provisions under the WTO.[4] This allows the U.S. to impose tariffs on Chinese products if an increase in imports causes or threatens to cause disruption of U.S. markets. This provision applies to all industries and allows action based upon a lesser showing of injury than existing rules.

- **Anti-dumping rules.** For a period of 15 years, the U.S. may use special methods to counteract dumping by Chinese firms.

- **Elimination of barriers to U.S. companies.** A mechanism is provided, enforceable under WTO rules, to prevent certain actions by Chinese companies and government such as forced technology transfer, mandated offsets, local content requirements and similar practices that may result in loss of U.S. jobs and technology.

- **New WTO rules.** New rules will allow the U.S. to continue to bar imports of goods made with prison labor, maintain its export control policies, and apply its trade laws, when dealing with a country holding MFN status.

> **The Russian Federation.** At the end of 2004, twenty-seven countries were engaged in negotiations to join the WTO, including the Russian Federation and six other former members of the Soviet Union. Although the Working Party on Russia's accession was established in 1993, negotiations still continue into 2005. Although it is likely that Russia will accede in 2005, it will be the last major economic power to join the WTO.

[c] Organization

WTO decisions are made directly by its member nations through a variety of committees and councils comprised of all members. Decisions are arrived at by consensus rather than by majority vote. Although this can be cumbersome in an organization of more than 140 members, it does result in policies that all members can accept. Because all members are directly represented on its governing bodies, the WTO, unlike the IMF and World Bank, does not delegate decisions or power to a board of directors or a bureaucracy.

---

[3] *See* 3.02, 3.03.

[4] *See* 2.02[5].

The highest level of policy decisions are taken by the members' trade ministers at a *Ministerial Conference* that convenes every two years to discuss outstanding issues and negotiate new initiatives.[5] The Ministers appoint the WTO's director-general for a three year term. The current director general is Supachai Panitchpakdi, the former deputy prime minister and commerce minister of Thailand.

The first two meetings, in Singapore in 1996, and Geneva in 1998, were relatively uncontroversial and resulted in minor new agreements relating to information technology products[6] and electronic commerce.[7] However, certain issues raised, but not resolved, in Singapore regarding investment and competition became highly contentious at subsequent Ministerial Conferences. Indeed, these subsequent meetings revealed significant policy disagreements between economically developed and developing countries and have become a focal point for public demonstrations of dissatisfaction with WTO policies and anti-globalization sentiment.

At the Seattle Ministerial Meeting in December, 1999, many developing countries complained that the benefits of WTO membership were not evenly distributed among members and that the organization's policies did not foster sustainable development. Specific areas of contention included trade barriers and subsidies in developed countries that restricted imports of agricultural products and textiles from developing nations that held a comparative advantage in these areas. The meeting also was marked by numerous street demonstrations, some violent, that focused on the lack of WTO labor and environmental standards. Because of the general geographic distributions of developed and developing countries, the persisting tensions about trade policy is often referred to as the "North-South" rift.

The fourth WTO Ministerial Conference, convened in Doha, Qatar, in November, 2001, focused on development issues and produced the Doha Development Agenda (DDA) setting forth specific negotiation objectives and deadlines for technical assistance and capacity-building programs.[8] However, these commitments to these programs in the DDA were not funded and could not be enforced through the dispute resolution mechanism. Accordingly, implementation of the agreed upon technical assistance and capacity building agenda depended on the amount and timing of the funds provided by the wealthiest WTO member nations.

The lack of progress on the Doha Agenda presaged the contentious Ministerial Conference held in Cancun, Mexico, in 2003. In Cancun,

---

[5] The meetings are required pursuant to the WTO Charter, Marrakesh Agreement Establishing the World Trade Organization, 15 April 1994, Final Act Embodying the Results of the Uruguay Round of Multilateral Trade Negotiations, art. IV, para 1.

[6] WTO, Ministerial Declaration on Trade in Information Technology Products, Singapore, 13 December 1996. The agreement requires tariff reductions on a range of information technology products.

[7] WTO, Declaration on Global Economic Commerce, adopted on 20 May 1998, WT/MIN(98)/DEC/2, The members agreed to examine trade-related aspects of electronic commerce and agreed to continue exempting tariffs on electronic transmissions.

[8] WTO, The Doha Ministerial Declaration, November 14, 2001, para 2.

representatives of developing countries as well as leaders of the IMF, World Bank and OECD, pressed the wealthier WTO members, particularly the United States and European Union, to eliminate the subsidies and protectionist policies regarding agricultural products and textiles. These subsidies and policies, it was vehemently argued, denied market access to the products that developing nations were able to export most competitively. The wealthier nations made few concessions regarding agriculture, but urged the conference to focus on the investment and competition issues raised at the Singapore meeting. The Cancun meeting adjourned with little progress, much rancor, and scant prospect of reaching a multilateral agreement on any issues.

The second level of decision is the *General Council*, also comprising all members, which conducts the organization's routine operations. The Council acts on behalf of and reports to the Ministerial Conference. It also convenes and acts as the WTO's Dispute Settlement Body and Trade Policy Review Body.

The General Council assigns the technical work needed to implement the WTO agreements to three subsidiary councils that act in specific trade areas. These include:

- The Council for Trade in Goods (Goods Council).

- The Council for Trade in Services (Services Council).

- The Council for Trade-Related Aspects of Intellectual Property (TRIPS Council).

These councils also comprise all member states and report to the General Council. A number of other committees and working groups responsible for specific areas, such environment, administration, investment and competition policy, transparency, etc., also comprise all members and report to the General Council.

[3] The Basic Agreements

The World Trade Organization is now the paramount forum for conducting multinational trade negotiations and implementing the resulting agreements. These negotiations and agreements are intended to encourage and enhance free trade by:

- removing national policies that obstruct international flows of goods, services and ideas;

- establishing clear, predictable, transparent trade rules for governments and businesses, and;

- providing a neutral, legal, dispute settlement process for resolving trade-related controversies.

To implement its policy of enhancing free trade, the WTO (and previously GATT) requires all its member states to adopt four basic principles (referred to as "pillars"):

1. *Most-favored nation treatment.* This principle prohibits a member from adopting discriminatory trade practices by requiring that a trade privilege (such as a lower tariff on a product) it grants to any country be granted to all WTO members. Thus, a country that eliminates a trade barrier or opens up a market to a particular product or service must do so for all WTO members. Generally, the MFN requirement applies to all the WTO agreements governing trade in goods (GATT), services (GATS), and intellectual property (TRIPS). Limited exceptions permit regional trade groups (such as the EU and NAFTA) to adopt trade agreements that only apply within the group and allow discrimination against products from countries that engage in unfair trade practices.

2. *National treatment.* Under this principle, foreign goods, services, and intellectual property, such as trademarks, copyrights, and patents that have legally entered a market must be treated in the same manner as domestic goods and services, and intellectual property.[9] National treatment applies after a product, service or idea enters a country, so that imposition of a tariff does not contravene the national treatment principle, even if domestic goods are not subject to a comparable charge.

3. *Tariff bindings.* WTO members must accept the principle of tariff binding (or concession), which are agreements to eliminate, reduce or limit tariff rates they will impose on imports over a given time period. By placing a ceiling on tariff increases, bindings create a stable and predictable market environment for international trade. Tariff rates are negotiated at WTO rounds, after which each member publishes a schedule that sets forth the tariff it agreed to maintain for a variety of specific goods. The schedules set forth the maximum tariffs that may be imposed, although developing countries sometimes charge lower rates. A nation can only change its bindings through negotiations, which may require it to compensate affected countries for any resulting loss in their trade revenues.

4. *Elimination of quotas and other non-tariff barriers.* WTO members are committed to eliminate or reduce a variety of non-tariff measures that restrict or impede free trade, including quotas and other numerical limitations on imports. Other barriers include excessive paperwork requirements and undisclosed or burdensome trade rules. WTO agreements often require governments to publicly disclose their trade rules and practices and the Trade Policy Review Mechanism scrutinizes national trade policies to encourage transparency and discourage restrictive policies.

---

[9] *See* GATT Article 3, GATS Article 17 and TRIPS Article 3.

[4] Specific Agreements

Membership in the WTO requires assent to three broad trade agreements: the General Agreement of Tariffs and Trade (GATT) that applies to goods, the General Agreement on Trade in Services (GATS), and the agreement on Trade Related Aspects o Intellectual Property Rights (TRIPS). The following sections describe the most important aspects of these agreements, but omit detailed explication of the lengthy annexes and special rules that apply in each area.

[a] GATT and Tariff Bindings

The purpose for the GATT is to reduce or eliminate the tariffs that impede free trade in goods. Under the GATT, as expanded by the Uruguay round, WTO members have substantially decreased tariffs on most products and significantly increased the number of bound tariffs. Generally, a tariff is bound under the GATT when a nation agrees (makes a concession) not to raise its rate above a specified level. Tariff bindings result from conferences between WTO members in which the parties make reciprocal concessions relating to their tariffs on items involved in their mutual trade. Ordinarily, the agreement results in lower tariff rates on all the products under discussion. Although a country can rescind a tariff binding, the process may be difficult and costly.

The Uruguay round resulted in significant tariff cuts and bindings for must products. Most of these tariff reductions have been phased in since 1995. Different amounts of reduction and different time periods apply to countries with developed and developing economies. At present, more than 98 percent of the products traded by WTO members are subject to tariff bindings and 100 percent of agricultural products are bound.

[b] Uruguay Round Agricultural Agreement (URAA)

The Uruguay Round began with a consensus that the rules governing international agricultural trade required dramatic reform. These reforms focused on three areas: market access; direct and indirect subsidies; and sanitary and phytosanitary measures. The trade problems in these areas had become particularly acute because government policies had greatly *distorted* the international agricultural markets.

Trade in agricultural products often is *distorted*, meaning that prices and production generally are higher or lower than they would be in a competitive market. Distortion occurs because governments protect farmers from foreign competition for a number of non-economic reasons, including:

- ensuring an adequate food supply for the country's long-term needs;

- protecting the incomes of farmers against risks such as weather and unpredictable price fluctuations, and;

- preservation of rural populations and cultures.

Agricultural distortions generally result from various policies that subsidize domestic growers and create barriers to imported products. These policies are likely to raise domestic prices, which in turn encourages overproduction. The resulting surplus often cannot be sold on world markets without export subsidies, which again promote overproduction. The consequence has been destructive agricultural trade wars involving high subsidies, quotas and other import restrictions, and tariffs.

The Uruguay Round Agricultural Agreement (URAA) implemented a market-oriented approach to establishing stable and predictable agricultural trade. Nearly all agricultural products are now subject to tariff bindings, and most quotas and other non-tariff import restrictions have been converted to tariffs (through tariffication) that provide the same level of protection against imports. Thus, the only permissible restriction on market access for imported agricultural goods is a tariff. Over time, most countries have agreed to reduce these tariffs. Beginning in 1995, developed countries began to reduce tariffs by an average of 36% over six years and developing countries by 24% over 10 years. The agreement also provides for tariff-quotas, designed to ensure that countries will not decrease the quantity of products that may be imported under the new rules.

To control subsidized overproduction, the URAA requires substantial reductions in agricultural support that directly affects production. Support that only minimally affects production, such as research, and environmental programs is unaffected. The URAA also prohibits most agricultural export subsidies.

The Cancun Ministerial Conference. Continuing agricultural subsidies for farmers in wealthy industrial countries are a very contentious issue within the WTO. Many developing countries argue that these subsidies deny market access to the products that they can export most competitively and ruin their small farmers by flooding their markets with cheap, subsidized food imports. The issue erupted at the 2003 Ministerial Conference in Cancun, Mexico, where many of the developing nations refused to continue negotiations on issues of concern to the wealthier countries, such as investment, competition policy and government procurement, until their agricultural policies are reformed.

Although the Uruguay and Doha Rounds of negotiations committed all countries to decrease supports for domestic agriculture, and increase market access for agricultural imports, little progress has been made in this area. Despite their commitments, the EU failed to reform its Common Agricultural Policy (CAP) that provides agricultural supports, and the U.S. Farm Bill dramatically increased support for agriculture. These actions were driven by complex, non-economic issues that affect agricultural policy in industrial countries, such as cultural preservation, food security, and biodiversity.

At Cancun a bloc of developing countries was formed to demand significant cuts in agricultural subsidies and tariffs by the developed countries. This bloc, called the G20 group, included large nations such as Brazil, India, China, Argentina, and South Africa, Nigeria and Indonesia and smaller countries like Bolivia, Chile, Cuba, Egypt, Mexico, Pakistan, Paraguay, the Philippines, Thailand, Venezuela, Tanzania and Zimbabwe. The bloc, supported by many other developing countries, insisted that the agricultural issues be settled before discussion of other investment and trade topics. Although the EU and U.S. made some concessions regarding agriculture, these were deemed insufficient and the Cancun meeting terminated without concluding any substantive agreements. There has been little progress on these issues since the Cancun meeting and they are again on the agenda for the ministerial meeting scheduled for December, 2005 in Hong Kong.

[c] Agreement on Sanitary and Phytosanitary Measures (SPS)

All countries adopt rules to ensure food safety and prevent the spread of pests or diseases among plants and animals. These *sanitary and phytosanitary* (plant health) measures may include inspection of products, requiring products to come from disease-free areas, special processing standards, setting maximum pesticide residue levels, quarantine requirements, restricting permissible additives in food and complete import bans. These rules generally apply to domestically produced products as well as imports.

Governments generally agree that trade restrictions required to protect human, animal or plant health are necessary and appropriate. In many cases, however, purported health measures actually are protectionist devices designed to reduce or exclude agricultural imports. The technical complexity of these rules makes them exceptionally deceptive and hard to dispute.

The Uruguay round adopted an *Agreement on Sanitary and Phytosanitary Measures* (SPS) to prevent the use of unwarranted sanitary and phytosanitary measures for trade protection purposes. Although each nation maintains the right to enact the health protection rules it deems appropriate, the SPS Agreement precludes rules adopted for protectionist purposes that create unnecessary trade barriers. Special rules allow limited exceptions for developing and least-developed countries, and longer time periods for them to reach compliance.

Under the SPS Agreement, a nation's sanitary and phytosanitary rules must be based upon an appropriate assessment of actual risks. Upon request, the government must show the risk factors considered, the assessment procedures used and the level of risk deemed acceptable. The SPS Agreement urges member nations to *harmonize* their risk assessment techniques with those developed by other international organizations. However, governments may adopt standards that are lower than the international standards. A country may adopt measures that provide higher protection than under international standards if there is scientific justification or the country's risk assessment shows that the international standard will not provide the appropriate protection level. A measure may be adopted provisionally as a precautionary step, if there is an immediate risk of disease but insufficient scientific evidence exists.

Generally, a country must utilize technically and economically feasible measures that are not more trade restrictive than necessary to achieve its domestic health objectives. For example, if feasible a suspect product should be quarantined rather than banned. Sanitary and phytosanitary measures may vary depending on origin of a product to account for differences in climate, pests, diseases, and food safety conditions in different regions.

To enhance transparency, the SPS Agreement contains a number of notification provisions. A country must notify other nations about any sanitary and phytosanitary requirement that restricts trade, and establish inquiry points to respond to requests for information about the application of its rules and its risk assessment findings. The WTO Secretariat must be notified about any new or modified SPS requirement a country plans to implement if it differs from international standards and may affect trade. These notices are circulated to all member nations, allowing them time to comment before implementation occurs. Also, every country must publish the sanitary and phytosanitary measures it adopts.

A prior GATT Agreement on Technical Barriers to Trade (TBT) governing technical standards for food safety, animal and plant health, inspections, and labeling have been incorporated into the WTO rules. Measures adopted to protect humans, animals, and plants from additives, toxins, or plant and animal-carried diseases, and a nation from the entry, establishment or spread of pests, are governed by the SPS Agreement. Other measures to protect human, animal, and plant life are covered by the TBT Agreement. For example, a food labeling requirement about the nutritional value or quality of a food product is subject to the TBT Agreement, while a labeling requirement about the safety of the product is governed by the SPS Agreement. Under the TBT, members generally agree to use international standards, such as the food safety standards established by the Codex Alimentarius Commission, and to notify other governments of any technical regulations that are not based on international standards.

Disputes under the SPS. Several alleged violations of the SPS have been considered by or are pending before the WTO Dispute Settlement Mechanism (discussed below) and others have been brought to the dispute process but settled by the parties. One SPS dispute regarding hormone treated beef has attracted considerable attention and remains unresolved. The following description of that dispute illustrates the kind of issues likely to arise under the SPS Agreement.

Hormone beef. In 1996, the U.S. and Canada challenged a European Union (EU) measure that bans imported bovine meat and meat products from cattle treated with specified growth hormones. The EU prohibits the domestic use of these hormones as a threat to human health and has banned imports of hormone-treated beef since 1989. The U.S. and Canada assert that growth hormones pose no health threat and that the EU rule is scientifically unfounded and designed to protect its domestic producers from foreign competition.

In 1997, a dispute resolution panel concluded that the EU ban violated the SPS Agreement, because it was not based on international standards and had not been justified by a risk assessment.[10] This decision was upheld in 1998 after an appeal by the EU to the Appellate Body. The Appellate Body noted that a nation may impose a higher standard than set by international organizations (*e.g.*, the Codex Alimentarius), only if a risk assessment shows that a risk exists. The WTO Dispute Settlement Body accepted these findings and the EU was given 15 months, until May, 1999, to comply.

The EU has not complied, citing a need for additional risk assessments. The assessments it has completed to date have not been consistent with numerous scientific reviews by international organizations, including the FAO/WHO Joint Expert Committee on Food Additives and the WTO's consultants. Accordingly, WTO arbitrators ruled that the EU beef ban causes significant loss to U.S. beef exporters, and that the United States is entitled to suspend over $100 million in tariff concessions on EU trade per year. Based upon the WTO ruling, the U.S. and Canada imposed $125 in sanctions on European products, including French Roquefort cheese, truffles, and mustard, and has been holding discussions with the EU about possible methods to resolve the dispute.

In October, 2003, the EU announced that it had conducted a new review of the existing scientific evidence that conclusively established the risks of hormone residues. This review, the EU asserted, complied with the WTO Appellate Body ruling. Accordingly, a new EU directive banning hormone treated beef was issued[11] and the U.S. and Canada were asked to remove their sanctions on European products. Both countries disagree with the EU's conclusion and refused to lift their sanctions.

In November, 2004, the EU initiated a WTO dispute against the U.S. and Canada asserting that the continuation of the sanctions is illegal. In the EU view, the beef importing countries must lift the sanctions and then challenge the EU's directive through the special WTO Dispute Resolution procedure for compliance issues. To date, neither the U.S. nor Canada have agreed to this procedure. In any case, the procedures and associated appeals would go on for a number of years.

The hormone beef dispute raises serious questions about the effectiveness of the WTO as a trade-regulating body. WTO supporters believe that by

---

[10] *See* Articles 3.1, 3.3 and 5 of the SPS Agreement.

[11] EU Hormones Directive, September 22, 2003.

indefinitely delaying implementation of the Appellate Bodies decision, the EU's weakens the SPS Agreement, the dispute settlement mechanism and the credibility of the WTO system. In this view, any country can violate its WTO obligations simply by postponing their implementation. On the other hand, consumer and food safety organizations criticize the WTO decision as fostering a global "downward harmonization" of consumer protections. It is likely that the SPS Agreement will be amended in the near future to account for one or both of these concerns.

Genetically Modified Organisms and Food (GMO and GMF). Genetically modified organisms (GMO) are seeds and similar organisms created through genetic engineering. Typically, genes of one species are transplanted into the cells of another species to transfer desirable characteristics for agricultural purposes. Genetically modified food (GMF) is made from GMO in the form of a living organism, such as a bean or tomato, or a food product such as flour or oil made from GMO ingredients.

Supporters of GMO and GMF maintain that these products are safe to use and eat and provide significant benefits to poor and lesser developed countries. GMO crops often require less water, grow in poor soil, have high nutritional content, require fewer pesticides and produce high yields. However, many consumer groups and NGOs zealously resist the use and distribution of GMO and GMF and many seek to stringently regulate or ban these products. Opponents assert that these products have not been adequately tested for long term effects and may adversely affect bio-diversity of indigenous plant and animal species and increasingly transfer control of agriculture from local farmers to distant multinational enterprises.

The U.S. and other grain exporters such as Canada, Argentina and Brazil adopted this scientific approach to agriculture and have approved and grow many varieties of genetically modified crops. Generally, business and government in these countries promote the use and export of GM crops. Many countries, however, often motivated by consumer resistance, ban or stringently restrict planting or importing GMO and GMF.

Of particular importance is the moratorium on GM products that was imposed by the EU in 1998. The U.S. has claimed that the EU attitude has persuaded other countries not to allow imports of GMO or GMF. Indeed, in 2002, famine-stricken Zambia refused U.S. food aid that included genetically-modified corn. Some EU countries have been accused of making their economic aid to developing countries contingent on their banning GM crops.

The U.S., has been joined by a number of countries (including Argentina, Canada, Australia, Chile, Colombia, El Salvador, Honduras, Mexico, New Zealand, Peru and Uruguay) in challenging the EU ban before a WTO Panel, claiming that its rules do not comply with the Sanitary and Phytosanitary Measures Agreement (SPS) and the Technical Barriers to Trade (TBT) Agreement. The SPS Agreement requires a scientific risk assessment to be conducted before a product can be banned on health and safety grounds. The TBT agreement bars the use of trade-restrictive testing and approval standards.

In August, 2004, the WTO Panel agreed to hear a report from a scientific committee before issuing a ruling, thereby delaying any decision until mid-2005. However, the EU has partially removed the moratorium, allowing the sale of a few varieties of GM food and more applications are being reviewed. The EU action follows enactment of strict GM labeling and traceability rules.

[d] Agreement on Textiles and Clothing (ATC)

Before 1995, the textile trade was governed by the Multifiber Arrangement (MFA), which established quotas for imports to countries whose domestic industries were being hurt by increased imports. Although quotas ordinarily are not permissible under the GATT, MFA members agreed in the early 1970s to dispense with that rule with respect to textiles.

The Uruguay round implemented a new *Agreement on Textiles and Clothing* (ATC) that replaces the MFA and integrates the textile sector into the general WTO rules over a ten year period ending in 2005. At that time, all textile quotas will end, the ATC will terminate, and the general WTO rules will apply. The long phase-in period is deemed necessary to allow importers and exporters to adjust to the new open market situation.

The expiration of the ATC at the end of 2004 means that standard GATT and WTO rules now apply to the textile and clothing industries. Elimination of quotas will favor a few countries that manufacture textiles and clothing, most particularly, China. Within a short time, China is expected to provide more that half of the world's textile production and export.

Because of regional trade agreements, it is likely that Mexico, the Caribbean, Eastern Europe and North Africa will continue as important exporters to the U.S. and EU. However, exporters from Cambodia, Bangladesh, Sri Lanka, Philipines, Indonesia and sub-Saharan Africa may lose market share because of their distance from the U.S. and EU and lack of favorable trade agreements. Elimination of the quotas will have mixed effects. Certainly, a number of textile workers will lose their jobs. However, the cost of goods such as shirts and socks should decline substantially, allowing consumers to spend the money saved on these items in other, more productive areas.

China's great advantage in textiles stems from its low labor costs and integrated industrial base that allows it make all parts of the finished goods. These advantages will increase substantially after the quotas are lifted. In luggage production, for example, Chinese companies subject to quotas made the frame, fabric, handles, and wheels and shipped them to other countries for assembly. Now, all aspects of production and export will occur in China. It is estimated that the quotas significantly increase the cost of finished goods to consumers.

Many nations, NGOs and labor organizations warn that removal of tariffs and quotas on textiles will harm many workers in the world's poorest countries. Although some developing countries have asked the WTO to review the issue, any change to this long-standing commitment would require an emergency meeting of the organization. China has firmly resisted attempts to retain any aspects of the quotas at the WTO, arguing that such restrictions violate the fundamental principles of the WTO.

[e] The General Agreement on Trade in Services (GATS)

The Uruguay round introduced the General Agreement on Trade in Services (GATS) as the first multilateral rules governing international trade in services. The importance of the agreement is illustrated by the fact that services account for more than two-thirds of U.S. GDP and more than twenty percent of world trade. The Agreement is supervised by the WTO Council for Trade in Services.

Under the GATS, nations that trade in services generally obtain most favored nation (MFN) treatment, market access, and limited national treatment. Stable and predictable markets are ensured through national schedules that establish binding commitments regarding specific service sectors. A series of GATS rounds to begin at five-year intervals is expected to continue to liberalize the rules for trade in services.

The GATS applies to all internationally-traded services, including:

- *cross-border* supply services that are supplied by one country to another, such as *international* telephone calls;
- *consumption abroad* services that consumers or companies use in another country; such as tourism;
- *commercial presence* services that a foreign company may provide as a subsidiary or branch in another country, such as a local branch of a foreign bank, and;
- *presence of natural persons* services provided by individuals who travel from their home country to provide services in another, such as consultants or actors.

The most favored nation principle applies under the GATS, meaning that all WTO members trading in services must be treated equally. Accordingly, a country that permits foreign service providers in a sector generally must allow service providers from other countries to compete in that sector. However, the GATS contains a number of exceptions to this equal treatment principle that are necessary because many countries were parties to preexisting bilateral and plurilateral treaties on services. These exceptions for preexisting arrangements may not be renewed and cannot last more than ten years.

The national treatment principle is not fully applicable in the services area. Generally, national treatment should mean that a country that permits a foreign service provider to operate in its market must treat that provider in the same manner as domestic companies. Under GATS, however, a country must apply equal treatment to a foreign service provider only if it has made a specific commitment to do so. This differs markedly from the national treatment rules for goods and intellectual property, which require imported products to be treated in the same manner as domestic goods in all cases.

The specific commitments a country makes about opening its market to foreign service providers result from bilateral and multilateral negotiations. The commitments are set forth in schedules that state the sectors involved, the degree of market access to be allowed in each sector, and any special limitations on national treatment. An example of a commitment on market access is an agreement to allow financial consulting firms in the domestic market. Limiting these firms to one office where domestic firms may operate in many cities may be a permissible exception to the principle of national treatment. A country's commitments are bound in the same manner as tariffs, meaning that modification requires the consent of affected countries and compensation for resulting losses. Thus, the commitments create stable, predictable markets exporters and importers of services.

To provide transparency, the GATS requires governments to publish all relevant laws and regulations, and establish inquiry points where foreigners can obtain this information about all service sectors. The WTO must be notified about any changes in regulations governing services subject to specific commitments. The agreement asks members to apply reasonable, objective, and impartial regulations to services, and to provide an impartial mechanism for reviewing administrative decisions affecting services providers.

Many WTO members have or will conclude bilateral or plurilateral agreements to recognize the qualifications of specific kinds of service providers, such as licenses or certifications. Under the GATS, these qualification recognition arrangements cannot be discriminatory nor function as disguised protectionist devices. The WTO must be notified about these agreements and other members must be provided an opportunity to negotiate comparable arrangements.

A number of annexes to the GATS provide special rules for services in different sectors. These include:

- *Movement of natural persons.* This annex specifies rights of an individual to temporarily stay in a country to provide services. Although the scope of the agreement is quite limited, it does facilitate cross-border transit of senior executives. It does not apply to people seeking permanent employment, permanent residence or citizenship.

- *Financial services.* This annex among seventy nations covers nearly all international trade in banking, insurance, and securities. Although it provides for MFN treatment, the annex also allows countries to adopt prudent measures to protect investors, depositors, and insurance policy holders, and to ensure the integrity and stability of the financial system.

- *Telecommunications.* This annex generally requires nations to provide nondiscriminatory market access to foreign service suppliers. The annex applies to seventy countries that made commitments that relate to more than ninety percent of world telecommunications revenue. The commitments cover most telecommunications services including wire and wireless local, long distance, and international services.

- *Air transport services.* This annex excludes air traffic rights and directly related activities from GATS because they are subject to other bilateral arrangements. The GATS does apply to aircraft repair and maintenance services, air transport services and computer-reservation services.

[f] Trade Related Aspects of Intellectual Property Rights (TRIPS)

Information, ideas, and designs are an increasingly important component of international trade, particularly for the most developed economies. To encourage creative efforts, most nations grant inventors, writers, designers and other originators temporary, exclusive rights, called intellectual property rights, to use or sell their creations. The major categories of intellectual property rights include:

- *Copyrights.* These are the rights given to creators of literary and artistic works such as books, paintings, music, and movies. Computer programs and databases may also fall in this category. Generally, copyrights extend for at least 50 years after the creator's death.

- *Trademarks and geographical indications.* Trademark rights protect distinctive signs that distinguish one person's goods or services from another's. Geographical indication rights protect signs that identify a product's place origin when origin is an important attribute. These protections may last indefinitely.

- *Patents, industrial designs and trade secrets.* These rights protect inventions and similar industrial property. Protection usually lasts for a definite period, usually 20 years for patents.

National laws differ greatly in the amount of protection they afford intellectual property rights and even more greatly in how effectively these rights may be enforced. Because intellectual property is so important in modern trade, these differences have created significant non-tariff trade barriers. To address this problem, the Uruguay round implemented an extensive agreement on the *Trade Related Aspects of Intellectual Property Rights* (TRIPS). That agreement attempts to provide uniform international treatment of intellectual property rights as well as a forum for settling trade disputes in this area.

The TRIPS agreement establishes trade rights relating to patents, copyrights, trademarks, geographical indications, sound recordings, industrial designs, semiconductor chip layouts, and trade secrets. In addition to improving standards for protecting intellectual property, TRIPS requires governments to establish domestic legal procedures and remedies needed to effectively enforce these standards. Although most WTO members are fully subject to TRIPS, some of the least developed nations have a transition period until 2006 for implementation. The WTO and World Intellectual Property Organization (WIPO) are providing technical advice to help these countries meet the deadline.

The TRIPS agreement derives the basic standards of protection for intellectual property rights from the pre-existing international agreements in this area under the World Intellectual Property Organization (WIPO). The basic agreement governing patents, industrial designs, and similar property is the *Paris Convention for the Protection of Industrial Property;* for copyrights, the basic agreement is the *Berne Convention for the Protection of Literary and Artistic Works.* TRIPS provides its own standards for matters not covered by either convention and for standards that are not believed adequate for international trade purposes.

Under TRIPS, a country must ensure that intellectual property rights can be enforced and provide penalties that will deter future infringements. The enforcement procedures must be fair, equitable, not complicated or costly, and provide reasonable time periods. Administrative decisions and lower court rulings should be reviewable by appeal. The agreement provides detailed enforcement and procedural rules relating to evidence, injunctions, damages, and penalties. National courts must be authorized to mandate the destruction of pirated or counterfeit goods and local law must treat willful, commercial scale, trademark counterfeiting or copyright piracy as criminal offenses.

TRIPS adopts the following special rules for specific kinds of intellectual property:

- *Copyright.* Computer programs and databases are specifically protected as literary works under the rules of the Berne Convention. International copyright rules are extended to rental rights. Computer programmers and sound recording producers have the right to bar commercial rental of their works to the public. Owners of film copyrights may bar commercial rental if widespread copying has reduced the earnings potential of the films. Performers may prevent unauthorized recording, reproduction and broadcast of their live performances for 50 years. Sound recording producers may prevent unauthorized reproduction of their recordings for 50 years.

- *Trademarks.* The types of protected signs and the minimum trademark ownership rights are set forth. Service marks are given the same protection as trademarks. Additional protection is afforded marks and signs that are particularly well-known in a country.

- *Geographical indications.* A place name that describes a product in terms of geographical origin and characteristics is a *geographical indication.* Special provisions protect place names that identify a product, such as Champagne or Roquefort, and preventing their use in a manner that misleads consumers. Greater protection is afforded wines and spirit place names, even if consumers are not misled. Exceptions apply if the place name is trademarked or if it has become generic, such as cheddar cheese. These exceptions must be negotiated with the country that wishes to protect the geographical indication. Special registration rules apply to place names for wines.

- *Industrial designs.* Protection for a minimum of 10 years is afforded. Protected design owners can prohibit manufacture, sale or import of products that copy the protected design.

- *Patents.* Patent protection must apply to both products and processes and last for at least 20 years. A country may deny a patent for a product if commercial exploitation is forbidden by public order or morality rules. Governments can deny patents for diagnostic, therapeutic and surgical methods, plants and animals (other than microorganisms), and biological processes for producing plants or animals (other than microbiological processes). Plant varieties must be protectable by patent or other means, such as conventions under the International Union for the Protection of new Plant Varieties (UPOV). Exceptions to the minimum required patent protection may apply if the patent holder abuses its rights by failing to supply the product. In such cases, a government may issue a compulsory license that permits production by a competitor. Patents for production processes extend to the products directly obtained from the process.

- *Integrated circuit designs.* These rules incorporate the *Washington Treaty on Intellectual Property in Respect of Integrated Circuits* that is under WIPO. Protection must be afforded for a minimum of 10 years.

- *Trade Secrets.* Trade secrets and other commercially valuable undisclosed information are protected against breach of confidence and acts that do not conform to honest commercial practices. However, reasonable steps must be taken to keep the information secret. Test data submitted to governments for approval of pharmaceuticals or agricultural chemicals are protected against unfair commercial use.

- *Licensing contracts.* The owner of an intellectual property right may *license* another person to commercially use the right. A special rule applies to anti-competitive licensing contracts. Under TRIPS, a government may void certain license contracts that restrict competition or impede technology development.

Note: TRIPS and the Public Health Crisis in Developing Countries

An important issue involving international patent protection relates to the pubic health crises facing many developing countries because of alarming epidemics of HIV/AIDS, malaria and tuberculosis.[12] Many of these countries have been unable to fund the high costs of the drugs needed to treat these diseases and have sought some form of compulsory licensing that would bring down these costs without violating their obligations under the WTO and TRIPS. This issue was the focal point of the discussions at the Fourth WTO Ministerial Conference held in Qatar during November, 2001. The Conference reached a consensus on this matter that was published as the *Declaration on the TRIPS Agreement and Public Health* (Ministerial Declaration).[13]

The issue requires an appropriate balance between the rights of patent holders and national public health interests. On one side, pharmaceutical companies argue that patent protection is essential to the development of new and more effective drugs because it provides the incentive needed to attract the long-term investment required for research. Also, an effective patent system permits (and often requires) companies to disclose the results of their research into new drugs, thereby encouraging the flow of scientific information that facilitates new discoveries. Proponents of rigorous patent protection note that many drugs that are *off-patent* remain unaffordable in developing countries because of socio-economic, not patent, factors.

Contrary arguments by developing countries assert that current patent law regimes allow drug companies to maintain much higher prices than would be possible in a more competitive system. By providing an artificial monopoly for a patented drug, the patent system deters effective competition and causes higher prices and less innovation. The current system favors the interests of businesses and their owners in the developing countries over the health requirements of the rest of the world. The patent system, it is argued, is especially unfair to developing countries, which face difficult social and economic circumstances.

After considering these issues, the Ministerial Declaration indicates that the TRIPS Agreement must be interpreted as part of a

---

[12] *See generally*, Nolff, *Compulsory Patent Licensing In View Of The WTO Ministerial Conference Declaration On The Trips Agreement And Public Health*, 84 J. Pat. & Trademark Off. Soc'y 133 (February, 2002).

[13] WTO document WT/MIN(01)/DEC/W/2 (14 November 2001).

broad international effort to address the public health issues. Accordingly, members states may apply the Agreement with "flexibility," specifically meaning that each WTO member state may:

- Grant compulsory licenses and determine the grounds for granting them.

- Determine whether a situation constitutes a national emergency or other circumstance of extreme urgency. It is understood that public health crises, including HIV/AIDS, tuberculosis, malaria and other epidemics, may be included in these situations.

- Establish its own regime for determining when a patent holder's rights under the TRIPS Agreement have been exhausted, subject to the MFN and national treatment requirements.

In effect, the Ministerial Declaration allows a member state to determine when a national emergency has arisen and that a challenge to that determination is unlikely to be successful if public health is involved. Under a national emergency situation, a member state need not go through the procedures ordinarily required under TRIPS, such as consultation and negotiations with the patent holder, but may immediately grant a compulsory license. The only requirement is that the patent holder be notified as soon as practicable and be paid "adequate remuneration."

A problem that was not resolved at the Qatar Conference concerned Article 31 of the TRIPS Agreement, which provides that pharmaceuticals produced under a compulsory license cannot be exported outside the country issuing the license. Consequently, a country that lacked adequate manufacturing capabilities could not use compulsory licenses to obtain necessary medicines. This problem was rectified by an Implementation Agreement reached in September 2003, just prior to the WTO Ministerial Meeting in Cancun, Mexico.[14] That Agreement waives the Article 31 rule prohibiting export of compulsory licensed products if specific conditions are satisfied. These conditions are designed to preclude importation of drugs to avoid high domestic costs or to resell in other markets. Compulsory licensing is permitted only for the least-developed countries that notify the TRIPS Council of their intent to import a limited supply of medicines produced under compulsory license for use only in "situations of national emergency or other circumstances of extreme urgency."

---

[14] Implementation of Paragraph 6 of the Doha Declaration on the TRIPS Agreement and Public Health, Decision of 30 August 2003, WT/L/540, [hereinafter Implementation Decision], docsonline.wto.org/DDFDocuments/t/WT/L/540.doc (Sept. 2, 2003).

[5] Unfair Trade Practices and Safeguards

[a] Anti-Dumping Agreement

Dumping occurs when a company in one country sells its product in another country at a lower price than in its domestic market or lower than its cost of production. A company may do this to increase its market share in another country or to avoid domestic political or social problems that would result from production cutbacks or layoffs. Many governments, including the U.S., consider dumping an unfair trade practice that justifies anti-dumping measures to protect domestic industries. Others suggest that such pricing strategies are legitimate and particularly necessary to protect industries in developing countries.

The WTO Anti-Dumping Agreement, adopted in the Uruguay round, provides guidelines regarding the kinds of anti-dumping measures a government may engage in. The Agreement does not focus on preventing dumping, but rather on the allowable anti-dumping measures. Generally, the Agreement permits a country to take action against dumping that creates a *material injury* to a competing domestic industry.[15] Such action usually involves increasing the import duty on the product being dumped to raise its price to the *normal value*. Ordinarily, the normal value is the price of the product in the exporter's domestic market. If that price cannot be ascertained, the normal value may be determined from the price the exporter charges in another country or calculated from the exporter's production costs, other expenses and profit margins. The Agreement provides specific rules for comparing the actual export price with the normal value.

A country may impose anti-dumping measures only if a domestic industry is materially injured. The Agreement sets out detailed rules for investigating the existence and extent of an injury, which include an evaluation of all the economic factors that affect the industry in question. The investigation must allow all interested parties a chance to present evidence. The investigation must stop immediately if the dumping margin is found to be insignificant (*i.e.,* less than 2 percent of the product's export price), or if the volume of dumped imports is negligible (*i.e.,* less than 3 percent of total imports unless several countries together account for 7 percent or more of total imports).

If the investigation establishes that dumping is harming a domestic industry, the exporting company may increase its price to avert imposition of an import duty. If anti-dumping measures are imposed, they must expire within five years unless that would create additional injury. Countries contemplating an anti-dumping case must promptly inform the WTO Committee on Anti-Dumping Practices about all preliminary and final anti-dumping actions. Dumping disputes can be resolved through the WTO's Dispute Settlement Mechanism.

---

[15] The Agreement provides specific rules that expand and clarify the provisions of GATT Article 6.

[b]   Agreement on Subsidies and Countervailing Measures (SCM)

Generally, a *subsidy* involves government support for the production, use, or sale of a product. A domestic subsidy represents general support for the product, regardless of whether it is exported. Domestic subsidies reduce the price of the product in both the domestic and export market, making it more competitive against imports at home and as an export item. Export subsidies apply only to exported products, thereby reducing their price in foreign markets but not in the home market.

Many countries assert that subsidies, particularly export subsidies, are an unfair trade practice that distort international trade. In this view, a country whose industry is harmed by another nation's subsidized exports is entitled to take actions — called *countervailing measures* — to increase the price of the import to its unsubsidized level. Other countries, particularly those with developing economies, maintain that governments often use domestic subsidies to achieve important social and economic policy goals and that they are necessary to transform state-run economies to market economies.

Taking account of these different views, the *Agreement on Subsidies and Countervailing Measures* (SCM) establishes categories of prohibited, actionable, and non-actionable subsidies, and restricts the actions countries may take to neutralize the effect of subsidized imports. A country that is adversely affected by a prohibited or actionable subsidy may ask the WTO Dispute Resolution Body to require the subsidy to be withdrawn. Instead, it may initiate its own investigation to determine if domestic industries are being harmed and, if so, impose a countervailing duty. The rules governing these investigations are similar to those required for an anti-dumping action. Special exemptions and phase in rules apply to subsidies provided by the least-developed and developing countries.

Under the SCM, a subsidy includes a financial contribution by a government or any form of income or price support if it confers a benefit on the recipient.[16] However, only *specific* subsidies are prohibited or actionable, and all non-specific subsidies are allowed. A *specific* subsidy is a domestic or export subsidy that is only available to an enterprise, industry, group of enterprises, or group of industries in the country giving the subsidy. Thus, subsidies derived from general infrastructure improvements such as roads or schools are not taken into account.

The SCM Agreement applies to industrial and agricultural products, except to the extent that agricultural subsidies are permitted by the Agricultural Agreement (described above). The SCM provides different rules for the following three categories of subsidies:

- **Prohibited (red light) subsidies.** These include all export subsidies and subsidies that require the recipient to use domestic

---

[16] SCM Agreement, Article I.

goods in place of imported goods. They are banned without regard to whether any injury is established. Any member may use the WTO Dispute Settlement Procedure (DSP) to challenge a prohibited subsidy, without showing injury, and the matter proceeds under an accelerated timetable. If the DSP agrees that the subsidy is prohibited, it must be withdrawn within the time period allowed by the DSP. If withdrawal does not occur, the DSP may authorize the complaining member to implement countervailing measures. A countervailing duty may be imposed if domestic producers are hurt by imports of products having a prohibited subsidy.

- **Actionable (yellow light) subsidies.** For subsidies in this category, the complaining country must show that the subsidy adversely affects its interests. The Agreement sets forth complex tests for determining whether adverse effects exist. Generally, the adverse effect must harm the complainant by:

  ○ injuring its domestic industry;

  ○ injuring competing exporters from other countries when the two compete in third markets;

  ○ injuring exporters trying to compete in the subsidizing country's domestic market.

If the DSP finds that the subsidy has an adverse effect, it must be withdrawn or its adverse effect eliminated. If domestic producers are hurt by the subsidized imports, a countervailing duty may be imposed. Otherwise the subsidy is allowable.

- **Non-actionable (green light) subsidies.** These subsidies include all non-specific subsidies, and specific subsidies for:

  ○ industrial research and pre-competitive development activity;

  ○ assistance to disadvantaged regions;

  ○ certain assistance for adapting existing facilities to new environmental laws or regulations.

Non-actionable subsidies cannot be challenged in the DSP and countervailing duties cannot be imposed on imports.

The Foreign Sales Company Dispute

The EU has successfully challenged the U.S. *Foreign Sales Corporation* (FSC) tax provision as an impermissible export subsidy. A WTO panel ruled that the U.S. must change its FSC provisions or face compensatory damages or retaliatory measures. Although Congress has repealed the old FSC rules, the EU asserts that the statute Congress enacted as a replacement continues to violate the WTO ban on export subsidies. Thus, the controversy continues.

The FSC rules provided a tax benefit by exempting certain U.S.-owned foreign corporations from the general tax treatment that would apply to income derived from U.S. sources. Generally, a U.S. corporation is taxable on its worldwide income, including income from exports, regardless of where it is earned. A foreign corporation, by contrast, is subject to U.S. tax only on income it derives from conducting a U.S. trade or business.

A U.S. company could avoid U.S. tax on its export income by organizing a foreign subsidiary corporation that met specified criteria (the FSC) and selling its exports through that corporation. Although a foreign corporation is ordinarily subject to U.S. tax on its export income from U.S. sources, the FSC rules specified a portion of such income as not being from a U.S. trade or business. The FSC rules provided a subsequent benefit when the FSC paid the export income to its domestic parent company as a dividend, by allowing the parent to deduct the entire amount received. For a complete discussion of international tax policy and rules, *see* § 6.01.

The FSC rules were adopted in 1984 to replace the prior export tax incentive provided for Domestic International Sales Corporations (DISCs). The EU countries had previously challenged the DISC rules as an illegal export subsidy under the GATT dispute settlement rules. The U.S. responded by asserting that the territorial tax rules of Belgium, France, and the Netherlands, also constituted an export subsidy because the tax exemption for foreign source income had the effect of taxing exports more favorably than comparable domestic transactions. In 1976, a GATT panel ruled that both the DISC and the European laws provided impermissible export subsidies.

Because the panel ruling was unenforceable, the dispute continued until resolved on the basis of a GATT Council *Understanding* in 1981, holding that exempting foreign source income from taxation is not an export subsidy. The European countries interpreted the Understanding to support their territorial tax system, while the U.S. interpreted it to mean that it could adopt new FSC legislation (in 1984) that exempted foreign source export income. In the U.S. view, the FSC rules incorporate the territorial tax principle by providing a tax exemption for income earned by corporations organized in foreign countries.

The EU did not accept this view, and in 1998 it brought the FSC issue before the WTO dispute resolution process. The dispute resolution panel supported the EU, holding that FSC is a prohibited export subsidy that violates the SCM Agreement[17] by providing an exception to U.S. tax law that would otherwise have taxed FSC export income. The WTO Appellate Body upheld the panel's finding, requiring the U.S. to remove the subsidy by November 2000, or be subject to sanctions or retaliatory measures by the EU.

---

[17] Articles 3.1 and 1.1.

In May 2000, the U.S. proposed an alternative statute that would provide a partial tax exemption for all foreign-source income of branches of qualified U.S. firms, not just export income. The U.S. contended that the replacement legislation was consistent with the rulings in the FSC dispute. In the U.S. view, by excluding a particular category of foreign source income from domestic taxation, the statute simply adopted the territorial approach used by most European countries. Although the EU rejected the proposal, the U.S. Congress adopted the legislation in November 2000.[18]

The EU notified the U.S. that it did not consider the new legislation to comply with the WTO rules and brought a new action before the dispute resolution body. In August 2001, a panel concluded that the FSC statute violated the WTO Agreement[19] and that holding was affirmed by the Appellate Body in January 2002.[20] The next month, the WTO authorized the EU countries to impose up to $4 billion in sanctions against U.S. companies, the largest award in history.

The sanctions were first imposed in March 1, 2004 beginning at a rate of 5% on various U.S. products, and increasing by one percent each month to a maximum of 17% in March, 2005. However, the FSC and subsequent provisions were repealed in 2004, and replaced with a number of limited-time tax benefits for U.S. exporters and multinationals companies.[21] In response, the EU announced that it would lift the sanctions on U.S. goods, beginning in January, 2005, provided that the U.S. tax benefits were fully eliminated by the end of 2006.

However, one aspect of the new U.S. law remains controversial and may be challenged at the WTO. That provision provides for a 2-year transitional period to phase out tax benefits to a number of U.S. exporters and multinationals. The EU contends that this grandfathering clause will continue to provide illegal subsidies after 2006, and therefore is incompatible with the WTO ruling. In November, 2004, the EU requested WTO arbitration on this compliance issue, although any sanctions would be significantly lower than the initial $4 billion.

Interestingly, economic analysis suggests that the FSC-like rules probably have little or no impact on the balance of trade and are likely to reduce U.S. economic welfare.[22] Such export legislation usually is supported by specific business and labor groups that benefit from exports, notwithstanding the impact on the economy as

---

[18] Public Law No. 106-519.

[19] WT/DS108/RW.

[20] WT/DS108/AB/RW.

[21] The American Jobs Creation Act of 2004 (signed October 22, 2004 and effective January 1, 2005).

[22] U.S. Library of Congress, Congressional Research Service, *The Foreign Sales Corporation (FSC) Tax Benefit for Exporting: WTO Issues and an Economic Analysis,* Report No. RL30684, by David L. Brumbaugh, Sept. 14, 2000.

a whole. Although export subsidies may increase income and employment in certain sectors, they may cause economic contraction in sectors that compete with imports. Moreover, by lowering export prices,
they transfer economic welfare to foreign consumers.

[c] Agreement on Safeguards

Safeguards are selective measures such as tariffs or quotas that may be
deliberately imposed to restrict imports for a temporary period to allow a
domestic industry to adjust to increasing competition from imports. GATT
Article XIX provides such a safeguard or *escape clause* by permitting a
country to impose temporary trade restrictions if increased imports of a
product cause or threaten serious injury to domestic producers. The
restrictions can be maintained as long as required to prevent or remedy
the injury.[23] However, a country that imposes safeguard measures must
compensate the exporting country by making trade concessions in other
areas.

Although the safeguard measure has always been available under the
GATT, it has not been used very often. Invoking the rule may be undesirable because a number of vague tests must be satisfied, its application is
temporary, and the exporting nation must be compensated. To avoid these
problems, governments have chosen to protect their industries through
other means, including antidumping and countervailing measures. More
problematic have been the *gray-area* measures such as "voluntary" export
restraint agreements that have been bilaterally negotiated between importers and exporters to circumvent the GATT rules entirely. These restraint
agreements have affected trade in numerous products, including automobiles, steel, and semiconductors.

To address these problems, the Uruguay Round implemented an Agreement on Safeguards. This agreement prohibits new gray-area agreements,
including voluntary export restraints and similar measures, and has phased
out all existing agreements. The WTO's Safeguards Committee oversees the
agreement and the members' commitments. Members must report each
phase of a safeguard investigation for the committee's review.

Under the Agreement, industries or companies may request their government to implement a safeguard. In that situation, the Agreement provides
criteria for safeguard investigations requiring transparency, public hearings, and means for interested parties to present evidence, including
evidence as to whether the public interest will be served. The Agreement
also establishes criteria defining when "serious injury" is caused or threatened, and the factors for assessing the impact of imports on a domestic
industry. Specific guidelines are provided regarding the kind, amount, and
length of safeguard measures that are imposed.

---

[23] U.S. law provides a similar escape clause in Section 201 of the Trade Act of 1974.

The exporting country may seek compensation through consultations. If unsuccessful, the exporting country may retaliate by taking equivalent action such as increasing tariffs on exports from the country imposing the safeguard. In some situations, the exporting country cannot retaliate until three years after the safeguard measure was introduced. This rule applies if the safeguard measure complies with the Safeguard Agreement and results from an absolute increase in the quantity of imports from the exporting country.

Special rules mitigate the effect of the safeguard rules on developing countries. A safeguard cannot be imposed on imports from a developing country unless that country supplies more than 3 percent of the imports of the product or developing countries together account for more than 9 percent of the imports.

For discussion of U.S. rules on sanctions and safeguards, *see* 3.02.

[6] Non-Tariff Barriers

Trade barriers are government laws, regulations, policies, or practices that protect domestic products from foreign competition or artificially stimulate exports of domestic products.[24] Certain trade barriers, such as tariffs, are permissible under the WTO and other international trade agreements. Generally, non-tariff trade barriers, such as quotas and similar quantitative restrictions are prohibited under the WTO Agreement. Other non-tariff trade measures, such as testing standards or customs regulations that serve legitimate national policies, may purposely or inadvertently be applied in a trade restrictive manner. Common non-tariff trade barriers include:[25]

- Quantitative restrictions such as quotas or voluntary export restraint agreements;
- Import licensing;
- Customs regulations;
- Standards, testing, labeling and certification rules;
- Government procurement policies, such as "buy national" and closed bidding;
- Export subsidies;
- Investment barriers, such as limitations on foreign equity participation and restrictions on transfers of profits or capital, and;
- Local content and export performance requirements.

Many of these non-tariff trade barriers violate international trade rules and may give rise to actions under U.S. law or through the WTO. WTO Agreements governing nontariff trade barriers have been implemented for:

---

[24] 2000 National Trade Estimate Report on Foreign Trade Barriers (NTE).
[25] 2000 National Trade Estimate Report on Foreign Trade Barriers (NTE).

- sanitary and phytosanitary measures,
- technical barriers to trade,
- customs valuation,
- anti-dumping,
- preshipment inspection,
- rules of origin,
- import licensing procedures,
- subsidies and countervailing measures, and
- safeguards.

The WTO agreements described below define a number of permissible and impermissible non-tariff trade barriers and regulate the retaliatory measures that may be imposed by affected countries.

[a] Technical Barriers to Trade (TBT)

Obviously, a nation may adopt the standards it deems appropriate to protect its citizens and environment and to foster the interests of its consumers. However, the wide variety of technical regulations and industrial standards adopted by many countries makes it difficult for producers to efficiently produce and export uniform, *world standard* products. To the extent that a standard is more burdensome or complex than necessary, it acts as a barrier to efficient trade. Arbitrary standards that do not actually protect against defective or harmful products, are simply disguised protectionist devices.

The WTO's Agreement on Technical Barriers to Trade (TBT) provides rules designed to eliminate regulations, standards, testing, and certification procedures that pose unnecessary obstacles to trade. The agreement provides a code of good practice for governments to use in preparing, adopting, and applying standards. A country must adopt fair and equitable procedures for determining if a product meets its national standards.

Generally, countries cannot adopt procedures that confer unfair advantages on domestic products. To facilitate more uniform global standards, the TBT Agreement encourages countries to use appropriate international standards and to recognize each other's testing procedures. This would ensure that a product tested in the exporting country is likely to satisfy the importing country's standards. To enable producers and exporters to observe new standards in existing or prospective markets, WTO members must establish national enquiry points.

[i] Customs Valuations

Most tariffs are ad valorem, meaning that the tariff is imposed upon the value of an imported product. Thus, the real importation costs depends upon the method customs officials use to determine that value as well as upon the actual tariff rate. An unfair system that does not conform to commercial reality or which uses arbitrary or fictitious customs values poses a significant barrier to fair trade.

The GATT provides *harmonized* rules for determining tariff valuations. The harmonized system provides an international nomenclature developed by the World Customs Organization, that uses six digit codes for all participating countries to classify traded goods in a common manner. One set of rules applies in determining how a particular item must be classified by a nation's customs officials in deciding the tariff rate that will be applied. Generally, WTO members must use the rules set forth in the *Harmonized Commodity Description and Coding system* (HS). The HS is a detailed nomenclature system used in international trade to impose tariffs on goods and for describing them in transport documents. The U.S. has adopted *the Harmonized Tariff Schedule of the United States* (HTS), which is based upon the HS.[26] The GATT also establishes a harmonized methodology for determining the value of an item for tariff purposes.

A ministerial decision reached in the Uruguay round allows customs officials to request additional information if they have reason to doubt that the declared value of imported goods is accurate. If the additional information does not eliminate that reasonable doubt, the customs value of the imported goods is not determined from the declared value.

[ii] Rules of Origin

Rules of origin are the standards applied in determining where a product was made. The origin of a product is important in assessing the proper tariff rate, particularly for countries that have entered preferential trade areas such as NAFTA or the EU. Rules of origin also are important in applying trade measures such as quotas, anti-dumping actions, countervailing duties, and safeguard actions.

A WTO Committee on Rules of Origin (CRO), and a technical committee (TCRO) under the auspices of the Customs Cooperation Council in Brussels currently are working on an agreement to harmonize the various national rules of origin standards.[27] When completed, the harmonization agreement should provide a single set of rules of origin applicable to all non-preferential trading (*e.g.*, non trading bloc) conditions by all WTO members. Until the harmonization program is completed, the WTO Agreement requires members to ensure that their rules of origin are transparent and do not restrict, distort or disrupt international trade. A nation must administer the rules consistently, uniformly, impartially and reasonably. The Agreement indicates that rules of origin should be based on a positive standard that states what confers origin rather than what does not.

---

[26] *See* 19 U.S.C. § 1401a.

[27] The CRO and the TCRO could not finalize their work within the foreseen deadline of 1998. The CRO continued its work in 2000. In December 2000, the General Council Special Session agreed to set, as the new deadline for completion of the remainder of the work, the Fourth Session of the Ministerial Conference, or at the latest end of 2001.

[iii]   Import Licensing and Preshipment Inspection

The Agreement on Import Licensing Procedures sets forth a number of requirements designed to make the licensing procedure simple, transparent and predictable. Governments must publish the information needed for dealers to understand the licensing requirement and notify the WTO when they change or introduce new import licensing procedures. The agreement provides criteria for automatic licensing procedures (*i.e.,* licenses that issue automatically when specified criteria are met). For licenses that are not issued automatically, the agreement provides that the licensing agencies should normally handle an application within 30 days.

Pre-shipment inspection is the practice often used by developing countries that employs private companies to check shipment details such as price, quantity and quality of products to be exported. The private companies are necessary when government bureaucracies cannot adequately monitor capital transfers, commercial fraud or customs evasions. The WTO Agreement requires governments using preshipment inspections to ensure non-discrimination, transparency, protection of confidential business information, avoidance of unreasonable delay, and to use specific guidelines for price verification. The agreement establishes an independent review procedure.

[7]   Dispute Resolution Mechanism

A trade dispute arises when one or more WTO members consider that another member has adopted a trade measure or taken an action that violates the WTO Agreements, or has failed to meet its WTO obligations. Where possible, the WTO tries to settle trade disputes through consultations, and more than one-fourth of these disagreements are resolved in that manner. When consultations are not effective, WTO members must seek a resolution through, and abide by, the WTO *Dispute Settlement Mechanism* (DSM) rather than take unilateral action.

The WTO mechanism replaced the relatively ineffective dispute settlement system that existed under the GATT from 1947 to 1994. GATT proceedings lacked definite timetables and were lengthy. Because panel decisions required a consensus for adoption, any nation, including the country losing the dispute, could block adoption of its report.

The rules of the WTO Dispute Settlement Understanding (DSU), implemented in 1995, require prompt settlement of disputes under the following clearly defined timetables:

Stage of the dispute settlement process	Time allowed for stage
Consultations and mediation	60 days
Panel established and panelists appointed	45 days
Final panel report to parties	6 months
Final panel report to WTO members	3 weeks

Stage of the dispute settlement process	Time allowed for stage
Dispute Settlement Body adopts report (if no appeal)	60 days
Total	1 year without appeal
Appeals report	60–90 days
Dispute Settlement Body adopts appeals report	30 days
Total	1 year and 3 months with appeal

Thus, an initial ruling in a case usually is issued in one year, and a total of 15 months is required if the ruling is appealed.

[a] Dispute Resolution Procedure

A country involved in a trade dispute may call for consultations to resolve the issue through informal negotiations. If the consultations are not successful within 60 days, it may ask the Dispute Settlement Body to establish a panel to resolve the dispute. Ordinarily, a panel comprises three individuals who are experts in international trade law. The panelists are usually chosen in consultation with the countries in dispute. If they cannot agree, the WTO Director General may appoint them. As a safeguard for developing countries, in a dispute between a developing country and a developed country, the panel must include at least one member from a developing country. Within six months, the panel must complete taking evidence and present a report and recommendation to the Dispute Settlement Body (DSB). The DSB is the WTO's General Council sitting in this special role. The General Council comprises the delegation heads from all member countries, meaning that all members are represented on the DSB.

Although the panel may ask for information and technical advice other sources, it is only required to hear submissions from WTO members, including members not directly involved in the dispute. In a few cases, panels have read submissions from concerned non-governmental organizations. Third-party member nations may also involve themselves in the dispute settlement process. Panel deliberations are confidential, and only the final panel report is made public.

Panel reports are presented to the Dispute Settlement Body, which either adopts the report or, by consensus, rejects it. Thus, a country that wants to block a ruling must persuade all other members (including the member favored by the ruling). If a party to the dispute appeals the panel's ruling, however, the DSB does not consider the report until the appeal is completed. Appeals are taken to the Appellate Body, consisting of three members chosen from a standing pool of seven individuals. The Appellate Body only considers issues of law and does not review the evidence and sends its report to the DSB. The DSB must accept the Appellate Body report unconditionally unless, within 30 days, it unanimously decides to reject it.

Within 30 days of the report's adoption by the DSB, the unsuccessful country must state its intention to follow the ruling. If so, it is encouraged to change its legislation to comply with the ruling within a reasonable period of time. If not, it must negotiate with the complaining country about compensation for future losses caused by its actions. Compensation may be in the form of suspension of tariff commitments and concessions on exports from the complaining country to the violating member.

If no compensation agreement is reached after 20 days, the complaining country may ask the DSB to authorize trade sanctions, which is done within 30 days unless all members oppose them. Generally, the sanctions are imposed in the same economic sector as the dispute. If this is not practical or effective, sanctions can be directed to a different sector of same WTO agreement that governs the dispute. In limited situations, the action can be taken under another agreement. For example, Ecuador suspended its TRIPs commitments to the EU in retaliation for the EU's non-compliance with panel rulings relating to a dispute about bananas under the GATT. These penalty rules are designed to minimize the chance that sanctions related to trade in one sector will affect unrelated trades sectors.

The Banana Dispute

A recent case that illustrates the operation of the Dispute Resolution Mechanism and its sanctions provisions involves a disagreement over banana imports to the European Union (EU). Although the EU comprises many European countries, it currently acts as a separate member of the WTO. Based upon the historic attachments between some EU nations and their former colonies, the EU entered into the ACP Treaty (Africa, Caribbean and Pacific) that requires the EU to import specified amounts of bananas from these former colonies free of the tariffs it imposes on bananas from other countries. Some ACP countries are small-scale, high cost producers that depend on banana exports for much of their income.

This arrangement was challenged in 1993 by five large-scale, low-cost banana producing countries in Latin American whose products were subject to EU tariffs. That case was initiated under the pre-WTO GATT dispute settlement system. Although the GATT panel ruled that the EU arrangement was illegal, the former GATT rules allowed the EU to block the ruling and the panel report was not adopted. Instead, the EU negotiated an import agreement with most of the complainants in exchange for their withdrawing the complaint.

Because large U.S. companies with banana operations in other Latin American countries were still being hurt by the EU regime, the U.S. initiated proceedings under U.S. trade law.[28] The U.S. complained that the banana regime was causing several hundred million dollars of harm to its economic interests. The EU and some

---

[28] U.S. companies initiated action under § 302(a) of the 1974 Trade and the U.S. Trade Representative filed a petition under § 301 of that Act.

Caribbean nations countered that the ACP Treaty was a valuable foreign aid mechanism and that its elimination would destabilize the economies of some developing countries. After unsuccessful consultations in 1995, the U.S. joined four Latin American countries (Guatemala, Honduras, Mexico and Ecuador) in bringing an action to the new WTO Dispute Resolution Mechanism. The U.S. also terminated its actions under domestic trade law.

The WTO panel and Appeal Board agreed with the complainants and stated that the EU must change its policies.[29] The panel granted the EU 15 months, until January 1, 1999, to comply. Although the EU changed its import policies, the U.S. was not satisfied and repeatedly complained to the WTO that the EU was not complying with the panel decisions. The U.S. requested WTO authorization to retaliate 20 days after the panel's deadline expired. After a great deal of legal wrangling about the meaning of various WTO provisions, the parties agreed to allow the appropriate amount of retaliation to be determined through arbitration.

In early 1999, based upon the arbitrators' findings, the WTO authorized the U.S. to impose trade sanctions of $191.4 million against the EU. The U.S. quickly imposed high tariffs on a variety of European products, including handbags, coffee makers, bed linens, cardboard packing material, and felt paper. Many Europeans resented these sanctions because the products involved are unrelated to bananas. Nevertheless, the sanctions have brought pressure on the EU to comply with the WTO ruling. In April, 2001, the U.S. and EU announced their agreement to resolve the banana dispute. The EU agreed to a new import regime and the U.S. lifted its sanctions.

[b] Concerns About the Dispute Resolution Mechanism

The WTO's power to exercise binding authority over international trade disputes, including imposition of penalties and compensation, distinguishes it from most international institutions. It is this binding power that has made the WTO system more effective and widely used than the GATT system. A country that is not assured that all members will follow WTO agreements is less likely to obey the rules itself. Many nations would take their own actions, such as imposition of tariffs or quotas, to remedy perceived unfair trade practices, with developed countries in a stronger position to do so than the lesser developed. An effective dispute settlement system promotes a transparent, predictable trading system by encouraging nations to adopt and implement policies that conform to their WTO obligations.

However, many serious questions have been raised about the effectiveness and fairness of the Dispute Resolution Mechanism. A common

---

[29] The Appellate Body report and the panel report as modified by the Appellate Body were adopted on September 25, 1997. WT/DS27/AB/R.

criticism is that the process lacks transparency and accountability. Many WTO members, including the U.S., seem to concur, and it is likely that more open procedures will be adopted in the near future.

Other complaints are from groups maintaining that the procedure does not sufficiently account for important non-economic issues such as environmental concerns or social standards. Because the dispute panels include only lawyers and economists, they do not reflect the interests of workers or consumers who are most affected by the underlying trade issues. Some believe that the system puts developing countries at a disadvantage because the legal, economic and statistical expertise needed to present a case to a panel or Appellate Body is beyond their means.

These criticisms suggest a belief that the WTO's power is being used to override important national policies that conflict with its expanded view of *free trade*. Should a powerful international body focused on trade have the power to nullify national legislation that reflects other concerns, such as environmental, labor, and consumer protection laws? This question, however, may also be properly addressed to most other international organizations.

§ 2.03 Environmental Protection and Trade

National and international policies to enhance trade and economic development often conflict with the policies favored by groups focused on environmental issues.[30] These groups raise legitimate concerns about the association between increased trade and development and unregulated consumption of natural resources, strained ecosystems, and lower environmental standards designed to attract industry. Issues also arise about free trade regimes that provide means for *environmental dumping* that transfers polluting industries to poor countries that have little or no environmental regulation.

Generally, environmental protection is not a major issue for regional and international trade organizations such as the WTO and NAFTA, which focus on fostering free trade. These organizations are not likely to play a leading role in environmental protection because no consensus exists among their member nations.[31] Wealthier members, such as the U.S. and the EU, are more likely to raise environmental concerns because they can readily afford the burden of such quality of life issues. The poorer, developing countries that make up a majority of WTO membership tend to resist stringent global environmental rules because they are apprehensive about the impact on their fragile economies.

---

[30] *See* Brand, *Sustaining The Development Of International Trade And Environmental Law*, 21 Vt. L. Rev. 823 (Spring 1997).

[31] Yavitz, *The World Trade Organization Appellate Body Report, European Communities — Measures Affecting Asbestos And Asbestos-Containing Products*, Mar. 12, 2001, Wt/Ds135/Ab/R, 11 Minn. J. Global Trade 43.

Disputes under the WTO and NAFTA often arise because of conflicts between national environmental rules that restrict imports and international trade rules designed to eliminate trade barriers. Many national laws and multinational environmental agreements utilize trade restrictions to implement or enforce their environmental laws and regulations. These measures are bound to clash with WTO rules that provide only limited exceptions to the general requirement that member nations refrain from adopting trade restrictive rules.

[1] Multilateral Environmental Agreements

Most international cooperation on environmental issues is accomplished though *multilateral environmental agreements* (MEA) and conventions. At present, more than 500 international treaties and agreements relate to the environment. Over 300 of these agreements are regional rather global, and most have been adopted within the past 30 years. Most agreements relate to a few major areas of environmental concern, including:

- **Marine Environment.** The largest grouping of international agreements concerns the protection of the marine environment and sustainable use of marine and coastal resources. These agreements include the *United Nations Convention on the Law of the Sea* (1982), the *Global Program of Action for the Protection of the Marine Environment from Land-based Activities* (1995), and many regional fisheries conventions and protocols. Other important agreements are the *Marpol Convention* and *London Convention,* which limit ocean-going vessel discharges into the marine environment.[32] The conventions are implemented in the U.S by the Ocean Dumping Act[33] and the Act to Prevent Pollution from Ships.[34] Examples of regional agreements include the *Barcelona Convention for the Protection of the Marine Environment and the Coastal Region of the Mediterranean,* the *Cartagena Convention for the Protection and Development of the Marine Environment of the Wider Caribbean Region* and the *South Asia Cooperative Environment Program.*

- **Biodiversity.** A second large group of treaties relates to biodiversity and endangered species. These agreements are designed to protect species and ecosystems and promote their sustainable use. Agreements in this category include the *Convention Concerning the Protection of the World Cultural and Natural Heritage*, the *Convention on Biological Diversity, the Convention on the Conservation of Migratory Species of Wild Animals* and

---

[32] International Convention for the Prevention of Pollution from Ships, Nov. 2, 1973, 12 I.L.M. 1319, amended by Protocol of 1978 Relating to the International Convention for the Prevention of Pollution from Ships (MARPOL), 1973, Feb. 17, 1978, 17 I.L.M. 546.

[33] 33 U.S.C. §§ 1401–45 (1994).

[34] 33 U.S.C. §§ 1901–12 (1994).

the *Convention on Wetlands of International Importance.*[35] A key agreement is the *Convention on International Trade in Endangered Species.*[36] This Convention restricts trade in certain endangered animal and plant species by establishing export and import certificate requirements for international shipments of such species.

- **Atmosphere and Energy.** These agreements relate to the protection of the environment by eliminating or stabilizing human-generated emissions of substances that threaten to interfere with the atmosphere. This group includes key agreements such as the *Vienna Convention for the Protection of the Ozone Layer* and the *Montreal Protocol on Substances that Deplete the Ozone Layer.*[37] The *Montreal* protocol requires the parties to limit and reduce the use of chlorofluorocarbons and other chemicals that deplete the ozone layer and phases out their use by 2000. Another recent agreement is the *United Nations Framework Convention on Climate Change.*

- **Chemicals and Hazardous Waste.** The objective of the chemicals and hazardous wastes conventions is to protect human health and the environment by regulating trade or restricting the production and use of certain chemicals. Examples of treaties in this group include the *Basel Convention on the Control of Transboundary Movements of Hazardous Wastes and Their Disposal,* that provides rules for international transport of toxic wastes.[38] Also included are International Labor Organization conventions regarding occupational hazards in the workplace, the *Rotterdam Convention on the Prior Informed Consent Procedure for Certain Hazardous Chemicals and Pesticides in International Trade* and the *Stockholm Convention on Persistent Organic Pollutants.*

[2] The WTO Committee on Trade and Environment

The WTO does not have a separate, specific policy regarding controlling the environmental impact of international trade. Indeed, as a trade promotion organization, the WTO attempts to eliminate international trade restraints and focuses on the development of national resources and economic growth. The WTO is not an environmental agency and it is unlikely to intervene in national or international environmental policies or to set environmental standards.

Although the WTO established a *Committee on Trade and Environment* (CTE) to study environmental and sustainable development issues, the

---

[35] *See generally* Bodansky, *International Law and The Protection of Biological Diversity,* 28 Vanderbilt J Transitional Law 623.

[36] Convention on International Trade in Endangered Species of Wild Fauna and Flora, Mar. 3, 1973, 27 U.S.T. 1087, 993 U.N.T.S. 243.

[37] S. Treaty Doc. No. 10, 100th Cong., 1st Sess. 2 (1987).

[38] S. Treaty Doc. No. 5, 102d Cong., 1st Sess. (1991).

CTE's task is limited to studying the impact of environmental policies on trade. However, the CTE has expressed the view that trade restrictions are not necessarily the most effective environmental methods, preferring a program of financial assistance to help countries obtain environmentally-friendly technology and training.

It is possible that a country will impose a trade restriction pursuant to an MEA that conflicts with its free trade obligations under the WTO Agreement. Although the CTE indicates that such conflicts are unlikely, and no MEA action has yet been challenged under the GATT or WTO rules, the possibility nevertheless exists. Obviously, if a dispute about an environmental trade restriction arises between two parties to an MEA, the issue should be settled under the rules of that agreement. It is less clear, however, how disputes should be resolved when an MEA is invoked to justify trade restrictions against a country that has not signed that environmental agreement. The CTE indicates that the WTO dispute resolution mechanism must be utilized for trade restriction disputes that involve a country that has not signed the MEA. The WTO panel will not ignore the environmental issue, the CTE maintains, but will seek expert advice before rendering a decision.

A key concern of the CTE involves labeling of purported environmentally-friendly products. Although a country may adopt such labeling to encourage sound environmental practices, labeling can also be used in a manner that violates important WTO principles that bar discriminatory import policies. A labeling policy that discriminates against certain trading partners may violate the WTO obligation to provide *most-favored nation* treatment to all WTO members. Similarly, labeling that discriminates against imports in favor of domestic products may violate the WTO *national treatment* obligation. Labeling also raises issues under the WTO Technical Barriers to Trade Agreement concerning whether the label should describe the environmental impact of how a product is produced, as opposed to the environmental impact of the product itself. These labeling issues are discussed further in the next section.

[3] WTO Environmental-Trade Disputes

A nation's obligations under an international trade agreement may conflict with its sovereign right to enact national environmental protection laws that restrict the sale or importation of certain products. The sensitive and controversial nature of these conflicts is illustrated by the on-going disputes about environmental restrictions on tuna, sea turtles and gasoline discussed below. These disputes demonstrate the variety of circumstances in which national laws enacted to address regional or global environmental issues may be challenged by other countries as impermissible trade restrictions. One possible effect of these challenges is to inhibit countries from implementing legitimate environmental protection initiatives. Alternatively, they may create a backlash among groups sensitive to national sovereignty or environmental issues, resulting in demands for withdrawal from free-trade agreements such as WTO and NAFTA.

The Tuna-Dolphin Cases. Recent decisions by dispute resolution panels have raised concerns that the WTO is not appropriately sensitive to national environmental laws that conflict with its free trade principles. The first Tuna-Dolphin case involved a claim by Mexico that the US Marine Mammal Protection Act (MMPA) violated U.S. obligations under the GATT by imposing quantitative restriction and failing to provide national treatment for imported tuna products.[39] Under the MMPA, tuna may not be caught in U.S. waters or imported into the U.S. unless the best available methods are used to prevent accidental killing of dolphins. An important trade aspect of the Act prohibits imports of tuna from a country that cannot establish that the fish are caught in a manner that causes no more dolphin deaths than results under the rules applied to U.S. tuna boats. The MMPA also applies to intermediary countries that process tuna caught in an impermissible manner.

The MMPA rules resulted in a ban on tuna exports from Mexico and affected a number of intermediary countries that processed the Mexican catch. In 1991, Mexico brought its complaint to the GATT dispute settlement procedure, joined by the affected intermediary countries. The GATT panel report issued in September, 1991, concluded that the tuna embargo was an impermissible quantitative restriction on Mexican imports.

Although the U.S. may regulate the quality or content of imported products, the panel maintained that it cannot bar imports of an item from a foreign country because its production method does not conform to U.S. regulations. In the panel's view, GATT permits a country to regulate the quality or content of an imported product, not the process by which it is made. Trade restrictions may not be used to extra-territorially impose one country's domestic laws in another country, even if the laws are designed to protect global natural resources or animal or plant life. The WTO rules that permit a country to restrict trade in order to safeguard the life or health of humans, animals or plants are limited to the importing country's jurisdiction. From the WTO perspective, allowing a country to embargo imports based upon the exporting country's different environmental, health or social policies would open the door to all forms of unilateral trade restrictions, including many thinly disguised protectionist measures.

A second part of the GATT panel report considered the legality of a labeling provision of the Dolphin Protection Consumer Information Act of 1990.[40] That Act makes prohibits producers from labeling a tuna product as "dolphin safe" if certain harmful methods were used to catch the tuna. This provision did not violate the GATT most-favored nation requirement because the labeling rules did not restrict the sale of imported tuna products, but provides accurate information to consumers and prevents

---

[39] GATT Dispute Settlement Panel, United States — Restrictions on Imports of Tuna, GATT B.I.S.D. 39th Supp. at 155 (1991), *reprinted at* 30 I.L.M. 1594

[40] 16 U.S.C. § 1385.

deceptive advertising with respect to both domestic and imported tuna. Under the GATT rules in effect at the time of the ruling, the panel's decision could not be implemented over the objections of the U.S. Accordingly, the panel report was not adopted, the import ban remained in effect, and Mexico and the U.S. conducted separate bilateral negotiations to resolve the dispute.

In 1992 the European Union initiated a second GATT proceeding regarding U.S. tuna policy that resulted in another panel report in 1994.[41] The second report reiterated the holding that the U.S. ban violated the GATT and went on to conclude that the application of the ban to the intermediary tuna processors also violated the agreement. However, the report appears to modify the first panel's conclusions about the extraterritorial application of U.S. environmental laws and rejects the notion that a country's environmental protection regulations cannot apply to practices outside its territory. Thus, the U.S. could legitimately pursue a policy to protect endangered animal life inside and outside its borders. Nevertheless, the U.S. tuna ban was impermissible because it was designed primarily to force other countries to change their policies rather than to protect the endangered dolphins. It should be noted that neither Tuna-Dolphin panel report was adopted by the GATT Council. Neither report could be adopted over the U.S. objections, and so expired when the GATT merged into the WTO in 1995. Of course, under the current WTO rules, the U.S. cannot prevent implementation of an unfavorable dispute resolution decision.

After a great deal of debate and negotiation, Congress enacted the *International Dolphin Conservation Program Act* in 1997.[42] Under the Act, the U.S. sought and achieved a multilateral agreement with many of its tuna trading partners that allowed the lifting of some embargoes. Scientific studies have been undertaken to determine safe fishing practices which would be reflected in new "dolphin-safe" labeling rules. Although many environmental groups are not satisfied with the new programs, the majority seem to consider the multilateral agreements to reduce dolphin mortality as a model for international environmental cooperation. Notwithstanding these agreements, the U.S. continues its primary embargos under the MMPA against a number of countries that continue to use tuna netting methods that are not dolphin-safe.

Shrimp-Turtle Dispute. In a dispute similar to the Tuna-Dolphin controversy, the WTO Appellate Body ruled in 1999, that a provision of the U.S. Endangered Species Act[43] violated the GATT agreement. The dispute, called the *Shrimp-Turtle case*,[44] involved a statute that banned shrimp

---

[41] GATT Dispute Settlement Panel, United States-Restrictions on Imports of Tuna, 33 I.L.M. 839.

[42] 13 U.S.C.A. § 1385.

[43] Sea Turtle Conservation Amendments to the Endangered Species Act, Pub. L. 101-162, sec. 609, 103 Stat. 988, 1037 (Nov. 21, 1989) (amending 16 U.S.C. § 1537 (1994)).

[44] Report of the Appellate Body on U.S. Import Prohibition of Certain Shrimp and Shrimp Products, Oct. 12, 1998, 38 I.L.M. 118 (1999).

imports from countries that had not adopted regulations comparable to the U.S. rules for preventing endangered sea turtles from being accidentally caught in shrimping nets. Under the U.S. rules, trawlers must use turtle excluder devices (TEDs) on the nets to prevent the sea turtles from capture and drowning.

Four Asian countries brought the issue to a WTO dispute resolution panel, complaining that the U.S. ban was an impermissible quantitative import limitation.[45] The U.S. argued that the ban was permitted under a general exception to the GATT rules that allows a country to adopt measures to protect human, animal or plant life, or to conserve exhaustible natural resources.[46] That exception may not be applied, however, "in a manner which would constitute a means of arbitrary or unjustifiable discrimination between countries where the same conditions prevail, or a disguised restriction on international trade. . . ."[47]

In early 1998, the WTO panel ruled in favor of the Asian countries, basing its decision on the same broad grounds as in the Tuna-Dolphin cases; a country's environmental policies cannot have extra-territorially effect.[48] The U.S. appealed the decision to the Appellate Body, which upheld the panel's decision, but on much narrower grounds. The Appellate Body concluded that the U.S. shrimp embargo qualified as a measure to conserve an exhaustible natural resource, and that it was equally applicable to domestic and foreign producers. However, the ban did not meet the general requirement that such measures cannot be applied to create an arbitrary and unjustifiable discrimination between WTO members. The U.S. was deemed to have implemented its rules in an arbitrary and discriminatory manner by not permitting other countries to use their own sea turtle protection methods, failing to negotiate the issue with affected nations and by allowing some countries a longer phase-in period than others.[49]

Although the countries involved in the dispute acknowledged that sea turtles are endangered and that TEDs are effective and inexpensive, the U.S. could not bar shrimp imports from countries that did not require the device. In 1999, the State Department revised its certification guidelines to accord with the Appellate body ruling. These guidelines provide a simpler and more open process for countries to obtain a certification to export shrimp to the U.S.[50]

The legalities of the panel's decision may be less instructive than the tone of criticism it provoked among WTO detractors. A number of trade and

---

[45] The action was brought by India, Malaysia, Pakistan, and Thailand under GATT Article XI.

[46] GATT Article XX(b), (g).

[47] Introductory clause (chapeau) to GATT Article XX.

[48] *See* WTO Panel Report on U.S. Import Prohibition of Certain Shrimp and Shrimp Products, May 15, 1998, 37 I.L.M. 832 (1998).

[49] Appellate Body, *supra* note 2.

[50] *See* U.S. Department of State, Revised Guidelines for the Implementation of Section 609 of Public Law 101-162 Relating to the Protection of Sea Turtles in Shrimp Trawl Fishing Operations, 64 Fed. Reg. 36,946 (July 8, 1999).

environmental groups interpreted the decision as a defeat for the democratic process in the U.S. that allows other countries to overturn hard-won
environmental, consumer and health legislation.[51] On the other hand, the
decision has been applauded as applying a reasonable, case-by-case, approach to determining whether the terms or implementation of a nation's
environmental laws are unjustifiable trade restrictions.[52]

The Reformulated Gasoline Dispute. Pursuant to an amendment to
the Clean Air Act, the Environmental Protection Agency (EPA) issued new
regulations requiring gasoline refineries to use certain production methods
that would prevent harmful gasoline emissions from exceeding 1990 levels.[53] In establishing the method for meeting this goal, the regulations
allowed domestic producers to determine their 1990 baseline in a different
manner than would apply to imported gasoline. The purpose for this
different treatment was to reduce the administrative problems of enforcing
jurisdiction over foreign persons. Brazil and Venezuela complained to a
WTO dispute resolution panel that the standards applied to their imported
gasoline was a discriminatory violation of the GATT national treatment
requirement.[54]

The U.S. asserted that the restriction was justified under the GATT
exceptions permitting a nation to adopt measures to protect human, animal
or plant life or protect natural resources. The panel disagreed, holding that
the regulations did not serve to protect human health because foreign and
domestic gasoline are chemically identical. Accordingly, the regulations were
an impermissible violation of the national treatment requirement that
discriminated against foreign refiners.

On appeal, the Appellate Body agreed with the U.S. that the gasoline
regulations could be allowed under the GATT exceptions. However, the
panel's decision was upheld on the ground that implementation of the regulations failed to satisfy the general requirement that a rule not create an
arbitrary or unjustifiable discrimination between WTO countries.[55] Although the Appellate Body recognized the U.S. concerns about regulating
foreign companies, it considered them insubstantial in justifying the denial
of equal treatment to foreign refiners. It agreed with the panel's finding
that other reasonable measures were available to the U.S.

In accord with the Appellate Body ruling, the EPA changed the regulation
in question to allow foreign refiners to chose the same methods as domestic

---

[51] Olsen, *The New York Times,* May 16, 1998.

[52] *See* Chang, *Toward A Greener GATT: Environmental Trade Measures And The Shrimp-
Turtle Case,* 74 S. Cal. L. Rev. 31 (November, 2000).

[53] Regulation of Fuels and Fuel Additives: Standards for Reformulated and Conventional
Gasoline, 59 Fed. Reg. 7716 (Feb. 16, 1994); 40 C.F.R. § 80 (1999). Clean Air Act Amendments
of 1990, §§ 211, 212–221, 228(d), Pub. L. No. 101-549, 104 Stat. 2399, 2488–2500, 2510 (1990).

[54] Dispute Settlement Report, United States — Standards for Reformulated and Conventional Gasoline, WT/DS2/R (Jan. 29, 1996).

[55] Appellate Body Report, United States — Standards for Reformulated and Conventional
Gasoline, WT/DS2/AB/R (Apr. 22, 1996).

companies for determining the 1990 emissions baseline. The new regulations have raised concerns among environmental and health groups that certain foreign gasolines contain higher levels of pollutants than domestic products. The EPA addressed these concerns by establishing benchmarks for imported gasoline and monitoring the imports to ensure compliance.[56] However, some groups remain skeptical that he EPA has the resources to actually carry out the required inspections.[57]

[4] NAFTA Chapter 11 Disputes

The North American Free Trade Agreement (NAFTA) differs from the WTO and many other multilateral trade agreements by allowing private investors to bring direct actions for monetary damages against the signatory countries, the U.S., Canada, and Mexico, for violations of the treaty's investment rules.[58] This may be done without the consent or knowledge of the investor's government. Under the WTO rules, by contrast, only governments may bring actions for violation of the agreement, and the remedy is limited to imposition of tariffs and other trade sanctions against the nation in violation. Although absent in most multilateral treaties, a number of U.S. *bilateral investment treaties* (BITs) give investors a right to bring suit against a treaty-partner government.[59] If no such BIT provision exists, a dispute between a U.S. investor and a treaty-partner government must be resolved through the foreign nation's courts.

The investment-protection rules of NAFTA *Chapter 11* have engendered a number of controversial disputes between companies engaged in cross-border operations and government environmental protection measures. Under Chapter 11, a party from a NAFTA country that invests or does business in another NAFTA country is granted comprehensive and detailed protections against loss of its investment through government action, including protection from nationalization, expropriation or actions that are *tantamount to expropriation*.[60] These provisions were designed to encourage cross-border investments, particularly in Mexico, by assuring foreign investors that the host government will not act against their interests in an arbitrary and discriminatory manner.[61]

Generally, an investor may challenge a government action under Chapter 11 by bringing its disputes directly to a binding arbitration proceeding.[62]

---

[56] *See* Regulation of Fuels and Fuel Additives: Baseline Requirements for Gasoline Produced by Foreign Refiners, 62 Fed. Reg. 45,533 (Aug. 28, 1997).

[57] Cummins, *Trade Secrets: How The Charming Betsy Canon May Do More To Weaken U.S. Environmental Laws Than The WTO's Trade Rules*, 12 Fordham Envtl. L.J. 141.

[58] NAFTA Chapter 11; NAFTA Arts 1115–1138

[59] Williams, *The Next Frontier: Environmental Law In A Trade-Dominated World*, 20 Va. Envtl. L.J. 221 (2001).

[60] North American Free Trade Agreement, Dec. 17, 1992, U.S.-Can.-Mex., arts. 1102–1110.

[61] *See* Int'l Division, U.S. Chamber of Commerce, A Guide to the North American Free Trade Agreement 22 (1992).

[62] NAFTA, arts. 1116, 1117.

Thus, a foreign investor may seek damages from a government based upon its claim that the government has enacted laws, regulations or other rules that treat its business in a discriminatory or inequitable manner or that reduce the value of the investment in a manner that is tantamount to expropriation. The government's obligation to pay damages to a foreign investor that is adversely affected by its laws or regulations is not determined by any national court, but by a panel of private arbitrators in closed proceedings.

Critics of Chapter 11 maintain that its rules to protect investors are incompatible with the right and obligation of national and local governments to implement valid environmental protection laws and regulations.[63] The basic criticism is that businesses will challenge government health and environmental measures that may reduce their anticipated profits as being tantamount to expropriation. Some believe that the mere threat of a major damage award may deter governments from taking an action that it otherwise deems proper. Many environmental groups assert that allowing privates suits and money damages in trade disputes will inhibit governments from enacting environmental legislation that may require them to compensate companies subjected to public health or environmental regulations. In this view, a corporation's right to be compensated for loss of business should not be afforded equal status with the public's right to healthy environmental conditions.

On the other hand, governments have been known to use environmental or health concerns as a pretext for actions that are really motivated a desire to protect a domestic industry or discriminate against a foreign company or country. This is, of course, the heart of the dispute between the U.S. and the EU regarding hormone-treated beef. *See* 2.01[4][c]. The drafters of NAFTA Chapter 11 envisioned that arbitration panels empowered to award damages would deter discriminatory or protectionist government actions against foreign investors, without invalidating valid environmental regulation. Those favoring the NAFTA-type rules argue that this kind of legal threat is necessary to ensure that governments carefully consider the impact of environmental rules that may violate international agreements.[64]

Recent actions brought by private investors illustrate the potential conflicts between the goal of Chapter 11 to enhance international capital flow and investment and a government's right to enact valid regulations. NAFTA clearly states that its provisions may not be construed to prevent a party from implementing environmental protection measures "otherwise consistent with" Chapter 11.[65] Thus, the issue in these cases is whether the government rule is supported by sufficient scientific evidence to be consistent with Chapter 11, or is an arbitrary or discriminatory action that

---

[63] *See generally*, Gantz, *Potential Conflicts Between Investor Rights And Environmental Regulation Under Nafta's Chapter 11*, 33 Geo. Wash. Int'l L. Rev. 651 (2001).

[64] U.S. Department of Treasury Staff, Briefing on the MAI and the Financial Services Agreement to the Senate Committee on Banking, Housing and Urban Affairs, 4/21/97.

[65] NAFTA, art 1114.1

is inconsistent with the country's NAFTA obligations. The question then becomes whether country must compensate a foreign company if it bars its products as a precaution before a scientific risk assessment has been concluded.

The MMT Gasoline Additive Dispute. The NAFTA *private action* right was first used by a U.S. company, the Ethyl Corporation (Ethyl), to initiate an action against Canada for damages resulting from a ban on imports of a gasoline additive called MMT. Ethyl, the only producer of MMT, claimed that Canada's ban violated NAFTA's national treatment obligation and reduced the value the of the company's plant, sales, and corporate reputation to an extent that was tantamount to expropriation. Under NAFTA, a government may not expropriate business assets without paying fair compensation.

The Canadian ban was based upon two concerns; that the MMT additive created gasoline emissions that may endanger public health and that it resulted in increased emissions by damaging automobile emissions control equipment. The government could not ban MMT under its own environmental pollution act, however, because it lacked adequate data on the health risks of exposure to emissions from the additive. Thus, MMT was not considered a health risk under Canadian domestic law. Similarly, the basic issue regarding the emissions equipment was the cost of repairs to the Canadian automobile industry rather than concern about clean air standards. This added expense to the auto industry, however, would be offset by increased gasoline mileage consumers would obtain from MMT.

In July of 1998, the Canadian government settled its dispute with Ethyl, based upon its own internal investigation and report that the MMT ban was inconsistent with its obligations under NAFTA.[66] Canada paid Ethyl $13 million and agreed to allow MMT to be imported into the country. The government conceded that the automobile industry representations about damage to the emissions equipment were unsubstantiated. It also noted that the evidence did not show that MMT posed a health risk, that studies were under way to determine its health effect and that future action would depend upon the outcome of this research.

There is concern that cases like Ethyl will deter governments from enacting laws and regulations that can adversely affect the businesses of NAFTA or BIT trading partners. Conversely, the ban on MMT can be viewed as an impermissible attempt by the Canadian government to favor the interests of its domestic automobile industry over a foreign company's imports into Canada. Under this view, the government's decision that reduced repair costs to its domestic auto industry outweighed the enhanced gasoline mileage to Canadian consumers was tainted by consideration of the fact that a ban on MMT would harm only a foreign company. Thus,

---

[66] Government of Canada, Statement on MMT, July 20, 1998.

the ultimate issue is the degree of scientific evidence a nation must have before it can enact environmental rules that affect trade agreements.[67]

S.D. Myers v. Government of Canada. In this case, Meyers, an Ohio firm engaged in a joint venture with a Canadian subsidiary, asserted it was damaged when Canada banned exports of PCB waste from Canada for disposal in the U.S.[68] Although Canada asserted that its ban was required pursuant to its treaty obligations regarding transportation of hazardous waste, Meyers claimed that Canada acted to protect its only domestic PCB treatment facility. Canada allowed PCBs to be transported to the facility in Alberta even though the distance was greater than for Meyers' shipments to the U.S. Canada had not shown any greater hazard was involved in transporting PCBs to the U.S. than to Alberta. The arbitration panel held that Canada violated Meyers' rights under NAFTA Chapter 11, leaving assessment of damages for a later proceeding.

Metalclad Corporation v. United Mexican States. Metalclad Corporation purchased land and developed a hazardous waste disposal facility in the Mexican State of San Luis Potosi.[69] The Mexican federal government granted a permit for construction, which began in 1993. Although the state and municipal governments opposed construction of the plant, it was completed in March, 1995. In response to this opposition, Metalclad negotiated an agreement with the Mexican federal authorities under which the company would modify the site, allow local citizens and scientific committees to participate, employ local labor, and contribute toward local welfare and medical services.

Nevertheless, in a closed procedure the municipal government denied a construction permit to Metalclad. However, the Mexican federal authorities subsequently granted Metalclad a permit to substantially expand the site's capacity. Shortly afterward, the governor of San Luis Potosi declared the landfill area a "Natural Area for the protection of rare cactus," that precluded operation of a hazardous waste disposal plant. Metalclad brought an action under Chapter 11 and an arbitration panel awarded it partial compensation for its lost investment.

The Loewen Case. An interesting and illuminating non-environmental case under Chapter 11 is *Loewen v. U.S.*[70] That case was brought to a NAFTA panel to challenge a $500 million award (including punitive damages) by a Mississippi state court jury

---

[67] *See Methanex v. United States*, First Partial Award (NAFTA Ch. 11 Arb. Trib. August 7, 2022) available at www.state.gov/documents/organization/12613.pdf (last visited August 4, 2004) (Canadian producer challenged California regulations banning the use of methanol in gasoline).

[68] *See S.D. Myers, Inc. v. Canada*, NAFTA Arb., Trib. (2000).

[69] *Metalclad Corporation v. United Mexican States*, Aug. 26, 2000.

[70] *The Loewen Group, Inc. v. United States*, Final Award, ICSID Case No. ARB/(AF)/98/3 (June 26, 2003).

against a Canadian funeral home conglomerate. Loewen challenged the verdict under NAFTA, claiming that the state trial was a denial of justice under customary international law because the presiding judge encouraged the jury's prejudice against Canadians.

The NAFTA tribunal agreed that the judge's actions denied Loewen due process and that the punitive damages were greatly disproportionate. However, the panel dismissed the claim because Loewen did not exhaust its remedies in the U.S. by seeking review in the Supreme Court. Loewen later settled the case and the NAFTA panel dismissed it. It appears likely that the NAFTA panel was disinclined to rule in Loewen's favor because that decision could generate anti-NAFTA sentiment and serious political fallout.[71]

[5] The WTO and Labor Standards

A frequent and important criticism of the WTO is that its rules foster exploitation of labor and undermine national rules designed to protect their health and safety. Critics have urged the organization to adopt *core labor standards* regarding issues such as child and forced labor, freedom to organize unions and the right to strike. Current WTO agreements do not provide that trade barriers may be raised against a country that violates labor rights of its citizens or residents.

The WTO is unlikely to undertake serious initiatives in this area, however, asserting that the International Labor Organization (ILO) is the appropriate organization to deal with labor standards. The labor issue is not presently on the WTO's agenda and no committees are directly considering the issue. The WTO has framed the issues the ILO should address as follows:

- Should trade action be used to pressure countries deemed to severely violate core labor rights?

- Do lower labor standards provide an unfair advantage for a country's exports?

- Is the WTO the proper venue to resolve labor issues?

These questions were intensively discussed at the Singapore Ministerial Conference in 1996. The outcome was a Ministerial Declaration that labor issues were beyond the scope of the WTO, but it would work with the ILO to establish and enforce core labor standards for WTO members. The WTO is reluctant to deal with labor standards because the issue will be divisive, pitting the developed countries with high labor standards and costs against developing countries having lower standards and wages. Thus, the underlying political issue is whether WTO labor rules really will improve labor standards or merely serve as an excuse for protectionist actions.

---

[71] *See* Afilalo, *Towards A Common Law Of International Investment: How Nafta Chapter 11 Panels Should Solve Their Legitimacy Crisis*, 17 Geo. Int'l Envtl. L. Rev. 51 (Fall 2004).

Many industrialized countries argue that establishing WTO core labor standards will create important incentives for members to improve working conditions. These countries, including the U.S., the EU, and Canada contend that the threat of WTO economic sanctions is required to compel many nations to improve or enforce their labor standards. This position is supported by a number of NGOs and civil organizations, suggesting that including labor issues in the WTO will increase public support for the organization, or at least reduce some of the criticism directed at it by labor unions and activists.

Conversely, many developing nations assert that WTO labor rules would provide a façade for protectionism that will undercut the comparative advantage they obtain from lower wage costs. Although there is general agreement that forced labor and discrimination should be globally banned, issues such as collective bargaining and child labor are controversial. Some countries suggest that some child labor may be essential for extremely poor families that need income from every member. Similarly, many nations are concerned that unionization of their workers will deter investment by multinational companies seeking low labor costs and activism. Because many exports from developing countries are labor-intensive, trade restrictions based on labor standards will restrict access to markets in many developed countries. In this view, the key to improvement of labor conditions is economic growth rather than enforcement of global labor rules.

§ 2.04 International Intellectual Property Rights

Information, ideas, and designs are an increasingly important component of international trade, particularly for the most developed economies. To encourage creative efforts, most nations grant inventors, writers, designers and other originators temporary, exclusive rights, called intellectual property rights, to use or sell their creations. The major classifications of intellectual property in the U.S. and throughout the world are patents, trademarks, copyrights, trade secrets and industrial designs.

Generally, a creator of intellectual property may protect his property rights by complying with the legal process of the country where he seeks protection. Under certain international agreements, however, each country signing the agreement is obligated to respect and enforce the intellectual property rights granted to citizens of other treaty partners.

The U.S. has entered into numerous multilateral and bilateral agreements regarding intellectual property. These international treaties provide minimum standards for protection of intellectual property, but do not create uniform rules that prevent inconsistent treatment of intellectual property rights in different countries. Because treaty partners are not obligated to enforce each others judgments, a party seeking to protect against infringement frequently must pursue its claim in multiple jurisdictions, sometimes with different outcomes.

Attempts to develop a harmonized international intellectual property law have raised a number of contentious issues, particularly between the developed and developing countries. For developed nations that own and export most of the intellectual property, lack of protection results in substantial financial losses. These nations assert that rigorous protection is required if inventors and creators are to recover their research and development costs and earn a suitable risk-weighted investment return. Lack of such protection will cause reduced innovation and product development, less choice and higher costs to consumers around the world.

By contrast, many developing countries argue that rigorous intellectual property protection results in economic domination by the richer nations that can afford the high costs that research and development require. Under this view, it is in the interest of the wealthier nations that seek profits through sales and investments in the Third World to encourage economic development by providing knowledge and information at the lowest cost. These issues have become more urgent as the increasing rate of HIV/AIDS cases and similar epidemics suggest a moral obligation of wealthier nations to provide intellectual property at a price that will allow poor countries to cheaply produce medicines. For discussion of the recent WTO pronouncement on compulsory licensing in HIV/AIDS situations, see 2.02[4][f].

[1] The World Intellectual Property Organization (WIPO)

At present, no global system exists for harmonizing the intellectual property protection rights that one nation must afford to citizens of another nation. The organization that comes closest to filling that role is the *World Intellectual Property Organization* (WIPO), a specialized agency of the United Nations located in Geneva that was established by the WIPO Convention 1967.[72] WIPO, which has 179 member states, is charged with promoting and protecting worldwide intellectual property rights and is responsible for administering a number of multilateral intellectual property treaties.[73] The organization is self-supporting, raising most of its income from fees paid by users of its registration services. Pursuant to an agreement between WIPO and the WTO, the two organizations cooperate on implementing the TRIPS Agreement in areas such as notification of laws and regulations relating to intellectual property and technical assistance to developing countries

The WIPO Convention does not provide an independent dispute settlement mechanism. Accordingly, international disagreements about intellectual properties issues are generally subject to the WTO dispute resolution procedures pursuant to the TRIPS Agreement. A major drawback of this arrangement is that the dispute settlement mechanism excludes WIPO signatories that are not WTO members, such as Russia.

---

[72] Convention Establishing the World Intellectual Property Organization, July 14, 1967, 21 U.S.T. 1770, 828 U.N.T.S. 3. The Convention became effective in 1970.

[73] *See generally*, Kwakwa, *Some Comments On Rulemaking At The World Intellectual Property Organization*, 12 Duke J. Comp. & Int'l L. 179 (Winter 2002).

WIPO does provide an Arbitration and Mediation Center that is available to individuals and companies engaged in intellectual property disputes. The Center maintains a list of specialized mediators and arbitrators that conduct dispute resolution procedures under rules established by WIPO. It is particularly active in settling disputes related to abusive registration and use of Internet domain names (*cybersquatting*). These procedures may be conducted on-line, resulting in fast, enforceable decisions.

[2] Trade Related Intellectual Property Agreement (TRIPS)

The most comprehensive and important recent treaty is the *Trade Related Aspects of Intellectual Property Rights* (TRIPS) Agreement that was adopted in connection with the formation of the World Trade Organization in 1994. The TRIPS Agreement standardizes many intellectual property rights among its signatory countries, and U.S. intellectual property law has been significantly modified to accord with our obligations under the treaty. Generally, TRIPS provides a higher degree of protection for intellectual property that exists under the prior multilateral treaties. For complete discussion of the TRIPS Agreement, *see* 2.02[4][f].

[3] Patents

A patent grants an inventor the legal right to prevent other persons from making, using or selling the patented invention. Under U.S. law, a *utility patent* for "any new and useful process, machine, manufacture, or composition of matter" has a 20 year term from the date the first U.S. patent application is filed.[74] Additional time periods may be allowed to compensate for delays caused by interference proceedings, patent secrecy orders and review by courts or the Board of Patent Appeals and Interferences. A *design patent* has a 14 year term from the date it is granted.[75] The patented work enters the public domain when the patent registration expires.

An inventor obtains a U.S. patent by filing an application with the U.S. Patent and Trademark Office (PTO) and showing that the invention is non-obvious, novel, and useful.[76] The U.S. awards its patents under a *first to invent* standard relating to the inventor who first conceived an invention and reduced it to practice, which differs from the law in most other countries that apply a *first to file* standard relating to the first person who files a patent application. This unique characteristic of U.S. law is not affected by the TRIPS Agreement or other international conventions.

The key treaties and conventions relating to international patent protection are the *Paris Convention for the Protection of Industrial Property* (Paris Convention),[77] which applies to patents, industrial designs, and

---

[74] 35 U.S.C. § 154, *as amended by the Uruguay Round Agreements Act*, P.L. 103-465.

[75] 35 U.S.C. § 173.

[76] 35 U.S.C. §§ 101–03.

[77] Paris Convention for the Protection of Industrial Property, 1883.

trademarks and the *Patent Cooperation Treaty* (PCT) that simplifies the procedures for acquiring international patent rights. Both treaties are administered by WIPO, which facilitates registration of patent rights and applications, but does not itself grant patent rights. Some international harmonization of patent procedures also has been achieved through the *Patent Law Treaty* (PLT) that was adopted in 2000. The PLT standardizes different national and regional patent requirements to create a simpler and predictable international patent process.

The *Paris Convention* obligates the signatory states to afford *national treatment* to the intellectual property of citizens of other treaty partners, and provides a twelve-month priority period for filing patent applications (six months for trademarks) in other treaty countries. A patent or trademark application filed in one treaty country during the priority period generally is deemed to have been filed on the date that an application was previously submitted in another treaty country. The twelve month priority period for patents (and six month period for trademarks) runs from the application date and not from the date the patent is granted or the trademark registered.

Generally, the holder of a patent in one country does not obtain any patent rights in a foreign country. Accordingly, patent protection in other countries must be obtained by applying for a patent under the law and procedures of each other country. Under the *Patent Cooperation Treaty* (PCT),[78] however, a single international patent application may be filed that automatically becomes a national application in treaty countries that are designated by the applicant. Thus, the PCT allows for simultaneous filing of patent applications in member nations so that the filing or priority date is obtained in all those countries. Once the application is filed, WIPO conducts a search and issues a preliminary examination report regarding potential patentability of the invention. The single application may be registered with a number of countries for later examination and a national patent grant.

The PCT does not itself result in the grant of any international patent right, but is a method for filing numerous foreign patent applications and obtaining a preliminary search and patentability opinion.[79] After the preliminary examination, the applicant must proceed through each country's patent process, so that the actual examination occurs in each country. Thus, it is possible that an application be treated quite differently in each country even though the applications are identical. A patent application in the EU, however, may be granted by the European Patent Office that may become a valid patent in each EU member country.

---

[78] Patent Cooperation Treaty, June 19, 1970, 28 U.S.T. 7645, T.I.A.S. No. 8733.

[79] The U.S. differs from most countries by allowing a one-grace period for filing a patent application after publication, public disclosure, offer for sale, sale, public use, etc., of the invention. No grace period is allowed in other countries and any publication, disclosure, sale, etc., is an absolute bar to patentability.

[4] Trademarks

A trademark is a word, name, sign, symbol or device (or combination of these) that an enterprise uses to distinguish its goods and services from those of other businesses.[80] Most countries have national laws and regulations that allow trademarks to be registered and protected. These trademark protection laws grant the owner of a trademark the exclusive right to use or license the mark to identify goods or services. The initial protection period varies from country to country, but most nations permit the trademark to be renewed. In the U.S., for example, trademarks and service marks may be federally registered with the U.S. Patent and Trademark Office (PTO) if the applicant intends to use the mark in interstate or international commerce.[81] The mark is granted a renewable term of 10 years if it is actually used in commerce.

Unlike many other nations, U.S. law does not allow registration or renewal of a mark that is not used in commerce, and registrants must periodically establish such use.[82] U.S. trademark law also differs from the practice in other countries with respect to priority of registration. Most countries use a *first to file* registrations system, under which an applicant does not have to show any actual use of the mark to apply for or maintain its registration. In the U.S., priority is determined under a *first to use* basis.[83]

Ordinarily, a trademark registered in one country is not automatically protected in other nations. A party seeking to use or register a trademark in a specific country may determine if the mark is available by searching the national or regional office that maintains the trademark register. The EU, however, maintains a Community Trade Mark (CTM) procedure that allows for a single registration of trademarks for all EU countries.[84] As noted in the previous section, significant international trademark protection is provided by *the Paris Convention for the Protection of Industrial Property*, which obligates signatory states to afford *national treatment* to the trademarks of citizens of other treaty partners, and provides six-month priority period for filing trademark applications in other treaty countries.

WIPO administers two other treaties that create a system for international trademark registration that precludes the necessity for separate registration in each country. Under these treaties, the *Madrid Agreement Concerning the International Registration of Marks,* and the related *Madrid Protocol*, persons linked through nationality, domicile or establishment to a country that has signed either treaty may obtain an international

---

[80] *See* 15 U.S.C.A. § 1127 (2001).

[81] Trademark Law Revision Act of 1988. Pub. L. No. 100-667, 102 Stat. 3935 (codified at 15 U.S.C. §§ 1051–1127 (1988)), effective November 16, 1989.

[82] *See* 37 C.F.R. § 2.33(b)(2) and 15 U.S.C.A. § 1058.

[83] *See* Curci, *Protecting Your Intellectual Property Rights Overseas*, 15 Transnat'l Law. 15 (Winter 2002).

[84] *See* Council Regulation (EC) 40/94 of 20 December 1993 on the Community Trade Mark, 1994 O.J. (L 11) 1.

registration that is effective in all member countries of the *Madrid Union*.[85] Although more than 60 countries are currently parties to these agreements, the U.S. has not adopted the Madrid Protocol. Consequently, except for the CTM registration process in the EU, a U.S. company cannot centrally register its trademark for international protection and must submit a separate application in each country where it desires registration.

Additional harmonization of trademark protection has been achieved through the WIPO *Trademark Law Treaty* that the U.S. ratified in 1998.[86] The Treaty, which focuses on procedural rather than substantive issues, allows U.S. firms to register their marks in treaty partner countries using standardized application forms and other documents such as powers of attorney. Certain burdensome requirements are prohibited, such as notarizations and signature certifications.

[5] Copyrights

The term copyright refers to the legal rights a nation grants to creators of literary and artistic works. These rights arise as soon as the creative work exists, and no specific procedure is required. In the U.S., a copyright extends for a term that extends to fifty years after the author's death, but most other countries provide quite different periods of protection. Many countries, including the U.S., have enacted laws that allow works to be registered for identification purposes and provide national or regional copyright offices for this function. Such registration may be *prima facie* evidence in copyright disputes.

Copyright protection covers a wide variety of creative endeavors, including

- literary works such as fiction and nonfiction, poems, plays, reference materials, and newspapers and advertisements;
- motion pictures;
- musical compositions and choreography;
- artistic works such as paintings, drawings, photographs and sculpture;
- architecture;
- maps and technical drawings, and;
- computer programs and databases.

Only expressions may be copyrighted, not ideas, procedures, methods or concepts.

Unlike patents and trademarks, copyrights are automatically protected in all countries that have signed *the Berne Convention for the Protection*

---

[85] The Protocol Relating to the Madrid Agreement Concerning the International Registration of Marks, adopted June 27, 1989, WIPO Pub. No. 204(E).

[86] The United States became a party to the Trademark Law Treaty on August 12, 2000. Trademark Law Treaty Implementation Act, Pub. L. No. 105-330, 112 Stat. 3064 (1998).

of Literary and Artistic Works (Berne Convention)[87] without actual filing in each country. Accordingly, a U.S. author has the same copyright protection in a country that is a Berne Convention signatory as that country grants its own citizens. Because a copyright arises when a work is created, Berne Convention nations may not impose additional prerequisites for obtaining protection.

The Berne Convention does permit member countries to impose post-creation copyright formalities, such as a requirement that a work be registered before an infringement action may begin. This is the case in the U.S., where infringement actions regarding works of U.S. origin are barred unless the copyright has been registered at the U.S. copyright office.[88] These formalities cannot affect works from other treaty countries, however, so that a copyright infringement action relating to a work that is not of U.S. origin may be brought in a U.S. court even though the work is not registered.

Under the Berne Convention, member states must recognize an original author's *moral rights* with respect to a copyrighted work.[89] These moral rights include the *right of attribution,* which allows the original author always to claim authorship, and the *right of integrity,* which allows the original author to bar distortion, mutilation, modification or any other actions detrimental to the work. These moral rights continue even though the original author has transferred ownership of the work to others. A number of European countries provide substantial protection for these moral rights. The U.S., however, provides only minimal protection in this area and has been subject to a great deal of criticism from the EU regarding its alleged failure to meet its obligations under the Berne Convention.

A number of countries, not including the U.S., also protect certain rights — often called *neighboring rights* — related to copyrights, such as those of performing artists, sound recording producers, and broadcasters. Some of these rights are governed by *The International Convention for the Protection of Performers, Producers of Phonograms and Broadcasting Organizations* (Rome Convention). Although the U.S. is not a signatory to the Rome Convention, it is a party to the *Geneva Phonograms Convention* that protects sound recordings in foreign countries. Important U.S. laws affecting sound recording issues include the *Digital Performance Right in Sound Recordings Act of 1995* (public performance rights),[90] and the *Audio Home Recording Act of 1992* (requiring manufacturers of audio recorders to pay fees to artists).[91] To keep up with the requirements of new

---

[87] Berne Convention for the Protection of Literary and Artistic Works, Sept. 9, 1886, revised in Paris on July 24, 1971, 828 U.N.T.S. 221. The U.S. joined the Berne Convention effective March 1, 1989. The Berne Implementation Act of 1988, Pub. L. No. 100-568, 102 Stat. 2853, 2854 (1988).

[88] 17 U.S.C. §§ 101, 411(a).

[89] Berne Convention, art. 6bis.

[90] P.L. 104-39.

[91] P.L. 102-563.

technology, WIPO administers two *Internet Treaties*, the *WIPO Copyright Treaty* and the *WIPO Performances and Phonogram Treaty*, that establish rules to prevent the use of creative works on the Internet.

[6] Trade Secrets

Generally, a trade secret is confidential, proprietary information used in a business that affords the business an economic advantage, because the information is not known to the public and the owner has taken reasonable measures to keep the information secret.[92] In the U.S., the common and statutory laws of each state govern an owner's rights to protect trade secrets, most recently through the Uniform Trade Secrets Act. A similar federal law, the Economic Espionage Act of 1996,[93] makes it a federal crime to steal or misappropriate trade secrets. These aspects of U.S. law are not affected by the TRIPS Agreement.

Ordinarily, trade secrets are not protected by filing or registration with a government agency, but through the efforts of the business owner. Any rights to keep the secrets are not protected for any specific period, but for as long as the owner preserves their confidential nature. Although a number of countries have adopted laws to protect trade secrets, these rules are difficult to enforce. Thus, a U.S. business operating abroad should carefully consider the advantages and disadvantages of providing access to secret information. This is true regardless of the existence of a confidentiality agreement.

---

[92] *See* U.S. Patent and Trademark Office website, at www.uspto.gov/main/glossary/index.html.
[93] P.L. 104-294.

Chapter 3

UNITED STATES TRADE LAWS

§ 3.01   Import Restrictions

[1]   General Considerations

Most U.S. laws governing trade are ostensibly designed to protect domestic industries from foreign practices that allow imports to *unfairly* compete in the U.S. market, or *unfairly* prevent U.S. exports from competing in foreign markets. As noted later in this chapter, many of these domestic laws integrate, or are subordinated to, recent trade rules and obligations adopted in connection with U.S. membership in global or regional trade agreements such as the WTO and NAFTA. Consequently, obtaining a remedy for an alleged unfair trade practice often involves the dispute resolution procedures established in these agreements as well as any relevant U.S. statute.

U.S. trade laws regarding imports usually focus on practices, such as subsidies or dumping, that allow foreign exports to sell in U.S. markets at artificially low prices. The laws for exports target the practices of foreign governments that restrict market access for U.S. goods or fail to protect U.S. property rights. For both imports and exports, the laws typically provide remedies that increase the price of foreign goods in the U.S. by imposing a duty to increase the price of a subsidized or dumped foreign product or to retaliate against the products of a foreign country that discriminates against U.S. imports. Although it may be difficult to understand how trade is enhanced by raising the prices that U.S. consumers pay for their products, many industry, labor and political representatives argue that unfair practices inflict long-term injury on the U.S. economy and standard or living.

Most U.S. trade laws are amendments to the Tariff Act of 1930,[1] as amended by the Trade Act of 1974,[2] the Trade Agreements Act of 1979,[3] the Trade and Tariff Act of 1984,[4] the Omnibus Trade and Competitiveness Act of 1988,[5] and the Uruguay Round Agreements Act.[6] These statutes comprise the rules governing anti-dumping,[7] countervailing duties,[8] import safeguards,[9] Section 337 infringement actions,[10] and Section 301 actions.[11]

[2] Tariffs

In the U.S., Article I of the Constitution grants Congress the power to impose and collect tariffs, which are taxes imposed on foreign imports. For most of U.S. history, the tariffs enacted by Congress served two functions. The first was to provide a source of revenue to support the activities of the federal government. Indeed, tariffs were the principal source of federal revenues until the early 1900's, when revenues from the newly established federal income tax first exceeded the amounts raised from import duties. Today, federal income from tariffs is relatively small.

The second function of tariffs is to protect domestic industry from foreign competition by raising the costs of imported goods, or to retaliate against the goods of foreign countries that use tariffs to protect their industries from

---

[1] 19 U.S.C. § 1671 *et seq.*

[2] Pub. L. No. 93-618, 88; 19 U.S.C. §§ 1863, 2101-2495 (1988).

[3] Pub. L. No. 96-39, in various sections of 19 U.S.C.

[4] Pub. L. No. 98-573, in various sections of 19 U.S.C.

[5] Pub. L. No. 100-418, in various sections of 19 U.S.C.

[6] Pub. L. No. 100-465, 19 U.S.C. § 1671 *et seq.*

[7] 19 U.S.C. §§ 1673-1673h.

[8] 19 U.S.C. §§ 1671-1671h.

[9] 19 U.S.C. § 2251.

[10] 19 U.S.C. § 1337.

[11] 19 U.S.C. § 2411.

U.S. competition. This continues to be the primary purpose for U.S. tariff legislation.

Substantial penalties may be imposed for Customs Law violations. An importer must use reasonable care to correctly classify and value its goods and must keep extensive records. Illegally imported goods may be seized and substantial civil penalties assessed for the fraudulent, grossly negligent, or negligent entry or introduction of merchandise into the U. S. by means of any document, written or oral statement, or act or omission that is material and false.[12]

[a]　The Harmonized Tariff Schedule

Most goods imported into the U. S. must be declared with the U.S. Customs Service and are subject to tariff under the Harmonized Tariff Schedule of the United States (HTS). The HTS is based upon an international convention adopted by all major trading countries called the Harmonized Commodity Description and Coding System (Harmonized System or HS), which requires contracting states to apply the same nomenclature and code numbers to imported or exported products. Although contracting states use the same code system for identifying imported goods, each country applies its own tariff rates which it publishes in tariff *schedules*.[13]

The rate applied to a particular product depends upon its classification, value, origin and entry status. A product's *classification* refers to its HTS code, which determines the applicable tariff rate and eligibility for any preferential tariff treatment. Goods are classified in a pyramidal system, beginning with the Section (*e.g.*, textiles, vehicles, etc.) and then breaking down further to Chapter, Heading, and Subheading definition levels. A tariff number's first six digits, through the Heading level, are standardized by the international HS system, and each country may make additional Subheading classifications by adding up to four more digits.

The classification of a product is quite important because it determines the applicable tariff rate. Accordingly, the classification method is governed by national and international interpretation rules.[14] These rules are often applied when a product falls under more than one category or when different tariff rates may apply to a product in a finished or unfinished condition. The U.S. Customs Service will issue rulings to importers seeking an advance determination of classification.[15]

Under the recent WTO *Information Technology Agreement* (ITA), special dual-use HS classification codes apply to many computer and telecommunications components that can be used in a variety of equipment.[16] That

---

[12] 19 U.S.C. § 1592.

[13] The HTS schedule is published and updated regularly by the ITC in the *Harmonized Tariff Schedule of the United States: Annotated for Statistical Reporting Purposes. See* USITC Publication 3249 (2000).

[14] *See* General Rules of Interpretation, USITC Publication 3249 (2000).

[15] *See* 19 C.F.R. pt. 177.

[16] The Information Technology Agreement (ITA) is referred to formally as the *Ministerial*

agreement eliminated tariffs on most information technology, including hardware and software, and their parts, components, and semiconductors, as well as most of the equipment used in semiconductor manufacturing. Treaty signatories include the U.S., the EU and most WTO member states, and the agreement is subject to the WTO dispute settlement rules.[17]

Most U.S. tariffs are *ad valorem*, meaning that they are based upon the *value* of the imported goods. In determining the value of a product, the U.S. utilizes the valuation method in the WTO Agreement on Customs Valuation.[18] Under this method, the tariff is based upon the *transaction value* of the imported merchandise, which is the price actually paid or payable for the merchandise when sold for export to the U. S. in a commercially realistic transaction (adjusted for certain costs such as packing and shipping). If the transaction value method cannot be used for some reason, the regulations provide specified alternative methods.[19]

[b] Country of Origin Rules

The country of origin of a product is important because treaties may reduce the tariff rate applied to imports from certain countries. For example, special rates may apply to goods from Mexico or Canada under NAFTA. Goods from countries that are members of the WTO are eligible for tariffs at the *most favored nations* rate, while higher tariffs may apply to goods from non-member states.

Although U.S. law require that the origin of an imported product must be clearly and truthfully explained, this may be difficult for products that have been worked on in different countries. Traditionally, the origin of such goods has been gauged by determining if the process in a country resulted in a *substantial transformation* that changed the goods into a "new and different product." Because this test is often difficult to apply, customs officials generally will determine origin by considering the *value* of work done in a particular country. Despite these rules, different countries often conclude that the same goods have different countries of origin.

Special, detailed, country of origin provisions apply to imports under the NAFTA. These rules are necessary to ensure that the free trade benefits of NAFTA apply only to goods that are from the U.S., Canada, and Mexico. Goods containing non-regional materials may qualify if these materials are substantially transformed in North America to reach a specified change in tariff classification. Certain goods (*e.g.*, automobiles) also must meet a specified percentage of regional content as well as satisfy the substantial transformation rules.

Declaration on Trade in Information Technology Products, effective January 1, 2000. *See* Tasker *The Information Technology Agreement: Building A Global Information Infrastructure While Avoiding Customs Classification Disputes,* 26 Brook. J. Int'l L. 917 (2001).

[17] *See* 1999 USTR Annual Report, note 3.

[18] *See* Trade Agreements Act of 1979, 19 U.S.C. § 1401a.

[19] 19 C.F.R. §§ 152.104-107.

[c] Special Entry Status

Goods with special entry status, such as merchandise placed in a bonded warehouse, or a foreign trade zone, may be entitled to duty free or deferred duty treatment. This is because imported products are not subject to U.S. tariff until officially *entered* for consumption. Thus, duty is not paid on goods in a *bonded warehouse* until they are released, hopefully at a time when tariff rated are lower. A *foreign trade zone* is a "restricted-access site, in or adjacent to a Customs port of entry. . . ."[20] that is administered by the Foreign Trade Zones Board. These zones are useful for importing unfinished goods or components and then completing or assembling them. A substantial saving can be obtained if the duty on the finished product is lower than it would be on the imported parts.

[3] Preferential Tariff Rates

[a] Most Favored Nation (MFN) or Normal Trade Relations (NTR)

A country that confers *Most Favored Nation* status on a trading partner commits itself to impose the lowest tariff rates on imports from that partner that are applied to imports from any other nation. In 1998, U.S. law changed its term for MFN status to Normal Trade Relations (NTR) status. All goods from MFN status countries are subject to the same U.S. tariff rates and any reduction, elimination or other change to a U.S. tariff applies equally to imports from these countries. The U.S. accords NTR status to most of its trading partners, meaning that the significantly higher tariffs that result from denied NTR treatment is a form of *economic sanction.*

Pursuant to its obligations under the WTO Treaty, the U.S. extends NTR status to all members of that organization. Non-WTO countries seeking NTR status with the U.S. do so through a bilateral commercial agreement. However, under the *Jackson-Vanik* provisions of the Trade Act of 1974,[21] NTR status may not be granted to any country unless the president determines that the country does not deny or impede its citizens the right or opportunity to emigrate. The president may allow an annual waiver of this requirement and succeeding presidents have granted this waiver to China for more than 20 years. Beginning in 2002, China has been granted permanent NTR status with the U.S. and has become a member of the WTO.

[b] Special Tariff Reduction Programs

A number of U.S. laws afford preferential tariff treatment to certain products imported from developing countries. These special programs include the *Generalized System of Preferences* (GSP), the *African Growth*

---

[20] 15 C.F.R. § 400.2(g).

[21] 19 U.S.C. § 2432.

and Opportunity Act (AGOA), the *Caribbean Basin Initiative* (CBI), and the *Andean Trade Preferences Act* (ATPA). These initiatives are designed to integrate developing countries into the international trading system in order to enhance economic growth and alleviate poverty. To be eligible for a specific tariff preference program, a *beneficiary developing country* (BDC) must satisfy its statutory requirements. Although the requirements differ somewhat for each program, they generally call for the BDC to provide access to its market and recognize and enforce internationally-recognized worker rights and intellectual property rights.

The broadest program is the *Generalized System of Preferences* (GSP), which allows certain products from designated developing countries to be imported into the U.S. tariff free.[22] This program was begun by the U.S. and other industrial countries in the 1970's to promote economic growth in developing countries by stimulating their exports. The program is not permanent, but must be reauthorized by Congress periodically. Since 1993, the GSP has been extended six times and expired several times.[23] The program's lack of continuity may undermine the incentive to invest in export industries in the designated countries.

The GSP law authorizes the President to provide duty-free treatment for any eligible product from any BDC. In designating BDCs, the President takes into account a country's level of economic development, commitment to a liberal trade policy, and the adequacy of its protection of intellectual property rights and workers' rights. Generally, the President cannot extend GSP treatment to other industrial countries, Communist countries, countries that provide preferential treatment to a developed country, or countries that nationalize, expropriate or infringe the property rights of U.S. citizens. Congress has designated specific products that are not eligible for GSP exemption. Eligibility for BDC treatment and of products for exemption is reviewed annually. Tariff exemptions are limited for certain products if imports exceed a specified dollar value.

The Caribbean Basin Initiative (CBI) provides tariff exemptions and reductions for products from participating countries in the Central American and Caribbean region. Countries can lose their CBI benefits in some circumstances. The CBI trade preferences are not subject to annual reviews. The Andean Trade Preference Act (ATPA) grants tariff reductions to certain products from Bolivia, Colombia, Ecuador, and Peru. This program is subject to periodic renewal.

§ 3.02   Trade Remedy Laws

Trade remedies are measures governments use to protect domestic producers from being injured by certain foreign trade practices. A number of U.S. trade laws governing imports are designed to provide remedies when

---

[22] Title V of the Trade Act of 1974, P.L. 93-618.

[23] The 107th Congress will determine whether to reauthorize the GSP that expired in September of 2001.

foreign goods obtain an unfair competitive advantage in the U.S., or when U.S. exports face discrimination in foreign markets. These laws provide remedies in the form of countervailing duties on imports that are subsidized by foreign governments, anti-dumping duties to prevent injuries caused by unfairly priced imports, and temporary safeguards to provide temporary, emergency protection to domestic producers facing increased imports.

[1] Interaction of U.S. and WTO Rules

Safeguard (or escape clause) provisions have been in U.S. law for many years,[24] and at U.S. insistence, were included in Article XIX of the original GATT in 1947, and again in the GATT Uruguay Round Agreement in 1994.[25] However, the Uruguay Round negotiations resulted in a new Agreement on Safeguards that provides procedures for applying Article XIX safeguards. Thus, in applying a safeguard measure, the U.S. and other countries must consider and conform to their obligations as WTO members.

Section 301 — U.S. Law on Sanctions. Section 301 is the principal statutory authority for the U.S. to impose trade sanctions against foreign countries.[26] The statute may apply to a country whose acts, policies and practices violate, or deny U.S. rights or benefits under trade agreements, or are unjustifiable, unreasonable or discriminatory and burden or restrict U.S. commerce. A section 301 investigation may be initiated if:

- An interested party files a petition with the U.S. Trade Representative (USTR) requesting an investigation of a particular practice of a foreign country.

- The USTR begins an investigation on its own initiative.

If the issue involves a trade agreement that includes a dispute settlement mechanism, the USTR must complete its investigation and make its action recommendation at the earlier of 18 months after the initiation or 30 days after the dispute settlement procedures ends. In other cases, the report must be issued within 12 months after initiation. An investigation involving alleged violations of a trade agreement, such as the WTO or NAFTA, must follow the dispute settlement provisions in that agreement.

If the investigation determines that violation of a trade agreement has occurred, the statute mandates that retaliatory action be taken. Mandatory retaliation may be waived if:

---

[24] *See e.g.*, Section 350 of the Tariff Act of 1930, Section 7 of the Trade Agreement Extension Act of 1951; Sections 301, 351 and 352 of the Trade Expansion Act of 1962. The 1962 provisions were repealed and replaced by Sections 201-203 of the Trade Act of 1974.

[25] The language of GATT article XIX is as follows: "If, as a result of unforeseen developments and the effect of the obligations incurred by a contracting party under this agreement, including tariff concessions, any product imported into the territory of that contracting party in such increased quantities and under such conditions as to cause or threaten serious injury to domestic producers in that territory of like or directly competitive products, the contracting party shall be free, in respect of such product and to the extent and for such time as may be necessary to prevent such injury, to suspend the obligation in whole or in part or to withdraw or modify the concession."

[26] Section 301 of the Trade Act of 1974, *as amended*, 19 U.S.C. § 2411.

- A WTO panel has ruled that violation of a trade agreement has not occurred.

- The USTR finds that the foreign country is taking satisfactory measures to comply with a trade agreement.

- The foreign country has agreed to eliminate the violating practice or otherwise satisfactorily resolved the matter.

- The foreign country has agreed to provide compensatory trade benefits.

- In extraordinary cases, the USTR may find that the benefits from retaliation are outweighed by its adverse impact on the U.S. economy.

- The action would seriously harm U.S. national security.

The USTR has discretion about taking retaliatory action if the foreign country's action is unreasonable or discriminatory and burdens or restricts U.S. commerce. This may be the case even if the act does not violate U.S. rights under international law. Unreasonable practices include:

- denial of fair opportunities to establish enterprises;

- denial of adequate and effective protection of intellectual property rights (even if the country complies with the TRIPS Agreement);

- denial of fair and equitable market opportunities;

- export targeting, and;

- denial of worker rights.

A practice is not deemed unreasonable if the USTR determines that it is consistent with the country's economic development. Actions are discriminatory practices if they deny national or MFN treatment to U.S. goods, services or investment.

The retaliation may be in the form of suspended or withdrawn trade concessions, duties or other import restrictions, or reduction of special benefits to certain developing countries. The USTR may negotiate agreements to eliminate or phase out the offending practice or provide compensation. Retaliation may be against any goods or economic sector without regard to whether that sector was involved in the underlying dispute. It should be proportionate to the value of the economic loss to the U.S. Generally, the retaliatory action must occur within 30 days of the determination, unless negotiations are making substantial progress toward a satisfactory solution. Any action automatically terminates after 4 years unless the petitioner or other representative of the domestic industry requests continuation.

A *special 301* provision was enacted to enhance the United States' ability to negotiate improvements in foreign intellectual property regimes. This section requires investigations of *priority foreign countries* whose actions regarding intellectual property rights are egregious and do the greatest harm to the U.S. Other special rules apply to a *telecommunications 301* action.

A *super 301* process had been reenacted for successive two year periods, but expired at the end of 2001. The super 301 procedure identified priority foreign practices that cause the most detriment to U.S. exports.

EU challenge to Section 301

In 1998, the EU complained to the WTO that the time frames in Section 301 require the U.S. government to retaliate before the DSB has adopted panel and Appellate Body findings. The EU specifically noted the 18 month deadline imposed on the USTR to conclude its investigation conflicts with the WTO Dispute Settlement Understanding.

The WTO panel rejected the EU's claim, holding that Section 301 allows the USTR adequate discretion to comply with WTO rules. Although the statute does not specifically mandate that the discretion must conform to the WTO timetable, that becomes evident when the statute is read in light of the Uruguay Round Agreements. Those agreements express the U.S. intention to follow DSU procedures in WTO-related determinations under Section 301.

The EU has not appealed the ruling. Indeed, it appears to consider the panel's reasoning to be a vindication of its position. In that view, the panel's conclusion that Section 301 does not violate the DSU is based upon assurances from the U.S. that it would only use its discretion under the statute in compliance with WTO rules.

---

[2] Subsidies and Countervailing Duties (CVD)

The CVD law is designed to offset any competitive advantage a foreign importer might obtain over a U.S. producer as the result of a foreign subsidy. The U.S. may impose a countervailing duty (CVD) on an import if the foreign producer has received a *countervailable* governmental subsidy, and the importation of the subsidized product causes, or threatens to cause, material injury to a domestic industry that produces a comparable product.[27] The CVD law imposes an additional duty on the import equal to the amount that offsets (*countervails*) the foreign subsidy.[28] It is important to note, however, that U.S. law incorporates the treaty provision of the WTO *Agreement on Subsidies and Countervailing Measures.*[29]

---

[27] *See* Tariff Act of 1930, *as amended*, (19 U.S.C. §§ 1671-1673h) and the related regulations in Title 19 of the Code of Federal Regulations.

[28] Subtitle A of title VII of the Tariff Act of 1930, as added by the Trade Agreements Act of 1979 and amended by the Trade and Tariff Act of 1984, the Omnibus Trade and Competitiveness Act of 1988, and the Uruguay Round Agreements Act of 1994.

[29] *See* discussion at 2.02[5].

[a]   CVD Investigations

Ordinarily, a CVD investigation is initiated when a domestic industry files a petition with the U.S. Department of Commerce (DOC) and the U.S. International Trade Commission (ITC). However, the DOC may initiate its own case. Both the DOC and ITC must make affirmative determinations for an investigation to go forward.

The investigation proceeds in two phases. In the first phase, the DOC determines if the imported product has been subsidized and the amount of any subsidy. The DOC must find whether a government is providing a *countervailable* subsidy for the manufacture, export or production of the product under investigation. A *subsidy* is a direct or indirect *financial contribution* from a foreign government that *benefits* its recipient. A *financial contribution* may consist of a direct transfer of funds (*e.g.*, grants), not collecting revenue (*e.g.*, tax credits or deductions), provision of goods or services, or purchasing goods. Generally, a financial contribution confers a *benefit* if a private actor would not have made a similar financial contribution.

In the second phase, the ITC determines whether the imports have caused, or threaten to cause *material injury* to a U.S. industry, or materially retard the establishment of a U.S. industry. A material injury is defined as harm that is not inconsequential, immaterial, or unimportant. The material injury test was included in U.S. law to meet our obligations under the WTO Agreement on Subsidies and Countervailing Measures. Accordingly, that test only applies to products from countries that are WTO members or that have treaties with the U.S. requiring such treatment. For imports from other countries, only the subsidy determination is required.

[b]   Countervailable Subsidies

A subsidy is *countervailable* only if it is of a kind that national or international law permits to be offset by a remedial tariff. In general, this means that the subsidy must be *specific* to an enterprise or industry.[30] This specificity requirement accepts the fact that it is inappropriate to impose a countervailing duty to offset the benefits a business may receive from its government's general involvement in national economic affairs. A subsidy is *per se* specific if it is contingent on export performance or upon the use of domestic rather than imported products. A subsidy may be deemed specific if receipt is restricted to a limited group of enterprises or industries. Under the WTO Agreement on Agriculture, certain agricultural subsidies are deemed noncountervailable.[31]

Generally, a subsidy is not specific if it is provided pursuant to objective criteria that do not favor one enterprise or industry over another. This kind

---

[30] Pursuant to the WTO Treaty, certain specific subsidies are not countervailable and thus exempt from the CVD law.

[31] These are listed in Annex 1 of the Agreement on Agriculture and which meet the criteria listed on Annex 2 of the Subsidies Agreement.

of subsidy may be deemed *de facto* specific, however, if it is administered in a fashion that favors a particular industry or enterprise. To determine if this kind of administration occurs, the DOC considers whether:

- a limited number actually receive the subsidy;

- one enterprise or industry is a predominant user of the subsidy;

- one enterprise or industry receives a disproportionately large amount of the subsidy, or;

- the discretion exercised deciding to grant the subsidy indicates that one enterprise or industry is favored over others.

A countervailing duty may be applied to offset an *upstream subsidy* to the producer of an input used in producing or manufacturing an imported product. The DOC may investigate an upstream subsidy if the input supplier is affiliated with the product's manufacturer, the price of the input is lower than if it were unsubsidized, and the government sets a price for the input that ensures that the subsidy benefit passes through to the producer. Additionally, the subsidized input must affect the cost of production for the import by more than one percent.

If the DOC and ITC investigations determine that a countervailable subsidy has been provided, the DOC calculates the rate or amount of the subsidy. The DOC regulations provide detailed rules for making these calculations. The DOC then instructs the U.S. Customs Service to assess duties against imports of that product into the United States. The duties are assessed as a percentage of the value of the imports and are equivalent to subsidy (or dumping) margins. The margin is the decreased price of a product resulting from the illegal action. For example, if the subsidy margin is 20 percent, the Customs Service will impose a 20 percent duty on imports of the product to offset the subsidy.

[3] Anti-Dumping Law

The term *dumping* refers to a form of international price discrimination in which an exporter sells goods in one export market (such as the U.S.) at lower prices than for comparable goods in its home market or in its other export markets. Under U.S. law, anti-dumping duties may be imposed on imported goods sold, or likely to be sold in the U. S. for *less than fair value*. [32]

---

[32] The Anti-dumping Act of 1916 provides criminal and civil penalties for the sale of imported articles at a price substantially less than the actual market value or wholesale price, with the intent of destroying or injuring an industry in the United States. Title VII of the Tariff Act of 1930, as amended, provides for the assessment and collection of AD duties after an administrative determination that foreign merchandise is being sold in the U.S. market at less than fair value and that such imports are materially injuring the U.S. industry. Section 1317 of the Omnibus Trade and Competitiveness Act of 1988 establishes procedures for the U.S. Trade Representative to request a foreign government to take action against third-country dumping that is injuring a U.S. industry, and section 232 of the Uruguay Round Agreements Act permits a third country to request that an order be issued against dumped imports from another country that are materially injuring an industry in a third country.

Generally, this means that the price of the product in the U.S. is less than its price in the country of origin. Although U.S. law has contained anti-dumping measures since 1916, the current law was amended in 1995 to conform with our obligations under the WTO Anti-dumping Agreement.[33]

[a]　AD Proceedings

Anti-dumping proceedings are initiated in the same manner as for CVD cases. A domestic industry may file a petition with the DOC and ITC. However, the DOC may initiate its own case. Both the DOC and ITC must make affirmative determinations for an investigation to go forward.

For an anti-dumping duty to be imposed, both of the following determinations must be made:[34]

(1)　The DOC determines that foreign merchandise is being, or is likely to be, sold in the U. S. at less than its fair value. This is determined by comparing the *normal value* with the *export price* of each import sale made during a specific time period.

(2)　The ITC determines that the dumping has caused, or threatens to cause *material injury* to a U.S. industry or materially retard the establishment of a U.S. industry.

If both determinations are made, an anti-dumping (AD) order will be issued to impose anti-dumping duties equal to the amount by which normal value exceeds the export price of the product (the *dumping margin*).

Usually, the *normal value* of the import is determined by one of three methods. In order of preference, the methods are:

● The sale price of the product in its home market.

● The price at which the goods are exported to countries other than the U.S.

● A *constructed* value determined under a statutory formula that uses the sum of the cost of production plus additions for profits, selling commissions, and administrative expenses such as packing.

These prices are adjusted for any differences in the merchandise, quantities sold, circumstances of sale, and different levels of trade in the markets. Special rules apply in determining the normal value for goods exported from a country that has a non-market economy.

Typically, the *export price* is the price at which the product is purchased or agreed to be purchased for before it is imported to the U.S. If the purchaser and exporter are related parties, however, a *constructed export price* is used, which is the price at which the product is sold or agreed to be sold for in the U.S., before or after importation, to the first unrelated

---

[33] For discussion of the history of U.S. anti-dumping laws, *see* Congressional Budget Office, *How the GATT affects U.S. Anti-dumping and Countervailing-Duty Policy,* Sept. 1994.

[34] Section 731 of the Tariff Act of 1930, as amended. 19 U.S.C. § 1673.

purchaser. The export price is adjusted for a number of items, including certain delivery expenses and U.S. import duties.

China and Anti-Dumping Cases. China is the largest target of anti-dumping actions in the world, accounting for more than fifteen percent of all global anti-dumping cases. A key issue in cases involving China is the appropriate method for determining whether dumping has occurred. The usual method is to compare the price of goods sold in the U.S. to the price in the exporting country. However, because China is considered a *non-market economy*, the U.S. uses one of the following methods to determine the price in the exporting country:

- The *factors of production* method in which the non-market economy manufacturers provide cost data for all inputs to manufacturing the export product and these costs are then adjusted for a comparable market economy.

- The *surrogate country* method in which input data is derived from a surrogate country of comparable economic development because information from the non-market economy is not available.

China has vigorously protested the use of the surrogate country method, maintaining that it provides inaccurate comparisons with the Chinese market. Chinese companies have argued that the cost of materials is frequently higher in the nations that are used as surrogates, such as India, Pakistan, Philippines and Brazil. In China's view, U.S. bureaucrats can and do manipulate the comparative cost figures to find dumping where it does not truly exist.

The U.S. Court of International Trade has upheld use of the surrogate method, holding that a Chinese exporter must demonstrate absence of *de jure* and *de facto* government control over a product.[35] Generally, the Department of Commerce maintains that an item is produced in a market economy if all the producer's prices and costs are market-determined.[36] This requires (1) no government involvement in setting prices and volume of production; (2) an industry characterized by private or collective ownership; and (3) all material and nonmaterial inputs purchased at market-determined prices.

It is unclear how China's accession to the WTO will affect anti-dumping cases in the U.S. The final accession protocol provides a special rule for determining price in anti-dumping cases against China.[37] Under these rules, an importing country determines the

---

[35] *Sigma Corp. v. United States*, 841 F. Supp. 1255 (Ct. Int'l Trade 1993); *UCF America Inc. v. United States*, 870 F. Supp. 1120 (Ct. Int'l Trade 1994).

[36] Sulfanilic Acid from the PRC, 57 Fed. Reg. 9409 (1992).

[37] Protocol on the Accession of The People's Republic of China, Part I, Section 15.

comparable price for Chinese products under one of two methods. It uses Chinese prices or costs when the Chinese producers clearly show that market economy conditions prevail with respect to the manufacturer, production and sale of the product. The importing country may use another method not based on strict comparison when the Chinese company cannot make that showing. This provision appears to allow the U.S. to continue to apply its non-market economy rules in cases involving Chinese producers. However, use of the non-comparison method will not be allowed for any Chinese goods after the importing country's national law determines that China is a market economy.

[b]   Third Country Dumping

A U.S. industry may be injured when goods from a foreign country are dumped in a third country to which the U.S exports competing goods. A domestic industry that produces a competitive product may petition the U.S. Trade Representative (USTR) to pursue U.S. rights under the WTO Anti-dumping Agreement if it has reason to believe that such merchandise is being dumped in a third country market and such dumping is injuring the U.S. industry.[38]

After determining whether the petition has a reasonable basis, the USTR will apply to the third country government, asking it to take anti-dumping action on behalf of the United States. Under the Anti-dumping Agreement, the application must be supported by detailed information that establishes the dumping and the injury.[39] If the foreign government refuses to take anti-dumping action, USTR must consult with the domestic industry about possible action under any other U.S. law. Similarly, the government of a WTO member may petition the USTR determine if imports from another country are being dumped in the United States, causing material injury to an industry in the petitioning country. With the approval of the WTO Council for Trade in Goods, the USTR may investigate and, when appropriate, impose an AD duty.

[4]   CVD and AD Procedures

[a]   Investigations

Most AD or CVD investigations are initiated by a petition filed by an interested domestic industry, although DOC may do so on its own initiative. Before the investigation begins, the DOC must determine that the petition meets criteria concerning whether the petition is actually filed *by or on behalf of* the domestic industry. A petition is sufficient if the domestic producers or workers supporting the petition account for:

---

[38] Section 1318 of the Omnibus Trade and Competitiveness Act of 1988.
[39] Article 12.

(1)   at least 25 percent of the total production of the domestic product (or *like* product), and;

(2)   more than 50 percent of the portion of the industry expressing support for or opposition to the petition.[40]

The DOC may poll the industry to determine whether the petition has adequate support.

In determining industry support, the DOC must disregard opposition from domestic producers that are related to the foreign producers who would be investigated. Similarly, the DOC may disregard the opposition from U.S. producers who also import the foreign goods. If the management of a firm expresses a position in direct opposition to the views of the workers in that firm, the DOC considers the production of that firm as representing neither support for nor opposition to the petition.[41] An industry's standing may not be challenged at the agency level after an investigation is initiated, but may be later challenged in court.

[b]   Preliminary Determinations

If the DOC determines that the industry support criteria are satisfied, it publishes a notice of initiation in the Federal Register and informs the ITC of its finding. At this point, both agencies must make preliminary determinations about continuing or terminating the investigation. The ITC must determine if a reasonable indication of material injury exists, based on the information available at the time. The petitioner bears the burden of proof on this issue. Ordinarily, the ITC staff obtains information by sending questionnaires to foreign and U.S. producers and importers. A conference may be held with interested parties who may also submit informational briefs after the conference. If the ITC preliminary injury determination is negative, the investigation terminates. Given the relatively low legal standard, however, preliminary determinations usually are affirmative.

If the ITC's preliminary determination is positive, the DOC must make a preliminary determination about dumping or subsidization. In antidumping cases, the DOC must determine, based on the available information from questionnaires and similar sources, whether there is a reasonable basis to believe or suspect that the goods are being sold, or are likely to be sold, at less than fair value. If affirmative, the DOC also must estimate the average amount by which the normal value exceeds the export price. In subsidy cases, the DOC determines if there is a reasonable basis to believe or suspect that a countervailable subsidy is being provided. If affirmative, the DOC must estimate the amount of that subsidy.

If the DOC (and ITC) preliminary determinations are positive, the DOC instructs the Customs Service to: (1) suspend further sale of the foreign goods, and; (2) for subsequent imports, requires importers to post a cash

---

[40] Section 212 of the Uruguay Round Agreements Act.

[41] Uruguay Round Agreements Act Statement of Administrative Action at 862.

deposit, bond, or other security equal to the dumping margin or subsidy. If the DOC preliminary determination is negative, these actions are not taken and both agencies begin their final investigations.

If the domestic industry is concerned that foreign producers have shipped large quantities of goods to the U.S. in order to avoid a subsequent AD or CVD duty, it can make a *critical circumstances* allegation. In that case, the DOC may apply a cash deposit or bond requirement to goods imported before the DOC issued its preliminary determination.

[c] Final Determinations

Generally, AD and CVD investigations must be completed within specified time periods after the preliminary determinations are made, although limited extensions are permitted. The DOC final investigation may include a *verification*, which is an on-site audit, to confirm if the submitted information is accurate. The parties may then submit briefs about the factual and legal issues, and participate in a public hearing. Based on all the information, the DOC issues its final determination. If the DOC's final determination is negative, suspension of sales is lifted, any bonds or security is released, and the proceedings terminate. If the DOC's final determination is positive, it suspends sales and orders posting of a bond (if these steps have not yet be taken), and the issue is sent to the ITC for a final determination of material injury.

The ITC must make its final determination within the longer of 120 days of the DOC's positive preliminary determination or 45 days of the DOC's positive final determination. If the DOC's preliminary determination was negative but its final determination is positive, the ITC must complete its injury determination within 75 days of the DOC's final action. In its final investigation, the ITC allows parties to submit briefs, participate in a hearing, and submit comments on the factual record developed in the proceeding. Nonparties may also participate to a limited degree. If the ITC makes a negative final determination, the investigation terminates.

[d] Determining Material Injury for CVD and AD Purposes

Generally, a CVD or AD order may not be issued unless the ITC determines that the dumped or subsidized imports cause, or threaten to cause, *material injury* to a domestic industry, or will materially retard the establishment of a domestic industry. For this purpose, material injury is defined as harm which is not inconsequential, immaterial, or unimportant.[42] In effect, the ITC must make two determinations: (1) has or will a material injury occur, and; (2) is the injury caused by the subsidy or dumping in question. Note that in applying a CVD to offset a subsidy, the injury test only affects products from countries that are WTO members or

---

[42] Section 771(7) of the Tariff Act of 1930.

that have treaties with the U.S. requiring such treatment. For imports from other countries, only a subsidy determination is required.

In making injury determinations, the ITC usually collects data for the three year period before the petition was filed. The ITC analyzes the data with respect to factors such as the volume of imports, the effect of imports on U.S. prices of similar goods, lost sales, profits, productivity, return on investment, production capacity, and market share. It also considers the imports' effect on employment, inventories, wages, the ability to raise capital, and negative effects on the development and production activities of the U.S. industry. In AD investigations, the ITC also must consider the size of the dumping margin.

If more than one country is named in the CVD or AD petition, ITC must make a cumulative assessment of the volume and effect of the imports from the countries named if they compete with each other and with similar products in the U.S. market.[43] If imports from a country are negligible, generally defined as less than three percent of total imports of the investigated product, the ITC must terminate the investigation of that country. Some exemptions from the cumulation rules are provided (e.g., for countries in the Caribbean Basin Initiative and Israel).

[e] Termination or Suspension of Investigations

In specified circumstances, the DOC may reach an agreement with the parties to suspend or terminate an AD or CVD investigation. This is permitted only if the DOC is satisfied that such action is in the public interest and that the agreement can be effectively monitored. The DOC is responsible for overseeing compliance with any suspension agreement and intentional violations are subject to civil penalties.

A CVD investigation may be suspended if one of the following types of agreements has been reached with the foreign government or exporters that account for substantially all the imports under investigation:

(1) An agreement to completely eliminate or offset the subsidy within 6 months after the investigation is suspended;

(2) An agreement to cease exporting the subsidized merchandise to the U.S. within 6 months after the investigation is suspended, or;

(3) An agreement to completely eliminate the injurious effect of the subsidized exports to the U. S. (which may be based on quantitative restrictions).

An AD investigation may be suspended if one of the following types of agreements is reached with exporters that account for substantially all the imports under investigation:

(1) An agreement to cease exporting the merchandise to the U. S. within 6 months after the investigation is suspended;

---

[43] Section 771(7) of the Tariff Act of 1930.

   (2)   An agreement to revise prices to completely eliminate any sales at less than fair value, or;

   (3)   An agreement to revise prices to completely eliminate the injurious effect of exports of the dumped merchandise to the U. S.

Unlike CVD cases, AD investigations cannot be suspended on the basis of quantitative restriction agreements (except AD investigations of imports from a non-market economy country).

Interested parties must be notified of the DOC's intent to suspend an investigation and given an opportunity to comment. If, within 20 days of this notice, the DOC is requested to continue the proceeding by a domestic interested party or from exporters accounting for a significant proportion of exports of the product, then both the DOC and ITC must continue their investigations. If a suspension agreement is not accepted, the exporter is entitled to an explanation of the DOC's reasons and an opportunity to submit comments.

[f] The AD or CVD Order

Within seven days of a final positive ITC determination about material injury, the DOC issues a CVD or AD duty order.[44] An AD order:

- directs the Customs Service to assess AD duties equal to the dumping margin (*i.e.,* the excess of the normal value over the export price);

- describes the merchandise to which the AD duty applies; and

- requires a cash deposit of the estimated AD duties.

The CVD order:

- directs the Customs Service to assess countervailing duties equal to the amount of the net countervailable subsidy;

- describes the merchandise to which the CVD applies, and;

- requires a cash deposit of estimated CVD's.

The required cash deposits are based upon estimates of the final AD or CVD duties.

[g] Administrative Review

Upon request, the DOC must conduct an annual review of outstanding AD and CVD orders and suspension agreements. An AD review includes a re-determination of the dumping margin and a CVD review re-determines the amount of the countervailable subsidy. The procedures and standards used in these reviews are similar to those used in the initial investigation. Suspended investigations are reviewed to determine the status of and compliance with the agreement. Unless good cause is shown, a final

---

[44] The DOC and ITC must issue affirmative final determinations, in both title VII AD and CVD investigations and in section 303 CVD investigations requiring an injury test.

determination or suspension agreement cannot be reviewed within 24 months of its notice.

A review also must be conducted if the DOC or ITC receives information or a request that shows sufficient changed circumstances to warrant modification or revocation of the order. In many cases, changed circumstances reviews are commenced after the U.S. industry informs the DOC that it is no longer interested in maintaining the AD or CVD order. In an AD review, the principal factors the DOC considers are the magnitude of the dumping margins found in the investigation and subsequent administrative reviews, and the volume of imports of the subject merchandise both before and after the effective date of the order/agreement. The DOC also has the discretion to consider price, cost, market or other economic factors it deems appropriate, for good cause.

In a review of a CVD order/agreement, the DOC considers the net countervailable subsidy received by the respondent in the investigation and whether there have been any changes in the program(s) examined in the investigation that would likely affect the CVD margin. The DOC may also consider programs maintained by the government investigated by the DOC in other investigations or reviews, but only if they did not exist at the time of the original investigation, and only if they could potentially be used by the respondent. In addition to these new programs, petitioners may also allege that other subsidies are being received, but the DOC must make an affirmative determination with respect to those programs for them to be included in the agency's determination of whether subsidization is likely to continue or recur.

[h] Sunset Review

Under a *sunset* rule required by the WTO, AD and CVD orders and suspension agreements terminate after 5 years unless termination is likely to result in continuation or recurrence of dumping, subsidization or injury.[45] The sunset review consists of both DOC and ITC proceedings. If either agency's determination is negative, the AD or CVD order or agreement is revoked or terminated. Although many economic factors are considered, the sunset reviews tend to focus on certain principal factors. In an AD sunset review, the principal factors are the magnitude of the dumping margins and the volume of imports of the goods before and after the order or agreement. In a CVD sunset review, the factors are the amount of the subsidy and any changes in the subsidy program that change its market impact.

The DOC must publish a notice of initiation of a sunset review within 30 days before the fifth anniversary of the order. A party wishing to maintain the order must provide information about the likely effects of revocation. The DOC must complete its sunset investigation within 240 days and the ITC within 360 days, although the deadlines may be extended for complex investigations.

---

[45] Section 220 of the Uruguay Round Agreements.

[i] Anti-Circumvention Authority

In some situations it may be unclear as to whether a particular product is covered by an AD or CVD order. At the request of an interested party, the DOC may address this issue through an inquiry regarding the *scope* of the order. The scope inquiry usually involves an investigation regarding the similarity of the product in question to the product subject to the order. Ordinarily, the scope inquiry is completed within 120 days.

Another kind of scope inquiry may be conducted to determine if a product should be subject to the AD or CVD order in order to prevent its *circumvention*. An order may be circumvented if a party changes its commercial or manufacturing practices to import products that are not clearly within the scope of the order, but which diminish the remedy the order provides. To prevent such circumvention, the DOC is authorized to extend the scope of an AD or CVD order to cover a new product. This authority addresses four situations:

(1) *Products assembled in the U.S.* Component parts of the product can be included in the scope of the order if —

- the completed goods are of the same *class or kind* as the goods subject to the order;

- the goods are assembled from parts produced in the foreign country subject to the order;

- the process of assembly or completion in the U.S. is minor or insignificant, and;

- the value of the parts or components is a significant portion of the total value of the goods.

(2) *Products assembled in a third country.* These imports can be included in the scope of the order if —

- the goods are of the same class or kind as the goods subject to the order;

- the goods are completed or assembled from products covered by the order, or from products of the foreign country to which the order applies;

- the process of assembly or completion in the third country is minor or insignificant, and;

- the value of the parts or components produced in the foreign country is a significant portion of the total value of the goods exported to the U.S.

(3) *Minor alterations to a product.* These imports can be included in the scope of the order if the alteration or modification is minor.

(4) *Later-developed products.* A product developed after an investigation can be included in the scope of an order if —

- the product has the same general physical characteristics as the *earlier product* subject to the order;

- the ultimate purchasers' expectations of the later product are the same as for the earlier product;

- the ultimate use of the earlier and the later products are the same;

- the later product is sold through the same trade channels as the earlier product, and;

- the later product is advertised and displayed in a similar manner to the earlier product.

The DOC consults with the ITC to determine whether inclusion of the product is consistent with the determination made in the original investigation. If possible, the DOC should issue a determination in an anti-circumvention scope inquiry within 300 days.

[j] Appeals

Judicial. Parties who are dissatisfied with the final DOC or ITC determination in AD or CVD cases may appeal to in the U.S. Court of International Trade (CIT) in New York City. The CIT has exclusive jurisdiction over U.S. tariff and customs issues, including AD and CVD matters. In reviewing a DOC or ITC final decision, the CIT must affirm the agency's determination if it is supported by substantial evidence on the record and is in accordance with law.[46] An appeal of a negative preliminary determination will not succeed unless it was "arbitrary, capricious, an abuse of discretion, or otherwise not in accordance with law." CIT decisions may be appealed to the U.S. Court of Appeals for the Federal Circuit in Washington, D.C.

NAFTA Controversies. A DOC or ITC determination involving imports from Mexico or Canada may be appealed to a bi-national dispute settlement panel convened under NAFTA Article 19 if either the United States, Canadian or Mexican government so requests. The panel applies U.S. law and U.S. judicial review standards to decide whether the DOC or ITC applied U.S. law correctly.

Like the CIT, a NAFTA panel will affirm an agency determination if it is supported by substantial evidence and is in accordance with law. The NAFTA panel decisions may be appealed to a NAFTA Extraordinary Challenge Committee which may determine if the NAFTA Panel's decision exceeded its authority

WTO Controversies. A party from a country that is a WTO member may ask its government to invoke its rights under the WTO Dispute Settlement Understanding (DSU). In that case, the WTO member country whose rights are infringed, rather than the party subject to the order, may appeal an adverse determination of the DOC or ITC. The WTO case may be initiated in addition to any appeal to the CIT or to a NAFTA panel.

---

[46] Section 516A of the Tariff Act of 1930.

Pursuant to the DSU, the action is brought before a panel to find whether the DOC or ITC determination was contrary to U.S. obligations under the WTO Agreement. DSU panel decisions may be appealed to the WTO Appellate Body. If the panel or Appellate Body rule against the U.S., the U.S. Trade Representative (USTR) may ask the DOC or ITC to issue a new determination consistent with the WTO decision. Following that determination, the original order may be revoked or modified.[47]

[5] *Safeguard* Import Relief

Under *safeguard* provisions of U.S. trade law, the President has authority to take action when increasing imports of a product cause or threaten serious injury to a U.S. industry that produces a competitive product.[48] The president may provide *import relief* to facilitate the domestic industry's efforts to adjust to the new foreign competition even if the imported product is fairly priced. Import relief may include the withdrawal or modification of trade concessions and the temporary imposition of duties or other restrictions on the imported product.

[a] Petitions and Investigations

The process may be initiated by an industry representative (*e.g.*, a trade association, firm, or union) that files a petition with the ITC describing the purposes for the desired action. These purposes may include facilitating an orderly transfer of resources to more productive pursuits, enhancing competitiveness, or other adjustments to new competition.[49] Alternatively, an investigation may be requested by the President, USTR, or the House Ways and Means or Senate Finance Committees, or self-initiated by the ITC.

The ITC then conducts an investigation, which must include public hearings, to determine if the product is being imported in such increased quantities to be the *substantial cause* or threat of *serious injury* to the competing domestic industry. For this purpose, *substantial cause* means a "cause which is important and not less than any other cause." This may be established by a showing that imports have increased (either actually or relative to domestic production) and that the proportion of domestic producers has declined.

In the first phase of the investigation, the ITC must determine whether there has been, or may be, a *serious injury* to a domestic injury. In making this injury determination, the ITC must consider all relevant economic factors and the condition of the domestic industry during the relevant

---

[47] Section 129 of the Uruguay Round Agreements Act.

[48] Sections 201-204 of the Trade Act of 1974, 19 U.S.C. §§ 2251-2254, *as amended* by section 1401 of the Omnibus Trade and Competitiveness Act of 1988, Public Law 100-418 and sections 301-304 of the Uruguay Round Agreements Act, Public Law 103-465, approved December 8, 1994.

[49] Under § 202 of the Trade Act of 1974.

business cycle. The statute requires the ITC to take account of the following factors concerning harm to the domestic industry:[50]

- significant idling of productive facilities;

- inability of a significant number of firms to operate at a reasonable profit level;

- significant unemployment or underemployment;

- decline in sales or market share;

- higher and growing inventory;

- downward trends in production, profits, wages, productivity or employment;

- whether firms can generate adequate capital to modernize plants and equipment, or; maintain research and development;

- whether exports of the product have been diverted to the U.S. because of trade restrictions in other countries.

For NAFTA partners, the ITC must also find whether the imports from Mexico or Canada account for a substantial share of total imports of the product and contribute importantly to the serious injury to the U.S. industry.[51] Unless this finding is positive, a relief action cannot apply to the NAFTA imports.

Ordinarily, the injury determination must be made within 120 days of the petition or request, although limited time extensions may be allowed. Before the injury report is issued, the petitioners may submit a plan describing how they intend to make the required adjustments to import competition. The plan may be prepared after consultation with the ITC, USTR, and other government officials and any party may individually submit its commitments regarding actions they intend to take to facilitate these adjustments.

The second phase of the investigation begins if the ITC makes a positive injury finding. In this phase, the ITC prepares a report recommending the most appropriate and effective action to address the injury and facilitate the domestic industry efforts to adjust to the competition. Recommended remedies may include tariffs, tariff-rate quotas, quantitative restrictions, adjustment measures, or any combination of these measures. The remedy recommendation report must be submitted to the President within 180 days of the petition and then made available to the public and published in summary form in the Federal Register.

[b] Action Decisions

The President must determine the action he will take within 60 days of receiving an affirmative ITC report. A Trade Policy Committee, chaired by the USTR also makes a recommendation as to the action that should be

---

[50] § 201 of the Trade Act of 1974.

[51] 19 U.S.C. § 3371.

taken. The President is not bound by this recommendation, but may act as he thinks appropriate to help the domestic industry cope with the new competitive situation.[52] In determining the appropriate action, the President must consider factors that include any adjustment plan or commitments submitted by the petitioners, the probable effectiveness of the proposed action, and the effect on national economic and security interests. If import relief is provided, it may not exceed the amount necessary to prevent or remedy the serious injury. Any action taken may apply for an initial period of up to four years, and may be extended one or more times for a total period of up to eight years.

Upon making his decision, the President reports the action he will take to the Congress along with an explanation of his reasons. A detailed explanation is required if the President's action differs from the ITC recommendation or if he decides that no action is appropriate and feasible. In these situations, Congress may pass a joint resolution of disapproval within 90 legislative days.[53] The resolutions are referred to the House Ways and Means and Senate Finance Committees, and reported out under special expedited procedures that allow no amendments. Within 30 days after such a resolution is enacted, the President must proclaim the relief recommended by the ITC.

[c] Monitoring, Modification, and Termination

After the President acts, the ITC monitors industry developments and, if the action exceeds 3 years, conducts a public hearing and submits a report at the midpoint of the initial period or extension. Based upon the report, the President may reduce, modify, or terminate the action if either: (1) the domestic industry makes the request based upon a positive adjustment, or; (2) he determines that such action is warranted by changed circumstances.

Before import relief is terminated, the President or a concerned industry may ask the ITC to conduct an investigation to determine whether the relief is still necessary to prevent or remedy serious injury and whether the industry is making a positive adjustment to import competition. The ITC must hold a public hearing send the report to the President within 60 days before termination of the relief action (unless the President specifies a different date.) If an action is terminated, the ITC evaluates its effectiveness in facilitating industry adjustment and must submit a report to the President and the Congress within 180 days of the termination.

If relief is provided, no new relief action may be taken about the same product for a period equal to the greater of the period of import relief, or two years. If the action was in effect for 180 days or less, however, the President may take a new action if at least 1 year has elapsed since the previous action, and an action has not been taken more than twice in the preceding 5-year period.

---

[52] The President may provide provisional relief for certain imports of perishable agricultural products. Section 202(d) of the Trade Act.

[53] Section 152 of the Trade Act.

Section 201 and Steel Tariffs

In 2002, the Bush administration used the authority granted by Section 201 to impose substantial tariffs on many types of steel products imported into the U.S. The administration claimed that the tariffs were needed to safeguard the U.S. steel industry which had suffered *substantial injury* from a surge in steel imports. This action, which appears to have been motivated by the political situation relating to the domestic steel industry, surprised and upset many U.S. trading partners who relied upon the president's oft-repeated commitment to free trade. The tariffs were swiftly and severely criticized by the most-affected trading partners, as well as by many economists and businesspeople in the U.S. who maintained that the tariffs were causing significant harm to domestic steel users.

Eight complainants — the EC, Brazil, China, Japan, New Zealand, Norway, South Korea, and Switzerland — challenged the steel safeguard measure before a WTO Dispute Resolution Panel. The Panel concluded that the tariff was inconsistent with the WTO Agreement on Safeguards and Article XIX of the GATT. Following a U.S. appeal, the WTO Appellate Body upheld most of the Panel's findings. The key factor underlying the Appellate decision was that the U.S. International Trade Commission (ITC) did not establish that the steel safeguard tariff actually was in response to a recent and sudden increase in steel imports or to unforeseen developments.

In its mid-term review report on the steel tariffs, the ITC concluded that the U.S. steel industry had restructured, consolidated, and upgraded its facilities and technologies since the tariffs were imposed. In December, 2003, President Bush lifted the steel safeguard tariffs (more than fifteen months before the scheduled expiration date). The administration stated that the ITC's mid-term review showed that the changed economic circumstances justified terminating the tariffs under section 204 of the Trade Act of 1974. Others have asserted, however, that the tariffs actually were terminated to avoid threatened retaliation by trading partners.

[6] Unfair Import Practices — Section 337

Section 337 of the Tariff Act of 1930 focuses on two different import issues: unfair import practices and imports that infringe intellectual property rights. Although the statute may apply to many kinds of unfair trade practices, an amendment in 1988 has made it particularly useful in cases involving imports that infringe intellectual property rights protected under U.S. law. Because the statute provides a relatively fast procedure with a lower burden of proof in intellectual property cases, administrative action often is preferable to seeking an injunction or damages in a U.S.

district court. Under Section 337, the ITC may block entry of goods that infringe intellectual property rights quickly and effectively before severe harm to a domestic industry occurs.

The pre-1988 portion of the statute relating to unfair trade practices, Section 337(a)(1)(a), is not limited to intellectual property issues, although it has often been used in patent infringement cases. Under this section, it is unlawful to engage in *unfair* methods of competition and *unfair* acts in the import and sale of products in the U.S., the threat or effect of which is to destroy or substantially injure a domestic industry or to restrain and monopolize trade and commerce in the U.S.[54] To be successful, an action in this category must establish that a trade act is unfair and that it has or will cause substantial injury to a domestic industry.

For intellectual property issues, the portion of the statute amended in 1988, Section 337(a)(1)(B), greatly simplifies the complainants burden. Under that section, it is unlawful to import or sell products that infringe a valid and enforceable —

- U.S. patent or registered copyright, or are produced under a process covered by a U.S. patent;
- U.S.-registered trademark, or;
- registered mask work of a semiconductor chip product.

Actions in this category need not establish injury, but only that a U.S. industry is producing, or is being established to produce, items covered by the infringed intellectual property right. A U.S. industry exists if there is: (1) significant investment in plant and equipment; (2) significant employment of labor or capital, or; (3) substantial investment in exploiting the patent, copyright, trademark, or mask work (*e.g.*, engineering, research and development, or licensing).[55]

[a] Procedure

Section 337 investigations are conducted by the ITC and may be initiated by a petition from a domestic producer or self-initiated by the ITC. The statute is the only trade law subject to the Administrative Procedure Act[56] and the ITC's investigation must be conducted on the record after published notice and a hearing in conformity with that act.[57] The statute confers *in rem* nationwide jurisdiction, meaning that exclusion orders relate to importation of the product, rather than to a foreign person. Accordingly,

---

[54] 19 U.S.C. § 1337(a)(1)(a).

[55] 19 U.S.C. § 1337(a)(3).

[56] 5 U.S.C. § 551 *et seq.*

[57] Amendments to Section 337 were enacted in conjunction with adoption of the Uruguay Round Agreement to conform the statute to U.S. obligations as a WTO member. 19 U.S.C. § 1337(c). A GATT panel previously had found that the statute violated the national treatment obligation. GATT Panel Report No. L/6439 (Jan. 16, 1989), summarized at 84 Am. J. Int'l L. 274 (Jan. 1990).

a complainant that brings an action against one importer obtains a remedy against all importers of the product.

No deadlines apply to the investigation, but within 45 days of initiation, the ITC must set a target date and conclude its investigation as soon as practicable. A respondent may raise counterclaims in a Section 337 investigation, but the claims must be removed to district court and cannot be litigated at the ITC. If the parties settle their dispute (*e.g.*, by a license agreement), the ITC may terminate the investigation after publishing a proposed consent in the Federal Register for comment.

The vast majority of Section 337 cases involve patent infringement. In deciding whether a U.S. patent has been infringed, the ITC must apply the domestic statutory and case law that a U.S. district court would use. Indeed, U.S. patent holders may file parallel actions with the ITC and in federal district court, although a respondent may obtain a stay of district court proceedings until the ITC issues a final decision. Antitrust issues may be raised by both the complainants and respondents, and the ITC may consider defenses based on antitrust theories.

If the ITC finds a violation of Section 337, it may issue an exclusion order and/or a cease and desist order. The President may disapprove the determination for *policy reasons* within 60 days after notification.[58] Although the statute does not define these policy reasons, the few times the President has disapproved, disapproval was based upon factors such as a duplicative or ineffective proceeding, an overly broad remedy, or that exclusion of the product was not in the public interest.[59] The President's determination is not subject to judicial review. If the President does not disapprove, the ITC's ruling becomes final and it may be appealed to the Court of Appeals for the Federal Circuit.

[b] Remedies

A complainant may not be awarded money damages in a Section 337 proceeding. The sole remedies are orders to exclude the products from the U.S. and orders to cease and desist for importers.

During the proceeding, the ITC may issue a *Temporary Exclusion Order* (TEO) to prohibit the entry of goods into the U.S., unless a bond is posted. Generally, the ITC must decide whether to grant a complainant's petition for a TEO within 90 days after the investigation begins. To prevent frivolous requests for a TEO, the ITC may request the complainant to post a bond that may be forfeited if no statutory violation is found.

If a violation is found, the ITC may issue a Permanent Exclusion Order (PEO) that prohibits the products in question from entering the U.S. Goods may be ordered seized and forfeited if an attempt has been made to import

---

[58] 19 U.S.C. § 1337(j).

[59] *See e.g., In re Spring Assemblies and Components Thereof*, 46 Fed. Reg. 42,217 (Aug. 19, 1981).

the goods and the owner or importer has been warned about the consequences of another attempt. Ordinarily, the ITC issues an exclusion order unless it concludes that exclusion would adversely affect:

- public health and welfare;

- U.S. competitive conditions;

- production of competitive products in the U.S., or;

- U.S. consumers.

Although a PEO usually applies to identified parties and products, it can be made applicable to an entire class of goods if a risk of evasion is present because the goods are imported from many sources and the producers cannot be identified. A cease and desist order may be issued by the ITC to stop the unfair methods or acts. Civil penalties may be imposed for violation of either or both orders. The ITC may not issue a general exclusion order (*i.e.*, an order affecting all shipments of the product, as opposed to one that only affects goods from the persons determined to violate section 337), unless the general order is necessary to prevent circumvention of specific orders, and there is a pattern of violation and it is difficult to identify the persons responsible for the infringement.

[7] Section 301 Proceedings

Section 301 of the Trade Act of 1974 is the principal U.S. statutory means for counteracting actions of foreign governments that impede exports of U.S. goods or services. The statute may be invoked to enforce the rights of U.S. companies under international trade agreements, to obtain access to foreign markets, and to respond to practices of foreign government that improperly restrict U.S. trade. The law establishes procedures for the USTR to investigate foreign practices and consult with foreign governments to resolve disputes by stopping the disapproved practice or providing compensation to the injured U.S. industry.

If the consultations do not achieve a satisfactory agreement, the USTR must invoke any dispute settlement procedures to which the U.S. is bound by treaty or trade agreements. Generally, this requires the dispute to be taken to the WTO dispute resolution procedures. If a satisfactory resolution still is not obtained, the USTR may take actions such as suspension of trade concessions or imposition of tariffs, fees or other import restrictions.

Special and Super 301 Proceedings. The statute has evolved through various amendments to include provisions that are targeted at particular trade problems. One provision, referred to as *Special 301*,[60] focuses on intellectual property issues by requiring the USTR to annually identify the countries that lack appropriate intellectual property (IP) protection or that deny fair market access to IP products from the U.S. The identified countries are divided into three categories — Priority Foreign Country, Priority Watch List, and Watch List — depending upon the severity of the

---

[60] Section 182 of the Trade Act of 1974.

IP issues involved. A country with the most severe problems in the Priority Foreign Countries category will be subject to a Section 301 investigation within 30 days of that designation. *See* discussion below.

A second targeted provision, referred to as Super 301,[61] establishes procedures by which the USTR conducts an annual review of U.S. trade priorities and determines the specific export impediments that will be focused upon in the near future. The USTR's Super 301 report serves as the basis for many U.S. trade negotiations during the subsequent year.

[a] Petitions and Investigations

Any interested person may ask the USTR to take action under Section 301 by filing a petition that states the allegations that support the request.[62] The USTR must determine whether to initiate an investigation within 45 days of receiving the petition. Alternatively, the USTR may self-initiate an investigation. The USTR must give public notice of its determinations and, in the case of a decision to proceed with an investigation, it must publish a summary of the petition and provide opportunities for presentation of views and a public hearing. In determining whether to conduct an investigation, the USTR may consider whether a Section 301 action would effectively address the offending policy, or practice.

A domestic investigation by the USTR must be coordinated with any relevant international dispute resolution procedures.[63] Pursuant to U.S. obligations under the WTO and other trade agreements, this usually requires opening of consultations with the relevant foreign government. Accordingly, on the day it determines to initiate an investigation, the USTR must request consultations with the foreign country regarding the alleged issues. The request may be delayed for up to 90 days if needed to verify or improve the petition so that an adequate basis for consultation exists. If the dispute is not resolved during the consultation period provided in the trade agreement, the USTR must request formal dispute settlement under the agreement by the earlier of the end of that consultation period or 150 days after consultations began.

[b] Mandatory and Discretionary Action

Subject to the important exceptions described below, Section 302 requires the USTR to take action to enforce U.S. rights against foreign countries that:

- Violate trade agreements, and;

- Engage in unjustifiable, unreasonable, or discriminatory trade practices that burden or restrict U.S. commerce.

---

[61] Originally enacted as Section 310 of the Omnibus Trade Act of 1988, the law has expired a number of times and has been reestablished by subsequent executive orders. The last was Executive Order 13116 (March 31, 1999).

[62] *See* § 302.

[63] Section 303

This mandatory implementation of the statute extends to countries that are members of the WTO or other trade agreements even if the trade measure in question is covered by that agreement.[64] Accordingly, the USTR must take action if it finds that a country's practices or policies falls under the rules of Section 301, unless otherwise directed by the President.

Pursuant to four important exceptions, the USTR is not mandated to take action under Section 301 if:

(1)   A panel authorized under the dispute resolution rules of the WTO[65] or other trade agreement has found that U.S. rights under the trade agreement have not been denied or violated. If the dispute resolution panel makes recommendations for action by the foreign country, the USTR may subsequently determine that the country has failed to implement the recommendation. After consulting with the petitioner, industry representatives and other interested parties, the USTR may, within 30 days after the end of the time period for implementing the recommendation, determine that further action is required.

(2)   The USTR concludes that the foreign country is satisfactorily acting to grant U.S. trade agreement rights, or has agreed to eliminate the offending practice, to quickly resolve the burden or restriction on U.S. commerce, or to provide compensatory trade benefits. The USTR monitors the implementation of these settlement agreements to determine whether further action is required.[66] A foreign country that is not in compliance, is deemed to violate a trade agreement, and becomes subject to mandatory action under Section 301.

(3)   In extraordinary cases, the USTR may find that the adverse impact of an action on the U.S. economy would be disproportionate to its benefits, or that the action would seriously harm U.S. national security.

(4)   The USTR determines that the foreign country's actions are *unreasonable* or *discriminatory* and burdens or restricts U.S. commerce, and action by the United States is appropriate.

Any action the USTR does take must have an economic effect on the foreign country that is equivalent to the burden or restriction imposed on U.S. commerce. The form of action the USTR may take includes:

(1)   denial of trade agreement concessions;

(2)   imposition of duties or other import restrictions or fees or restrictions on services from the foreign country for a specified time period;

---

[64] Sections 301–309 of the Trade Act of 1974.

[65] As a WTO member, the U.S. is a party to the *Dispute Settlement Understanding* (DSU) which establishes procedures for dealing with disputes arising under any of the WTO agreements. *See* 2.02[5]. Public Law 103-465, approved December 8, 1993.

[66] Section 306.

(3)   withdrawal or suspension of preferential tariffs under the GSP or similar trade preference acts, or;

(4)   entering binding agreements committing the foreign country to

   (a)   eliminate or phase out the offending practice,

   (b)   eliminate any burden or restriction on U.S. commerce, or

   (c)   provide compensatory trade benefits.

(5)   other appropriate and feasible action as directed by the President.

If import restrictions are imposed, the USTR must give preference to tariffs over other kinds of restrictions. Restrictions on services may include prospective denial of authorizations to enter the U.S. market, such as licenses or permits, that are issued under federal law.

[c] Implementation of Action

The USTR must implement a Section 301 action within 30 days after it makes a positive determination.[67] Implementation may be delayed up to 180 days if requested by the petitioner, or for self-initiated cases, by a majority of the domestic industry. A 180 day delay also is permitted if the USTR determines that substantial progress is being made toward a satisfactory solution. In Special 301 cases involving intellectual property rights in a Priority Country, the delay cannot exceed 90 days.

The USTR may modify or terminate a Section 301 action if:

•   an exception to mandatory Section 301 action for trade agreement violations or unjustifiable practices applies;

•   the effect of the unfair practice on U.S. has changed, or;

•   discretionary section 301 action is no longer appropriate.

A Section 301 action automatically terminates after 4 years if neither the petitioner nor any industry representative submit a written request to the USTR within the final 60 days of that period. If a request is submitted, the USTR reviews the effectiveness of any trade actions in achieving their objectives, and the effects of the actions on the U.S. economy and consumers.

[d] Special 301: Intellectual Property Rights Disputes

Under the provisions of the law called *Special 301*,[68] the USTR must identify foreign countries that deny adequate and effective protection of intellectual property rights or fair and equitable market access for U.S. persons that rely on intellectual property protection. The statute was amended in connection with U.S. adoption of the Uruguay Round Agreements Act to clarify that a country may be considered to deny adequate

---

[67] Section 305.

[68] Section 182 of the Trade Act of 1974, added by section 1303 of the Omnibus Trade and Competitiveness Act of 1988, 19 U.S.C. § 2242.

and effective intellectual property protection even if it complies with the TRIPS Agreement. *See* § 2.02[4][f]. In applying Special 301, the USTR must take into account a country's history with respect to intellectual property laws, prior U.S. efforts to obtain effective intellectual property protection there, and the country's response to these efforts.

After identifying these countries, the USTR determines if any should be designated a *Priority Foreign Country,* meaning a country that—

(1)   has the most onerous and egregious acts, policies and practices that have the greatest adverse impact (actual or potential) on relevant U.S. products, and;

(2)   are not engaged in good faith negotiations or making significant progress in negotiations to address these problems.

The USTR's decision to make or revoke the identification of a Priority Country must be detailed in its semiannual report to the Congress under Section 301.

Once a nation is identified as a Priority Foreign Country, the USTR must decide within 30 days whether to initiate an investigation of the matters that were the basis for that classification. If the USTR determines that initiation of an investigation would be detrimental to U.S. economic interests, it must submit a detailed report of the reasons to the Congress. The procedures for a Special 301 investigation are similar an investigation pursuant to a Section 301 petition, except that a shorter time period is allowed under Special 301. Generally, only six months are allowed for the USTR determination, with an extension of up to 9 months if certain criteria are met.

In conjunction with its duties under Special 301, the USTR maintains separate categories of countries whose intellectual property practices are of concern. Countries whose practices are serious but have less impact on U.S. trade are placed on a priority watch list. Other countries are placed on a watch list or in a special mention category, depending upon the severity of the issues involved. These designations change from year to year as a result of the annual review the USTR conducts for Special 301 purposes.

[8] The Court of International Trade

The Customs Court Act of 1980 expanded the jurisdiction of the U.S. Court of International Trade (CIT) to decide cases involving international trade and customs duties.[69] Under that Act, the CIT reviews decisions of the U.S. Customs Service, the International Trade Administration and the International Trade Commission involving matters such as classification rates and duties, antidumping and countervailing duties and unfair import practices by trading partners. Generally, the CIT upholds an agency decision unless it is unsupported by substantial evidence or otherwise not in accordance with law.

---

[69] 28 U.S.C. §§ 1581-1585.

The CIT has exclusive jurisdiction to decide any civil action against the United States, its officers, or its agencies arising out of any international trade law. Its powers, both in law and equity, include entry of money judgments, remanding agency determinations for further action, reviewing antidumping and countervailing duty (AD/CVD) determinations and granting other relief available in district courts. The CIT also reviews customs and AD/CVD determinations, executive decisions concerning customs broker's licenses, eligibility for trade adjustment assistance under the Trade Act of 1974, and requests for confidential information. It also has exclusive jurisdiction for judgments on any counterclaim, crossclaim, or third-party action and civil actions commenced by the U.S. to enforce administrative sanctions. The 1980 Act also continued the CIT's de novo review in customs cases and the deferential standard of review in AD/CVD cases. These jurisdictional changes were designed to provide a comprehensive judicial review system for actions arising from import transactions and U.S. statutes affecting international trade.

The CIT, which was called the U.S. Customs Court until 1980, is an Article III court and its nine justices are appointed by the President with the advice and consent of the Senate. The offices of the court are located in New York City, but its geographical jurisdiction extends nationwide. The court may hold hearings in foreign countries. Its nine judges are appointed for life by the President with the advice and consent of the Senate. Appeals from the court are heard by the U.S. Court of Appeals for the Federal Circuit and then may be heard by the U.S. Supreme Court.

§ 3.03 Export Controls

[1] Multi-Lateral Export Control Regimes

Many nations, including the U.S., restrict exports of certain items and limit the countries to which specific exports may be exported. These restrictions may cover diverse items such as weapons, natural resources, national treasures or relics, strategic commodities or technology. Governments usually implement export restrictions by requiring a license for exporting specified items to certain countries.

[a] Background

The current U.S. export control regime began to be developed during the Cold War to prevent the Soviet Union and its allies from obtaining western technology. The first such law was the Export Control Act of 1949, which restricted exports of military-use items as well as scarce products needed in the domestic economy. Soon after, NATO established a *Coordinating Committee* (CoCom) to control exports of similar items to Eastern Europe. A number of U.S. and European export control laws were adopted during the Cold War period to implement and enforce the CoCom controls over shipments of strategically important items.

With the end of the Cold War, CoCom was terminated and many of the restrictions on exports to Russia and Eastern Europe were relaxed or eliminated. Although the CoCom multi-lateral export control regime ended, individual governments, including the U.S., continued to impose their own national export restrictions. As a result of political developments, however, the target of the controls shifted from the Soviet Union and Eastern Europe to a number of Middle East and Asian countries. These new control regimes focused on technology that could be useful in developing nuclear, chemical and biological weapons, and missile delivery systems.

[b] Wassenaar Arrangement

The fast pace of developments in technology also stimulated a new round of multi-lateral discussions about exports controls on arms, and *dual use* technology that has both civilian and military applications. In 1996, the discussions resulted in the *Wassenaar Arrangement on Export Controls for Conventional Arms and Dual-Use Goods and Technologies* (Wassenaar Arrangement). The Wassenaar Arrangement was signed by thirty-three countries and implemented in the U.S. by final regulations issued in January, 2002.[70]

The Wassenaar Arrangement is designed to enhance regional and international security by encouraging transparent and responsible transfers of conventional arms and dual-use products and technologies. It is not oriented against Eastern Europe — indeed, Russia is a founding participant — and there are no specific target countries. However, the U.S. hopes it will restrain imports to so-called *rogue nations* that support terrorism or are developing weapons of mass destruction.

Participating states have agreed to exchange information about exports of dual-use goods and technologies to other countries so that the risks associated with these transfers can be assessed. The Arrangement is headquartered in Vienna, Austria, and operates through a permanent secretariat in that city. Working groups from member countries attend annual meetings to develop organizational policy. An annual Plenary meeting is held to approve or reject the policies recommended by the working groups.

The U.S. also is a party to a number of other multi-lateral and bi-lateral arrangements to restrict exports that may proliferate nuclear, biological and chemical weapons, and missile technology. For example, the Biological and Toxin Weapons Convention, the Chemical Weapons Convention, and the Nuclear Nonproliferation Treaty commit the signatory States to refrain from actions, such as the exportation of products that will facilitate development, production, or acquisition of these weapons by other nations.

Other commitments between governments are not provided by treaty or convention, but nevertheless obligate the parties to limit certain exports. These commitments provide a multi-lateral mechanism for coordination

---

[70] 15 C.F.R. Parts 743, 752, *et al.*; 67 FR 2 (January 3, 2002).

and control of strategic exports. Arrangements of this type include the Australia Group, the Missile Technology Control Regime, and the Nuclear Suppliers Group. Each of these groups has developed an agreed list of exports that should be restricted that is implemented through national controls.

[2]　U.S. Export Controls

Ordinarily, the U.S. imposes export controls because of concerns about how a particular export will affect national security, foreign policy, or domestic supply shortages. These controls are authorized by statutes that empower the President to regulate the export of various commodities and technologies. The range of products affected by an export control often depends upon the country involved, so that most products and technologies may be exported to Canada without a license, while nearly all trade with Cuba is subject to stringent licensing restrictions.

Whether an export license is required depends upon the nature of the product, the destination and end-user, the intended use, and the probability and effect of a diversion to military use. An exporter must determine whether any technology used in the product is subject to export controls. It should be noted that only a small percentage of exports require an export license. Given the penalties involved, however, companies that sell or ship goods abroad must take care to comply with all export control provisions.

[a]　Regulatory Agencies

Export controls are authorized by various statutes and implemented by government agencies that are responsible for issuing export licenses for specified products. For example, the Food and Drug Administration controls exports of drugs and medical devices, and the Department of the Interior governs exports of fish and wildlife. Despite these diverse responsibilities, most export controls fall into the following categories:

- **Nuclear Materials.** A number of agencies govern various types of exports related to nuclear technology. Exports of nuclear reactors and associated materials and technology are governed by the Atomic Energy Act and require a license issued by the Nuclear Regulatory Commission,[71] while transfers of technical information are controlled by the Department of Energy.[72] Other nuclear-related commodities and dual use technologies are controlled by the Department of Commerce (DOC).[73]

- **Weapons and Military Technology.** Under the *Arms Export Control Act*,[74] a license from the State Department's Office of

---

[71] 10 C.F.R. § 110.

[72] 10 C.F.R. § 810.

[73] 15 C.F.R. §§ 742.3, 744.2, 744.5.

[74] 22 U.S.C. §§ 2778-2994.

Defense Trade Controls (ODTC) is required for exporting defense articles and services, including weapons and military technology set forth in the *Munitions Control List* in the *International Traffic in Arms Regulations*.[75] The Munitions List includes items developed for military application. However, items converted to primary civilian use and dual use items are under the jurisdiction of the DOC. The Defense Department's Defense Technology Security Administration and Defense Threat Reduction Agency also review many license applications.

• **Foreign Assets.** The Treasury Department's Office of Foreign Assets Control (OFAC) administers trade sanctions and embargoes against targeted foreign countries. These include Cuba and North Korea under the Trading With the Enemy Act and other countries such as Libya, Iraq, and Iran, under the International Emergency Economic Powers Act. The OFAC also applies other economic measures, such as freezing assets and restricting imports to terrorist organizations and narcotics traffickers.

[b] Department of Commerce Export Controls

The broadest range of products and technologies are subject to export controls administered by the Department of Commerce (DOC) pursuant to the Export Administration Act of 1979 (EAA).[76] The EAA expired in 1994 and has been kept in force by successive Presidents pursuant to their authority under the International Emergency Economic Powers Act.[77]

The EAA is administered by the Bureau of Export Administration (BXA).[78] Export licenses are issued by the BXA under guidelines set forth in the Export Administration Regulations (EAR).[79] The EAR applies to exports and re-exports of items from abroad, either as exported from the U.S., or included in the content of a foreign-produced product.

Items or technology for which a license may be required are identified on a *Commodity Control List* (CCL) maintained by the BXA. The CCL lists more than 200 categories of goods and technologies applied to seven country groups, with the most stringent controls applied to exports to Cuba and North Korea. In effect, the CCL describes the products that are most likely to require an export license.[80] Items are identified on the CCL by an Export

---

[75] 22 C.F.R. § 120.

[76] 50 U.S.C. app. § 2410(c).

[77] 50 U.S.C. § 1702; Exec Order 13,222; 66 FR 44025 (2001). Both houses of Congress have introduced a new Export Administration Act of 2001, H.R. 2568, is identical to S. 149 as reported out of the Senate Banking Committee on March 22, 2001.

[78] Export Administration Act Of 1979 (EAA) allows the President to control exports of U.S. goods and technology to all foreign destinations, as necessary for national security, foreign policy, and supply purposes. Although the EAA expired in August 1994. these controls have been kept in force since then by executive order under the International Emergency Economic Powers Act (IEEPA).

[79] 15 C.F.R. §§ 730-774. The EAR were extensively restructured and rewritten in 1996.

[80] 15 C.F.R. § 774.

Control Classification Number which is used to determine whether a license is required for its export to a specific country, end use, or end user.

The BXA's enforcement duties include maintaining a Denied Persons List of parties who have been denied export privileges.[81] Exporters must consult this list to ascertain whether they are violating the EAR by a transaction with an ineligible person. The Proliferation Entities List identifies foreign organizations that may be involved in developing or producing weapons of mass destruction.

Dual use products. Some of the most comprehensive controls apply to *dual use* products, such as computers, software, electronics and communications equipment, that may have both military and civilian functions. The CCL has been updated over the years by the U.S. in conjunction with its allies to decontrol a number of items that are widely available and to concentrate on restricting access to high-technology and scarce strategic materials. Recent amendments reflect the *Wassenaar Arrangement* relating to exports of munitions and dual use items discussed above.

[c]　Items and Activities Subject to Export Control Rules

The BXA jurisdiction extends to all *items and activities* that are *subject to the EAR*.[82] Generally, the term *items* refers to all domestic products and foreign-origin goods that have more than a *de minimus* U.S. content.[83] This includes tangible commodities and products, software, technology, technical data, and technical know-how.[84] As discussed below, the EAR also applies to non-export *activities* that result in a transfer of technology or services to a foreign country.

Items or activities that are subject to the EAR may require a license for export or re-export. A license is not required, however, if one of the following exceptions applies:

- The item is not described on the Commodity Control List (CCL).

- The item appears on the CCL, but the EAR country chart states that a license is not required to export that item to the importing country.

- The CCL and country chart would require a license, but a specific *License Exception* in the EAR applies to the transaction in question.[85] Situations in which a License Exception may apply include low value exports, and exports to a U.S. agency or allied government.

---

[81] 15 C.F.R. pt. 764, Supp. 2 (2001).

[82] 15 C.F.R. § 734.2.

[83] 15 C.F.R. § 734.3.

[84] 15 C.F.R. § 732.2.

[85] The exceptions are set forth in 17 C.F.R. § 740.

For purposes of the EAR, the following activities are considered to be exports:

- A shipment or transmission of an item out of the U.S.[86] A *transmission* includes items sent by e-mail or Internet *(e.g.,* software), cable, photo-optical and similar communications facilities.[87]

- Release of software or technology in a foreign country;

- Release of technology or source code to a foreign national.[88] *(See* subsection [c] Deemed Exports below.)

- Items produced in a foreign country using U.S.-origin technology.[89]

- Re-export of previously exported items.[90]

[d] Deemed Exports

The EAR also apply to *activities* that are not exports but nevertheless result in a transfer of technology or services to a foreign country. The most important activity is the *deemed export* of technology that is considered to occur when there is a *release* of technology or software to a foreign national in the U.S. or another country.[91] The technology transfer is a *deemed* export to the foreign national's home country, or a *deemed* re-export, if the release occurs in a third country. The deemed export rule does not apply to aliens that are permanent residents in the U.S..

The technology release can occur through oral or written communication or by a visual inspection. For example, allowing a visiting foreign national to see a computer program that would require a license to export may violate the EAR[92] Under a special rule for *encryption sources codes*, the EAR is not violated unless the code is actually transferred outside the U.S. (which encompasses foreign embassies).[93] This special rule reflects recent judicial decisions suggesting that encryption source codes are expressions that are protected by the Constitution.[94]

[e] End-Use or End-User Restrictions

A number of EAR controls relate to the identity of the end user or end use of the export.[95] These rules prohibit unlicensed exports of any product

---

[86] 15 C.F.R. § 734.2(b)(1).

[87] *See* 15 C.F.R. § 730.5(c), 15 C.F.R. § 734.2(b)(9)(ii).

[88] 15 C.F.R. § 734.2(b)(2)(ii).

[89] 15 C.F.R. § 734.3(a)(4).

[90] 15 C.F.R. § 734.2(b)(4).

[91] 15 C.F.R. § 734.2(b)(1), (b)(2)(ii).

[92] *See* 15 C.F.R. §§ 734.2(b)(2)(ii)-(3)(i).

[93] 15 C.F.R. §§ 734.2 (b)(9)(i)(A)-(B).

[94] *See Junger v. Daley,* 209 F.3d 481, 485 (6th Cir. 2000); *Bernstein v. United States Dep't of Justice,* 176 F.3d 1132, 1147 (9th Cir. 1999).

[95] 15 C.F.R. § 744.

to any person the exporter knows that the product will be directly or indirectly used in the research or production of nuclear, chemical, or biological weapons.[96] Thus, a license is required to export laboratory equipment to a biological weapons factory even though the equipment is not on the CCL and it is being shipped to a country allied with the U.S. Other end user controls ban exports of missile, chemical and biological technologies to specific countries. Similar rules applicable to encryption software have been removed recently.[97]

[f] Restricted Persons

The BXA and other export regulating agencies maintain lists of specific persons and entities that may not receive unlicensed exports from the U.S. The major lists include:

- *Specially Designated Nationals* (SDN) set forth on a list published by the Treasury Department's Office of Foreign Assets Control (OFAC).[98] These are persons, vessels and entities determined to be agents of terrorists, drug dealers, organizations proliferating weapons of mass destruction, and embargoed countries.

- *Debarred Parties* listed by the State Department's Office of Defense Trade Controls (ODTC). These persons are debarred from engaging in export activities related to defense items or services. U.S. persons who export defense articles may not engage in transactions with these people.[99]

- *Denied Parties* set forth on a list maintained by the BXA are denied export privileges.[100] These parties are subject to *denial orders* that prohibit U.S. persons from engaging in any export-related activity to or for the denied party.[101]

- *Proliferation Entities* are set forth on a list maintained by the BXA and published in the EAR. The list sets forth entities that the U.S. government has determined to be involved in the research into or production of weapons of mass destruction.[102]

[g] Country Controls

The U.S. maintains many forms of trade and export sanctions against specific nations and organizations. Most arms embargoes are administered by the State Department ODTC.[103] The ODTC list of embargoed countries

---

[96] 15 C.F.R. § 744.6.

[97] 15 C.F.R. parts 732, 734,740, 742, 744, 748, 770, 774.

[98] 31 C.F.R. ch. V, app. A.

[99] 22 C.F.R. § 126.7(a)(6).

[100] 15 C.F.R. § 764.

[101] 15 C.F.R. § 764, Supp. 1 and 2.

[102] 15 C.F.R. § 744.

[103] 22 C.F.R. § 126.1.

is periodically updated in the Federal Register. U.S. persons, regardless of where located, are prohibited from entering into export, sales, or broker activities with these countries, their citizens, or agents. The Treasury Department's Office of Foreign Assets Control also maintains a list of embargoed countries that are subject to sanctions under a variety of U.S. laws, Presidential executive orders, and United Nations Security Council Resolutions.

[h] Penalties

Violations of the export control rules can result in substantial civil and criminal penalties. The EAR imposes a $10,000 per violation civil fine for most infractions,[104] increasing to as much as $100,000 for a violation of National Security Controls.[105] Much greater fines can be imposed for violations of the International Traffic in Arms Regulations, which allows for a civil penalty of up to $500,000.[106] The civil penalties can be imposed on a strict liability basis, without regard to the violator's knowledge or intent.[107] To encourage voluntary self-disclosure of violations, the EAR provides that such disclosure is a mitigating factor in determining the administrative sanctions the BXA's *Office of Export Enforcement (OEE)* will seek.[108]

Violators also may be subject to a denial of export privileges, which prohibits them for engaging in export activities for any third party.[109] Attorneys, accountants, consultants, freight forwarders, and others acting in a representative capacity for an exporter may be *excluded by order* from being involved in a license application or other activity before the BXA.[110]

For criminal violations involving general intent, fines may be imposed of the greater of $50,000, or five times the value of the export, and imprisonment for up to five years.[111] If the violation is *willful*, an organization may be fined up to the greater of $1,000,000 per violation, or five times the value of the export, and an individual may be fined up to $250,000, and be imprisoned for up to ten years.[112] If the violation involves the *International Traffic in Arms Regulations*, the penalty may be a fine of up to $1,000,000 and up to ten years imprisonment.[113]

The Customs Service may detain goods that it believes are being shipped in violation of the export control rules.[114] If an investigation shows that the export is legal, the goods are released. If illegal, they may be seized.

---

[104] 10 C.F.R. § 110.

[105] 10 C.F.R. § 810.

[106] 15 C.F.R. §§ 744.2-744.4, 744.6(a)(1), (2).

[107] *Iran Air v. Kugelman,* 996 F.2d 1253 (D.C. Cir. 1993).

[108] 15 C.F.R. § 764.5.

[109] 15 C.F.R. §§ 742.3, 744.2, 744.5.

[110] 50 U.S.C. §§ 1701-1706

[111] 15 C.F.R. § 740.3(d).

[112] 15 C.F.R. § 740.7.

[113] 50 U.S.C. app. § 2404.

[114] 22 U.S.C. § 401.

[3] Economic Sanctions

Generally, the term *economic sanctions* refers to restrictions that a government maintains regarding a foreign country's economic activity for foreign policy reasons. Common forms of economic sanctions include:

- embargoes on trade and investment;

- prohibitions on property transactions such as *blocking* or *freezing* of assets;

- suspension of government trade or investment assistance;

- denial of normal trade relations (or MFN status), and;

- rescission of preferential import treatment.

Economic sanctions are not trade remedies, but are used as foreign policy tools to change, or retaliate for another nations political or military activities.

The U.S. may implement economic sanctions pursuant to a direct statute or through a statute that authorizes the President to impose the sanction. A recent example of a Congressionally imposed sanction is the *Cuban Liberty and Democratic Solidarity (LIBERTAD) Act* (Helms-Burton Act) that authorizes lawsuits against foreign persons who deal in or benefit from property that was confiscated by Cuba under the Castro regime. Another example, is the law enacted after the Tiananmen Square incident in Beijing that forbade granting of licenses for a variety of exports to China.

A few examples of the numerous statutes that authorize the executive branch to impose economic sanctions include:

- The *International Emergency Economic Powers Act* (IEEPA), which is the primary authority for executively established economic sanctions. The President may impose sanctions to respond to *an unusual and extraordinary threat to the national security, foreign policy, or economy*. Since 1977, presidents have used the IEEPA to establish embargoes and freeze assets of countries and organizations for foreign policy reasons. These sanctions include asset-blocking orders and embargoes against Iraq, Libya, Serbia and Sudan; asset-blocking orders against Latin American narcotics dealers and Middle Eastern terrorists; embargo measures against Iran; and a ban on investment in Burma.

- The *United Nations Participation Act* provides authority to implement U.N. Security Council measures. It is also serves as authority for the Iraq sanctions.

- The *Marine Mammal Protection Act* prohibits imports of yellowfin tuna from countries that do not maintain adequate marine mammal protection policies.

- The *Narcotics Control Trade Act* generally requires the president to raise tariffs on imports from major drug-producing countries unless he certifies that the country is, among other things, cooperating to prevent drug shipments to the United States.

- The *International Religious Freedom Act (Wolf-Burton Act)* directs the president to issue sanctions against countries that engage in or tolerate certain actions deemed to violate religious freedom.

- The *Trading With the Enemy Act* authorizes the president to impose *economic sanctions* and is applied to impose *embargoes* against Cuba and North Korea. An amendment in 1977 limits its authority to imposing new *economic sanctions* to times of war.

Waivers. Most sanctions laws authorize the President to *waive* application of sanctions otherwise mandated by law. Typically, sanctions may be waived upon a determination that doing so is in the *national interest* or the *national security interest* (a more restrictive standard).

Criticism of U.S. Sanctions. Many international groups commend the U.S. sanctions policy as an exercise in leadership to address violations of human rights and other injustices and seek more aggressive application of sanctions for such purposes. Political leaders also maintain that economic sanctions are an important foreign policy tool that may eliminate the need for more forceful measures. They are used when diplomatic methods are insufficient and their imposition is likely to change the offending state's behavior.

There has been, however, substantial international criticism of U.S. economic sanctions. One criticism is that the U.S. often imposes its sanctions *unilaterally* rather than in harmony with similar measures taken by other countries. A more frequent and strident complaint is that certain U.S. sanctions are *extraterritorial* in that they attempt to limit the actions of foreign persons and businesses outside of the U.S.

This last concern prompted the EU to commence a proceeding against the U.S. alleging that the Helms-Burton Act violates the WTO Agreement by applying extraterritorial sanctions on foreign businesses that operate in Cuba. Similar issues have been raised by Canada and Mexico under the NAFTA. None of these cases were continued because the President has suspended application of the Act in many areas. The EU also brought, and then suspended, a WTO challenge to a Massachusetts law that sanctions companies that do business in Burma. Although the cases have not gone forward, the underlying concerns about U.S. extraterritorial sanctions have not been resolved. On the other hand, many U.S. criticisms regarding the EU's lack of response to many countries human rights violations have not been addressed.

[4] Anti-Boycott Laws

Although U.S. anti-boycott laws apply to all economic boycotts that are not sanctioned by the U.S. government, their principal focus is the boycott of Israel organized by a number of Arab nations. These laws are designed to discourage U.S. companies from participating in boycotts that implement policies of foreign countries that do not conform to U.S. policy. The U.S. recognizes that Arab nations may refuse to trade with Israel, but will not allow these countries to prescribe the conditions under which U.S. companies do business.

The anti-boycott rules are authorized by the Export Administration Act (EAA)[115] and expanded and explained in the Export Administration Regulations (EAR).[116] Generally, these provisions apply very broadly to all *U.S. persons* engaged in interstate or foreign commerce, which includes individuals and companies in the United States and their foreign affiliates. U.S. persons are subject to the law if their activities relate to the sale, purchase, or transfer of goods, services, or information in the U.S. or with a foreign country. This includes exports and imports, financing, forwarding and shipping, and certain offshore transactions.

[a] Prohibited Activities

A U.S. person may be deemed to violate the regulations if:[117]

- a boycott is imposed by a foreign country that is directed toward a country friendly to the U.S.;
- the person is aware of the boycott, and;
- the boycott is part of the reason for the action the person takes.

A violation may occur even if the U.S. person does not intend to break the law or agree with the boycott. It is sufficient that the person intends to comply with, further, or support the unsanctioned boycott, even if there are other business reasons for acquiescing to the boycott request. This intent may be inferred from a reference in a document to the boycott or phrases such as "eligible for business in Arab countries."

Conduct prohibited under the EAR includes:[118]

- Refusing or agreeing to refuse to do business with Israel or with a company blacklisted by the boycott. An agreement to refuse can be inferred from terms or conditions in a contract or letter of credit (*e.g.*, "do not use blacklisted contractors").

- Discriminating or agreeing to discriminate against U.S. persons based on race, religion, sex, national origin or nationality. Disparate treatment of an individual on religious or national origin grounds also is a violation. These nondiscrimination rules apply whether or not the act is in response to a request.

- Furnishing or agreeing to furnish information with respect to the race, religion, sex or national origin of a U.S. person.

---

[115] 50 App U.S.C.A § 2407.

[116] EAR, Part 760, 15 C.F.R. § 760.

[117] *Id.*

[118] 15 C.F.R. § 760.2.

- Furnishing or agreeing to furnish information about past, present or proposed business relationships with a boycotted country or with any person known or believed to be restricted from doing business in a boycotting country. An example of prohibited information about business relationships is a *negative certificate of origin* certifying that a shipment does not contain items made in Israel. This prohibition accounts for most violations of the Act.

- Paying or otherwise implementing letters of credit containing prohibited boycott terms or conditions. Banks are explicitly covered by the statute and regulations. Note that if the prohibited terms are in a pre-printed in a letter of credit issued by a foreign bank, a cooperating U.S. bank may violate the Act numerous times in a short period of time.

- Furnishing or knowingly agreeing to furnish information concerning charitable or fraternal organizations which support a boycotted country. This applies to information provided voluntarily or in response to a request or requirement.

- Acting with intent to evade the regulations.[119] U.S. persons also may not assist other U.S. persons in violating or evading the regulations.

The regulations provide a number of express exceptions to the above prohibitions. These include:[120]

- Compliance with the import requirements of a boycotting country. This does not permit an agreement not to ship the goods of blacklisted firms outside of Israel, negative certificates of origin, or a general refusal to deal with Israel.

- Compliance with import and shipping document requirements of a boycotting country. This allows a company to provide a positive certificate of origin, a positive statement of the name of supplier of the goods or services; and a statement as to the route of shipment or the name of the carrier. The information may be provided on the shipping documents, but not in contract negotiations or letters of credit.

- Compliance with unilateral and specific selections regarding carriers, insurers, suppliers, and similar persons within the boycotting country. The unilateral and specific selection must be made by a bona fide resident or national of the boycotting country.

- Compliance with export requirements relating to shipments or transshipments of exports to Israel.

- Compliance with the immigration, employment or passport requirements of any country. This is limited to information about

---

[119] 15 C.F.R. § 760.4.
[120] 15 C.F.R. § 760.3.

the U.S. person or its immediate family. A company may substitute employees if another employee is denied entry into a boycotting country, but cannot select employees for assignments based on assumptions about whether a country will issue a visa or work permit to persons of a particular religion, sex, race or national origin.

- Compliance with local laws that only apply to activities within that foreign country. These activities include, making contracts, employing local residents, and furnishing information. A U.S. person can make boycott-based selections of goods imported into and used within the boycotting country if for his own use or use in performing contractual services within that country. The exception does not allow boycott based selections for goods to be resold in the form in which they are received. It also does not permit furnishing information about, or discriminating against, any U.S. person on the basis of race, religion, sex or national origin.

[b] Reporting Requirements

U.S. persons must to report any requests they receive to take actions to comply with or support a foreign boycott. Reporting is required even if the recipient does not intend to comply with the request. The reports are made on forms provided by the Department of Commerce's *Office of Antiboycott Compliance* (OAC) and filed with that agency.[121] For persons in the U.S., the report must be made by the end of the quarter in which the request was received. The deadline is two months later for persons outside the U.S.

These reports are available for public inspection and copying. Disclosure may be withheld if the reporting person certifies that such disclosure of information about the quantity, description or value of the items being shipped would place a U.S. person at a competitive disadvantage. The person furnishing the information must provide both an unedited version and a redacted version of the report. However, the Secretary of Commerce has discretion to disclose the report if he determines that no competitive disadvantage would result, or that the national interest requires disclosure.

[c] Penalties

Violations of the anti-boycott regulations can result in substantial administrative and criminal penalties. These include:

- **Criminal.** A fine of up to $50,000 or five times the value of exports involved, whichever is greater, and imprisonment of up to five years (ten years if during a period when an Executive Order under the International Emergency Economic Powers Act is in effect.)

---

[121] 15 C.F.R. § 760.5.

- **Administrative.** For each violation of the EAR any or all of the following penalties may be imposed:

  - General denial of export privileges.

  - Fines of up to $12,000 per violation (adjusted annually for inflation).

  - Exclusion from practice.

[d] Anti-Boycott Tax Legislation

Tax legislation related to the Arab boycott of Israel was enacted in 1976.[122] The legislation does not prohibit specific conduct, but denies tax benefits associated with certain boycott-related agreements. These penalties may affect a taxpayer's foreign tax credit, foreign subsidiary deferral, and Foreign Sales Corporation tax benefits.

These tax rules apply to U.S. taxpayers and their related companies. Reporting requirements apply to a taxpayer's operations in, with, or related to boycotting countries or their nationals. These reports must specify requests received to participate in or cooperate with a foreign boycott. The reports are filed with tax returns on IRS Form 5713.

[5] Foreign Corrupt Practices Act

Under the *Foreign Corrupt Practices Act* (FCPA) enacted in 1977, it is a criminal act for a U.S. business or individual to make an illegal payment to a foreign public official.[123] Congress passed the FCPA after a series of bribery scandals revealed that many, if not most, American companies doing business abroad regularly bribed foreign officials to obtain contracts. Indeed, an SEC study before the law was passed showed that nearly 600 U.S. firms commonly paid substantial foreign bribes each year.[124]

[a] Coordination with the OECD Bribery Convention

The FCPA created a substantial disadvantage for American companies in competing against firms from the many other countries that do not prohibit bribing foreign officials. As a remedy, the U.S. Congress and President pressed wealthier trading partners to enact similar anti-bribery rules.[125] The outcome was the *Convention on Combating Bribery of Foreign Public Officials in International Business Transactions* (Bribery Convention) adopted by the Organization for Economic Cooperation and

---

[122] IRC § 999.

[123] Foreign Corrupt Practices Act of 1977, Pub. L. No. 95-23, 91 Stat. 1494, (codified *as amended* at 15 U.S.C. §§ 78m(b), (d)(1), (g)-(h), 78dd-2, 78ff (1994)), *amended by* International Anti-Bribery and Fair Competition Act of 1998, 15 U.S.C. §§ 78dd-1 to 78dd-3, 78ff (1999).

[124] *See* Heifetz, *Japan's Implementation Of The OECD Anti-Bribery Convention: Weaker And Less Effective Than The U.S. Foreign Corrupt Practices Act*, 11 Pac. Rim L. & Pol'y J. 209 (2002).

[125] *See* Foreign Corrupt Practices Act Amendments of 1988, Pub. L. No. 100-418, at 924.

Development (OECD) in 1997. The OECD membership encompasses more than thirty of the world's wealthier industrialized countries.

The Bribery Convention recognizes that bribery raises serious moral and political concerns, and distorts international trade, and required signatory countries to enact implementing legislation by 1999. The U.S. Congress ratified the Convention and amended the FCPA to implement its rules, which became effective in 1999.[126] These amendments increase the range of acts that may violate the FCPA and provide stronger enforcement tools to U.S. prosecutors.

Signatory nations to the Bribery Convention must:

- apply "effective, proportionate and dissuasive criminal penalties" to persons engaged in bribery;

- establish liability for legal persons such as corporations, partnerships, and similar business entities;

- include bribery as a predicate offense for money laundering legislation;

- improve national accounting procedures;

- prohibit off-the-books accounts, and;

- provide mutual legal assistance and extradition in cases subject to the Convention.

Signatory countries must participate in a mutual evaluation process to monitor their implementation of their obligations under the Convention.

[b] Accounting Rules

The FCPA provides two different sets of anti-corruption rules. One set mandates certain accounting procedures designed to enable enforcement officials to determine if illegal payments have been made. The second set contains specific anti-bribery provisions. The FCPA accounting provisions require companies whose securities are listed on U.S. markets to maintain books and records that fairly report the corporation's transactions.[127] These provisions only apply to *issuers,* defined as companies that have issued securities subject to Sections 12 and 15(d) of the Securities and Exchange Act.[128] Accurate accounts must be maintained for all of the issuer's business undertakings, whether domestic or foreign, legal or illegal. An issuer also is responsible for the maintenance of accurate books and records by a foreign subsidiary that it controls.

The issuer's books, records, and accounts must be kept in reasonable detail and accurately reflect its transactions and asset dispositions.[129] In

---

[126] International Anti-Bribery and Fair Competition Act of 1998, 15 U.S.C. §§ 78dd-1 to 78dd-3, 78ff (1999).

[127] 15 U.S.C. § 78m(b).

[128] 15 U.S.C. §§ 78a-78ll; 15 U.S.C. § 78l(g).

[129] 15 U.S.C. § 78m(b)(2)(A)

general, the records must provide any information that would alert the Securities and Exchange Commission about possible improprieties. Thus, issuers cannot defend their failure to keep records on the basis of lack of materiality. Issuers also must establish an internal accounting control system to reasonably assure that unauthorized or unrecorded transactions do not occur.

Criminal liability for falsifying a book or record or failing to maintain adequate accounting controls may be imposed only if an individual *knowingly* took such action.[130] Thus, criminal sanctions cannot be imposed for inadvertent violations of the Act, but an individual may act knowingly if he willfully or consciously attempts to avoid such knowledge.[131] Criminal penalties do not apply to violations that are technical or insignificant accounting errors.

[c] Bribery Rules

The FCPA was amended in 1998 to incorporate the provisions of the OECD Bribery Convention.[132] The SEC and Department of Justice can prosecute individual corporate employees regardless of whether the corporation is guilty of violating the Act. Note that the Act applies to the bribe payer, but does not reach the foreign officials who take bribes from American companies, and foreign officials cannot be prosecuted for conspiracy to violate the Act.

The FCPA applies to most U.S. persons and entities. The crime of bribing a foreign official may be committed by any *domestic concern*, which includes:

- an individual who is a U.S. citizen, national, or resident, and;

- any corporation, partnership, association, joint-stock company, business trust, unincorporated organization, or sole proprietorship having its principal place of business in the U. S., or that is organized under the laws of a U.S. state territory, possession, or commonwealth.[133]

As amended, the FCPA makes it a federal crime for a U.S. person or entity to offer or pay anything of value, directly or through an intermediary, to a foreign official for the purpose of gaining an improper commercial advantage in obtaining or retaining business or directing business to another person.[134] The statute applies to payments or offers to foreign officials, government employees, officers of a public international organization, foreign political parties, candidates, or any agents of those entities. These acts are criminal if made with the intent to:

---

[130] 15 U.S.C. § 78m(b)(5).

[131] *See* Foreign Corrupt Practices Act Amendments of 1988, Pub. L. No. 100-418, at 916, 920–21 (1988).

[132] 15 U.S.C. § 78dd-1(g).

[133] 15 U.S.C.S. § 78dd-2(h)(1)(B).

[134] 15 U.S.C. § 78dd-1(a),(f).

- influence a foreign official's act or decision,
- induce a foreign official to violate a lawful duty,
- secure an improper advantage, or;
- induce a foreign official to use his influence with a foreign government to affect or influence that government's act or decision. [135]

The FCPA does not criminalize payments made to expedite or to secure performance of a routine government action. [136] This seems to cover small payments made to motivate a government official to perform his lawful duty. Similarly, the Act does not apply to payments that are lawful under the written laws of the official's country and it is a valid defense to show compliance with such laws. [137]

[d] Penalties

The FCPA provides substantial penalties for violations. A domestic concern that is not a natural person may be subject to a criminal fine up to $2,000,000, and civil penalties up to $10,000. [138] A natural person who is an officer, director, employee, agent, or stockholder acting for a domestic concern faces criminal fines up to $100,000, and civil penalties up to $10,000. The Act also authorizes the Attorney General to seek injunctions against entities that are or will be engaged in prohibited acts. [139]

[e] Company Compliance Programs

Many companies avoid problems under the FCPA by establishing internal procedures for avoiding, detecting, and dealing with corruption issues. This involves publication and dissemination of guidelines that describe the FCPA rules and sanctions as well as the corporate policies and procedures for reporting and responding to situations involving actual or requested questionable payments.

Steps that can be taken to implement a compliance program include:

- Creation of a compliance *culture* in which employees know and understand that liability cannot be avoided by willful ignorance or conscious disregard of FCPA violations. Supervisors must avoid inadvertent authorization of bribery through statements such as "do what you have to do to get the sale."
- Companies must perform due diligence about their potential business partners to avoid inadvertent dealing with ventures indirectly owned or controlled by foreign officials or governments.

---

[135] 15 U.S.C.S. §§ 78dd-1(a)(1), (a)(2), (a)(3).

[136] 15 U.S.C.S. § 78dd-1(b).

[137] 15 U.S.C.S. § 78dd-1(c)(1).

[138] 15 U.S.C.S. § 78dd-2(g)(1).

[139] 15 U.S.C.S. § 78dd-2(d).

The due-diligence efforts should be fully documented to establish the reasonable scope of the investigation.

- Contracts may require their business partners to comply with the FCPA and to inform the U.S. company of any questionable acts or practices.

- Consistent surveillance and questioning of managers and employees is required. This is especially true if the business is conducted in a country known to tolerate official corruption. Transactions that can conceal questionable payments, such as excessive commissions or consultation payments, should be scrutinized.

Chapter 4

INTERNATIONAL SALES

§ 4.01 International Contracts for the Sale of Goods

[1] In General

Generally, a domestic contract for the sale of goods is governed by Article 2 of the *Uniform Commercial Code* (UCC). If the parties are located in different states, a particular state's version of the UCC will be selected as the applicable law. Although state versions may differ slightly, both parties and their lawyers can clearly understand the rights, obligations and risks the contract creates under the applicable law. Because the social and legal environment is similar in both states, the parties have accurate expectations about how the contract will be performed and disputes resolved.

If one of the parties is in a different country, however, social, cultural and legal values and practices may be quite different. The contractual difficulties created by these differences may be compounded by distance, language barriers, and lack of personal contact. Obviously, in this situation the U.S. party would prefer to have the contract governed by the familiar UCC rules and disputes resolved in a U.S. forum. Just as obviously, the foreign party would prefer to apply its own national rules and courts.

Recognizing the difficulties that choice of law issues pose in cross-border transactions, international organizations have promulgated uniform rules for contacts involving parties in different countries. For sales of goods, these rules are provided by the *Convention on Contracts for the International Sale of Goods* (CISG), described below. Although the CISG generally applies to international sales contracts (*i.e.*, contracts between parties in different countries), the parties may agree to opt out of all or some of its provisions. They can do so by supplying their own terms that derogate from the CISG provisions, or choose another law such as the UCC to govern their contract.

In practice, the parties should specifically define their rights and obligations in the contract and not rely on any implied terms that must be determined from the law. If the contract is explicit, there is little scope for legal interpretation and the parties expectations will be fulfilled regardless of the applicable law. Because omissions and unforeseen events are always possible (or probable), however, the parties should carefully choose the applicable law and reflect their decision in an appropriate contract clause.

In making that choice, U.S. contract parties must note the significant differences between the UCC and CISG provisions. Although both codes establish uniform rules for sales contracts and reflect modern commercial practices, they arise from different legal traditions and vary in scope, structure and substance. The CISG generally is narrower than the UCC and does not cover issues relating to contract validity, sales of consumer goods, or title to goods sold.[1] Because many terms are undefined, contracts must refer to the rules of other organizations such as the International Chamber of Commerce (ICC) for *Incoterms* (described below). The UCC has a broader scope, Article 2 being only one part of a comprehensive commercial code that covers numerous areas, including leases, commercial paper, letters of credit, documents of title, and secured transactions.[2]

In many cases, the decision to opt out of all or part of the CISG in favor of the UCC is based upon lack of familiarity with the CISG rather than an aversion to any specific provisions. For that reason, the discussion below focuses on the CISG, comparing it to the UCC where relevant.

[2] The Convention on Contracts for the International Sale of Goods (CISG)

The *Convention on Contracts for the International Sale of Goods* (CISG) is an international treaty that governs contracts for the sale of goods between U.S. persons and persons in other countries that have ratified the convention.[3] The Convention was first proposed in 1980, and took effect in 1988, after ratification by the U.S. and many other countries. More than sixty nations have adopted the convention and a number of others are expected to do so in the near future.

The CISG culminates a lengthy international effort to harmonize the rules for international sale of goods. These efforts began with the formation of *the International Institute for the Unification of Private Law* (UNIDROIT) in 1930, which made several unsuccessful attempts to produce an internationally acceptable sales law. Its last attempt, at the Hague Conference in 1964, resulted in two codes, the Uniform Law for the International Sale of Goods and the Uniform Law for the Formation of Contracts, which was ratified by only ten countries, not including the U.S. Ultimately, these laws affected few contracts and had little impact on world trade.

---

[1] Speidel, *The Revision of UCC Article 2, Sales in Light of the United Nations Convention on the International Sale of Goods*, 16 Nw. J. Int'l L. & Bus. 165 (1995).

[2] *Id.*

[3] The U.S. did not ratify CISG Article 1(1)(b), which would apply the treaty "when the rules of private international law lead to the application of the law of a Contracting State."

The failure of these uniform laws prompted formation of *the United Nations Commission on International Trade Law* (UNCITRAL), which began in 1968 to develop an effective, widely-acceptable set of international sales rules. It accomplished this by consulting with representatives of the corporate, government, and academic sectors from different geographical regions, stages of economic development, and legal, social, and economic systems. The draft text was proposed and adopted at the *Vienna Convention* in 1980, and ratified by the U.S. in 1986. As a treaty, the convention has the effect of a federal statute that may apply to an international sales contract unless the parties opt out of its provisions.

The CISG consist of four parts:

- Part One governs its the scope of application and contains general provisions.

- Part Two provides rules governing the formation of contracts for the international sale of goods.

- Part Three establishes the contract parties' substantive rights and obligations that arise from the contract.

- Part Four contains specific reservations and declarations about the convention and how it applies if the States involved in a contract have the same or similar law on the subject.

[a] "Opting out" of the CISG

At the outset, it is important to note that the parties may freely choose not to apply the CISG to their contract or to derogate from or vary any treaty provision.[4] However, unless the parties expressly "opt out" of the CISG (*e.g.*, by stating that another law will govern), or derogate from its provisions (*e.g.*, by a contrary clause in the contract), the Convention will apply to any international contract that meets its jurisdictional rules.[5] In deciding whether to opt out, the parties to a sales transaction should compare the CISG provisions with the law that would otherwise govern their contracts (*e.g.*, the UCC).[6]

An acceptable opt-out clauses is:[7]

→   *The rights and obligations of the parties under this agreement shall not be governed by the provisions of the United Nations Convention on Contracts for the International Sale of Goods (CISG). These rights and obligations shall be governed by the law of* _____.

For contracts that do not opt out of the CISG, the parties should consider clauses governing items that are not covered by the convention (*e.g.*, validity: mistake, duress, fraud) and choice of language. Examples are:

---

[4] CISG Art. 6.

[5] CISG Art. 94.

[6] *See* Winship, *Changing Contract Practices in Light of the United Nations Sales Convention: A Guide for Practitioners*, 29 Int'l Lawyer 525, 538 (1995).

[7] The State Department recommends the application of the CIGS be expressly negated.

→ *This Agreement shall be governed by the CISG. Any ambiguities or items not covered by the CISG shall be governed by* _____.

→ *This Agreement shall be covered by the English version of the CISG.*

Choice of forum may be important, particularly with respect to possible remedies. Civil law countries are more likely to require specific performance where common law countries would impose money damages.

[b] Scope of Application of the CISG

Generally, the CISG applies to contracts of *sale of goods* between parties whose *places of business* are in different countries if both countries have signed the convention (Contracting States). The nationalities of the parties or the movement or location of the goods are not considered in determining whether the Convention applies. Many countries, not including the U.S., also apply the CISG if the choice of law rules of private international law lead to the law of a Contracting State.[8] For a U.S. business person, therefore, the CISG governs a contract only if: (1) the other party's place of business is in a Contracting State, and; (2) the contract does not opt out of the CISG.[9]

For parties having more than one place of business, the place with the closest relationship to the transaction is used.[10] This may be an important consideration for multi-national enterprises that maintain divisions in many countries and for parent-subsidiary relationships that may be vulnerable to being treated as a single enterprise. The CISG may apply even if the goods do not move across international boundaries. For example, the convention applies if a U.S. buyer purchases goods already in the U.S. from a foreign seller.

The CISG does not apply to contracts for services, distribution agreements, contracts of carriage or insurance, letters of credit, or to dispute resolution clauses in a contract.[11] A contract is deemed to be for services, rather than for goods, if the purchaser will supply a substantial part of the materials needed to manufacture or produce the goods. Similarly, a contract is for services if supplying labor or other services is a preponderant part of the seller's obligations.

Specific kinds of sales are excluded from the CISG, including: sales for personal, family or household use, sales by auction, on execution or by law, and sales of stocks, shares, investment securities, negotiable instruments, money, ships, vessels, hovercraft, aircraft or electricity. The CISG governs only the formation of a contract and the parties' rights and duties that arise from the contract. Its provisions do not relate to contract validity, title to

---

[8] CISG Art. 1.

[9] CISG Art. 1(b).

[10] CISG Art. 10.

[11] CISG Art. 3.

the goods sold, or to the seller's tort liability with respect to users of the goods.

In resolving disputes about the meaning and application of the CISG, national courts are asked to observe its international character and apply it to promote uniformity and good faith in international trade.[12] Unsettled issues should be settled in conformity with the general principles of the CISG. If these principles are not evident, such issues may be resolved by reference to the law applicable under private international law. The parties to a sales contract may be bound by trade usages and practices they have agreed to or established, and by usages they know or should know about that are widely known and regularly observed with respect to similar contracts in their trade.[13]

[c] Contract Formation

Under the CISG, a sales contract need not be in writing and does not require consideration.[14] A writing may be necessary, however, if a party's place of business is in a Contracting State that has made a formal declaration that its law requires written contracts of sale.[15] The United States has not made this declaration, so that the UCC's Statue of Frauds rules[16] do not apply to contracts governed by the CISG. Note, however, that other international conventions may require specific contract provisions to be written. For example, the New York Convention on the Recognition and Enforcement of Foreign Arbitral Awards requires written arbitration clauses and jurisdiction clauses must be in writing under the Brussels Convention on Jurisdiction and Enforcement of Judgments in Civil and Commercial Matters.

The existence and provisions of a contract under the CISG may be proven by any means, including witnesses.[17] Thus, the parol evidence rule (which bars evidence of an earlier oral contract contradicting or varying a subsequent written contract) is inapplicable and testimony about the parties' negotiations, prior dealings and intention is permitted. Ordinarily, a person's intent is determined by applying a reasonable person standard, considering all relevant circumstances.[18] However, a party's subjective intent may be considered in interpreting its statements and conduct "where

---

[12] CISG Art. 7.

[13] CISG Art. 9.

[14] CISG Art. 11.

[15] CISG Arts 12 and 96. The few countries making such declarations include Argentina, Belarus, Chile, China, Estonia, Hungary, Lithuania, the Russian Federation, and the Ukraine., pursuant to the Article 12 exclusion. *See* Eiselen, *Electronic Commerce and the UN Convention on Contracts for the International Sale of Goods*, 5 Edi L. Rev. 21, 36 (1999).

[16] Under UCC § 2-201-1, a contract for the sale of goods for $500 or more is not enforceable absent a sufficient writing indicating a contract for sale that is signed by the party against whom enforcement is sought.

[17] CISG Art. 11.

[18] CISG Art. 8.

the other party knew or could not have been unaware what that intent was."[19]

Generally, a contract may be modified or terminated by the "mere agreement" of the parties.[20] This contravenes the common law requirement that contract modification must be supported by consideration. However, a written contract clause requiring specific formalities for modification or termination will be enforced unless one party's conduct has induced the other party to rely on contrary statements or conduct.

A contract formed by acceptance of an offer is concluded when the acceptance becomes effective under the CISG.[21] A proposal constitutes an offer if it is addressed to specific persons and is sufficiently definite, meaning that it indicates the goods and expressly or implicitly fixes or provides a means for determining the quantity and price.[22] An offer is effective when it reaches the offeree[23] and is terminated when it is rejected.[24]

Generally, an offer may be revoked if the revocation reaches the offeree before he sends an acceptance.[25] However, an offer cannot be revoked if: (1) it indicates that it is irrevocable (*e.g.*, by stating a fixed time for acceptance), or; (2) the offeree reasonably relied on the offer being irrevocable and acted in reliance on the offer.[26]

→   Offers are more likely to be irrevocable under the CISG than under the UCC. Under the UCC, an offer may be revoked unless a signed writing assures that it will be held open. The period of irrevocability, however, is limited to three months. The CISG does not impose any writing requirement or time limit, and an offer that states a fixed time for acceptance may be irrevocable until that time even if does not expressly state that it will be held open.

An offer may be accepted by a statement or other conduct indicating assent to the offer, but not by silence or inactivity.[27] The acceptance is effective when the indication of assent reaches the offeror. That must occur within a reasonable time, unless a time for acceptance is fixed in the offer. If the parties have established the practice, acceptance may occur when an act is performed, such as dispatch of the goods or payment of the price.[28] Generally, an oral offer must be accepted immediately.

---

[19] CISG Art. 8(1).

[20] CISG Art. 29.

[21] CISG Art. 23.

[22] CISG Art. 14.

[23] CISG Art. 15.

[24] CISG Art.17.

[25] CISG Art. 16(1).

[26] CISG Art. 16(2).

[27] CISG Art. 18.

[28] CISG Art. 18(3).

[d]   Battle of the Forms

Exporters and importers usually prepare and use forms that set forth the terms they prefer to have in a purchase contract. The party receiving an offer on the other party's form may return it with changes, or perhaps reply on its own form. This exchange of additions, deletions, confirmations and revisions, called the *battle of the forms*, often raises the issue of whether a particular reply constitutes an acceptance, rejection, or counteroffer. If the reply is an acceptance, questions may arise as to the final terms of the contract.

→   Under U.S. common law, a purported acceptance that stated terms that differed from the offer was considered to reject the offer. No contract was deemed to arise unless the acceptance was the *mirror image* of the offer. The UCC overturns this demanding common law rule by providing that an expression of acceptance creates a contract unless: (1) the acceptance is conditioned on the offeror accepting the changed terms, or; (2) the offeror limited acceptance to the terms of the offer, or; (3) the offeror objects to the changed terms.[29] If the offeror does not object, the changed terms become part of the accepted offer. An additional term is not included in the contract, however, if it is *material.*

The CISG does not accept the UCC position, but applies a standard similar to the mirror image rule.[30] Generally, a purported acceptance containing terms that change or add to the offer is deemed to reject the offer and constitute a counteroffer. An acceptance does occur, however, if the changed terms are not material and the offeror does not object to them.[31] For this purpose, terms relating to price, payment, quality and quantity of the goods, place and time of delivery, extent of liability, or settlement of disputes are considered material.[32]

To illustrate the difference between the UCC and CISG rules, assume that an offer is accepted with the addition of a clause requiring arbitration of disputes. Under the UCC a contract is formed; whether the arbitration clause is included in the contract depends upon whether it is *material.* Since the clause probably is material, the terms of the contract are the original offer. Under the CISG, by contrast, no contract is formed because the arbitration clause relates to dispute resolution and therefore is material.[33]

Courts have applied the CISG rule in two different manners.[34] Under

---

[29] U.C.C. § 2-207.

[30] CISG Art. 19.

[31] *See generally*, Gabriel, *The Battle of the Forms: A Comparison of the United Nations Convention for the Sale of Goods and the Uniform Commercial Code*, 49 Bus. Lawyer 1053 (1994).

[32] CISG Art. 19(3).

[33] *See* McMahon, *When the U.N. Sales Convention Applies and Some of the Reasons Why it Matters to You and Your Clients* (Presentation to Mecklenburg County Bar, International Sales CLE, 1996).

[34] DiMatteo, et al, *The Interpretive Turn In International Sales Law: An Analysis Of Fifteen Years Of Cisg Jurisprudence*, 24 Nw J Intl L & Bus 299 (Winter 2004).

the so-called "knock out" approach, a valid contract is deemed formed if the parties agreed to the essential terms such as identity, quantity and price of the goods *and* commenced performance, but the conflicting terms are ignored (knocked-out). The contract is deemed valid even if the conflicting terms are material because the parties' performance indicates their intent to form a contract. Under the so-called "second shot" approach, the terms including in the acceptance to the offer control the contract. The offeror's failure to object to the conflicting terms is deemed an implied consent to their inclusion in the contract.[35]

[e] Statute of Frauds and Parol Evidence

The CISG does not include statute of frauds or parol evidence provisions. This reflects the civil law tradition that does not require a writing to enforce a contract. Under the CISG, a contract need not be in writing and any evidence may be admitted that bears on the issue of contract formation, including witnesses.[36]

> → By contrast, the UCC requires a sale of goods for $500 or more be evidenced by a writing signed by the party against whom it will be enforced.[37] Between *merchants*, a written confirmation of a contract is binding on the sender if the recipient does not object in writing within ten days.[38]

A country may opt out of the oral agreement and evidence provisions if its domestic law requires written sales contracts.[39] China, the Russian Federation and Argentina have done so. The U.S., however, has not, meaning that U.S. parties to a contract governed by the CISG cannot rely on these affirmative defenses.

With respect to parol evidence, the CISG permits evidence to be presented about any relevant statement made in negotiations prior to the signing of the contract. This may include pre-contract letters, proposals, or letters of intent. However, the parties may agree by contract that all modifications to their written agreement must be in writing.[40]

> → Under the UCC, a written agreement cannot be contradicted by evidence of a prior agreement or a contemporaneous oral agreement.[41]

---

[35] *See e.g., Filanto v. Chilewich*, 789 F Supp 1229 (S.D.N.Y. 1992) (dealings followed by silence and obtaining letter of credit constitute acceptance of agreement with arbitration clause).

[36] CISG Art. 11.

[37] U.C.C. § 2-201(1).

[38] U.C.C. § 2-201(2).

[39] CISG Arts.12, 96.

[40] CISG Art. 29.

[41] U.C.C. § 2-202.

[f] Assurances of Performance

The common law doctrine of *anticipatory repudiation* allowed a party to terminate a contract if the other party unequivocally expressed its intent not to perform, or the circumstances indicated that nonperformance was nearly certain. However, the terminating party was liable for breach of contract if its grounds for repudiation subsequently proved unreasonable. Thus, a party who became uneasy about the other party's ability or willingness to perform a contract could not readily make other arrangements even though the anticipated breach would cause serious financial loss.

→   The UCC resolves this issue by allowing a party to demand adequate assurance of due performance and to suspend its own performance until the assurance is received.[42] The demand can be made if, applying commercial standards, reasonable grounds for insecurity arise about the other party's performance. A party that does not provide adequate assurance of performance is deemed to repudiate the contract.[43]

Under the CISG, a party may suspend its performance if it is apparent that the other party will not perform a substantial part of its obligations.[44] This standard is more stringent than the UCC, requiring objective grounds that show a high probability of non-performance.[45] Moreover, a party may suspend its performance only if the basis for the insecurity arises after the contract is made. The suspending party must continue its performance once adequate assurance is provided.

Unlike the UCC, the CISG does not consider a failure to provide assurances of performance as a repudiation of the contract[46] Thus, reasonable insecurity about the other party's performance is not, in itself, a ground for *avoiding* a contract. A contract may be avoided under the CISG only if it is clear that the other party's action will create a *fundamental breach*.[47] This position is similar to the common law.

[g] Buyer's and Seller's Obligations and Remedies

A properly drawn sales contract will contain provisions governing when, where, and how the seller must perform its obligations to deliver the goods, provide requisite documents, and transfer title. It also will specify the buyer's obligations about payment and taking delivery. Thus, the CIGS rules relating to these issues should only apply in the unfortunate situations where the contract fails to adequately cover these matters.

---

[42] U.C.C. § 2-609.

[43] U.C.C. § 2-609(4).

[44] CISG Art. 71.

[45] Honnold, *Uniform Law for International Sales Under the 1980 United Nations Convention* 389 (2nd ed. 1991).

[46] CISG Art. 71.

[47] CISG Art. 71(1).

Generally, under the CISG the buyer must inspect the goods "within as short a period as is practicable" and notify the seller of the specific non-conformity within a reasonable time after the problem is, or should be, discovered, but no later than two years from the date the goods were handed over to the buyer (unless the contract provides otherwise). [48] A buyer that does not comply with these inspection and notice provisions may not raise the defense of non-conformity against the seller. However, the buyer may reduce its payment to the seller or claim damages (except lost profits) if a "reasonable excuse" exists for not providing the required notice. [49] The buyer also must take reasonable steps to preserve the non-conforming goods for the seller's benefit. [50]

Generally, under the CISG the seller must deliver goods of the quantity, quality, description and packaging set forth in the contract. [51] The goods must be free from any right or claim of a third party, including intellectual or industrial property rights. [52] If the contract requires delivery to a carrier, the seller must hand the goods over to the first carrier. [53] Where the contract does not require delivery to a carrier, the goods must be placed at the buyer's disposal at the place where the goods are known to be manufactured or warehoused or at the sellers place of business. [54] If the seller must deliver the goods or arrange for shipment by a carrier, its obligations are defined by the contract. [55] A seller must take reasonable steps to preserve the goods for the benefit of a buyer who delays taking delivery (as by nonpayment). [56]

Warranties. A seller's obligation to deliver goods is subject to any warranties expressed in the contract or implied by the CISG. [57] Under the CISG implied warranty, goods must be "fit for the purposes for which goods of the same description would ordinarily be used." They must fit the buyer's special purpose if expressly or impliedly made known to the seller when the contract is made. Unless otherwise agreed, the goods must be packaged in the usual manner for such goods or in a manner adequate to preserve and protect them. Implied warranties do not apply if the buyer did not rely on the seller's skill or judgment or if it would be unreasonable for the buyer to do so.

Third-party claims. Generally, a seller must deliver goods free from any third party rights or claims unless the buyer agreed to take the goods

---

[48] CISG Art. 39(2).

[49] CISG Art. 44.

[50] CISG Art. 86(1).

[51] CISG Art. 41.

[52] CISG Art. 42.

[53] CISG Arts 30–34.

[54] CISG Arts 31.

[55] The obligations regarding terms of carriage usually are set forth by Incoterms as described in §4.02.

[56] CISG Art. 85.

[57] CISG Art. 35.

subject to such claims.[58] A special rule applies third party industrial or intellectual property rights or claims. In such cases, the seller must deliver the goods free of claims that the seller knew or could not have been unaware of at the time the contract was concluded.[59] The third party claim must be based upon the law of the country where the buyer has its place of business or where the parties contemplated that the goods will be resold or used. Generally, the buyer must notify the seller of the right or claim within a reasonable time after he is or should be aware of it.

Remedies. It is important to note that some remedies are allowed under the CIGS only in the case of a *fundamental breach*. This occurs if the detriment to the aggrieved party substantially deprives him of what he is entitled to expect from the contract, unless the result was not foreseen nor reasonably foreseeable by the party in breach.[60] For example, a buyer may not demand substitution of nonconforming goods unless the breach is fundamental.

> → This is a more stringent standard for revocation than under the UCC, which provides a *perfect tender rule* that allows a buyer to reject nonconforming goods without contention about the extent of the nonconformity.[61] Although a buyer may reject the goods and cancel a contract even for minor deficiencies, the UCC imposes an obligation of good faith in the performance or enforcement of a contract.[62]

The remedies for breach of contract are similar for buyer and seller. Generally, the aggrieved party may *require the other party to perform its obligations, claim damages* or *avoid* (cancel) the contract. In addition to damages, the buyer may reduce the price for nonconforming goods even though the price has already been paid.[63]

Demand Performance. Under the CISG, a buyer may demand performance of incomplete elements of a contract.[64] If the lack of conformity of goods constitutes as fundamental breach, the buyer may demand delivery of substitute goods upon notice within a reasonable time. However, this right to substitute goods may be limited by courts in countries that would not grant such specific performance under local law.[65] If reasonable, a buyer may require the seller to repair the lack of conformity.

Additional Time. A buyer may set a reasonable additional time period for the seller to perform its contractual obligations.[66] By setting such a

[58] CISG Art. 41.
[59] CISG Art. 42.
[60] CISG Art. 25.
[61] UCC 2-601.
[62] UCC § 1-203.
[63] CISG Art. 50.
[64] CISG Art. 46.
[65] CISG Art. 28.
[66] CISG Art. 47.

period, that the buyer may overcome the presumption that delayed performance generally is not a fundamental breach. During that period specified,
the buyer may not use other remedies unless notified that the seller will
not perform.

Similarly, a seller may cure a non-conformity after the delivery date if
done without unreasonable delay or inconvenience to the buyer.[67] The seller
must notify the buyer about the late delivery and the buyer must then notify
the seller if he will accept late delivery. If the buyer does not respond, the
seller obtains an automatic time extension.

Avoid Contract. A contract may not be avoided under the CISG unless
a fundamental breach occurs. The less restrictive CISG rules take into
account the international setting of the sale, where rejection of goods with
a minor defect can impose a substantial loss on a seller thousands of miles
away. If a seller fails to deliver within the contract period, the buyer may
fix a reasonable additional time for performance and avoid the contract if
that date is not met.[68]

A buyer's right to avoid a contract changes, however, if the goods are in
fact delivered. If delivery is late, the buyer must declare the contract void
within a reasonable time after it becomes aware of the late delivery.[69] If
the goods are otherwise nonconforming, the buyer must avoid the contract
within a reasonable time after it knew or should have known of the breach
or after the seller has failed to cure the breach as provided by the CISG.

Price Reduction. A buyer may reduce the price of nonconforming goods
even if the price has already been paid.[70] The buyer must disclose the
reduction, but is not precluded from claiming damages attributable to the
nonconformity. The amount of price reduction is computed in the proportion
that the value of the goods delivered bears to the value the conforming goods
would have had. The price reduction rule does not apply to conforming
goods, even if the delivery is late.

→   The UCC rule differs somewhat, providing that a buyer who gives
    notice may deduct its damages from any portion of the unpaid
    amount.[71] This right to *setoff* damages may not be a meaningful
    remedy to a buyer that has paid for the goods, as is typically the
    case.

The CISG does not contain a statute of limitations. However, *the Convention on the Limitation Period in the International Sale of Goods,* provides
a four year limitation period.[72] This rule is similar to the period provided
by the UCC.[73]

---

[67] CISG Art. 48.

[68] CISG Arts. 49(1)(b), 47.

[69] CISG Art. 49(2).

[70] CISG Art. 50.

[71] UCC 2-717.

[72] The U.S. became a party to this treaty in 1994.

[73] UCC 2-725.

[h] Seller's Right to Cure

Under the CISG, a seller has fairly wide latitude to cure a defective delivery of documents or goods that occurs before performance is due. The seller may remedy a tender of defective documents up to the time fixed for handing them over, if the buyer is not subjected to unreasonable inconvenience or expense.[74] Similarly, a seller that delivers non-conforming goods before the contractual delivery date may replace the goods or remedy the nonconformity up to the delivery date if the buyer is not caused unreasonable inconvenience or expense.[75]

After the contractual delivery date, a seller may remedy a failure to deliver goods on time if it can do so without unreasonable delay and without causing the buyer unreasonable inconvenience or uncertainty about reimbursement of expenses it advanced.[76] The seller must ask the buyer whether it will accept delivery within a specified time and the buyer must respond to that question within a reasonable time. A buyer who does not respond to a seller's notice of late delivery is in breach of contract if it refuses to accept delivery.[77]

> →   The UCC provides a more limited right to cure. If a seller makes a nonconforming delivery that the buyer rejects before the contractual delivery date, the seller can make a conforming delivery before that time.[78] The seller may cure within a reasonable time beyond the contractual delivery time if it had reasonable grounds to believe that the buyer would accept a nonconforming delivery. In other situations, however, late delivery is not a curable breach.

[i] Risk of Loss

International sales contracts should contain terms governing the time that the risk of loss or damage to goods passes from the seller to the buyer. (See discussion of Incoterms, below.) In the absence of such terms, the CISG provides a general rule that risk passes to the buyer at the earlier of the time he takes over the goods or the time that he breaches the contract by failing to take delivery when the goods are placed at his disposal. Special rules apply when a contract involves carriage of the goods or when the goods are sold in transit. Both parties must preserve and account for any goods in their possession belonging to the other party.

[j] *Force Majeure*

Under the CISG, a party may be exempt from paying damages if its failure to perform is due to an impediment beyond his control that he could

---

[74] CISG Art. 34.

[75] CISG Art. 37.

[76] CISG Art. 48.

[77] CISG Art. 48(3).

[78] U.C.C. § 2-508(1).

not reasonably take into account when the contract was concluded and that he could not have avoided or overcome.[79] This exemption can apply if the failure is attributable to a third person engaged to perform all or part of the contract. In effect, the CISG shields a seller from damages if it cannot perform because a third party, such as a supplier or carrier, failed to perform.[80] Although the seller is not liable for damages, the buyer may avoid the contract or seek to reduce the price for the goods.[81] The party whose performance is affected by the unforeseeable force must notify the other party or remain liable for damages.[82]

→ Under the UCC, by contrast, a seller may be liable for breach of contact damages even though its failure to perform is due to an unforeseeable interruption in its source of supply, caused by factors such as a casualty, fire, or delay by the carrier of the goods.[83] Nonperformance may be excused, however, if the seller relied upon an exclusive source of supply and used due diligence to ensure that the source did not fail. These UCC provisions mirror the common law rule. Many contracts override these rules through a *force majeure* clause that relieves a party whose failure to perform is attributable to unexpected events beyond its control.

Note on *force majeure*. Under the UNIDROIT model code for international commercial transactions *force majeure* is defined as an impediment so severe as to justify a party's nonperformance. In that case, a *hardship* exemption to contractual performance may apply. Hardship exists "where the occurrence of events fundamentally alters the equilibrium of the contract either because the cost of a party's performance has increased or because the value of the performance received has diminished" and the events occur or become known to the disadvantaged party after the conclusion of the contract, the disadvantaged party could not reasonably have been taken the events into account when the contract was concluded, the events are beyond the disadvantaged party's control, and the risk of the events was not assumed by the disadvantaged party.

---

§ 4.02 Incoterms

A contract for the sale of goods should set forth and describe the parties rights and obligations regarding delivery of the goods, covering matters such as the place, method, insurance and risk associated with carriage.

---

[79] *See* CISG Art. 6.2.2.

[80] CISG Art. 79.

[81] *See* CISG Art. 50.

[82] CISG Art. 79(4).

[83] U.C.C. §§ 2-613 through 2-616.

Merchants have long used abbreviated trade terms such as FOB (Free on Board) or CIF (Cost, Insurance and Freight) as a convenient way to express detailed provisions related to delivery. Because countries often define trade terms differently, contracts should specify the terms or incorporate terms from a published set of rules that defines the principal trade terms.

Although definitions of some trade terms are found in the UCC, these statutory terms are somewhat obsolete and are infrequently applied in international transactions.[84] The most widely-used international trade terms are the *Incoterms* published by the International Chamber of Commerce (ICC). Incoterms provide a uniform set rules and definitions for common abbreviated contract provisions related to transportation of goods under a contract of sale. The Incoterms were first published in 1936 and are periodically revised and republished to reflect recent developments. The most recent revision is Incoterms 2000.[85]

Incoterms are not implied in a contract for the sale of goods, but must be specifically included. For example, a contract may provide the delivery term as "C.I.F. (Incoterms, 2000)." This specificity avoids having the desired Incoterm confused with a similar UCC term that has a different meaning.

Incoterms may be included in a contract to indicate transport terms such as:

- the method of transportation,
- who must pay the transportation costs,
- when and where delivery will occur,
- who bears the risk of loss during each phase of carriage,
- who must insure the goods and pay the premiums,
- when is delivery deemed completed and what proof of delivery is required,
- what notice and documents must each party provide regarding transportation and delivery,
- which party must obtain licenses or satisfy other government regulations or formalities.

Incoterms generally do not to cover all elements of delivery required in a contract, so that other specific clauses are necessary to express the parties' intentions. For example, Incoterms do not describe how title to the goods will pass, nor provide remedies for breach of delivery terms. The terms apply only to sales of goods and not to contracts for services.

The Incoterms are classified into the following four groups by reference to the transport obligations each trade term imposes:

---

[84] *See* U.C.C. §§ 2-319-22.

[85] International Chamber of Commerce, Incoterms 2000 (ICC Pub. No. 560, 2000).

[1] Group E — Departure

Under the sole term in this category, the seller makes the goods available to the buyer at the seller's own premises.

[a] EXW (Ex Works, Factory, . . . [name of place])

This term imposes the minimum obligation on the seller. The seller must make the goods available at its premises, but need not load the goods on the buyer's vehicle unless so agreed. Title and risk pass to buyer, including the obligation to pay transportation and insurance costs from the seller's location. The buyer bears the costs and risk of collecting the goods and transporting them to their destination. This term may apply to any mode of transportation.

It is important to note that the buyer must obtain all documents and pay and arrange all customs clearances. Since the goods will be picked up in the seller's country, the buyer may find these arrangements quite difficult in practice.

> → Under the UCC term *ex ship,* the risk of loss passes when the goods "leave the ship's tackle or are otherwise properly unloaded."[86]

[2] Group F — Carriage Unpaid

Under the terms in this category, the seller delivers the goods to a carrier the buyer designates.

[a] FCA (Free Carrier . . . [name of place])

This term obligates the seller to deliver the goods to the custody of the buyer's designated carrier at the named place or to load the goods on the buyer's vehicle. It is useful for multi-modal transportation, such as containers, or rolling traffic onto trailers and ferries. It also permits the parties to divide the freight charges and other costs in a logical manner.

- Title to the goods, risk of loss, and transportation and insurance costs pass to the buyer when the seller delivers the goods to the carrier cleared for export. The *carrier* is any person that has made a contract of carriage by road, rail, air, sea, or a combination of methods. The seller meets its obligation by giving the buyer the bill of lading or other required document issued by the carrier. The carriage contract is made by the buyer. The seller must furnish required export licenses.

- Generally, the seller must bring its truck to the loading platform and place the goods at the importer's disposal at the truck's rear. The buyer bears the risk of unloading the goods from the seller's vehicle to the freight terminal. If the terms state *FCA Exporter's*

---

[86] *See* U.C.C. § 2-322(2)(b).

Place, the seller bears the risk and obligation of loading the goods onto the buyer's vehicle.

[b] FAS (Free Alongside Ship . . . [name of port of shipment])

This term is used for sea and inland water transport and requires the seller to deliver the goods alongside the ship on the dock. After that point, the buyer obtains title and bears all costs and risk of loss to the goods. The buyer must clear the goods for export and pay the cost of loading the goods.

→ The UCC uses a similar term, *FAS Vessel*, indicating that delivery will be on a dock the buyer designates.[87] The seller must provide the required documents, such as the bill of lading, and assist the buyer in obtaining export documents.[88]

[c] FOB (Free Onboard Ship . . . [name of port of shipment])

This term is used for sea and inland water transport and requires the seller to place the goods on board the ship at the shipment port designated in the contract. The seller pays the cost of loading the goods. The buyer pays the transportation costs and obtains title and bears risk of loss when the goods are off the dock and placed on the ship (*i.e.*, over the ship's rail).

→ This term is comparable to *FOB vessel* under the UCC.[89] In a contract governed by the UCC, omitting the word "vessel" may obligate the seller to ship to the designated FOB point. The UCC requires the Seller to furnish a negotiable bill of lading and bear the expense and risk of loading the goods onto the ship.

[3] Group C — Carriage Paid

Under the terms in this category, the seller contracts with the carrier, but does not bear additional costs or risk of loss for the goods for events that occur after the goods are shipped. Although the seller bears the cost of shipment, the buyer bears the risk of loss after the goods are handed over to the carrier.

[a] CFR (Cost & Freight . . . [name of destination port])

This term is used for sea and inland water transport and requires the seller to pay the transportation costs for shipping the goods to the named destination. The buyer obtains title and bears the risk of loss when the goods are off the dock and placed on the ship. The buyer pays for insurance and the cost of unloading the goods at the destination.

---

[87] U.C.C. § 2-319(1).

[88] *See* U.C.C. § 2-311.

[89] U.C.C. § 2-319(4).

[b] CIF (Cost, Insurance & Freight . . . [name of destination port])

This term is used for sea and inland water transport and imposes the same requirements as CFR except that the seller also must insure the goods against loss or damage and pay the required premium. The buyer obtains title and bears the risk of loss when the goods are off the dock and placed on the ship. The buyer should take care to ensure that the insurance coverage is adequate.

→ Under the UCC, the CIF terms obligates the seller to provide evidence that the goods have been received for shipment. Apparently, the risk of loss passes to the buyer when delivery is made to the carrier.[90] The UCC provides that an invoice is a required CIF document. The insurance provided must include terms that are current at the port of shipment and be for an amount equal to the value of the goods at the time and place of shipment.[91]

[c] CPT (Carriage Paid To . . . [name of destination])

This term is used for any mode of transportation including container or roll-on roll-off traffic by trailers and ferries. It requires the seller to pay the freight costs for shipping the goods to the named destination. The buyer must pay for insurance. The buyer bears the risk of loss to the goods after they are delivered to the custody of the carrier, as well as any additional costs attributable to events after delivery to the carrier. If more than one carrier is to be used, title and risk transfer to the buyer when the goods are in the custody of the first carrier. The seller must clear the goods for export.

[d] CIP (Carriage & Insurance Paid To . . . [name of destination])

This term is used for any mode of transportation and imposes the same requirements as CPT except that the seller also must insure the goods against loss or damage and pay the premium. The buyer obtains title and bears the risk of loss when the goods are delivered to the custody of the carrier. The buyer should take care to ensure that the insurance coverage is adequate.

[4] Group D — Arrival

Under the terms in this category, the seller bears all costs and risks associated with bringing the goods to the destination country.

---

[90] *See* U.C.C. § 2-302 Official Comment 1.

[91] U.C.C. § 2-302(2)(c).

[a] DAF (Deliver At Frontier . . . [name of place])

This term is used for any mode of transportation, but primarily for rail and truck. The seller must bear all costs and risks for delivering the goods to the designated border. The buyer obtains title and bears all costs and risks, including customs, duties, and clearance, after the goods are delivered to that point.

[b] DES (Delivered Ex Ship . . . [name of destination port])

This term is used for sea or inland water transport. The seller bears all costs and risks of bringing the goods to the designated port and making them available to the buyer on board the ship at that point. The buyer obtains title and bears the cost of unloading the goods, customs duties, and risk of loss after the seller delivers the goods on board the ship at the destination.

[c] DEQ (Delivered Ex Quay . . . [name of destination port])

This term is used for sea or inland water transportation. The seller bears the costs and risks of bringing the goods onto the quay or wharf, including unloading and customs clearance at the designated port, and making the goods available to the buyer at that point. The buyer obtains title and bears the risk of loss when the goods are delivered on the dock cleared of customs.

[d] DDU (Delivered Duty Unpaid . . . [name of destination])

This term is used for any transportation method. The seller bears all costs and risks of bringing the goods to the designated place, other than customs clearance, and making them available to the buyer at that point. The buyer obtains title and bears the risk of loss after the seller delivers the goods to the designated point and must clear the goods through customs.

[e] DDP (Delivered Duty Paid . . . [name of destination])

This term imposes the maximum obligation upon the seller. It may be used for any transportation method. Ordinarily, the named destination is the buyer's premises. The seller bears all costs and risks until the goods are delivered to the designated place, clear of customs. The parties can shift specified costs to the buyer through additional terms such as *delivered duty paid exclusive of VAT*. Buyer obtains title and bears the risk of loss after the seller delivers the goods to the designated point cleared for import.

§ 4.03 Dispute Resolution

[1] In General

Although most international contracts are performed with no, or few, disagreements, disputes are not uncommon and parties should plan how they will be resolved. The basic issues to be addressed are where the controversy will be decided and who will render the decision. These two choices will determine whether the common, civil, or other law will govern the parties rights, whether the issues will be decided by a judge, jury, or third party, and what procedural rules will apply.

Because these issues are so important, international contracts often include clauses governing the manner that disputes between the parties will be resolved. These commercial dispute resolution provisions generally take one of two forms: (1) *forum selection* clauses, or (2) *arbitration* agreements. A forum selection clause provides that the parties will litigate their dispute in the courts of a specified country. Usually, this means that the dispute will be governed by that country's substantive and procedural rules in proceedings conducted by its citizens. Under an arbitration clause, the parties select the third parties that will adjudicate their dispute as well as the applicable arbitration rules and procedures.

[2] Litigation and Forum Selection

Numerous factors must be considered in determining whether contract disputes should be resolved through litigation. These include:

- Which courts have jurisdiction over the issues involved?
- What rules of evidence and discovery apply in these courts?
- How long will the process take?
- How knowledgeable are the judges and local lawyers about the technical aspects of the dispute?
- What costs are involved, including lawyers, translators and court fees?
- Is a judgment of that court readily enforceable domestically and internationally?

A contract party is likely to believe that the most favorable forum for litigating a dispute is the court closest to its place of business. Presumably, the local court will prove more convenient and predictable. Obviously, these same reasons should make that choice of forum unacceptable to the other contract party. It is possible, and not uncommon, for the parties to choose the law and courts of a country where neither is a resident.

The forum selection clause may be *exclusive* or *non-exclusive*. Under an exclusive clause, the dispute must be resolved in the specified forum. This is the typical choice, because it reduces the risk of being forced to litigate in an unanticipated forum. A non-exclusive clause allows the parties to litigate their dispute in the specified forum, but does not require them to do so. Thus, they also may bring the litigation in other courts that have jurisdiction over the parties and the dispute. This may be desirable if a party anticipates multi-venue litigation to pursue the other party's assets or to prevent it from improperly using intellectual property rights in many places. Examples of these forum selection clauses are:

- The courts of _____ shall have exclusive jurisdiction over all actions relating to this Agreement.

- The courts of _____ shall have nonexclusive jurisdiction over all disputes relating to this Agreement.

[3] Alternate Dispute Resolution

Although litigation is always an option, international lawsuits can be time-consuming, expensive and very uncertain. Moreover, residents of the many countries where litigation is far less common than in the U.S. may not be amenable to that form of dispute resolution. With increasing frequency, international contract disputes are being resolved through various alternate dispute resolution (ADR) methods, including *mediation* and *arbitration*.

[a] International Commercial Mediation

Mediation usually involves voluntary negotiations between the contract parties that are facilitated by a neutral third party. The process is non-binding, so that the parties actually settle their own disagreement with the assistance of a mediator who helps them identify the important issues and communicate effectively. This method is often adopted by parties who expect to have a continuing relationship. The goal is to resolve the dispute constructively, with both parties making compromises that will allow them to work together in the future. Generally, the mediation process is informal and relatively fast and inexpensive. Because there is no public record, all negotiations and outcomes are confidential.

Parties who choose to mediate their dispute begin by selecting the mediator. They may be assisted in this choice by national or international mediation organizations or by the recommendation of the court where they intend to litigate. After meeting with the parties, both separately and together, the mediator may recommend various ways to resolve their disagreement. If the parties do not voluntarily accept these recommendations or reach their own solution, the mediation terminates unsuccessfully and the parties are free to seek other remedies.

The parties may provide for mediation of future disputes by inserting a clause similar to the following into their contract:

The parties agree that they will endeavor to settle any dispute, controversy or claim arising out of or relating to this contract, which they are unable to settle through direct discussions, by mediation administered by _____ *before resorting to arbitration, litigation or other dispute resolution procedure. The requirement of filing a notice of claim with respect to the dispute submitted to mediation shall be suspended until the conclusion of the mediation process.*

[b] International Commercial Arbitration

Arbitration is a method of alternate dispute resolution in which the parties agree to abide by the decision of neutral third parties called arbitrators. The arbitrators adjudicate the dispute based upon the evidence presented by the parties and pursuant to the applicable arbitration rules. In many cases, these rules and the method for selecting the arbitrators are set forth in the parties' original contract.

Although arbitration proceedings usually are less formal than litigation, they are conducted under comprehensive rules that address the parties' basic concerns, including the selection and powers of the arbitrators, applicable law, rules of evidence, confidentiality, and the extent to which the decision is binding. Arbitration proceedings may be *ad hoc* or *institutional.* Ad hoc arbitration is not conducted under the auspices or rules of any particular arbitration institution and the parties agree among themselves about the procedural rules and selection of arbitrators. Under *institutional arbitration*, the parties agree to resolve their dispute through an established arbitration institution that will administer the proceeding under its own rules.

Ad hoc arbitration allows the parties to set-up their own proceedings in a neutral setting, at an agreed location, and in a manner that suits their particular requirements. It also may reduce costs and accelerate the dispute resolution process. The parties may appoint one mutually agreed arbitrator, or usually, use three arbitrators; one chosen by each party and the third chosen by those two arbitrators. The parties may agree to ad hoc arbitration in their contract or after their disagreement occurs.

When choosing ad hoc arbitration, parties should specify in the arbitration clause all aspects of the arbitration, including applicable law, rules under which the arbitration will be conducted, number of arbitrators, method for selecting the arbitrators, language for the proceeding and place of arbitration. Parties may either develop their own rules or select established arbitration rules to govern the arbitration. Parties may use the rules of an arbitration institution without submitting the dispute to that institution. When technical information is involved, arbitrators with a specialized background may be selected. Quite often the arbitration rules are derived from the Model Rules issued by the *United Nations Commission on International Trade Law* (UNCITRAL).

Institutional arbitration allows the parties to utilize the rules and procedures that many institutions have established to assist parties with dispute resolution. Prominent international arbitration institutions include the International Chamber of Commerce (ICC), the London Court of

International Arbitration, and the American Arbitration Association. Many arbitration organizations specialize in disputes involving particular regions, such as the Commercial Arbitration and Mediation Center for the Americas (CAMCA), or economic sectors, such as the International Center for the Settlement of Financial Disputes (ISCID) or the World Intellectual Property Organization (WIPO).

The advantages of institutional arbitration include administrative assistance and support services in conducting the proceedings, lists of experienced arbitrators with special expertise and an established, workable format. However, the costs for the services and support may be high and the bureaucratic nature of some organizations may cause unwanted delays.

Arbitration is an effective method for resolving international commercial disputes only if the arbitral decision will be recognized and enforced by a court if a party does not satisfy the award. Accordingly, contracting parties should determine whether the country where a potential award must be enforced (typically the losing party's country) has an effective legal structure and has signed a treaty obligating it to enforce arbitral awards.

[c]　Arbitration Treaties

The New York Convention. The use of arbitration has grown enormously in recent years, facilitated by many treaties and conventions that have created a predictable legal environment for settling international commercial disputes. The most important arbitration treaty is the *United Nations Convention on the Recognition and Enforcement of Foreign Arbitral Awards of 1958*[92] (New York Convention), which has been signed by more than 120 countries. Pursuant to the New York Convention, local courts will recognize and enforce contractual agreements to arbitrate disputes as well as the arbitration awards that result from the process. A party seeking enforcement must provide the local court with an authenticated original or certified copy of the award and the original or a certified copy of the arbitration agreement. U.S. Courts will enforce an arbitral award only if it is commercial in nature and was rendered in a country that is a party to the New York Convention.

The Convention permits a national court to refuse to enforce arbitration awards on the following grounds:

- The agreement to arbitrate is invalid under the law applicable to a party.
- Proper notice of the arbitration proceeding or the appointments of the arbitrators was not provided.
- The tribunal did not restrict itself to agreed issues.
- The composition of the tribunal contradicts the arbitration agreement or applicable law.

---

[92] 21 U.S.T. 2517, T.I.A.S. No. 6997.

- The arbitration award is not a final award under applicable law.
- The arbitration award is contrary to the public policy of the country where enforcement is sought.

The ICSID Convention. A number of legal and enforcement issues arise when a private party engages in a contract with the governmental of the country where the contract is to be performed. In such cases, the contract should require the contracting government to resolve disputes through arbitration procedures in which it cannot use its state power to unilaterally affect the parties' rights and duties. The government also should explicitly waive its sovereign immunity against enforcement and execution of any award and agree that an unsatisfied award may be enforced against it in the courts of any nation.

The *International Convention for the Settlement of Investment Disputes* (ICSID) was established in 1966 to provide a neutral forum for resolving investment-related disputes between private investors and States that are parties to the Convention.[93] The Convention seeks to facilitate investment in developing countries by reducing concerns that local governments will assert sovereign immunity or similar defenses to avoid liability in disputes. A country that ratifies the Convention must enforce an ICSID award as a final judgment of of its courts. Although ICSID is an autonomous international organization, it is closely linked to the World Bank.

Generally, ICSID jurisdiction extends to investment disputes between a contracting State and a national of another contracting State. In 1978, ICSID adopted *Additional Facility Rules* that expanded its jurisdiction to include disputes involving only one ISCID signatory State or national and to certain non-investment disputes. Under the Additional Facility rules, the arbitration must be conducted in countries that are party to the New York Convention.

Although ICSID arbitrations were infrequent for many years after the Treaty's inception, the number of cases has greatly increased during the past ten years. More than 150 countries are now contracting states or signatories. Quite importantly, ICSID expressly applies to disputes between a signatory state to the North American Free Trade Agreement (NAFTA) and a citizen of a NAFTA country. ISCID jurisdication also extends to signatories of the Cartagena Free Trade Agreement and the Colonia Investment Protocol of Mercosur. Similarly, more than 900 bilateral investment treaties (BIT) specifically refer to resolution of investment disputes through ICSID arbitration.

The Panama Convention. Another recent treaty, the Inter-American Convention on International Commercial Arbitration (Panama Convention),[94] provides default arbitration procedures for commercial disputes involving members of the Organization of American States (including the U.S.). These rules apply to an arbitration unless the parties expressly agree

---

[93] 17 U.S.T. 1270.
[94] 104 Stat. 449, 42 O.A.S.T.S. 1.

to use other rules. The Panama Convention also provides for reciprocal recognition and enforcement of international commercial arbitration agreements and awards.

[d] Arbitration Clause

Many international contracts contain clauses requiring the parties to resolve commercial disputes through arbitration. Obviously, parties can agree to arbitrate a dispute after it arises even though not obligated by contract. However, to avoid disputes about resolving disputes, it is best to include the arbitration provision in the initial agreement.

To ensure a successful arbitration, parties should draft an arbitration clause that applies to and meets the needs of their specific contract. In ad hoc arbitration, all aspects of the arbitration should be specified in the arbitration agreement. The agreement should address the following issues:

- Scope of the issues subject to arbitration.
- Selection process for arbitrators.
- Choice of substantive and procedural law that will apply to the arbitration. If no choice is expressed, the law of the place of the arbitration applies.
- Location of arbitration. The location may affect the enforceability of any award as well as practical matters such as ease of travel, availability of documents and witnesses, etc.
- Language used in the arbitration proceedings and rights to interpretations.
- Procedures for initiating arbitration.
- Allocation of costs among parties.
- Procedures for enforcement of any award and currency for payment.

Parties to ad hoc arbitration may use the rules of an arbitration institution without submitting the dispute to that institution. The institutions and rules include:

- Arbitration Rules of the United Nations Commission on International Trade Law (UNCITRAL)
- American Arbitration Association International Arbitration Rules
- International Chamber of Commerce Rules of Conciliation and Arbitration

If institutional arbitration will be used, the institution provides the arbitral rules and administers the proceedings. In that case, some acceptable contract arbitration clauses are:

- For ICC Arbitration:

All disputes arising out of or in connection with the present contract shall be finally settle under the Rules of Arbitration of the International Chamber of Commerce by one or more arbitrators appointed in accordance with the said Rules.

- For UNCITRAL Arbitration:

Any dispute, controversy or claim arising out of or relating to this contract, or the breach, termination or invalidity thereof, shall be settled by arbitration in accordance with the UNCITRAL Arbitration Rules as at present in force.

Parties may wish to consider adding:

- *The appointing authority shall be . . . (name of institution or person).*
- *The number of arbitrators shall be . . . (one or three).*
- *The place of arbitration shall be . . . (town or country).*
- *The language (s) to be used in the arbitral proceedings shall be. . . .*

[e] Advantages and Disadvantages of Arbitration

Advantages of arbitration include:

- *Uniform, simpler, faster procedures.* When arbitration is conducted through, or under the rules of, an international arbitration organization, both parties may be equally familiar with the procedures. By contrast, knowledge of local litigation procedures affords one party a significant advantage when a dispute is litigated in its home country. Generally, arbitration procedures are faster and far less complex and than the civil procedures of most nations.
- *Arbitral expertise.* Parties to dispute may choose arbitrators with technical backgrounds who understand the specific issues in the case;
- *Elimination of national bias.* Whether or not justified, a party is likely to have misgivings about the impartiality of a tribunal in the opposing party's country. A related problem is that local judges are likely to know and favor their own national laws and may be disinclined to base their decisions international rules and commercial practices. Arbitration generally provides nonaligned adjudicators and the procedures may be conducted in a neutral country.
- *Elimination of jurisdictional issues.* An arbitration clause conclusively establishes the forum in which a dispute will be resolved. If this issue is left open, a great deal of time and money may be expended to determine the jurisdiction to which the underlying dispute will be brought.

- *Enforcement of judgment.* Enforcing the judgment of a foreign court in the opposing party's country can be time-consuming, expensive, and perhaps futile. By contrast, many countries have signed the New York Convention, which makes the enforcement of an arbitration award easier and more certain than enforcing a judgment issued by another nation's court.

- *Confidentiality.* Ordinarily, arbitration proceedings and awards are confidential. This protects business secrets and may facilitate settlement by reducing publicity.

- *International Acceptance.* Most countries recognize and understand arbitration as an accepted form of dispute resolution. Many countries, including Russia, China, Japan and most Latin American nations prefer and utilize arbitration as the principal method for resolving international disputes.

- *Shorter duration.* Arbitration often produces a faster decision litigation.

- *Less adversarial.* Arbitration is often less adversarial, allowing long-term business relationships to continue despite a dispute.

Some disadvantages of arbitration include:

- *High Costs.* The costs of conducting an international arbitration are considerable. Actually, with the legal fees, administration costs and arbitration fees, an arbitration can be more expensive than a lawsuit!

- *Limited Judicial Review.* Judicial review of arbitration proceedings and awards often are limited to procedural issues and do not focus on the merits of the case. Because most countries will enforce an arbitration award, a party seeking review may have to do so separately in every country where it has assets. Many arbitration agreements call for binding arbitration, which significantly limits appeal rights. A party seeking to appeal a binding arbitration decision bears a high burden of proof, often requiring a showing of bad faith or abuse of authority by the arbitrator.

- *Limited Discovery.* A party requiring information or documents from the other party to prove its case may find that its discovery rights are far more restricted than in a comparable U.S. lawsuit. The parties must often rely on evidence in their possession when the arbitration begins. Of course, many foreign courts also impose limited discovery rules.

§ 4.04 Transport Documents

An international import or export transaction, which includes delivery of the goods to the carrier, shipping, delivery, and payment, requires preparation of a number of documents. The kind of documents needed will depend upon the nature of the goods, the method of shipping, and the manner of payment involved. The following discussion describes the various documents that may be utilized in an international sale of goods, and summarizes their legal effect.

[1] Bill of Lading

When goods are shipped by sea, the shipper (usually the seller or exporter) packs and delivers the goods to the vessel. After the goods are loaded on board and inspected, the ship's owner, captain, or agent prepares and signs a *bill of lading* and gives it to the shipper. The bill of lading is a document that lists the goods that are being shipped, describes the carrier's contractual obligation to transport the goods in exchange for payment of the freight charge, and sets forth the carrier's commitment to deliver the goods at the destination port. Thus, the bill of lading serves as a receipt for the goods and as a contract for transport and delivery.

A *nonnegotiable bill of lading* (formerly known as a *straight bill of lading*) states that the shipper will carry the goods to their destination and deliver them to a specified person or *consignee*.[95] The document is marked as *nonnegotiable*, meaning that it cannot transfer title or any rights to the goods by endorsement or delivery to another person. The named consignee does not need the document to obtain the goods, but may claim them after showing proper identification. Because the buyer can obtain the goods without evidence of payment, the nonnegotiable document is used when the goods are shipped prepaid or on an open account.

A *sea waybill* is a transport document that is similar to a nonnegotiable bill of lading. For air shipments, the document is called an *air waybill*. The consignee does not need the document to take delivery of the goods, but must only identify himself at the destination. The waybill is marked nonnegotiable, and serves as a receipt and contract of carriage for the goods delivered to the carrier. Sea (or air) waybills often are used for containerized shipments or other fast transport methods that may result in the cargo arriving before the documents. If banking documents or other proof of payment is not required, such as for shipments to related companies or long-standing customers, waybills allow the goods to be picked up without the delays that may be associated with negotiable bills of lading.

A *negotiable bill of lading* (or *order* bill of lading) is a document that confers title to the goods to the order of a specified person.[96] Ordinarily, that person is the shipper, but it may be the importer or a bank that is operating on behalf of one of the parties. The person named on the bill of lading may transfer title to the goods (*i.e.*, negotiate the bill) by endorsing the document and giving it to the endorsee, who becomes a *holder*. If the endorsement is in *blank*, the goods belong to the person in possession of the bill of lading. Because it is negotiable, the bill of lading, and title to the goods, may be transferred while they are still in transit. The bill of

---

[95] *See* 49 U.S.C. § 80103(b).

[96] 49 U.S.C. § 80103(a).

lading eventually must be given to the buyer to take delivery of the goods at their destination.

Generally, the buyer does not get the bill of lading, and therefore cannot obtain the goods, until the seller has been paid or credit arrangements have been made. The negotiable bill of lading frequently is used in conjunction with a *letter of credit*, in which case the document is presented to the buyer's bank for payment before it is released to the buyer. The bill of lading and associated documents are often sent in advance of the goods by air or express mail. In many cases, the importer requires the bill of lading to clear the goods through customs, so that late arrival of the documents may result in unnecessary storage charges.

Other terminology may be used with respect to a bill of lading to note the condition of the goods when delivered to the carrier or the method of transport. A *clean bill of lading* indicates that the merchandise appeared to be in good condition when given to the carrier. A *claused bill of lading* indicates any specific issues concerning the quality or quantity of the goods. A *multi-modal bill of lading* (or *through bill of lading*) covers more than one means of transport for the goods, for example, goods that will be carried by truck, rail, and ship to the final destination.

[2] Other Documents

Documents other than a bill of lading that may be required or associated with an export include:

- **Commercial Invoice.** The is a key document issued by the seller that sets forth in detail the essential terms of the transaction. It provides the names and addresses of the parties; the quantity and description of the goods; the unit and total price, other charges, and total sale price; packing and shipping details; and the form of delivery and payment.

- **Shipper's Export Declaration.** The shipper provides this document to the government of the export country, specifying the type, quantity, origin, and value of the goods being exported. The declaration usually is a required document used by customs officials for assessing duties and statistical purposes.

- **Export License.** Whether a license is required depends upon the nature of the goods and the export and import countries involved. A license usually is required for exports of arms or dual use goods, national treasures, drugs and strategic commodities.

- **Cargo manifest or packing list.** These are not generally required, but are usual when the weights or contents of packing cases vary. The list also may provide the outside dimension of each case and the total cubic content and weight of the shipment. Shipping marks and numbers also are noted.

- **Insurance Certificate.** The certificate provides the type and amount of insurance covering the shipped goods. The commercial terms of the contract determine how much insurance is required and which party is responsible for obtaining and paying for the policy.

- **Certificate of Origin.** Many countries require all imports to be accompanied by a certificate of origin describing where the goods were produced. The origin is needed to determine whether the import is allowed and the appropriate duty that should be imposed. Generally, the certificate is prepared on a standard form that is certified by an appropriate authority.

- **Inspection Certificate.** These are often required for animal or plant products or other goods that must meet certain specifications. Ordinarily, the certificate is issued by a government or private testing organization.

- **Import License.** A country may require an import license if it restricts imports of the goods involved. Usually, the license is obtained by the foreign importer and sent to the exporter who may be required to have it certified by the local consul for the import country.

[3] Carrier's Liability Under the Carriage of Goods by Sea Act (COGSA)

In transport law, the term *carrier* refers to one in the business of transporting goods or passengers. A carrier's liability for loss of damage to goods in its possession is governed by two U.S. statutes. The *Harter Act*, applies to domestic shipping, such as coastal trade, and also may apply to a carrier's liability for goods before and after they are loaded.[97] The *Carriage of Goods by Sea Act* (COGSA) applies only to foreign trade and is incorporated into every bill of lading for a shipment to or from the U.S.[98]

Under COGSA, a shipowner cannot be relieved by contract of its duties to carefully put its vessel in good shape, or to take proper care of the goods it carries. The carrier's duties in this regard are to use due diligence to: (1) make the vessel seaworthy; (2) properly equip, supply, and man the vessel, and; (3) make the holds and other storage areas fit and safe for the reception, preservation, and carriage of the goods. Thus, the carrier may be liable for damage caused by negligence in loading, storing, and unloading cargo. The carrier has the burden of proof in showing due diligence was exercised.

If due diligence is exercised in these matters, the carrier is not liable for loss or damage arising from most other causes.[99] The exemption from liability extends to negligence by employees in management or navigation; the vessel's unseaworthiness; fire (unless the carrier's fault); perils of the sea;

---

[97] 46 U.S.Code app. § 190-196.

[98] 46 U.S.C. app. § 1300 *et seq.*

[99] COGSA, § 4(1).

acts of God, war, or public enemies; seizure under legal process; quarantine restrictions; strikes, lockouts, and work stoppages; and any other acts or omissions of the owner or shipper of the goods.[100]

The COGSA liability rules, enacted in 1936, are adopted from the *Hague Rules,* an international convention that was adopted by most larger trading nations.[101] To account for major changes in the shipping industry, particularly the wide-spread use of containers, the Hague Rules were amended by the *Visby Protocol*[102] in 1968, and the amended text is referred to as the *Hague-Visby Rules.* Although most of our major trading partners adopted the amended Hague/Visby text, the U.S. has not changed the original COGSA.

Another revision of the Hague rules, the *United Nations Convention on the Carriage of Goods by Sea,* was completed in 1978 and became effective in 1992.[103] This convention, known as the *Hamburg Rules,* has been adopted by a number of developing countries. It imposes somewhat greater liability on carriers than the Hague/Visby Rules.

The U.S. is unlikely to adopt the Hamburg rules and Congress is considering a new COGSA that would greatly change the responsibilities and liabilities of carriers.[104]

§ 4.05 Payment Methods

[1] In General

In a sales transactions, the seller risks not being paid for its goods, and the buyer risks not getting the goods paid for. These risks often increase in international transactions because the parties must exchange well known domestic business practices, laws and regulations for unfamiliar foreign kinds. The amount of risk a party bears often depends upon the payment method used, as different methods provide varying degrees of security for ensuring payment to a seller and delivery to a buyer.

Common international payment methods are described below.

[a] Cash in Advance

The best payment method for an export seller is to require payment before goods are shipped. The seller bears no credit risk and reduces the likelihood that the goods will be refused or returned as non-conforming. The buyer

---

[100] COGSA, §§ 4(2)a-p.

[101] The Hague rules were adopted at the International Convention for the Unification of Certain Rules of Law Relating to Bills of Lading, 51 Stat. 233, 120 L.N.T.S. 155.

[102] Protocol to Amend the International Convention for the Unification of Certain Rules of Law Relating to Bills of Lading, Signed at Brussels on 25th August 1924 (Feb. 23, 1968).

[103] The United Nations Convention on the Carriage of Goods by Sea, adopted at Hamburg on March 30, 1978 and in force as of November 1, 1992.

[104] The Carriage of Goods by Sea Act of 1999.

obtains the shipping documents quickly and can take possession of the goods immediately upon delivery. These terms may be used in a new business relationship, in relatively small transactions, or when the buyer has no choice but to pre-pay. The buyer should have confidence in the seller's ability to deliver, considering the economic and political conditions in the seller's country. Note that many import purchasers will not accept advance payment arrangements in a competitive market.

[b] Open Account

The buyer agrees to pay for the goods within a designated period (ordinarily 30, 60, or 90 days) after shipment or delivery. The buyer ships the goods, forwards the shipping documents to the buyer, and awaits payment under the credit terms provided. The seller should be confident that the buyer can and will pay for the goods, considering the economic and political conditions in the buyer's country. The seller incurs a loss if the buyer fails or delays payment or refuses the goods.

[c] Consignment

The seller retains title to the goods even after they have been delivered to the buyer. The seller does not receive payment until the buyer sells the goods to a third party. The seller may bear post-delivery costs, such as warehousing. The seller has a substantial risk of loss or nonpayment unless the consignment is made through a foreign branch or subsidiary. The buyer bears little risk.

[d] Documentary Collection — Document Against Payment

The seller ships the goods and sends the shipping documents to its bank (remitting bank) with instructions to forward them to a bank (collecting bank) near the buyer for collection. The collecting bank may not give the documents to the buyer until payment is made. The buyer is presented with the seller's Sight Draft, which must be paid before the documents are released. The buyer can then present the appropriate documents (usually a bill of lading) to the carrier for possession of the goods.

The seller risks non-payment by the buyer, which may force him to dispose of the goods at a loss. However, the seller retains title to the goods until payment is received and may seek any remedies available under contract law. The buyer risks receiving nonconforming goods unless he can inspect them before paying. If the buyer does not pay for some reason, its legal obligation is determined by contract law. Banks may facilitate, but do not guarantee payment.

Documentary collection terms are often used in continuing business relationships. Banks involved in documentary collections follow *the International Chamber of Commerce's Uniform Rules for Collections.*

[e] Documentary Collection — Trade Acceptance

A Trade Acceptance (or Document against Acceptance) is a form of documentary collection that allows the buyer to pay at a specified future date. The collecting bank releases the documents upon the buyer's acceptance — *i.e.*, the buyer signs a *time draft* promising to pay the amount of the draft at its maturity. The accepted draft is referred to as a *trade acceptance*, which is a negotiable instrument. The seller may be able to sell the trade acceptance to its bank or another party at a discounted price.

The seller risks nonpayment of the draft after he has given up title to the goods. Although the seller's accepted draft is an enforceable legal obligation, collection depends on the buyer's creditworthiness. The buyer acquires the goods before payment and bears little risk.

[f] Documentary Letter of Credit

A letter of credit is a bank's promise to pay a seller on behalf of the buyer when the seller satisfies all the conditions specified in the letter. The letter of credit is a separate contract that is independent from the underlying sales transaction. It establishes the bank's obligation to pay money to a specific person if and when specified documents are presented. The bank's obligation relates to the documents, rather than to the goods the documents refer to. The bank that issues the letter of credit (issuing bank) is liable for the payment, not the buyer. The letter of credit assures the seller that it will be paid after shipping its goods and the buyer is assured that payment will not occur until he receives the shipping documents required to obtain possession of the goods. Letters of credit are a common form of international payment because they provide security to both sellers and buyers.

Generally, a seller will obtain an irrevocable letter of credit, *i.e.*, one that cannot be amended or cancelled without the seller's permission. A seller dealing with an unknown bank, particularly in a foreign country, may wish to have the letter of credit confirmed by its own local bank (Confirming bank). In that case, the Confirming bank becomes obligated to pay the seller. A seller must be aware that the right to payment is conditioned on satisfying *all* the documentary requirements specified in the letter of credit — shipment of the goods is not sufficient.

By guaranteeing payment to the seller, a bank that issues a letter of credit assumes the risk of the buyer's creditworthiness. A local bank that confirms a letter of credit bears a risk of nonpayment by the issuing foreign bank. Accordingly, bank fees for certain documentary credits can be high, particularly if the letter of credit is irrevocable and confirmed. In many cases, the buyer and seller will adopt a less cumbersome and costly payment method after a stable business relationship is formed.

Although the letter of credit often is disparaged as a costly and slow payment method, it is effective in mitigating many substantial risks in international sales transactions. Because letters of credit continue to be so widely used in international transaction, they are discussed in detail in the next section.

[2] The Letter of Credit

Business operations usually involve some degree of risk, often arising from changes in the economic or political climate, contractual nonperformance, unreliable transportation, and lack of creditworthiness. International transactions increase the likelihood and severity of such risks because they also involve geographic distance, cultural misunderstanding, numerous intermediary parties, unfamiliar regulations and procedures, lengthy transportation times, and foreign political instability. The letter of credit is commonly used to reduce international risk, particularly in transactions that involve new relationships or unfamiliar countries. If the terms of the letter of credit are satisfied, the buyer is assured that he will receive the merchandise, and the seller is assured of payment for the goods he ships.

A letter of credit presented for immediate payment is accompanied by the seller's *sight draft,* which is paid as soon as the bank determines that the required documents are in order. If payment will occur at a later time, the seller presents a *time draft* which, after reviewing the documents, the bank accepts by its stamp and signature, and returns to the seller. The draft is now a *banker's acceptance* that carries the banks unconditional payment obligation. The seller can present it for payment at its maturity date or sell it at a discount in financial markets to obtain funds immediately.

Two basic types of letters of credit are discussed below. The *commercial* (or documentary) letter of credit is frequently used in international sales transactions as a method of payment for goods that have been shipped or delivered. Ordinarily the parties expect the letter of credit to be drawn upon. A *standby* letter of credit is used to assure payment or performance that is expected at some future time. The letter is drawn upon only if the expected payment or performance does not occur. Ordinarily the parties do not anticipate drawing upon the standby letter of credit.

The following terminology is used with respect to letters of credit:

- *Account party or Applicant*: The person for whose account the letter of credit is issued. Usually, this refers to the party who is purchasing the goods or services that are being paid for.

- *Beneficiary:* The party for whom the letter of credit is issued and who is entitled to payment under the terms of the letter of credit. Ordinarily, only the beneficiary may claim payment.

- *Issuer or issuing bank*: The bank or other person that issues the letter of credit for the account party. The issuer must honor a draft or payment demand if the stipulated documents are presented and the conditions of the letter of credit are satisfied.

- *Advising or notifying bank*: If the issuing bank is geographically distant from the beneficiary, the issuer may have a local corresponding bank advise the beneficiary about the letter of credit issuance and terms. The advising bank is not obligated to make any payments to the beneficiary, but does undertake to provide accurate information.

- *Confirming bank*: A confirming bank agrees to pay the beneficiary when the conditions in the letter of credit are satisfied, regardless of whether the issuing bank pays. A confirming bank has the same payment obligation to the beneficiary as the issuing bank. The confirming bank may seek reimbursement from the issuing bank. A seller may wish to have a local confirming bank engaged if the issuing bank is geographically distant or its creditworthiness is unknown. The beneficiary can then obtain or enforce payment locally.

- *Negotiating bank*: A bank that purchases drafts under a letter of credit (usually at a discounted value). Generally, the negotiating bank is local to the beneficiary, allowing the beneficiary to obtain local payment. The negotiating bank will pay the beneficiary when it determines that the documents are in order and then seek reimbursement from the issuing bank. The letter of credit must specify that it is a negotiation credit that allows the negotiating bank or another party to purchase the draft.

- *Paying or nominated bank*: A bank authorized in the letter of credit to make payment on presentation of drafts and documents specified in the letter of credit. The paying bank then obtains reimbursement from the issuing bank. Usually, the paying bank is local to the beneficiary. This transactions utilizes a negotiation letter of credit, which allows a third party to pay the beneficiary to take possession of the documents with the same rights that the beneficiary would have.

[a] Commercial Letter of Credit

A commercial letter of credit is a technique for ensuring that payment will be made upon the occurrence of specified events, such as shipment or delivery of goods. The following steps usually are involved in sales transactions using a letter of credit:

- The buyer and seller agree on the terms of a sale.

- The buyer arranges for its bank (Issuing bank) to issue a letter of credit that guarantees payment to the seller when a specified set of documents (typically a commercial invoice, bill of lading, insurance, and inspection certificates) are presented to the bank. The buyer may be required to secure the letter of credit with a bank account or other assets.

- The Issuing bank prepares an irrevocable letter of credit that includes instructions to the seller about the documents required for payment.

- The Issuing bank sends the letter of credit to a corresponding bank (Advising bank) in the seller's locale, and the Advising bank informs the seller of its issuance.

- If the letter of credit is to be confirmed, it is sent to a Confirming bank in the seller's locale. The seller may require that its own bank act as Confirming bank. The Confirming bank sends a letter of confirmation to the seller with the letter of credit.

- The seller then arranges for shipment of the goods and has the required shipping documents forwarded to the local Advising or Confirming bank, along with a draft for the agreed amount of payment.

- If the documents are in order and properly presented (*i.e.*, to the correct bank and before the letter's expiration date), the Advising or Confirming bank pays the draft.

- The documents are sent (by air or wire) to the Issuing bank, which collects payment from (or extends credit to) the buyer and gives it the documents needed to obtain possession of the goods.

By this method, the seller is assured of prompt payment before the buyer obtains title to the goods, and the buyer is assured by the documents that the goods have been inspected, insured, and shipped.

[b] Issuance of Letter of Credit

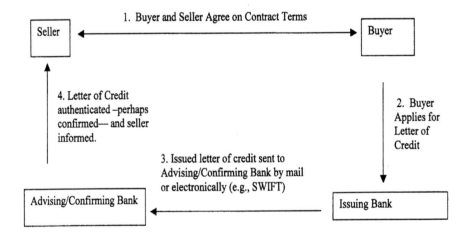

[c] Payment on Letter of Credit

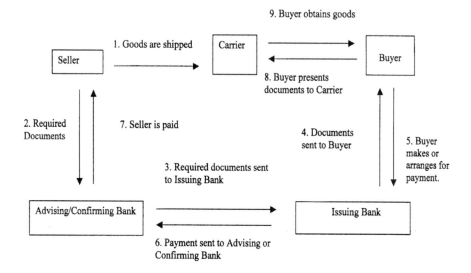

[d] Law Governing Commercial Letter of Credit

The law governing letters of credit generally derives from two sources: revised Article 5 of the *Uniform Commercial Code* (UCC),[105] which has been adopted by most states, and the *Uniform Customs and Practice for Documentary Credits* (UCP) issued by the International Chamber of Commerce.[106] Although the UCP is not truly a law, its provisions are internationally accepted and are binding when expressly incorporated into a letter of credit.

Principle of Independence. Transactions involving letters of credit have three parts:

1. The underlying business transaction for which the letter of credit is required, *i.e.*, the contract for goods or services that will be paid for in the future.

2. A transaction in which the party establishing the letter of credit (account party) agrees to pay or reimburse his bank (issuing bank) for issuing a letter of credit on his behalf.

---

[105] *See e.g.*, the Illinois statute at 810 ILCS 5/5-101, *et seq.* A United Nations Convention on Independent Guarantees and Standby Letters of Credit governs standby letters of credit and independent guarantees. A publication on International Standby Practices ("ISP98") published in 1998 by The Institute of International Banking Law & Practice and endorsed by the International Chamber of Commerce also applies to standby letters of credit.

[106] International Chamber of Commerce's ICC Uniform Customs and Practice for Documentary Credits (rev. 1993) (ICC Publication No. 500) (UCP).

3. The issuance of the letter of credit by which the issuing bank
    agrees to honor drafts for payment to the person designated in
    the letter (beneficiary) when all the terms and conditions of the
    letter of credit are satisfied.

Under the independence principle, each of these transactions is independent of the others, and the parties' rights and obligations in one transaction
are not affected by a breach or non-performance in another transaction.
Consequently, a bank is obligated to pay in accordance with the terms of
the letter of credit even if a dispute about the underlying sales contract
exists. These disputes are settled only after payment occurs. A bank must
disregard nondocumentary conditions in a letter of credit and will not
accept conditions requiring it to assess or certify goods.[107] These rules
reflect the underlying purpose of letters of credit — to protect the beneficiary from having to litigate for payment after he ships goods to a foreign
destination.[108]

[e] Drafting a Letter of Credit

A letter of credit is construed without reference to other documents.
Accordingly, the letter of credit should include all required terms and
conditions and not refer to or incorporate other documents by reference.
Express reference to the UCP is permitted, however, if the parties want
to be subject to its rules. All documents that the beneficiary must present
to receive payment must be clearly indicated.

A letter of credit should clearly state whether it is revocable or irrevocable. An irrevocable letter of credit cannot be modified or revoked without
the beneficiary's consent. Revocable letters of credit are not commonly used
because they may be revoked by the issuer without notice to the account
party or beneficiary. A letter of credit that does not expressly state that
it is revocable is deemed irrevocable.[109]

In many situations a seller may wish to have a letter of credit issued by
an unknown foreign bank confirmed by a known local bank. The issuing
bank requests confirmation by a bank in the seller's country through its
international network of corresponding banks. A confirmed letter of credit
gives the seller two guarantees of payment and provides a local site to
obtain immediate payment on his draft.

A letter of credit should clearly state its expiration date. After that date,
the issuer is not obligated to pay the beneficiary's drafts or payment

---

[107] U.C.C. § 5-108(g).

[108] UCP 500 art. 3; U.C.C. § 5-103(d). The UCC states the independence principle as follows:
Rights and obligations of an issuer to a beneficiary or a nominated person under a letter of
credit are independent of the existence, performance, or nonperformance of a contract or
arrangement out of which the letter of credit arises or which underlies it, including contracts
or arrangements between the issuer and the applicant and between the applicant and the
beneficiary. *See* Comment, *The Independence Rule in Standby Letters of Credit*, 52 U. Chi.
L. Rev. 218, 245 (1985).

[109] UCP Art. 6.c.; U.C.C. § 5-106(a).

demand. Absent a specified expiration date, a letter of credit expires one year after its issuance date.[110] A letter of credit that purports to be perpetual is deemed to expire five years after the issuance date.[111]

In planning a letter of credit transaction, be sure that the seller can meet the obligations the buyer states in the letter of credit. If the terms of the letter of credit are difficult or impossible to meet, it may be necessary to ask the buyer to amend it. Since a letter of credit is usually irrevocable, the seller may be at a disadvantage in seeking to renegotiate the terms. The beneficiary should closely examine the letter of credit to ensure that it states:

- Correct names and addresses.

- An adequate credit amount.

- Documents that are required and obtainable under the terms of sale. Payment problems may arise if the documents are difficult or impossible to obtain.

- Correct points of shipment and destination. The seller may wish the letter of credit to permit transshipment and partial shipments.

- Insurance coverage requirements that are obtainable under the terms of sale.

- Expiration date that allows sufficient time for shipping of goods and presentation of documents and draft.

- Correct, simple description of goods and quantities.

[f] Issuer's Obligations

As noted above, the issuer of a letter of credit must pay the beneficiary if the terms of the credit are satisfied, without regard to any disputes about the underlying contract. If payment is made in accordance with the letter of credit terms, the issuer is entitled to reimbursement from the account party. If, however, the issuer's payment does not accord with the terms of the letter of credit, reimbursement from the account party is not required. With the consent of the account party, an issuer may waive a beneficiary's failure to satisfy a term in the letter of credit.

The issuer must examine the documents listed in the letter of credit in good faith and in accord with general banking usage.[112] Although the issuer should reject documents that clearly do not satisfy the letter of credit, it bears no liability for payment on documents that appear to be genuine.[113] Most banks are inclined to honor their letters of credit, lest they become commercially unacceptable. Generally, slight differences between the

---

[110] U.C.C. § 5-106(c).

[111] U.C.C. § 5-106(d).

[112] UCP Art. 13(a); U.C.C. §§ 5-108(a), 5-108(e).

[113] U.C.C. §§ 5-109(a)(1), 5-109(a)(2); UCP 500 Art. 13.

description of a document in the letter of credit requirements and the document actually presented will not result in nonpayment.

An issuer that refuses to pay the beneficiary must state the reason, and provide expeditious notice and time to cure any defect.[114] If no reason is stated, the issuer may be precluded from later asserting that ground. This preclusion rule applies to the issuer and does not prevent the account party from challenging the issuer's actions.

Under the UCC, an issuer need not pay on a timely-presented document until the close of the seventh business day after it receives the documents.[115] The UCP allows the issuer to hold payment for three business days after it receives the documents. No payment is required with respect to documents presented after the letter of credit expires.

A beneficiary that succeeds in an action for wrongful nonpayment may recover the amount under the letter of credit plus incidental damages and interest. The action is brought in the state where the issuer is located or doing business.[116] The law of the issuing bank's jurisdiction applies unless the letter of credit stipulates the governing law.

[g] Fraud

An issuer that believes documents are forged may refuse to pay and require the beneficiary to sue. As noted above, however, the issuer may pay on documents that appear genuine on their face. This is true even if the issuer is notified about a fraud or forgery that is not evident on the documents. Although the issuer may refuse to pay because of forgery or fraud, there is no duty to the account party.

Under the UCC, an account party alleging fraud or forgery may attempt to enjoin the issuer from making payment.[117] The standard is that the documents are "materially fraudulent" or would "facilitate a material fraud by the beneficiary on the issuer or applicant." To obtain an injunction, the account party must show irreparable injury and the lack of adequate remedies at law. If the account party cannot obtain an injunction, its only recourse is to assert that the issuer's decision to pay was not made in good faith. Although the UCP does not contain any provisions about fraud or other grounds to stop payment, it is likely that the fraud exception will apply to a letter of credit dispute if any U.S. state law governs the issue.

---

[114] UCP Art.14; U.C.C. § 5-108(c).

[115] U.C.C. § 5-108(b).

[116] U.C.C. § 5-116.

[117] U.C.C. § 5-109(b).

[h] Confirmed Letter of Credit — Sample

First Trust Bank
15 Dearfoot Street
Chicago, Illinois

Dated: *June 1, 2001*
Advice Number: *DE000000011*
Issue Bank Ref: *1234/BJ/5678*   **Amount**: *US$*** 500,000****
Expire Date: *September 1, 2001*
Beneficiary: **Applicant:**
Chicago Insert Company, Inc.   *Beijing Shoe Company*
25 East Jackson Blvd.   *25 N. Xisanhuan Avenue*
Chicago, Illinois 60604   *Beijing, China 11180003*
000-000-0000   *000-0000-0000*
FAX 000-000-0000   *FAX +000-0000-0000*

We have been requested to advise you of the following letter of credit issued by:

China Evergreen Bank
16 Foujimenlu
Beijing, China 11180003

Please be guided by its terms and conditions and by the following:

Credit is available by negotiation of your draft(s) in duplicate at sight for 100% of invoice value drawn on us accompanied by the following documents:

- *Signed commercial invoice, one (1) original and three (3) copies.*

- *Full set ocean bills of lading consigned to the order of China Evergreen Bank notify applicant and marked freight collect.*

- *Packing list, two (2) copies.*

Evidencing Shipment of: *100,000 Foam Shoe Inserts*
                                      FOB Seattle
Shipment From: **Shipment To:**
Chicago, IL via Seattle, WA   *Beijing, China*

Partial Shipments not allowed. Transshipment not allowed.

All banking charges outside China are for beneficiary's account.

Documents must be presented within 21 days from Bill of Lading date.

At the request of our correspondent, we confirm this credit and engage with you that all drafts drawn under and in compliance with the terms of this credit will be duly honored by us.

Please examine this instrument carefully. If you are unable to comply with the terms or conditions, please communicate with your buyer to arrange for an amendment.

Sincerely yours,

Vice President

[i] Standby Letter of Credit

A standby letter of credit is not a true payment method, but acts as back-up to be called upon only if a party does not perform its obligations in the underlying transaction. If the account party meets these obligations, no payment demand occurs, and the letter of credit expires. The standby letter of credit must be paid when the documents specified in the letter of credit (*e.g.*, affidavits of noncompliance) are presented to show that the account party has not performed a specified obligation. The transaction generally anticipates that the letter of credit will not be drawn upon.

The beneficiary may demand payment when specified contingent events occur, such as a default in the underlying transaction. The issuer's payment obligation arises when the appropriate document specified in the standby letter of credit is presented, not when the contingent event occurs. In many cases, the required document is the beneficiary's written certification that a payment-triggering event has occurred. The independence principle described above applies to standby letters of credit as well as commercial ones.[118]

Standby letters of credit are not surety or guarantees contracts and are not governed by surety law. Under a surety contract, the surety is secondarily liable — payment is required when and if the beneficiary establishes that the primary obligor has defaulted. The surety need not pay until the default is established, which may require litigation. In contrast, the issuer of a letter of credit is primarily obligated pay and may have to do so even if a guarantor or surety would not be liable. The issuer's payment obligation under a letter of credit arises when the documents or certifications specified in the letter are timely presented. Disputes between the beneficiary and account party about whether the default actually occurred are resolved after the beneficiary is paid.

[j] Standby Letter of Credit — Sample

First Trust Bank
15 Dearfoot Street
Chicago, Illinois

Dated: *July 20, 2001.*

Expiration Date: *July 20, 2003.*

Beneficiary: *Global Drilling and Pipe Company, Inc.*

To Whom It May Concern:

---

[118] *See* Comment, *The Independence Rule in Standby Letters of Credit,* 52 U. Chi. L. Rev. 218, 245 (1985).

We establish our irrevocable standby letter of credit Number 112233 in your favor for the account of_____ for an amount up to $600,000. This amount is available upon presentation of your sight drafts or drafts drawn upon us and accompanied by the following documents:

1. Your letter certifying that Local Pipe Specialty Fabricators, Inc. has defaulted on its obligation under contract 33355, Dated July 18, 2001, and has failed to cure said default within 10 days after your written notice of such default; and certifying that the amount stated in the accompanying draft is due and owing to you.

2. A certified copy of the written notice of default referred to in paragraph (1) above, together with proof of delivery of such notice to Local Pipe Specialty Fabricators, Inc.

A draft drawn under this letter of credit must state: "Drawn under First Trust Bank Irrevocable Letter of Credit No. 112233, dated July 20, 2001."

We engage with you that all drafts drawn under and in compliance with the terms of this credit will be honored if drawn and presented for payment at First Trust Bank, 15 Dearfoot Street, Chicago Illinois, on or before the expiration date of this credit.

This credit is subject to the Uniform Customs and Practice for Documentary Credits (2000 revision) of the International Chamber of Commerce, Publication No. 500.

Sincerely yours,

Vice President

§ 4.06 Electronic Contracts and Documents

With increasing frequency, international transactions are documented through electronic means using computers and computer technology.[119] Most electronic commercial transactions utilize the *electronic data interchange* (EDI) system, which provides a relatively simple international standard for computerized message transmissions. Electronic documents associated with these transactions may include purchase orders, pricing schedules, shipping and receiving confirmation, invoices and payments. EDI is often used to transmit financial instructions, such as those conducted through SWIFT, to communicate letters of credit and similar payment and funds transfer instructions to banks and other financial institutions throughout the world. *See* discussion of SWIFT at 1.02[2][c].

Although the law relating to electronic commerce is rapidly developing, many issues are unresolved regarding the legality and enforceability of EDI contracts. These issues are becoming more acute as many companies seek to cut costs by requiring transactions with their suppliers and trading partners to be conducted electronically. These transactions require all the

---

[119] *See* Livermore, *et al., Electronic Bills of Lading and Functional Equivalence,* Journal of Information, Law and Technology (1998).

parties to obtain the appropriate technological hardware and software, train their personnel and take steps to protect their systems from hackers and fraud.

Although certain technical and legal issues must be resolved, it is likely that electronic bills of lading and other shipping documents will soon replace paper documentation. The technical issues generally relate to the ability and willingness of banks and financial institutions to forgo the security and transactional value associated with paper documents. For example, a bank in possession of a paper bill of lading may sell the goods in transit while it is unclear that this is possible with an electronic document. The legal issues require changes to many national and international laws that require and refer to paper documents and manual signatures.

[1] UNCITRAL Model Law on Electronic Data Interchange (EDI)

To facilitate adoption of EDI in international transactions, *the United Nations Commission on International Trade Law* (UNCITRAL) has adopted a *Model Law on Legal Aspects of Electronic Data Interchange (EDI) and Related Means of Communication.* [120] The Model Law is intended as a guide for governments in drafting and legislation related to all forms of electronic commercial activity, including shipping and transport documents such as bills of lading. A number of governments are in the process of adopting legislation that incorporates features of the Model Law. [121]

The Model Law is broad in scope, covering "any kind of information in the form of a data message used in the context of commercial activities." Its purpose is to permit these activities to be conducted though EDI, which is defined as the electronic transfer between computers of information using an agreed standard to structure the information. Because EDI does not replicate a paper document, the Model Law adopts a *functional equivalence* method which analyzes the functions of paper documents and provides analogous EDI means for accomplishing those functions. [122]

Under the Model Law, EDI may be used with respect to all aspects of a contract, including offer and acceptance, unless the parties have agreed not to use electronic means or such means are expressly prohibited by legislation (*e.g.*, a contract for marriage or to sell a personal residence). [123] Thus, a contract cannot be held invalid or unenforceable solely because it was formed through electronic messages. [124]

---

[120] *See* Report of the United Nations Commission on International Trade Law on the Work of its Twenty-Ninth Session, U.N. GAOR, 51st Sess., Supp. No. 17, Annex I at 70, U.N. Doc. A/51/17 (1996). The model law is available on the Internet at UNCITRAL Model Law on Electronic Commerce.

[121] UNCITRAL has adopted a Guide to enactment of the Model Law.

[122] *See* Guide to enactment of the Model Law, no. 16.

[123] Model Law, Article 11.

[124] Model Law, Article 5.

The first part of the Model Law provides general rules applicable to electronic commerce and the legal requirements for creating and communicating data messages. The second part sets forth rules relating to specific commercial areas, such as carriage of goods.

[a] Legal Requirements Applicable to Data Messages

The basic legal issue raised in most electronic commercial transactions is how laws and judicial procedures that require specified information to be in writing can be satisfied by an EDI message. The Model Law resolves this issue by providing that electronic transmissions must be afforded the same legal status as writings.[125] To the extent that a national law or rule requires information to be written, an EDI message satisfies that rule if the information is accessible so as to be useable for future reference. Information cannot be denied legal effect, validity or enforcement solely on the ground: (1) that it is in the form of a data message, or; (2) that it is not contained in the data message, but merely referred to therein.[126] The second part refers to situations that would be equivalent to items that are incorporated by reference into a paper document.[127]

Similarly, the Model Law protects the admissibility and evidentiary value of EDI by requiring the rules of evidence to be applied in a manner that does not deny admission of a data message on the ground that it is not in writing or that it is not an original document.[128] Thus, the legal recognition and evidentiary value of EDI cannot be challenged under the *hearsay* or *best evidence* rules.

[b] Electronic Signatures

Obviously, a major issue in electronic commerce is how a data message can serve as the functional equivalent of a manual signature, which authenticates the parties and indicates their intention to be legally bound. The Model Law addresses this issue by providing that a data message satisfies the legal requirement for a signature if it uses a method to identify the signer and indicates the signer's approval of the information in the message. The method used must be as reliable as appropriate for the purpose for which the data message was generated or communicated, in light of all the circumstances, including any agreements between the message's originator and addressee.[129]

The Model Law does not require the use of any specific electronic signature technique, allowing various methods to be used and changed as needed to keep consistent with current technology. Existing EDI signature methods include:

---

[125] Model Law, Article 5.

[126] Model Law, Chapters II & III. Articles 4 and 5.

[127] Model Law, Article 5bis (added in June 1998).

[128] Model Law, Article 8.

[129] Model Law, Article 7(1)(a).

- secret digital codes, similar to the PIN numbers used for many electronic banking or Internet transactions;

- cryptographic methods that use mathematical systems to arrange computer data;

- computer software that allows a person to physically sign a computer screen and then encrypts the signature;

- legislatively authorized public key encryption licensed by government authorities, as under the *Uniform Electronic Transmission Act* described below.

[c] Communicating Data Messages

The Model Law provides rules for situations that raise questions about whether a data message actually was sent by the person indicated as the originator.[130] Obviously, a person will be treated as the originator of a message he sends it himself. A person also will be deemed the originator of a data message sent by another person or information system acting on its behalf. An addressee may assume that a data message is from the originator, and act accordingly, if:

- the addressee used an authentication procedure previously agreed to by the originator, and;

- the data message was sent as a result of actions by persons authorized to access the originator's authentication procedure.

This assumption is not valid if the originator notified the addressee that it was not his data message and the addressee has reasonable time to act accordingly.[131] Similarly, the addressee cannot rely on a message it knows or should know is not the originator's.

An addressee may regard a data message as representing the message intended by the originator and act on that assumption.[132] This is not the case if the addressee knows or should know that a transmission error has occurred. A message must be acknowledged if acknowledgment has been agreed upon or requested.

Unless agreed otherwise, the time that a message is dispatched occurs when it enters an information system outside the originator's control.[133] The time of receipt ordinarily is when the data message enters the addressee's information system. However, if an information system is designated and the message is not sent there, the time of receipt is when the addressee actually retrieves the message. The Model Law provides that the place of a message is the parties' place of business, which is assumed to be the place where the data message is dispatched or received unless the parties agree

---

[130] Model Law, Article 13. *See* Guide to enactment of the Model Law, No. 83.

[131] Model Law, Article 13, par 4(a).

[132] Model Law, Article 13, par 5.

[133] Model Law, Article 15, par 1.

otherwise. Thus, the physical location of the information system equipment does not determine the where the data is received.

A number of countries have adopted legislation based on the Model Law, including Australia, Bermuda, Colombia, France, Hong Kong, Ireland, Philippines, Korea, Singapore, and Slovenia. The U.S. and Canada have adopted their own Model Laws (*See* Uniform Electronic Commerce Act, adopted by the Uniform Law Conference of Canada and the Uniform Electronic Transactions Act adopted by the National Conference of Commissioners on Uniform State Law) which are greatly influenced by the UN document.

[2] Uniform Electronic Transactions Act (UETA)

In 1999, the National Conference of Commissioners on Uniform State Laws approved the *Uniform Electronic Transactions Act* (UETA), which has now been adopted by nearly 40 state legislatures.[134] The purpose for UETA is to validate the use of electronic documents and signatures for many purposes by granting them the same status as paper-based, manually signed documents. The Act permits parties to use electronic signatures and records in commercial transactions with a high degree of certainty about their legal status.

Generally, UETA applies to electronic records and signatures relating to actions between persons conducting business, commercial, or governmental affairs.[135] It does not apply to the creation and execution of wills, codicils, testamentary trusts, or any other laws specifically identified by an enacting State. The Act also is inapplicable to transactions subject to certain portions of the UCC, including the sections relating to payment systems,[136] documents of title,[137] and sections that already account for electronic documentation.[138]

The operative section of UETA provides that a record, signature or contract may not be denied legal effect or enforceability solely because it is in electronic form or an electronic record was used in its formation. Under UETA, any law, including the statute of frauds, that requires a written record or signature is deemed satisfied by an electronic record or signature.[139] The effect of these rules is to equate electronic signatures, contracts, and records with written counterparts. The Act does not grant an electronic record or signature any particular effect, because other factors may cause a contract or signature to be invalid. As with paper documents, the effect of an electronic record is determined from the surrounding

---

[134] *See* Beattie, *Facilitating Electronic Commerce — The Uniform Electronic Transactions Act*, 32 UCC L.J. 3.

[135] UETA §§ 2(16), 3(a).

[136] Articles 3, 4 and 4A.

[137] Article 7.

[138] Articles 5, 8 and 9.

[139] UETA § 7.

circumstances, including the parties' intent, applicable laws, and commercial practice.

UETA applies only to parties that have agreed to conduct their transactions by electronic means.[140] Thus, the parties must *opt-in* to the statute for it to apply. However, this does not require an express agreement; the parties' agreement may be determined from the surrounding circumstances, including their conduct. A party that agrees to conduct an electronic transaction may refuse to conduct future transactions electronically, and this right cannot be contractually waived.

Under UETA, when parties agree to conduct a transaction electronically, any law related to the transaction that requires information to be provided in writing is satisfied if, at the time of receipt —

- the recipient can access and read the electronic record, and;
- the information is sent in a form and manner that is *capable of retention* by the recipient for subsequent review.[141]

An electronic record is not capable of retention if sent in a manner that inhibits the recipient's ability to print or store it. A record that cannot be retained is not enforceable against the recipient.

An electronic record must be sent in the specific manner or format required by law.[142] For example, UETA does not affect a statute that requires a notice to be delivered by first class U.S. mail, unless the law permits the parties to change that requirement by agreement.[143] Although the information may be provided in electronic form, the delivery must still be through the U.S. Post Office. Similarly, the Act does not change display, delivery or formatting requirements.

An electronic record or electronic signature is attributable to a person if it was that person's act.[144] This include the acts of a person's human or electronic agents, meaning that records or signatures generated by computers are attributed to the operator or programmer.[145] For example, an e-mail signature on a purchase order is attributable to a person even though it is generated by an authorized employee, or by a computer programmed to automatically respond to inventory levels.

[a] Electronic Signatures

Under UETA, an electronic signature satisfies all signature requirements imposed by law, and the legal effect and enforceability of a signature may not be denied solely because it is in electronic form.[146] An electronic

---

[140] UETA § 5(b).

[141] UETA § 8(a).

[142] UETA § 8(b).

[143] UETA § 8(d)(2).

[144] UETA § 9(a).

[145] Reporter's Note to § 108 of the 1999 annual meeting draft of UETA; UETA § 9.

[146] UETA § 7.

signature is defined as "an electronic sound, symbol, or process attached to or logically associated with a record and executed or adopted by a person with the intent to sign the record." The signing symbol must be attached to, or associated with, the electronic record being signed. Essentially, the signature is valid if the signer executes or adopts electronic means with the intent to sign.

Valid electronic signatures may be executed as encrypted digital signatures, by signing a name to an e-mail message or by transmitting a signature facsimile. It also includes a final enter or mouse click that is intended to agree to an order of goods or services over the Internet.[147]

[b] Errors in Transmission

Several UETA provisions address problems that may arise when electronic records are exchanged. These provisions deal with situations such as the method for correcting errors and the risk of loss when an error is not detected. Generally, the effect of an error by an individual may be avoided if he or she: (i) promptly notifies the other person of the error and the lack of intent to be bound by the mistaken electronic record; (ii) takes reasonable steps to return or destroy (as instructed) any consideration received as a result of the error, and; (iii) has not used or received any benefit or value from the consideration received.[148] These rules do not apply to errors that are machine or computer generated because the operator has the opportunity to build in appropriate safeguards.

[c] Automated Contract Formation

Under UETA, a contract may be formed by the action of two electronic agents in an automated transaction even though no individual was aware of or reviewed these actions. It is sufficient that individuals programmed and placed the computers into operation with the intent that such actions would occur and contracts be formed. Similarly, a contract may be formed between an individual and electronic agent, such as occurs during most Internet transactions.[149] The terms of automated contracts are determined by applicable contract law.

[d] Electronic Records

Time of Electronic Messages. Generally, an electronic record is sent when it: (i) is addressed or directed properly to an information processing system the recipient has designated or uses for receiving electronic records or information; (ii) is in a form capable of being processed by that system, and; (iii) enters an information processing system outside the control of the sender or the information processing system designated or used by the

---

[147] Reporter's Note to § 102 of the 1999 annual meeting draft of UETA; UETA § 2.

[148] UETA § 10(2).

[149] Reporter's Note to § 113 of the 1999 annual meeting draft of UETA; UETA § 14.

recipient which is under the recipient's control.[150] An electronic record is received when it enters the recipient's information processing system in a form capable of being processed by that system. An electronic record is considered to be received even if no individual is aware of its receipt. This is consistent with the UCC mailbox rule that provides that a message is effective when it is sent.

Retention of Electronic Records. For purposes of a law that requires a record to be retained, an electronic record is satisfactory if it accurately reflects the original information and is accessible for later reference.[151] This UETA provision allows written records to be converted to electronic form. Unless a specific retention requirement applies, the written records may be destroyed after the electronic conversion occurs. The retained electronic record is satisfactory for legal evidentiary purposes, unless prohibited by a law enacted after UETA. A requirement regarding the retention of a check is satisfied by an electronic record of the information on both sides of the instrument.[152]

Transferable Records. UETA governs certain electronic records, called transferable records that represent ownership rights, such as notes and documents.[153] A transferable record is an electronic record that, if in writing, would be a note under UCC Article 3 or a document under UCC Article 7, which the issuer expressly agrees is subject to UETA.[154] The necessity for an express agreement means that the obligor's consent must be obtained before a paper note or document is converted to electronic form.

A person may control a transferable record if a system for evidencing transfers of interests reliably establishes that the transferable record was issued or transferred to that person.[155] A system meets the reliability standard if the transferable record is created, stored, and assigned so that:[156]

- A single authoritative copy of the transferable record exists which is unique, identifiable, and, except as noted below, unalterable.

- The authoritative copy identifies the person asserting control as the person to whom the transferable record was issued or most recently transferred.

- The authoritative copy is communicated to and maintained by the person asserting control or a designated custodian.

- Consent of the person asserting control is required before any copy or revision that adds or changes an assignee of the authoritative copy can be made.

---

[150] UETA § 15(a).

[151] UETA § 12(a).

[152] UETA § 12(e).

[153] Generally the act does not apply to payments systems transactions governed by UCC Articles 3 and 4 or related federal regulations.

[154] UETA § 16(a). Chattel paper governed by UCC Article 9 is excluded from this definition.

[155] UETA § 16(b).

[156] 107 UETA § 16(c). These provisions are derived from Revised U.C.C. § 9-105.

- Any copies of the authoritative copy must be readily identifiable as not being the authoritative copy.

- Any revision of the authoritative copy must be readily identifiable as authorized or unauthorized.

Generally, a person having control of a transferable record is the *holder* (as defined in the UCC)[157] of the transferable record, and has the same rights and defenses as a holder of an equivalent written record under the UCC.[158] This includes the rights and defenses of a holder in due course, a holder to which a negotiable document of title has been duly negotiated, or a purchaser, respectively.[159] An obligor under a transferable record has the same rights and defenses as would apply to written records under the UCC.[160]

Notarization. If a record or signature must by notarized, acknowledged, verified, or made under oath, an authorized person may satisfy these requirements through an electronic signature that is attached or logically associated with the signature or record.[161] Additional requirements, such as an affixed seal are governed by local law, meaning that legislatures that adopt UETA also must revise their notarization laws.

[3] Electronic Signatures in Global and National Commerce Act (E-sign)

In October 2000, the federal Electronic Signatures in Global and National Commerce Act (E-sign) became effective.[162] When E-sign was enacted, many states had not yet adopted UETA and some of the adopting states had significantly changed some of its core provisions. Thus, an important impetus for the federal act was the array of non-uniform state laws relating to electronic commerce that was creating confusion and unwarranted expense in the technology and financial sectors.

Like the state laws based upon UETA, E-sign is intended to encourage the use and acceptance of electronic records and signatures by affording them the same legal status as written and manually signed documents.[163] Both acts provide that transactions may not be denied legal effect solely because they are conducted in electronic form. Neither law requires the use of any specific technology nor compels anyone to use or accept electronic records and signatures. Because the state and federal acts contain many comparable provisions, the discussion below focuses on the differences between the statutes and the extent to which the state laws are preempted by the federal act.

---

[157] U.C.C. § 1-201(20).

[158] UETA § 16(f).

[159] UETA § 16(d). *See* the requirements under U.C.C. §§ 3-302(a), 7-501, or 9-308.

[160] UETA § 16(e).

[161] 113 UETA § 11.

[162] Pub. L. No. 106-229, 114 Stat. 464 (2000).

[163] § 101(a)(1).

[a] E-sign Operating Provisions

The basic operating provisions of E-sign and UETA are similar. Under both acts, a record, signature, or contract may not be denied legal effect or enforceability solely because it is conducted, executed, or prepared in electronic form or an electronic record was used in its formation. Similarly, both acts validate the use of an electronic record or signature to satisfy any requirement for a written record or signature. Both acts define electronic signatures and records broadly to cover a variety of communication methods, including undeveloped future technologies. The acts apply only to transactions between parties that have agreed to conduct transactions by electronic means (*i.e.*, parties that *opt-in*), and any party may refuse to conduct future transactions by such means.

E-sign applies broadly to transactions between two or more persons conducting business, commercial or governmental affairs. Certain transactions are not covered by E-sign, including:[164]

- wills, codicils, testamentary trusts and documents related to adoption, and family law;

- proceedings and filings with various state and federal agencies;

- a variety of consumer cancellation notices, including those to shut off utility services or cancel health or life insurance benefits;

- notices of default, acceleration, repossession, foreclosure, eviction, or the right to cure under a credit or rental agreement relating to primary residence, or;

- recall notices regarding a product that may endanger health or safety.

Both E-SIGN and UETA affect UCC transaction in the same manner. Both acts expressly apply to the sale of goods and leases (under UCC Articles 2 and 2A), and to the statute of frauds for the sale of most personal property.[165] Neither act applies to electronic signatures or records used for commercial paper transactions (under UCC Article 3) nor to bank deposit and collections (under UCC Article 4), documents of title (under UCC Article 7), and security interests in personal property (under UCC Article 9).

E-sign contains consumer protection rules for situations that require specific information to be provided in written form. If a law requires a record to be given to a consumer in writing, the document may be provided electronically if the consumer *affirmatively consents* to receive it in that manner and, prior to consenting, is provided with a statement that describes:[166]

- the consumer's right to obtain a paper copy;

---

[164] § 103(b)(2)(A),(B),(C).

[165] Excluding goods under U.C.C. § 1-206.

[166] § 101(c).

- the consumer's right to withdraw consent to receive electronic documents and the consequences of withdrawal;

- the procedures for withdrawing consent;

- information regarding whether consent applies only to the specific transaction or to other categories of records;

- how the consumer may obtain a paper copy in addition to an electronic record, and;

- the hardware and software requirements to access and retain electronic records (including any changes or updates).

A consumer's consent to do business electronically must be provided in a manner that demonstrates his or her ability to access electronic information (*e.g.*, by e-mail rather than a written consent).[167] Under E-sign, but not UETA, recordings of oral communications may not be used to obtain consumer consent to electronic records.

Like UETA, E-sign validates automated contracts that are formed by the action of two electronic agents (*e.g.*, computers) even though no individual was aware of or reviewed these actions. However, E-sign does not contain any specific attribution rules, providing only that the electronic agent's action must be attributable to the person intended to be bound. As noted above, UETA contains specific attribution rules that depend upon the interaction between an individual and electronic agent and explicitly validates *click through* transactions conducted over the Internet.

Under UETA and E-sign, records may be copied to and retained in electronic form if the electronic record:

- accurately reflects the information in the original records,

- are accessible to persons entitled such access under applicable law, and

- are stored in a manner which permits them to be accurately reproduced.

UETA requires accessibility to the records for later reference. E-sign expands that requirement by providing that the electronic records must remain accessible to all persons who are entitled to access by statute, regulation, or other rule of law for the time specified in that rule.[168]

[b] E-sign Preemption of UETA

The interaction between the federal E-sign legislation and state UETA statues is somewhat uncertain and is likely to require judicial clarification. In general, E-sign specifically does not preempt a state law that reflects the version of UETA as it was initially approved and recommended.[169]

---

[167] § 101(c)(1)(C)(ii).

[168] § 107(a).

[169] 102(a).

Thus, a state law that is consistent with the authorized UETA will govern. However, E-sign does supercede any other state statutes governing electronic signatures and records, and any variations of the UETA statute. For example, it appears that the Utah Digital Signature Act of 1995,[170] which is the first U.S. statute to authorize digital signatures, is now preempted. The Utah act seems inconsistent with E-sign because it requires the use of a particular digital encryption technology, whereas E-sign does not mandate a particular form of technology. A state law or UETA version that differs from E-sign is invalid unless it:[171]

- specifies alternative procedures or requirements for the use or acceptance of electronic records or signatures, and

- these alternatives are consistent with E-sign, and

- do not require, or give greater legal status or effect to a specific technology or technological specification.

[4] Electronic Commerce in the EU

The EU has begun a campaign called the *eEurope Initiative* that hopes to bring every European citizen, home, school and business on-line and into the digital era. The impetus for the initiative is that U.S. e-commerce revenues are expected to be more than three times greater than Europe's by the year 2003. This may be explained by the fact that more than half the homes in the U.S. are Internet-connected, while only 12 percent of EU homes are on-line.

To realize its goal, the EU has issued a series of Council Directives, described below, that will create a regulatory framework governing electronic commerce throughout Europe. The Directive on E-Commerce, issued in 1997, provides rules to ensure businesses and consumers that their communications are secure, that buyer and seller are identified to each other, and that the transaction mechanism is secure. Because cryptographically secure communications are central to a secure electronic commerce system, a Directive on Digital signatures was adopted in 1999.

These Directives require member states to enact legislation in a variety of areas related to electronic commerce, including automated (distance) contracts, computer software, and digital signatures. Although the U.S. is not subject to these directives, U.S. businesses are likely to be affected by laws enacted by EU member countries. Accordingly, many U.S. companies engaged in electronic commerce, such as Internet sales, will adopt practices that are consistent with the EU directives.

[a] Directive on Distance Contracts

As part of its consumer protection regulation, the EU has issued a directive governing electronic distance contracts.[172] A distance contract is

---

[170] Utah Code Ann. §§ 46-3-101 to 504.

[171] § 102(a)(2).

[172] Council Directive 97/7 on EU Distance Contracts, 1997 O.J. (L 144), 0019-0027.

defined as "any contract concerning goods or services concluded between a supplier and a consumer under an organized distance sales or service-provision scheme run by the supplier, who, for the purpose of the contract, makes exclusive use of one or more means of distance communication up to and including the moment at which the contract is concluded." The directive establishes numerous consumer protection rules requiring prior information, written confirmation, right of withdrawal, performance, payment, and inertia sales. It also restricts certain methods of distance contracts and provides judicial and administrative procedures and remedies.

The directive sets forth specific information that must be given to the consumer, the manner by which the information is communicated, and the obligations of the supplier before and after the contract is formed. The directive also requires EU member states to ensure that consumers have access to judicial or administrative redress that protect them under the laws of a non-member country. EU countries may adopt stricter provisions than those established in the directive, such as a ban on marketing of certain goods through distant contracts.

Under the directive, a consumer must be informed of the supplier's identity, the characteristics of the goods or services, the price, delivery costs, method of payment, withdrawal rights, cost of the distance communication, the time period that the offer is valid, and the duration of the contract.[173] This information must be provided in a clear and comprehensible manner as appropriate to the distance communication method used, with particular regard to good faith principles in commercial transactions and the principles governing members state legislation for the protection of persons legally unable to consent (*e.g.*, minors).

Written confirmation of the required information must be provided by another durable method that is available and accessible to the consumer.[174] If written confirmation is not provided, the consumer's right to withdraw from the contract is extended from the normal seven days to three months. Unless otherwise agreed, the contract must be performed within 30 days.[175] The directive also contains a number of provisions to protect consumers from liability for goods or services they did not order.

[b] Directive on Electronic Commerce

The EU *Directive on Electronic Commerce* was issued to provide a legal framework for electronic commerce that is clear, simple, predictable and consistent with international rules.[176] The key provisions of the directive include:

---

[173] Directive, Article 4.

[174] Directive, Article 5.

[175] Directive, Article 7.

[176] Directive 2000/31/EC.

- **Place of Establishment.** A business is established where its operator actually pursues an economic activity through a fixed establishment, not the location of web-sites or servers or the operator's mailbox. Operators are subject to supervision in the EU country where they are established. A member states may not impose special authorization schemes for information services that are not applied to the same services provided by other means.

- **On-line contracts.** Member states must remove prohibitions or restrictions on the use of electronic contracts.[177] The Directive sets forth the following information the service provider must make available before a contract is concluded:[178]

  - the steps to follow to conclude the contract;

  - whether the concluded contract will be filed and whether it will be accessible;

  - the methods for correcting handling errors;

  - any codes of conduct to which they subscribe, and information on how those codes can be consulted electronically.

Pursuant to the Directive, EU member states must enact legislation that precisely describes the steps to be followed in forming an electronic contract. The legislation must provide a form that ensures that parties can give full and informed consent.

- **Liability of intermediaries.** The Directive exempts *intermediaries* from liability for acts of the operators. Intermediaries are defined to have only a passive role as a "mere conduit" of information from third parties. Similarly, a service provider's liability is limited with respect to its intermediary activities, such as information storage.

- **Commercial communications.** Under the Directive, commercial communications such as advertising and direct marketing are subject to transparency requirements to ensure fair trading and enhance consumer confidence. E-mailed commercial communications must be clearly identifiable. A general principle set forth in the Directive allows regulated professions (*e.g.*, lawyers or accountants) to provide on-line services and national rules regarding advertising cannot prevent professions from operating web-sites. The sites must respect professional ethics rules reflected in codes of conduct to be drawn up by professional associations.

- **Implementation.** To ensure enforcement of the required national legislation, EU states must provide fast, efficient legal

---

[177] Directive Article 9.
[178] Directive Article 10.

remedies that are appropriate to the on-line environment. Sanctions for violations of the Directive's rules must be effective, proportionate, and dissuasive.

- **Recognition.** Generally, national laws regarding information services must be mutually recognized among EU states, meaning that the law of the country of origin is applied. However, on a case by case basis, member states may impose restrictions on information services from another member state if necessary to protect the public interest. These restrictions must be proportionate to their stated objective and imposed only after specified measures have been taken.

[c] Directive on Digital Signatures

The Directive on Digital Signatures focuses on establishing minimum requirements for electronic signature certificates and certification services in order to ensure a level of security and still allow for their free use in the EU.[179] The computerized *certificates* used to send and authenticate electronic signatures are issued by *certification-service-providers*. This may be any entity or legal or natural person who issues certificates or provides other services related to electronic signatures. An EU member sate may grant legal recognition to a signature only if the certification-service-provider passed tests set out in the Directive and monitored by the EU Commission and its Electronic Signature Committee.

The basic rules established by the directive are:

- If an electronic signature certificate and its service provider satisfy specific requirements, an assumption arises that the resulting electronic signature is legally valid. A valid electronic signature cannot be discriminated against solely on the grounds that it is in electronic form and may be used as evidence in legal proceedings.

- A certification-service-provider who issues or guarantees a qualified certificate to the public is liable for damage caused to any entity or person who reasonably relies on that certificate for statutorily specified assurances regarding the reliability of the certificate.

- Products and services related to electronic signatures can circulate freely and are only subject to the legislation and control by the country of origin. Member states cannot make services related to electronic signatures subject to mandatory licensing.

- An electronic signature must be granted legal recognition regardless of the kind of technology used.

---

[179] Directive 1999/93/EC.

[5] Electronic Transport Documents

A number of countries and regional organizations have adopted rules and commenced projects that support the use of electronic bills of lading and other transport documents. Many of these systems are described below. It must be noted, however, that the use of electronic messages is limited in many situations because international shipments usually involve numerous parties that have different documentary requirements. In addition to the exporter and importer, a shipment contract may involve several banks, insurance companies, carriers, forwarders, and port and customs authorities. These parties may be subject to laws, regulations, and systems in different countries that mandate paper documentation.

The main obstacle to electronic bills of lading relates to the fact that the documents usually are negotiable. A bill of lading generally is a negotiable commercial paper that allows title to the goods to be transferred while they are in transit. It is a document of title that entitles the holder to take delivery of the goods. Few issues arise when EDI is used for a non-negotiable bills of lading, such as a *sea waybill.* For example, an exporter may easily provide an electronic shipping instruction to a carrier who will then issue an electronic sea waybill. The cargo can be unloaded when the ship arrives at the port of destination because presentation of the document is not required for delivery and a bank will generally accept a non-negotiable sea waybill if it satisfies the requirements stated in a letter of credit.

Another limitation on the use of EDI shipping documents is the existence of many international conventions that were adopted well before the information technology revolution. These conventions usually refer to and require *writings, signatures, documents,* and other words that preclude the use of EDI messages. Although these conventions eventually will be amended to accommodate EDI, the process is slowed by the necessary participation of many countries whose national policies and technological situation must be accommodated. Accordingly, electronic bills of lading are unlikely to fully eliminate the need for paper documents until a global EDI system is established.

Global implementation of EDI transport documents will require establishment of a common standard data format that can be processed and understood by the computers used by all the parties. Currently, two different standards are being developed and used. In the U.S., the prevailing standard is promulgated by the American National Standards Institute Accredited Standards Committee (ANSI). The U.N., in conjunction with the International Standards Organization has developed a computer language standard called EDIFACT (EDI For Administration, Commerce and Trade). However, the absence of an agreed standard will not greatly impede the use of EDI, because software can be utilized to make the different systems compatible.

Despite these limitations, EDI transport messages provide significant advantages over paper based transport documents. These advantages include:

- Eliminate costly delays created by paper-based documentation. This would ensure that goods are not held up after arriving at their destination because the paper documents have not arrived or been processed.

- Ensure the accuracy of information by requiring EDI messages to be structured to an agreed format. A message will be rejected if it does not conform to this format and can be instantly verified by a *private key* or *electronic signature*.

- Reduce fraud by digitally encrypting all electronic messages.

Until a global system is in place, parties wishing to use EDI may enter company-to-company *trading partner agreements* in which they contractually agree about the legal effect of the EDI messages they will use in their commercial activities. These agreements generally are utilized between parties that expect to maintain a long-standing commercial relationship. For isolated transactions, however, the time and effort needed to establish a trading partner agreement may not be justified. Consequently, many of the legal issues involving electronic commercial messages are likely to arise from transactions between smaller enterprises.

Many larger companies now require such trading partner agreements with their customers and suppliers, mandating the use of EDI as a condition of doing business with them. For existing commercial relationships, a letter may be sent advising the partner or supplier that future shipments must be arranged through EDI. Generally, the recipient is given a specific time period to obtain EDI capabilities.

A number of U.S. air carriers and forwarders have adopted an *Interchange Agreement* for processing electronic entries of goods through the U.S. Customs Automated Manifest System. The agreement governs most legal aspects of EDI messages, including their validity, evidentiary admissibility, confidentiality, authentication, and technical specifications, and provides remedies for non-compliance and methods for dispute resolution. Although air shipments are processed through electronic documents, the parties still must provide paper air waybills for international deliveries to comply with the provisions of the Warsaw Convention, which has not been amended to accommodate EDI messages.

[a] CMI Rules for Electronic Bills of Lading

The *Comité Maritime International* (CMI) is a private organization of over 40 national maritime law associations that has been instrumental in adopting many important international conventions. It was established in 1897 in Antwerp as a committee of the International Law Association. The CMI has adopted Rules for Electronic Bills of Lading that parties may voluntarily apply to their contract. If agreed by the parties, the CMI rules are deemed incorporated into their contract. The CMI Rules establish a private registry system for electronic bills of lading. The system operates by having the carrier send the exporter an electronic message with a private code (key) that allows the holder to obtain possession of the goods. The exporter may transfer control over the goods by notifying the carrier, who then cancels the original key and provides a new key to the person designated by the exporter.

Parties using the CMI Rules agree that all national and local laws, customs, and practices that require a written, signed bill of lading are satisfied by the CMI procedures. The parties also agree that they will not assert the lack of a writing or signature as a defense in any action relating to the contract. The CMI Rules do not cover issues such as offer, acceptance or receipt.

[b] The Bolero (Bills of Lading for Europe) System

The Bolero (Bills of Lading for Europe) system is operated by a consortium of shipping companies, banks, and telecommunications companies that utilize an on-line computerized title registry to replace paper shipping documents. The title registry is a database that only records ownership of goods covered by electronic bills of lading. The system is based upon the CMI Rules for Electronic Bills of Lading.

The Bolero system focuses on creating negotiable EDI documents that allow a holder of the document to transfer title of the underlying goods to a purchaser.The system operates by exchanging EDI messages between a *title registry* and its *users* (typically, carriers, shippers, freight forwarders, and banks). Through computers, the users send and receive messages from the title registry and directly between themselves.

In a typical transaction, a Bolero carrier sends a message to a Bolero shipper that confirms the carrier's receipt of the goods and provides the data required in a bill of lading. The message also is sent to the title registry where the shipper is recorded as the holder of the electronic document. The shipper may transfer ownership of the goods by sending an electronic message to the title registry in Bolero format that identifies the new owner (who must be a Bolero user). Upon receipt of the message, the title registry sends a message confirming the new owner as the holder that has rights over the goods.

Bolero implements a number of security controls and procedures to protect the system and authenticate its electronic messages. Most important are the digital signature procedures that authenticate the message sender and prevent it from being modified during transmission. A digitally-signed Bolero message has the following attributes:

- A user can authenticate the origin of a message digitally signed by another user.

- The originator of a digitally signed message cannot repudiate its transmission.

- A recipient of a digitally-signed message can detect that it has been altered.

- Digital signatures operate across communication platforms.

These digital signature features allow a signed message to be considered authentic and binding on the sender. After a message to the title registry records a party as a holder, only that party may send subsequent message instructions to transfer rights to the goods. Consequently, the title registry allows bills of lading and ownership of goods to be transferred quickly and securely.

Chapter 5

OPERATING IN FOREIGN MARKETS

SYNOPSIS

§ 5.01   Entering a Foreign Market

[1]   General Considerations

A U.S. company that wishes to expand into a foreign market must develop an appropriate method for distributing or producing its goods or services in the chosen country. If the goods will be exported from the U.S., distribution methods may include direct sales to foreign retailers or consumers, or indirect sales through local sales representatives, agents, or distributors. For products or services that will be produced or rendered in the foreign country, a licensing agreement, franchise, joint venture, or foreign branch or subsidiary may be utilized.

A business contemplating a foreign transaction should carefully research the people and companies it may be involved with as well as the government and legal system of the country in question. In many countries, contracts with foreigners must be approved by government agencies and may be subject to important restrictions. Important factors to consider about the host country include:

- The extent and effectiveness of its intellectual property protection laws.

- The existence of controls on foreign exchange, including limits on the repatriation of dividends and royalties.

- The nature of its product liability laws.

- The prevailing antitrust rules.

- The applicable tax laws and rates, and the provisions of any bilateral tax treaty.

[2]   Direct Sales

If the company knows the foreign market and has experience with international transactions, it can sell its products directly to foreign retailers. The products can be introduced to the foreign market by traveling sales representatives, or through mailed brochures and similar literature. Some products can be sold directly to large volume foreign consumers, such as governments, hospitals, schools, or corporations. These potential buyers often can be identified through trade conventions or international publications (including the Internet).

For discussion of the contract issues related to such sales, *see* 4.01. For discussion of shipping and payment issues, *see* 4.05.

[3]   Sales Representative

An effective way for a business to expand its sales operations to a foreign country is through a local commercial representative who is familiar with the local market, culture, people, and laws. The relationship between the exporter and the local sales representative frequently is structured as either an *sales representative, sales agency,* or a *distributorship.* Because these are distinct methods for distributing goods with different legal consequences, it is important to draft documents that clearly establish the desired business and legal relationship.

Generally, a foreign *sales representative* is a local resident who introduces the exporter's products to potential buyers. Pursuant to a contract with the exporter, the sales representative typically acts within a defined territory for a specified time period and is compensated by sales commissions. The sales representative may work for the exporter on an exclusive or a nonexclusive basis.

The contract should carefully define the relationship as a representation rather than an agency. As described below, an agent is usually authorized to make binding commitments on behalf of the exporter. Unless the exporter wishes to be bound by the representatives actions, the terms *agent* or *agency* should be avoided.

[4]   Sales Agency

An international sales agency refers to a relationship in which an exporter (principal) authorizes an agent to act independently to engage the exporter in a contractual relationship with a buyer (importer). The agent is not a salaried employee of the exporter, but is self-employed and earns commissions based on the amount of goods that are sold. The distinction may be important in excluding the arrangement from coverage by local labor laws applicable to employees. Generally, the term agent does not apply to a party that acquires goods in its own name for resale to its own customers.

Generally, a sales agent acts on behalf of the exporter in the foreign country by finding and soliciting customers for its goods. The agent is expected to take orders from the potential customers which, depending on the scope of the agents authority, may or may not be subject to acceptance or rejection by the exporter. Ordinarily, the agent does not have title or possession to the goods, which are shipped directly from the exporter to the buyer.

The buyer makes its payment to the exporter who bears all the risk of nonpayment. However, the agency contract may require the agent to provide information about a potential customer's credit. Typically, the agent is compensated by a commission on the sale, which is paid after the exporter is paid by the buyer.

An agent may bind the exporter to a contract if he acts within the scope of the powers defined in the agency agreement. This means that an exporter who grants the agent authority to negotiate purchase orders will be bound to accept the resulting arrangement. If the scope of the agent's authority is ambiguous, the exporter may find itself bound to an unanticipated contract with consequential liability to a buyer it has never dealt with directly. Similarly, an agent may bind an exporter who acts in a manner that allows a potential customer to reasonably believe that the agent had authority to act.

To preclude an agent from binding the exporter to an undesirable arrangement, the agency contract should clearly define all aspects of the agent's authority. The parties also must account for how local law, in both the exporter's and agent's countries, may affect the scope of the agent's authority. An agency contract should specify whether the agent is authorized to:[1]

- Enter binding agreements with third parties.
- Provide guarantees, assurances, warranties, or other representations.
- Settle claims relating to the exporter.
- Collect funds for the exporter.
- Provide credit on behalf of the exporter.
- State that it is the exporter's agent or legal representative.

The agency contract should clearly describe the products covered by the agreement and the sales territory. It should also define the extent to which the agent's territory is exclusive or non-exclusive. The agent's duties should be stated in detail, including its obligations to increase sales, advertise, submit orders on time, make periodic reports on market conditions, maintain contact with customers, keep proper records, etc. The agent's remuneration should be specified, including the amount of each commission, and when the payment is due.

Many commercial agency contracts prohibit the agent from entering into a similar arrangement with a competitor. This kind of *non-competition* clause should specify whether the agent is barred from all other agency agreements or only to agencies involving competing products. If the non-competition obligation extends beyond the termination of the contract, the clause should clearly state the expiration date and the amount of additional compensation being paid for the non-competition agreement.

The contract should require the agent to satisfy any local registration requirements and obtain necessary licenses and approvals. Note that many

---

[1] *See* Guide for the Drawing Up of Contracts, 6–7 (International Chamber of Commerce Publication No. 410, 1983).

countries require commercial agents to register with a governmental agency, some only permit state bodies to enter into agency agreements, and others only allow their nationals to act as commercial agents. Where necessary, the agent should be responsible for facilitating the movement of goods through customs.

Other matters that may have to be addressed in a sales agency contract include:

- Restriction of the agent to a particular customer base, such as manufacturers, wholesalers, retailers, governments, etc.

- The exporter's obligations to inform the agent about sales policies and procedures, products, and prices. Samples, advertising material, manuals, catalogues, and similar sales promotion materials that either party must provide should be specified, along with the agent's responsibility to protect and return these materials.

- The agent's obligations to protect any patents, trademarks, or other proprietary rights of the exporter.

- The exporter's obligation to provide the agent with regular statements of its account. These statement s are required by many countries, including the EU nations.

- The costs to be borne by each party, such as travel expenses, telephone, and similar expenses incurred in the commercial agency business. The principal should not assume too many agent expenses or risk creating an employment relationship under local law.

- The agent's duty to inform the exporter about changes in market conditions, new laws or regulations affecting its products, and the financial situation of existing or potential customers.

- The parties' obligation to maintain confidentiality with respect to information about each other's businesses during and after the contract period.

- The agent's *del credere* obligations. An agent who works on a *del credere* basis, guarantees to indemnify the exporter against a buyer's failure to pay for the goods. This clause should clearly state the amount and nature of the guarantee and when a debt will be considered unpaid.

- Any minimum sales quotas involved, and the consequences of a failure to meet the quota. This provision can be subject to periodic review to reflect economic changes.

Agency agreements often provide for a probation period that allow for termination if specific performance criteria are not met. After that period, termination of an agency may be more difficult in a country whose legislation restricts the termination of agency agreements. Under some labor laws, an agent who is an individual is afforded termination rights similar to employees, including pension and other benefits. An agent terminated without just cause also may seek damages for lost profits and goodwill. The agency agreement should state that any authority granted to the agent is revoked when the agency contract is terminated.

[5] Distributorship

In a international distributorship, an exporter contracts with a local person to sell (distribute) its products in a specific territory. The distributor purchases and takes title to the exporter's goods and resells them either to retailers or directly to end-users. Most distributors are responsible for warehousing and delivering the products. A distributor is legally independent of the exporter and, unlike an agent, has little power to bind the exporter to contracts with third parties. Ordinarily, the distributor must ensure that the product it sells complies with local laws and regulations, including packaging and labeling requirements. Of course, the exporter may be liable in the foreign jurisdiction for any damage or injuries caused by its products.

An exporter wishing to enter a number of foreign outlets may use distributorships to create an international marketing network. This can be done by:

- Designating a major company as its sole international distributor with worldwide distribution rights.
- Appointing a number of independent distributors to operate exclusively within specific geographic territories.
- Creating a wholly-owned subsidiary with worldwide distribution rights.
- Creating a number of wholly-owned subsidiaries, each having distribution rights within a specified territory.

Unlike an agency, the exporter does not enter into a direct contractual relationship with the persons who buy the goods. The distributor is the seller in the foreign country, and as such, must provide support and maintenance services to the buyers, and also bear any credit risks. In many countries, local law precludes the exporter from controlling the price of its goods in the foreign market or the distributor's profit. In the U.S., Canada, and the EU, for example, a contract allowing an exporter to control a distributor's pricing may be unenforceable.

Under its contract, a distributor may be required to take affirmative actions to meet specific performance objectives. This may include promoting the exporter's product, maintaining sufficient inventory, providing post-sale service, or achieving minimum sales levels. To ensure quality control, the distributor may be required to train its personnel and follow the exporter's or manufacturer's procedures regarding storage, delivery, installation, and maintenance of the product.

The distributorship agreement should specify which party will bear specific expenses related to the goods. The exporter typically provides free technical and sales literature, and possibly technical support, and warranty service. In some countries, local law obligates the exporter or manufacturer to provide specific product support for retail customers. If the distributor has confidential information about the exporter's products, the contract should provide for strict confidentiality during and after the term of the contract. Similarly, the agreement should preclude the distributor from working for a competing exporter for a specified period. An explicit provision should indicate that the distributor is not be entitled to any permanent rights to use the exporter's trademark or trade name.

[6] Licensing

An increasingly important method for entering a foreign market is by licensing the use of a legally protected property right in connection with the production or sale of a product or service. Many well-known licensing arrangements involve sports or entertainment names, fashion designs, trademarks, logos, pictures, and characters, as well as software, pharmaceutical formulae, manufacturing processes, and similar intellectual property. Licensing has proven to be an effective marketing tool that enhances the ability of a local enterprise to reach global markets without exporting their products or making substantial foreign investments.

Through a licensing agreement, a licensee immediately obtains the marketing benefits of an established brand name or the ability to use a process that has taken years of research to develop. Thus, the expense and time needed for research and product development are saved in return for a relatively small percentage of future sales. Indeed, the increased price, sales, and profits associated with a licensed product usually exceeds the required payment to the licensor. The licensee's major risk is the possible financial loss of the royalty guarantee and marketing expenses incurred in connection with obtaining the license and marketing the product. Of course, unlicensed products involve similar risks.

In many cases, the licensor and licensee share responsibilities for advertising, promotion, and marketing the licensed products. The licensors may provide general advertising about the product to strengthen their brand image. The licensees ordinarily conduct specific advertising and promotional campaigns for the products in their local market.

The licensor benefits by having any number of established foreign businesses manufacture or distribute its products for the local market. Thus, the licensor can enter a foreign market without making a large investment in capital equipment and personnel. By avoiding foreign production and marketing costs, the licensors royalties are equivalent to net profits. In effect, the license arrangement allows the licensor to avoid many of the risks associated with entrance to a new market.

A significant benefit to the licensor is the degree of control it affords over the use of the licensed property. This control is exercised through appropriate contractual provisions and, more importantly, by the licensor's right to refuse to renew the license if the licensee's performance is inadequate. Lack of adequate control over the quality of licensed products can substantially diminish the value of a brand, trademark, or similar property right. In some developing countries, however, it may be difficult to adequately protect the licensed product from unauthorized use by third parties.

[a] Technology Licenses

Because licensing agreements usually involve intellectual property rights, it is essential that this kind of property is recognized and protected by law in the countries of the licensor and licensee. Licenses relating to the use of technology usually entail patented (or patentable) property, trade secrets, know-how, confidential information, and copyrighted technical items such as software, databases, or instruction handbooks. Merchandising licenses cover trademarks, trade names, packaging, and publicity rights. Licenses related to publishing and entertainment generally pertain to copyrighted material such as books, plays, movies, videotapes, and music.

Many licensing agreements involve rights to use a licensor's technology such as patented or copyrighted material. U.S. companies often license their technology to foreign companies that use it to manufacture and sell products in countries defined in the licensing agreement. This arrangement allows a technology company to enter a foreign market quickly with far less risk than would be entailed by participating in a foreign joint venture or ownership of a foreign plant. Some licensing agreements are reciprocal, meaning that the a *cross-licensing* or *grantback* provision allows the licensor to benefit from any technological improvements to the licensed product that are developed by the licensee.

[b] License Contracts

Generally, a *license* is a contractual agreement by which a *licensor* that owns a property right permits a *licensee* to utilize that property right in manufacturing or selling its products and services. Most licenses involve intellectual property rights that are protected by patent, copyright, or trademark laws. Usually, the licensee's authorization to use the licensed property is limited to a specific territory and time period. The licensor is remunerated through a *royalty* agreement that provides for periodic payments based upon a percentage of the licensee's sales of licensed products or a *running royalty* based on the volume of production. License agreements often require a minimum guaranteed royalty that must be paid regardless of the level of the licensee's sales.

In preparing an international licensing agreement, the following factors should be considered:

- *The scope of the license.* The contract should specify the products covered by the license, including any new products that may be developed during the term of the license. The licensor may wish to obtain the rights to new products associated with the license.

In some situations, it may be desirable to allow the licensee to sublicense the property right within a specified territory.

- *Territorial restrictions.* The license should be limited to areas that the licensee can reasonably be expected to exploit. Other areas should be reserved for other licensees. However, local law restrictions on territorial licensees must be considered.

- *The exclusivity or non-exclusivity of the license.* An exclusive license often is granted only on a reciprocal basis, meaning that the exclusive licensee agrees not to produce or sell competing products and the licensor agrees not to license others in the same territory. This arrangement, however, may be restricted by local competition laws. Similarly, an exclusive license can be granted in exchange for an agreement to meet specified sales targets within a particular time period.

- Other contractual obligations of the licensee may include:

  o Best efforts to develop the local market.

  o Quality control, inspection and reporting requirements for licensed goods.

  o Warranty and similar customer service.

  o Indemnity to the licensor for liability related to licensed products, such as improper manufacture, or violation of government laws or regulations.

  o Proper use of licensor's trademarks.

Other contractual obligations of the licensor may include:

  o Provide technical assistance to licensee, including transfer of know-how.

  o Protect the value of the license by taking legal action against infringement.

[7] Franchising

A franchise is a marketing and distribution system in which an independent business owner (the franchisee) obtains the right to market the franchisor's goods or services and associated standards and practices. The franchise usually involves a recognized trademark that is associated with a uniform product or service. Through this arrangement, the franchisee acquires the name-recognition, products, training advertising, and expertise of a successful large company, and the franchisor acquires expansion capital, additional distribution outlets, and highly-motivated small business owners to market its products.

Most franchises involve dealers whose operations focus on selling one company's products, so that their business is closely identified with the suppliers. This kind of *product and trade name* franchising includes automobile dealers, gas stations, and soft drink bottlers. In a second type of arrangement, *business format* franchising, the franchisor provides the training and assistance needed to begin a business, and then operate it in accordance with specific standards during the entire franchise relationship. This is a fast-growing type of franchise that includes many restaurants, convenience stores, hotels, auto repair shops, photocopying and printing services, and real estate brokers.

[a] Franchise Contracts

The duties and obligations of the franchisee and franchisor should be set forth in a comprehensive franchise contract. Under a typical contract, the franchisor provides to the franchisee:

- The right to operate a franchised unit for a fixed period of time (perhaps with renewal rights).

- The know-how, techniques, instructions, manuals, procedures, and systems required to operate a unit in accordance with the franchisor's established methods. Ordinarily, the franchisee is obligated to adhere to these directions.

- A dependable supply of products.

- Territorial exclusivity.

- A right to use and display its proprietary marks.

- Specifications regarding a wide variety of operating matters, such as site selection, design, construction, fixtures, furniture, equipment, signs, accounting procedures, insurance, licensing, management, employee training, hours of operation, uniforms, advertising, sales techniques, and maintenance.

- A national or regional advertising program.

In many cases, the contract obligates the franchisor to provide a specified amount of financing. The contract also may state the grounds that permit the franchisor to terminate the arrangement, along with any notice requirements. It may grant the franchisor a right of first refusal or otherwise restrict the franchisees right to transfer the franchise.

The franchisee's obligations under the contract usually include:

- An initial fee for to obtain the franchise and the associated rights.

- An obligation to pay a continuing royalty for using the franchise or to purchase a specified amount of products or services from the franchisor.

- A promise to conduct the franchised business in strict compliance with franchisor's standards, procedures, and policies during the franchise relationship.

- A promise not to sell any product or service not authorized by the franchisor.

- A promise to successfully complete the franchisor's training programs.

- A promise not to divulge any information obtained from the franchisor.

- Obligations to contribute to national or regional advertising funds administered by the franchisor.

- A promise not to relocate the franchise without the franchisor's approval.

- An obligation to indemnify the franchisor for liability arising solely from the franchisee's acts and to obtain a specified amount of liability insurance.

- An undertaking not to compete with the franchise during the term of the franchise and for a specified period after its termination.

- A promise that, upon termination of the franchise, it will not use the franchisor's trade secrets, procedures, or trademark, or similar mark or name.

[b] Master Franchise Arrangements

A franchisor that wishes to expand its operations into a foreign country must consider whether to do so directly or indirectly by arranging to have a local person or company develop all the franchises within the country. Factors to consider in making this decision include the availability of personnel to work abroad, the expenses that will be incurred, the geographic distance involved and the differences between the language, culture, business, and legal systems of the franchisor' home base and the foreign country. The direct method may be preferable if the foreign country is geographically close to the franchior's home base or if the countries share similar language and customs. If the foreign country is far away or culturally dissimilar, a *master franchise* arrangement with a local developer or a *joint venture* with a local company may facilitate entry to the new market.

Under the *direct* franchise method, the franchisor enters a *unit franchise* agreement with a foreign franchisee who will establish a franchise outlet in the foreign country. A unit franchise allows the franchisee to operate one outlet within a designated territory, perhaps with an option to purchase additional outlets in a reserved territory during a specified time period. In some cases, the contract will allow the foreign franchisee to develop and own all the franchise outlets its country.

In effect, a franchisor grants a foreign direct franchise in the same manner that it would grant a franchise in its home nation. By contracting directly with the foreign franchisee, the franchisor obtains significant control over many important aspects of the relationship, particularly the implementation of franchise standards, local advertising and the appropriate use of its trademark. It may prove disadvantageous, however, if local law, commercial practices, or politics makes it difficult for a foreigner to operate. These problems are exacerbated to the extent that the franchisor's unfamiliarity with local culture and customs make potential local franchisees reluctant to deal with him directly.

Most international franchises are structured as *master franchise* arrangements, rather than as direct contracts. In a *master franchise*, the franchisee obtains an exclusive right to operate and sell all the outlets that are planned for a specified territory. The master franchisee is granted an exclusive territory in which it is obligated to sell franchises to local business people pursuant to a development schedule. The master franchisee thus becomes a *subfranchisor* that enters into unit franchise contracts with the *subfranchisees* to whom it has sold units.

Master franchises are necessary in many foreign countries where the cultural or political situation prevents the franchisor from effectively establishing and supervising its franchise system. In effect, development of the franchise system in the country is delegated to an experienced local person or company that can manage the difficulties created by different languages, cultures, legal systems, and commercial practices. The franchisor also may need to rely on a local developer because it lacks the finances, personnel, or expertise required for an extensive foreign operation.

In some situations, the franchisor first forms a *joint venture* company or partnership with a person in the foreign country and the joint venture then enters into the master franchise contract. This may be desirable if the local person lacks sufficient financial or managerial resources to develop the franchise system on its own. Similarly, the franchisor may wish to engage a local partner to obtain financing or limit its financial exposure in the foreign country.

The master franchise arrangement entails some significant disadvantages. Most importantly, the franchisor must surrender a good deal of control over its franchise system and trademark in the foreign country. Although the master franchise contract may contain detailed provisions relating to operating standards and trademark usage, these may be difficult to enforce in practice. Similarly, the contracts with third party subfranchisees can make it difficult for the franchisor to terminate an unsuccessful master franchise arrangement. An unrelated business failure or bankruptcy of the subfranchisor may damage or destroy the entire franchise system in the foreign country.

Note on Anti-Trust Rules

In structuring arrangements for selling, producing or licensing, or franchising products or services in a foreign country, the effect of U.S. *anti-trust* and foreign *competition* laws must be taken into account. While U.S counsel may be familiar with the U.S. rules, many other countries — including the European Union, Canada, Mexico, Japan, and Australia — approach competition law quite differently. A U.S. firm that enters a foreign market generally must comply with both the U.S. and foreign rules.

Most agency, distribution, and license arrangements are *vertical* agreements — that is, an agreement between a supplier and its customer — that may violate *competition* or *anti-trust* laws of some countries. *Vertical* agreements often contain one or more of the following restrictions that may raise competition law issues:

● The buyer may be prohibited from buying goods from anyone except the seller.

● The seller may be constrained from supplying goods to anyone except the buyer.

● The buyer may not be free to establish its resale price or it may be limited with respect to where, or to whom it may resell the goods.

Under U.S. antitrust law, a vertical restraint may be permissible unless it unreasonably restricts imports of competing goods or technology, or restrains domestic competition or exports. The criteria for determining if this occurs is the *rule of reason*. Under the rule of reason, an arrangement is analyzed to determine if the acts that occurred had an anti-competitive effect. The factors taken into account include the impact on market prices and output, barriers to market entry, the parties' market shares, and the business justification for the contractual restraint. A U.S. court's authority over the foreign activities of a U.S. exporter may be limited by statutes such as the Export Trading Company Act.[2]

The U.S. Department of Justice and the Federal Trade Commission have issued *Antitrust Guidelines for the Licensing of Intellectual Property (1995)* which set forth enforcement policies regarding the licensing of intellectual property protected by patent, copyright, and trade secret law, and know-how. If an arrangement may involve antitrust issues, a U.S. licensor may apply for an export trade certificate of review from the Department of Commerce.[3]

In contrast to U.S. law, the EU competition law does not analyze the impact of restraints, but bars agreements containing vertical restrictions unless allowed by a specific exemption. EU law generally precludes agreements that fix prices or trading conditions, limit or control production, or share markets or sources of supply.[4] Such agreements are null and void[5] unless an exemption is specifically granted by the European Commission.[6]

---

[2] *See* Export Trading Company Act of 1982, Titles II and IV.

[3] Alternatively, a request can be made for a Department of Justice business review letter pursuant to 28 CFR50.6.

[4] Treaty of Rome, Article 85(1).

[5] Treaty or Rome, Article 85(2).

[6] Treaty or Rome, Article 85(3).

The Commission has issued a number of *block exemption* regulations covering a variety of vertical arrangements.[7] Before drafting an agency, distributorship, license or other vertical agreement contract, counsel should carefully examine the regulations to determine whether the arrangement falls under a block exemption. These regulations describe the type of agreement and the permitted or prohibited restrictions they may contain.

Some of the areas covered by block exemption regulations are exclusive distribution agreements, exclusive purchasing agreements, patent and know-how licenses, and franchising agreements. Some exemptions apply only if the restriction does not exceed a specified time limit, typically five years.[8] If the arrangement does not fall under a block exemption, an individual exemption must be obtained from the European Commission.

[8] Joint Ventures

As described above, sales representatives, distributorships and licenses are common methods for a U.S. company to enter a foreign market without bearing the expense or risk entailed by a direct investment of capital or personnel in an unfamiliar country. In many cases, however, access to the foreign market requires a direct commitment of substantial resources to the foreign operation. This can be accomplished through an investment in a wholly-owned foreign branch or subsidiary, or through a *joint venture* arrangement with a local person or firm.

Joint ventures work best when each party makes a different, but necessary, contribution to the foreign operation. The U.S. partner often contributes skills and resources such as capital, managerial expertise, and intellectual property, such as technology or trademarks, and experience in the industry. The local partner can diminish many problems and risks an outsider might otherwise encounter in an unfamiliar market. It can provide knowledge about the market, an established distribution system, and valuable links to the business and political community. In many countries, a local partner is required, by law or custom, to conduct a particular activity or obtain government contracts or subsidies.

Most international joint ventures are *equity* transactions in which the parties contribute money, personnel, or property (including intellectual property) to a separate business entity, such as a corporation or partnership, that is organized in the foreign country. In return for their contributions, each party obtains a percentage of ownership. Generally, an equity arrangement is formed between parties that expect a long-term relationship involving substantial amounts of capital and time. Some international joint

---

[7] These block exemption regulations are "Commission Regulation (EC) No. 240/96 of 31 January 1997 on the Application of Article 85(3) of the Treaty of Rome."

[8] *See* Commission Regulation (EC) No. 240/96 (Technology Block Exemption).

ventures are *nonequity* transactions in which the parties do not make substantial contributions, but contractually agree to work together toward specified common business goals, such as research and development of a product.

To allow for an effective working relationship, the parties to the joint venture must consider how their entity will be controlled and managed, and how future capital needs will be met. Typically, joint ventures are organized under the laws of the host country as corporations, partnerships, or limited liability companies, or as local entities that have similar characteristics to these business forms. Tax considerations are quite important in determining the best form of entity for the joint venture.

Many aspects of the joint venture may be affected by local laws regulating foreign investments. For example, a country may prohibit foreign control over domestic companies, or require that its nationals occupy specified management positions. These kind of rules will greatly affect the rights of the U.S. partner to manage the enterprise or continue its operations if the foreign partner withdraws. In some countries, specific kinds of property contributed by the host country partner may not be transferable to the expatriate partner. This complicates the negotiation and drafting of certain joint venture provisions such as termination.

In many joint ventures, the partners usually have different roles in operating the business and may have different objectives and expectations regarding its success. In the research and development area, for example, the company that is the major source of technology may wish to operate as a joint venture in order to obtain more control over the use of the technology than could be achieved in a license relationship. The foreign partner, particularly if located in a developing country, may prefer a joint venture to ensure that its workers receive a high level of technical training. Indeed, the degree of technology transfer and training involved is often the most important factor governments consider in approving joint venture arrangements. Similar considerations arise in joint ventures to develop natural resources in developing countries. Although most of the capital and expertise may come from the U.S. participant, local governments often require high levels of local ownership and management, and significant investment in infrastructure such as roads, schools, or housing.

[a] Disadvantages of Joint Ventures

A potential disadvantage of a joint venture is the loss of managerial control that may occur in a country that limits foreign companies to minority ownership. This can lower product quality control to a point that damages the trademark, reduces sales, and exposes the manufacturer to product liability suits. Similarly, improper environmental management can result in expensive litigation and penalties. A U.S. firms that wants to retain managerial control must raise these issues with the local government and prospective joint venture partner.

Many countries impose significant restrictions on foreign ownership of local firms. These restrictions may limit foreign ownership to a minority interest or prohibit foreign investment in specific economic sectors such as communications or transportation. In recent years, governments have tended to relax many of these restrictions to attract foreign capital or comply with WTO requirements for *national treatment* of foreign investment.[9] Thus, governments often waive the minority interest limitation for foreign companies that bring new capital or technology into their country.

[b] Joint Venture Agreements

An international joint venture agreement should clearly state and define its provisions in a manner that can be understood by parties from different language, cultural, and legal backgrounds. For that reason, most joint venture agreements define all terms and set forth the parties' obligations and rights in great detail. In many cases, the agreement is based upon a prior memorandum of understanding or letter of intent that provides a detailed outline of the parties intentions regarding the purpose and operation of the joint venture. This should be done with great care because such letters or memos can be treated as binding agreements under the law of some countries.

Management and control. The most important provisions of a joint venture agreement relate to management and control issues. In many cases, practical considerations or local law will require that majority ownership and specific management positions be vested in the local partner. This regime is generally acceptable for most routine operational decisions. For certain key decisions, however, the joint venture agreement should grant all parties a right to notice and to *veto* unacceptable choices. These key decisions may include items such as selection of upper management, mergers and acquisitions, issuing new shares and incurring debt above a specified level. The veto may be implemented by requiring a super-majority of the board of directors, management committee, or shareholders for the key actions.

Given their different backgrounds and objectives, the parties should consider the possibility that they may disagree about a fundamental matter that threatens the venture's continuation. If the issues cannot be resolved, the parties will resort to the detailed termination provisions of the joint venture agreement discussed below. In many situations, however, the parties may wish to continue an otherwise successful venture. Contract provisions may be included to refer these kinds of disputes to the equity owners or to a resolution process, such as mediation or arbitration.

Capital contributions. The joint venture agreement should set forth the contributions each party will make, including technology transfers, when, and what form the contributions will be made, and the method for determining the value of contributed property or services. In some situations, one

---

[9] *See* the discussion at 2.02[3].

party will lack sufficient resources to make a contribution equal to its proportionate ownership interest. In that case, the other party can provide its funds or property to the venture in a non-contribution manner, such as a lease or loan. If a loan from a third party is needed, one or both parties may be have to provide a guarantee. The agreement also should address how much additional capital the parties may be required to contribute, and the process for determining whether and how much capital is needed. If only one party contributes additional capital, the agreement should specify how ownership and control arrangements are affected.

Profit interests. In negotiating their agreement, the parties should consider how they expect to utilize future profits. For example, a U.S. partner may wish to distribute the profits currently in order to enhance its domestic balance sheet, while a foreign partner with a longer investment horizon may seek to reinvest the profits in growth of the venture. Both parties may wish to distribute profits currently if the value of the local currency is unstable. Cultural differences can be important in this regard, because U.S. firms often seek quicker returns than their foreign counterparts.

Force majeure. Joint venture contracts often include *force majeure* clauses that preclude the parties from claiming damages for nonperformance attributable to unforeseeable forces beyond their control. International contracts should be quite specific about the events covered by the clause, which may include political disorder, revolution, war, expropriation, new trade sanctions or restrictions, and similar laws or events that frustrate the joint venture.

Choice of law and forum. Although the joint venture entity is organized under local law, the parties may choose the law of another country to control all, or portions of, their contract. For example, local law may to apply to employee matters, while U.S. law is chosen for patent or trademark issues. Obviously, a choice of law provision will not be effective if local law specifically controls an issue, such as import or antitrust rules. Similar considerations apply to the choice of forum for dispute resolution.

[c] Termination of Joint Ventures

The parties to a joint venture often recognize that unforeseen events may convince one or both of them that the relationship should be terminated.[10] Arguably, contractual termination provisions may induce parties to end a venture over minor differences that can be resolved through negotiation, mediation or arbitration. The better view, however, is that explicit provisions governing the actions and rights of the parties upon termination allow the parties to separate without expensive, time-consuming, and contentious procedures.[11] Obviously, termination provisions are required for a joint

---

[10] One study of joint ventures showed that the majority terminate within 5 years. *See* Bleeke and Ernst, *The Way to Win in Cross-Border Alliances*, 69 Harv. Bus. Rev. 127 (Nov.-Dec. 1991).

[11] *See* Ehrenhaft, *International Joint Ventures: Setting Them Up, Taking Them Apart*, ALI-ABA Course of Study, July 12, 1999.

venture that has a known termination date, such as the completion of construction or the end of a research project.

A party to an international joint venture may wish to terminate the relationship for a variety of reasons. These reasons may include:

- The market that prompted the venture has changed to the point that one or both parties no longer believe their project is viable.

- The laws or regulations of the host country have changed (*e.g.*, taxation, environmental regulations, or currency controls) in a manner that adversely affects the venture.

- The parties cannot work together effectively because of different business culture or practices.

- The business objectives of one or both parties have changed in a manner that cannot be realized through the venture.

In planning for a joint venture's termination the parties should consider the disposition of the entity's capital, inventory, and intangibles, such as technical know-how and goodwill. Other concerns relate to winding up current orders and activities, paying debts and negotiating continuing relationships with key employees. If one party is state-run or owned, the interests of local workers and related state enterprises may be paramount.

One method for terminating a joint venture is for one party to buy the other's interest. A formula for setting the purchase price (*e.g.*, book value or a multiple of earnings) should be set forth in the initial agreement, as well as the accounting method that will be used. A buyout may not be practical, however, if the U.S. partner cannot acquire full ownership under local law. Similarly, an advance buyout provision is not a secure termination arrangement if the local government must approve sales of business interests to nonresidents.

A buyout is not possible if the enterprise will cease operations and liquidate. In that case, the agreement should provide that the parties' capital contributions will be restored to them. This includes invested capital, equipment, technology, patents, copyrights, trademarks, and similar intangibles.

[9] Foreign Direct Investment

A *foreign direct investment* (FDI) is made when an investor in one country acquires and *manages* an asset in another country. Assets that are passively held and not managed, such as foreign stocks, bonds, and financial instruments, are considered portfolio, rather than direct investments. Typically, a foreign direct investment occurs when a company in one country is actively involved in a business located in another country. If the interest is controlling, a parent-subsidiary relationship is formed. If it is not controlling, the two business are said to be affiliated. The resulting firm is usually referred to as a *multi-national enterprise* (MNE).

Interests in foreign businesses may be obtained through mergers and acquisitions of existing companies or by creating new facilities. Ordinarily, the amount of direct investment equals the value of the *equity capital* — stocks or other ownership interests — the MNE owns in the foreign business entity. An MNE's investment in a foreign venture may increase substantially to the extent that its share of earnings is retained and reinvested in a foreign subsidiary or affiliate. Other capital may be invested in the form of short or long-term loans between the MNE and subsidiary or affiliate.

The global economic importance of FDI is immense, involving nearly two-thirds of all world trade.[12] Approximately one-third of global trade involves intra-firm transactions between affiliates of MNEs, and another one-third involves exports by MNEs to non-affiliated businesses. Thus, national, non-MNE companies only account for one-third of international business transactions.

[a] FDI in Developing Economies

Until the end of the Cold War in the early 1980s, many developing countries excluded most foreign investment in order to foster state-controlled, rather than market-driven, economic development. Socialist and communist countries barred FDI on ideological grounds and many post-colonial nations avoided foreign investment in order to regain control over their industries and natural resources. Developing countries that permitted FDI usually imposed substantial restrictions on the entry and operations of foreign companies, often in conjunction with policies designed to limit imports by substituting local products. These restrictions, many of which are still in effect, include:

- Limits on foreign business ownership and property rights of foreign investors.

- Limits on legal national treatment for MNEs.

- Discriminatory treatment among MNEs based upon home country.

- Restrictions on economic sectors open to foreign investment.

- Performance requirements regarding amount of exports and employment expected from MNEs.

The shift to market-based economies that began in the 1980s has induced many developing countries to implement policies designed to attract, rather than discourage, foreign investment. These policies require governments to eliminate most restrictions on the entry and operations of foreign enterprises, and to provide guarantees that they will not adopt new measures that will significantly harm the interests of foreign investors. Accordingly, most recent national legislation regulating FDI is designed to

---

[12] Blackhurst and Otten, *Trade and Foreign Investment,* WTO Report (October 16, 1996).

create a predictable and secure environment for foreign capital investment.[13] In addition, many developing counties have offered special tax breaks and other subsidies to attract specific kinds of direct investment projects, often competing with each another for these projects.[14]

This legislative trend reflects the view that laws that hinder foreign investment obstruct economic growth by preventing the most efficient producers from participating in the local market. Investment liberalization measures have contributed to the worldwide growth of FDI, so that nearly a $1 trillion of capital was involved in new cross-border investment during 1999, of which almost $200 billion was directed to developing countries. It should be noted, however, that much of this growth in FDI is attributable to international mergers and acquisitions rather than new plants and facilities.[15]

It seems clear that FDI flows to developing countries enhances competition, innovation, capital formation, and job creation more effectively than traditional trade patterns.[16] The most significant advantage of FDI to developing economies is the access that is provided to world capital that would not be available through loans or international aid. Because these funds are invested in permanent productive facilities, they can integrate the local market into the world economy more effectively than traditional trade activities.

In addition to increased trade and business activity, foreign investment allows a developing country to obtain a number of intangible resources that are not readily tradable on international markets. These resources include technology, managerial expertise, labor skills, and access to international production networks, markets, and established brand names. These investments in technology and modern business know-how have allowed many developing economies to modernize their production capabilities to the point that their goods and services are competitive in the global market.

Foreign investment can have a negative impact on a developing economy if it eliminates or disrupts local competition. Large flows of FDI that cannot be readily absorbed by the local economy may increase the exchange rate of the nation's currency, resulting in a lower exports and increased imports. Foreign investment that merely exploits local natural resources without creating new productive and technological capacity is unlikely to result in sustained development. Investments in developing nations that lack effective competition laws and regulations may result in monopolization of local markets by foreign companies. These problems may be exacerbated if the

---

[13] *See* U.N. Conference on Trade & Dev., World Investment Report 1998: U.N. Doc. UNC-TAD/WIR/1998, U.N. Sales No. E.98.II.D.5 (1998).

[14] *See* Hanson, *Should Countries Promote Foreign Direct Investment?* United Nations Conference On Trade And Development, No. 9, February 2001.

[15] *See* 17 Int'l Trade Rep. (BNA) 234 (Feb. 10, 2000).

[16] *See generally*, WTO, Working Group on the Relationship between Trade and Investment, Foreign Direct Investment and Economic Development 4–5, WT/WGTI/W/26 (Mar. 23, 1998).

size and importance of FDI to the local economy weakens the government's ability to manage its economic development.

[b] Bilateral Investment Treaties (BITs)

Most countries are now parties to one or more *bilateral investment treaties* (BITs) that liberalize and promote investments in their territory by investors residing in the treaty partner's country. Indeed, this global network of BITs currently involves more than 1,500 separate arrangements.[17] The increasing adoption of these treaties reflects the view of both developed and developing countries that foreign investment provides a significant catalyst to economic growth.

Generally, BITs focus on two issues: (1) the protection of investments against expropriation, nationalization, or other major property right infringements, and; (2) the free transferability of capital and personnel into and out of each country. Accordingly, many treaties assure fair treatment to investors, reject expropriation without full compensation and provide extensive dispute settlement procedures. The treaties also provide that profits, capital, royalties and other funds may be freely transferred outside the host country, and that foreign managers and other personnel may be employed without significant restriction.

The key provision of a BIT is the application of *most favored nation* (MFN) treatment to investments from the treaty partners. Accordingly, investors from a treaty partner nation must be afforded the most favorable investment terms that are given to investors from any other country. Essentially, this standard precludes most forms of discrimination by the host government against investors from the treaty partner and allows their investments to compete effectively in the host country. Many treaties provide exceptions to the MFN standard for certain kinds of investments, such as those involving national security, and other exceptions based on reciprocal treatment, such as in the taxation and intellectual property areas.

MFN treatment for treaty-partner investors raises important ancillary issues. One is the *free rider* problem, which describes the host country's obligation to unilaterally extend to its existing treaty partners any additional rights that it provides to other countries in future agreements. A second issue concerns the increasingly difficult task of identifying companies and investors that are actually from the treaty partner country. Because many MNEs hold large investments throughout the world, the nation in which the parent company is organized or incorporated may not accurately reflect its true nationality. Although nationality is usually based on the country of organization, many treaties also refer to the country where the MNE is owned or controlled.

In addition to MFN treatment, most BITs provide some form of national treatment to foreign investors. The national treatment principle requires

---

[17] U.N. Conference on Trade & Dev., World Investment Report 1998: Trends and Determinants. U.N. Doc. UNCTAD/WIR/1998, U.N. Sales No. E.98.II.D.5 (1998).

a host country to treat foreign investors as favorably as its own national investors. Ordinarily, treaties limit national treatment by listing specific economic areas in which it will not apply. Often these are areas in which local industries are being developed and require protection from foreign competition. Many treaties also provide general exceptions to investments in areas of national concern such as public health and safety, morals, and national security.

Generally, a BIT identifies the investment assets to which the treaty applies and establishes the obligations created by the treaty. The assets are often defined broadly to include tangible property, and intangibles such as contract rights and intellectual property. Some treaties, however, exclude or provide different treatment for certain investments that do not further the economic development policies of the treaty partners. For example, a treaty may exclude investments made before its effective date, short-term investments, investments that do not meet specific minimum capital standards, or investments in certain economic sectors.

Many recent BITs include clauses requiring treaty partners to provide *fair and equitable treatment* to each other's investors. Although this standard is not precisely defined, it does indicate that the government of the host country is willing to accommodate the interests of foreign investors. Indeed, failure to incorporate this provision into a BIT may raise questions about a government's intention to treat foreign investors fairly and equitably.

It is important to determine how the parties intend to implement this clause. One approach is to interpret the phrase non-technically, to simply require fairness and equity as determined under local circumstances. Another view, is that the phrase implies that investors will be afforded protections that accord with minimum international standards. Many developing countries prefer the former definition, and are not prepared to afford foreign investors international standards, particularly if that standard will entitle foreigners to more favorable treatment than local investors.

[c] Multilateral Agreement on Investment (MAI)

Many of the difficult issues raised by expanding scope of foreign investments are illustrated by the failed attempt of the *Organization for Economic Cooperation and Development* (OECD) to formulate a *Multilateral Agreement on Investment* (MAI) that was acceptable to both developed and developing countries. The OECD represents the nations having the world's largest economies, and at the end of 1996 its members were the source of 85 percent of global FDI. The organization began negotiations to develop an MAI in 1995, with the goal of creating a unitary set of global rules that would replace the many hundreds of bilateral investment treaties that were in place or being negotiated. If adopted, the MAI would include all the OECD members and allow non-OECD countries to join by accession..

The thrust of the MAI proposal was application of the MFN and national treatment principles to foreign investment. Accordingly, all foreign investors would be treated equally, regardless of their home country, and foreign and domestic investors in the host country would be subject to the same rules. To ensure this treatment, an effective dispute resolution procedure would be implemented.

Substantial disagreements among the negotiators, stimulated by fierce (and sometimes violent) anti-globalization protests by outside groups, resulted in a recess and then abandonment of the negotiations in 1998. Arguments against the MAI focused on its potential adverse effect upon the environment, employment and labor rights, light industries intimately related to local culture, and the ultimate inability of national governments to regulate or tax MNEs. In some developed countries, including the U.S., opposition groups expressed concern that the treaty would encourage businesses to transfer their facilities abroad, resulting in fewer jobs and lower wages. Other objections related to the negotiating process, which many viewed as secretive and lacking in sufficient representation for many groups that would be affected by its outcome.

[d]   Trade Related Investment Measures (TRIMs)

The WTO Agreement on *Trade-Related Investment Measures* (TRIMs) is a narrowly-drawn treaty that governs investment measures that violate the GATT rules regarding national treatment or elimination of quantitative restrictions. The Agreement prohibits national laws or regulations that favor domestic products over imports, particularly government incentive programs that encourage businesses to use local products to create or protect domestic employment. The narrow scope of the TRIMs agreement is attributable to the same disagreements between developed and developing countries that caused the termination of the MAI negotiations.

The effectiveness of the agreement is enhanced, however, by the fact that disputes are subject to resolution through the WTO dispute resolution mechanism. Similarly, a review mechanism functions through a Committee on Trade-Related Investment Measures that meets at least once a year to monitor the implementation of the agreement.[18] The Committee reports to the WTO Council for Trade in Goods.

Parties to the treaty must inform the WTO and its members about any investment measures that do not conform to the agreement. Nonconforming provisions had to be repealed over a transition period that depended on a country's state of economic development. Developed countries had until the end of 1996, developing countries until the end of 1999, and least developed countries until January, 2002. Developing and least-developed countries may apply for an extension of the transition period and a few such requests have been submitted.[19]

The TRIMs agreement does not define the term "trade-related investment measure" but provides an illustrative list of laws, regulations, and actions

---

[18] TRIM Agreement, Article 7.

[19] TRIM Agreement, Article 5.3.

that are subject to the treaty. Generally, these examples indicate that a TRIM may be any government measure that discriminates between domestic and foreign goods, including:

- Local content requirements mandating that businesses use or purchase domestic products to avoid a penalty or obtain a benefit.

- Trade balance rules that restrict importation of inputs by a business in relation to its level of exports.

- Foreign exchange balance rules that tie the level of a business' imports to the value of its exports.

It is important to note that the TRIMs Agreement is limited to goods; services and technology transfers are not covered by the TRIMs agreement.

[10] Financing International Transactions — The Export Import Bank

Ideally, companies engaged in domestic or international transactions could avoid financing costs by receiving payment from its customers before it must pay its own suppliers. Because this is usually not the case, financing often represents a significant business cost that must be included in the price charged for goods and services. The funding requirements in an international transaction may begin with the working capital to produce goods for export and end with collection of the foreign account receivable.

The most common source of financing for international transactions are the international departments of commercial banks. Special international finance programs also are provided by a number of government agencies, such as the Export Import Bank and the Small Business Administration. Many of these programs are designed to enhance export activity and therefore offer relatively low-cost, subsidized, financing.

The Export–Import Bank of the United States (Ex-Im Bank) is a U.S. Government agency that was established in 1934, during the Great Depression, for the purpose of creating jobs in the U.S. by enhancing the export of U.S. products. The Bank supports U.S. exports through loan and loan guarantee programs that finance a foreign company's purchase of U.S. products, or support the U.S. exporter's costs of producing its products. It also provides credit insurance that protects U.S. exporters against the risks of non-payment by foreign buyers.

The Ex-Im Bank is managed by a Board of Directors consisting of a Chairman, Vice Chairman, and three other members who are chosen by the President. Generally, the Ex-Im Bank may not compete with commercial lenders, but assumes risks they cannot accept. However, the Bank may not extend credit in a transaction unless there is a reasonable assurance of repayment.

A transaction may qualify for Ex-Im Ban financial support if it —

- satisfies specific credit standards,

- involves goods that have at least 50 percent U.S. content, and
- does not adversely affect the U.S. economy.

The Bank may finance exports of most types of goods and services, including commodities, other than military-related items.

In recent years, the Bank has focused on supporting exports to developing nations. Its finance programs frequently cooperate with other institutions, such as the U.S. Agency for International Development, the World Bank, and regional development banks to allow U.S. firms to participate in projects in developing countries.

Working Capital Guarantees. The Ex-Im Bank's *Working Capital Guarantee Program* is designed to encourage commercial lenders to make loans to U.S. businesses for export-related activities. It provides guarantees for working capital loans to creditworthy small and medium sized U.S. businesses if the lender establishes that the loan would not be made without the guarantee. The exporter may use the guaranteed financing to:

- Purchase finished products for export.
- Pay for raw materials, labor and overhead to produce goods or services for export.
- Cover standby letters of credit serving as bid bonds, performance bonds, or payment guarantees.
- Cover retainages and warranties.
- Finance foreign receivables.

The Ex-Im Bank will provide a working capital guarantee to an exporter that establishes it ability to perform satisfactorily and a presents a reasonable assurance of repayment. Generally, an exporter must show successful past performance, including one full year of operations, and a positive net worth. Financial statements must demonstrate an ability to service the requested loan. Guaranteed loans must be collateralized by assets, such as export-related inventory or accounts receivable, including inventory purchased with the proceeds of the guaranteed loan or the receivables from the sale of such inventory. Services companies may collateralize the loan with engineering, design, or similar items.

Working capital guarantees cover up to 90 percent of the principal and interest on commercial loans to creditworthy small and medium-sized companies that need funds to produce or market U.S. goods or services abroad. The loan guarantees may apply to a single transaction or to a revolving line of credit. The EX-Im Bank has authorized certain experienced private lenders to commit its guarantee.

A U.S. manufacturer or exporter that has an Ex-Im Bank working capital guarantee can more easily obtain the best financing terms from a private lender. After the Ex-Im Bank approves a preliminary commitment for a guarantee, the exporter may negotiate with lenders to secure the best loan arrangement. Because 90 percent of the loan is guaranteed by a U.S.

government agency, reasonable terms usually are available. The preliminary commitment is valid for six months and the lender must apply for the final commitment.

The Ex-Im Bank also guarantees commercial loans to foreign buyers of U.S. goods or services. The guarantees cover political and commercial risks of nonpayment up to 100 percent of principal and interest. The guarantees for medium-term loans (up to five years) apply to sales of capital items such as construction equipment, scientific apparatus, food processing and medical equipment, and project-related services such as architectural, industrial design, and engineering services. Long-term guarantees (up to ten years) may apply to major projects, capital goods and project-related services. The Ex-Im Bank also provides competitive, fixed-rate direct loans to foreign buyers to finance their purchases from the U.S.

§ 5.02 Managing International Investment Risk

[1] Risks of Foreign Investment

Although any business enterprise involves risk, foreign ventures present distinct hazards. This is particularly true for transactions in developing countries where the threat of unstable currencies, government action or political violence create significant risk of loss. For example, an exporter who sell goods on credit terms may sustain losses when its foreign buyer cannot meet its obligations because of local currency restrictions. Similarly, an investment in a foreign venture may substantially loose its value as a result of local regulatory action or civil unrest. Assessment of the risks in an international transaction requires due diligence to ascertain the applicable local and international laws and rules, and to obtain pertinent information about the debtor, the country in which the contract is to be performed, and the specific risks involved in that market.

[a] Credit Risk

Although every exporter would prefer to be paid for its goods before they are shipped, the fact is that most international sales involve credit terms that allow payment to occur at a later time. In many competitive foreign markets it is not feasible for an exporter to require a letter of credit or similar device to secure payment on delivery when other local and foreign companies are willing to finance the purchase of their goods.

An exporter that extends credit must consider two important factors: (1) the cost incurred because of the time value of the delayed payment, and; (2) the risk of nonpayment arising from the debtor's financial condition, and from changed political or currency conditions in the debtor's country. These nonpayment or *credit risks* may be mitigated by structuring the transaction to ensure the likelihood of prompt payment, and by shifting the other types of risks to governmental or private institutions that provide political and currency risk insurance.

Exporters may adopt a number of credit policies to reduce credit risks associated with the importer's failure to meet its payment obligations. Most important is a comprehensive credit analysis of the foreign customer. Other credit policies should account for the important differences between foreign and domestic transactions, including dissimilar business and legal systems, and the increased travel costs that may restrict the seller's ability to monitor performance. In arranging security for the payment, it is important to note that many countries do not utilize or respect security interests in goods that may apply under the Uniform Commercial Code. In many civil law nations, for example, the seller's security interest requires retention of title to the goods.

U.S. companies often find that export transactions generate lower profit margins than domestic sales because of the increased financing costs resulting from payment delays. To increase these margins, many companies implement internal controls designed to monitor international credit transactions. These controls should identify the risks of non-performance by a specific customer and determine a price that compensates for the full cost of the credit.

[b] Political Risk

Transactions in developing countries and countries in transition from socialist to market economies often entail significant political risks for creditors and investors. These political risks arise when the local government officials and judicial system do not effectively enforce contractual rights and obligations or protect property rights. Although many nations are in the process of developing their commercial legal systems, the rapidity of these changes often creates an insecure, unpredictable environment for foreign creditors and investors.

Political risks may be insured through a variety of national and international, and public and private institutions, some of which are described below. The major U.S. government source of political risk insurance is the *Overseas Private Investment Corporation* (OPIC), which often cooperates with the *Export Import Bank of the United States* (Ex-Im Bank) . Similar insurance is available from governmental and private groups in most industrialized trading nations, particularly members of the OECD. As discussed below, the World Bank provides risk insurance for transactions in developing countries through the *Multilateral Investment Guarantee Agency* (MIGA).

[c] Currency Risk

Generally, a U.S. business venture in a foreign country must conduct its operations in that nation's currency. The local currency will be used to buy and sell goods and services, pay wages and taxes, and account for local income, profit, or loss. Economic and political factors may create a substantial risk of loss, however, when the U.S. investor attempts to convert the local currency to dollars and remit the funds back to the U.S. or to another country.

These currency-based risks are of three basic kinds:

- *Inconvertibility.* The investor may be unable to convert the local currency to dollars or other hard currencies if the host country lacks sufficient foreign exchange. This may pose particular difficulties if the local business has debts that must be paid in a hard currency. A country that lacks sufficient foreign exchange may actively prevent conversion of its own currency by imposing official exchange controls or passively by administratively delaying the investor's currency exchange application.

- *Non-transferability.* Although a host country may appear to convert the investor's local currency into foreign exchange on its books, it may not actually be willing to transfer the foreign exchange out of the country. This is particularly true for countries that are having difficulties in meeting their foreign exchange obligations. This kind of transfer risk raises the same issues as clear-cut inconvertibility.

- *Devaluation.* The local currency depreciates in value, so that the investor sustains losses in converting that currency into foreign exchange. This risk is quite significant in many developing countries.

[d] Expropriation and Government Action

Under the customary international law governing foreign investments, a government may expropriate assets owned by foreign nationals if done for a public purpose, in a non-discriminatory manner, and with due process of law.[20] However, the expropriating host government must promptly pay the foreign owner adequate and effective compensation. Generally, this standard entitles the owners to be paid in a hard currency in an amount equal to the going concern value of the expropriated property. Outright, uncompensated expropriations of foreign-owned assets were commonplace for a few decades after World War II, particularly in Communist and post-colonial nations. This form of overt action has become rare since the 1980's, as these developing nations shift to market economies and commensurate policies designed to attract foreign investment.

Expropriatory actions may consist of expropriation, confiscation, nationalization, discriminatory legislative actions, requisition, condemnation, eminent domain, sequestration, or other governmental measures. Expropriation can occur by a single governmental act or through *creeping expropriation*, which is a series of actions that reduce the value of the project and ultimately compel the owners to abandon it.

---

[20] *See* Dattu, *A Journey From Havana To Paris: The Fifty-Year Quest For The Elusive Multilateral Agreement On Investment*, 24 Fordham Int'l L.J. 275 (2000).

It is important to note that legitimate actions by a host government that do not constitute an expropriation can significantly impair the value of a foreign investment. These may include price controls, restrictions on imports or exports, or reductions in governmentally provided goods and services such as transportation, electric power, or fuel. Similarly, increased local tax rates and fees can erode an investment's profitability.

[e] Political Violence and Instability

It is increasingly obvious that the value of investments in many countries are substantially affected by local political violence. This includes acts of war (declared or undeclared), revolution, civil war, terrorism, or sabotage that disrupt or terminate a project's ability to function in a profitable manner. Disruptive violence also may include politically motivated strikes and riots.

[2] Insuring Risks

Although no investment, domestic or foreign, is without risk, investors can insure against many of the distinct hazards of international investment through a variety of multinational, U.S. government, and private firm insurers. Generally, these insurance programs are designed to encourage foreign direct investment in developing countries by covering losses associated with political unrest and instability. This is accomplished through subsidized insurance that guarantees investors against risks arising from political acts, such as currency restrictions, expropriation, and civil unrest.

It is important to note that political risk insurance does not encompass the significant commercial risks that may arise when exporting to or investing in a developing country. Thus, it is necessary to distinguish between an uninsured commercial risk attributable to the host government's economic policies, and an insured political risk related to governmental actions that obstruct the ability of a foreign exporter or investor to receive payment or enforce its contract or property rights.

[a] Overseas Private Investment Corporation (OPIC)

The U.S. government agency that insures against political risks is the *Overseas Private Investment Corporation* (OPIC). OPIC is a self-funding U.S. government agency that provides risk insurance for U.S. businesses that invest in developing countries.[21] The agency also conducts a finance program that provides loans and loan guarantees for projects that cannot obtain funding from commercial lenders. These OPIC programs are available for investments in nearly 140 countries throughout the world. OPIC's insurance obligations and loan guaranties are backed by the full faith and credit of the U.S., meaning that they are U.S. government obligations.

OPIC benefits are available for new investments and for acquisitions of existing operations if the U.S. investor contributes additional capital for

---

[21] *See* OPIC website at www.opic.gov.

modernization or expansion. Coverage may be allowed for up to 90 percent of the U.S. investor's interest in a project (100 percent of a U.S. financial institution's exposure), up to a maximum of $200 million per project. The foreign enterprise need not be owned or controlled by U.S. parties, but OPIC insurance only covers the portion of the investment made by the U.S. investor. Insurance generally is not available for ventures that are controlled by a foreign government.

Although OPIC operates in the same manner as a private corporation, it is subject to the policy guidance of the State Department. Thus, a program does not qualify for assistance unless it is both beneficial to the host country and not detrimental to U.S. interests. A project may be deemed detrimental to the U.S. if it is likely to adversely affect U.S. employment or balance of payments, or if the host country imposes requirements that will reduce U.S. trade benefits from the investment.

OPIC is governed by the *Foreign Assistance Act of 1961*[22] (FAA), which provides that the following persons are eligible for its insurance and finance programs:

(1) U.S. citizens;

(2) U.S. corporations or other business entities that are substantially beneficially owned by U.S. citizens;

(3) a foreign corporation that is at least 95 percent owned by persons or business entities eligible under (1) or (2) above, and;

(4) a non-corporate foreign business entity that is 100 percent owned by persons or business entities eligible under (1) or (2) above.

OPIC insurance coverage extends to three basic risks associated with investments in developing countries:

- *Foreign Currency Inconvertibility.* OPIC inconvertibility coverage insures against the risk of adverse change in the terms and conditions for converting a foreign currency to U.S. dollars and transferring the funds out of the country. This applies to earnings on or returns of capital, principal, and interest payments, and fees and royalties. The insurance covers losses from regulatory changes that prevent the investor from converting local currency to dollars and sending the dollars abroad, and to passive failures by local authorities to permit conversion within a designated time period. Although OPIC does not guarantee the exchange rate at which a currency will be converted, the agency is considering a new product that will insure against certain devaluation risks. Generally, OPIC does not insure convertibility of a currency that is not effectively convertible to dollars on the date the contract is sought.

- *Expropriation.* OPIC expropriation coverage insures against the nationalization, confiscation, or expropriation of a project. For

---

[22] 22 U.S.C. § 2191 *et seq.*

this purpose, expropriation means an illegal government action that deprives an investor of fundamental rights or financial interests in a venture. This includes *creeping* (indirect) expropriation, but does not include minor events or general government action such as a changed tax rate (unless the tax rate was specifically set by advance agreement), or new regulatory measures. The government action must be discriminatory and violate international law.

Generally, OPIC only insures against total expropriation and does not pay compensation unless the expropriatory action continues for at least six months. As a condition of insurance, OPIC may require an investor to pursue any contractual dispute resolution procedures agreed to in the project agreement before seeking compensation. In that case, OPIC's obligation is limited to ensuring that the government engages in the dispute resolution procedures and pays any award granted through that process. However, the insured is not required to seek redress in the courts of the host country, even if that is required in the project agreement.

To receive compensation, the insured must assign its entire insured interest in the project to OPIC. This includes its equity investment in the project, free and clear of any encumbrances. Consequently, an investor is unlikely to present a claim to OPIC unless it is willing to abandon the project.

- *Political Violence.* OPIC political violence coverage insures against losses from violence conducted for political reasons. Covered losses include damage to property and lost business income resulting from violence due to declared or undeclared war, hostile actions by national or international forces, civil war, revolution, insurrection, and civil strife, including political terrorism and sabotage.

Compensation for damaged property may be based on replacement cost (limited to twice the original cost) or the lesser of original cost, fair market value at the time of loss, or the cost of repairs. Compensation for lost business income equals the net income lost as a result of the property damage caused by political violence. Compensation is paid until production is restored, limited to one year.

Risk Insurance for Contractors and Exporters. In addition to its investment insurance program, OPIC insures against political risks that can disrupt international contracting and export transactions. These policies may cover U.S. firms engaged as contractors in international construction, sales, or service contracts, and U.S. exporters of certain products. Generally, OPIC coverage is limited to contracts between U.S. companies and foreign governments. This kind of OPIC policy covers U.S. contractors and exporters against:

- Wrongfully called bid, performance, or advance payment guaranties, bonds, and other guaranties;

- Lost assets and bank accounts from confiscation or political violence and inconvertibility of proceeds from the sale of equipment, and;

- Losses from contractual disputes with the foreign buyer.

[b] Export-Import Bank of the U.S.

The Export–Import Bank of the United States (Ex-Im Bank) is a U.S. Government agency that supports U.S. exports through loan and loan guarantee programs. (For complete discussion of Ex-Im Bank financing programs, see 5.01[10].) The Ex-Im Bank also provides credit insurance that protects U.S. exporters against the commercial or political risks of non-payment by foreign buyers or debtors. Typically, these are short-and medium-term export credit insurance policies that are tailored to meet the specific insurance needs of exporters and financial institutions. The policies may apply to shipments to one buyer or to many buyers, provide comprehensive coverage of commercial and political credit risks, or only apply to specific risks, and cover short-term or medium-term sales. A number of policies are specifically designed for small businesses.

Credit insurance offered by the Ex-Im Bank include the following kind of policies:

- Multi-buyer policies for short-term export credit sales. These short-term policies generally cover political risks up to 100 percent of the principal, and commercial risks up to 90–95 percent of the principal, plus specified interest. They support the sale of consumer goods, raw materials, and spare parts on terms of up to 180 days, and bulk agricultural commodities, consumer durables, and capital goods up to 360 days.

- Single-buyer policies cover short-and medium-term repeat sales to the same buyer, and apply to losses from political risks, changes in import laws, foreign exchange convertibility, and commercial default. The medium-term policies may cover 100 percent of principal and interest on the financed portion, and capital goods may be insured for up to five years.

- Letter of credit policies insure U.S. banks against losses arising from confirmation or negotiation of irrevocable letters of credit issued by foreign banks relating to U.S. exports. This kind of policy covers political risks and commercial risks related to failure of a foreign private or public issuing bank.

- *Financial Institution Buyer Credit Export Insurance* covers risks of default on loans made by a financial institution to a foreign buyer to finance importation of U.S. goods. This type of policy insures against defaults attributable to political and commercial risks.

- *Small Business Credit Insurance* covers short-term credit sales by small companies. The policy insures losses from a buyer default arising from political risks, cancellation of an import or export license, currency inconvertibility, and commercial reasons.

[c] Multilateral Investment Guarantee Agency (MIGA)

The *Multilateral Investment Guarantee Agency* (MIGA) is an affiliate of the World Bank that was formed in 1988 to encourage foreign direct investment in developing countries. It does this by providing investment guarantees to foreign private investors and lenders that mitigate the political risks associated with their project or loan. The agency recently made a significant increase in the amount of risk coverage it provides, setting it up to $200 million per project and up to $620 million per host country. MIGA also offers technical assistance to host governments regarding methods that will enhance their ability to attract foreign capital.

MIGA insurance covers the following political risks:

- *Transfer Restriction.* This insures investors against losses from an inability to convert local currency into foreign exchange for transfer outside the host country. Coverage applies to losses from excessive delays in acquiring foreign exchange caused by action of the host government, adverse changes in exchange control laws, or regulations, and deterioration in conditions governing the conversion and transfer of local currency. Devaluation of the local currency is not covered. Upon receipt of the blocked currency from the investor, MIGA pays compensation in the currency stated in the guarantee contract.

- *Expropriation.* This covers losses arising from host government acts that reduce or eliminate ownership of, control over, or rights to the insured investment. The insurance applies to outright nationalization and confiscation, and to *creeping expropriation* through a series of acts over time. Limited coverage of partial expropriation or confiscation may be obtained. This insurance does not apply to bona fide, nondiscriminatory measures a government adopts pursuant to its legitimate regulatory authority. MIGA pays the net book value of a totally expropriated equity investment and the insured portion of expropriated funds. Loans are guaranteed in the amount of the outstanding principal, and any accrued and unpaid interest. The investor must assign its interest in the expropriated investment to MIGA to obtain compensation.

- *Breach of Contract.* This protection applies to losses from the host government's breach or repudiation of a contract with the investor. Compensation is paid only after the investor invokes its contractual dispute resolution procedures (such as arbitration) and either obtains an award for damages, or the dispute resolution method fails because of the actions of the host government. If damages are awarded, MIGA will pay if the government fails to do so within a specified time period — usually 90 days.

- *War and Civil Disturbance.* This coverage applies to losses from damage to, or the destruction or disappearance of, tangible assets caused by politically-motivated acts of war or civil disturbance in the host country, including revolution, insurrection, coups d'état, sabotage, and terrorism. MIGA insurance covers the investor's share of the lesser of the book value, replacement cost, or repair cost of the lost or damaged assets. Loans and loan guaranties are paid up to the insured principal and defaulted interest payments caused by war and civil disturbance. Coverage also extends to events that interrupt essential project operations or financial viability for a period of one year. If the interruption results in a total loss, MIGA pays the book value of the total insured investment.

Eligible Investments. MIGA insures international investments that originate in any member country with a destination in any developing member country. Coverage also is available for new investments that expand, modernize, or financially restructure an existing project, and for acquisitions of privatized state enterprises. The investment may be in the form of equity, shareholder loans, and loan guarantees by shareholders. Certain loans to unrelated parties may be guaranteed by MIGA. For involving technical assistance, management contracts, franchising and licensing agreements that have contractual commitment terms of at least three years, remuneration is tied to operating results. MIGA's policy is to insure investment projects that contribute to host country needs, such as job creation, technology transfer, and exports.

Eligible Investors. Investors are eligible for MIGA insurance if they are nationals of a member country other than the country where the investment will be made. Corporations and financial institutions are eligible if their place of incorporation or principal place of business is in a member country or if the entity is majority owned by nationals of a member country. Commercial state-owned companies also are eligible.

Coverage Terms. The standard insurance term is 15 years, but certain projects may be covered for 20 years. MIGA cannot terminate its guarantees unless the insured party defaults on its obligations, but the insured may reduce or cancel its coverage.

[d]   Cooperative Underwriting Program

Over the past few years, a few large private insurance companies have begun to offer long-term political risk insurance, either as separate policies or as co-insurers with institutions such as MIGA and OPIC. MIGA has collaborated with the private insurance industry to create the *Cooperative Underwriting Program* (CUP), which offers co-insurance policies in which MIGA is the insurer of record, and the private companies participate as underwriters. The CUP greatly increases the amount of insurance available to investors by attracting private insurers that would not guarantee such political risks without the MIGA's participation. Although the private companies must bear their share of the insurance liability, they also share in any amounts that MIGA subsequently recovers from the host government.

§ 5.03   Choosing the Appropriate Business Entity

[1]   U.S. Business Entities

Corporations. A corporation is established when its owners file articles of incorporation in accordance with local law. Most of the rules governing corporate management, capital structure, and shareholder rights are codified in extensive and well-understood state laws. The most significant aspect of a corporation is that its owners ordinarily are not personally liable for corporate debts. This feature makes the corporate format attractive to parties who wish to limit their potential losses to the capital that they invest in the venture.

Partnerships. Unincorporated ventures with multiple owners typically are considered partnerships. Most partnerships are general partnerships, meaning that each partner is an agent for the venture whose actions may bind the other partners. Every general partner is personally liable for all partnership obligations; a general partner's personal assets are potentially at risk if the venture is unsuccessful. Partners may organize and operate their partnership informally pursuant to an unwritten understanding, or they may formalize their arrangement through a written partnership agreement.

Limited Partnerships. A second kind of partnership is a limited partnership, which is formed by executing and filing a written instrument in accordance with state statutes. A limited partnership must have at least one general partner that bears personal liability for partnership obligations. The limited partner's status is similar to that of a corporate shareholder: limited partners cannot directly manage partnership business affairs; they cannot bind the partnership; and their liability for partnership obligations is limited to the capital they have invested.

Limited Liability Companies. All U.S. states have enacted statutes that permit the formation of a business entity called a Limited Liability Company (LLC). The LLC combines the limited liability of a corporation with the flexibility and tax advantages of a partnership. If the LLC is properly formed and operated under state law, its members are not personally liable for the entity's debts and obligations. Generally, a member's rights concerning matters such as the LLC's governance, operations, transfer of interests, income, distributions, and liquidation are set forth in an operating agreement that is similar to a partnership agreement. The members of an LLC may manage the business directly or they may delegate some or all managerial functions to other members or to hired managers. Unlike a limited partnership, an LLC member who participates in management does not forfeit limited liability under state law.

[2]　Characteristics of Business Entities

[a]　Limited Liability

Business owners often wish to protect their personal assets from business creditors' claims. Typically, this goal is attained by organizing the venture under a state law that limits the owners' liability to the amount of capital they have invested in the entity. The broadest form of statutory limited liability from all creditors is afforded to shareholders of a corporation and to members of a limited liability company (LLC). Many states have enacted statutes permitting a general partnership to register with a designated state office as a limited liability partnership (LLP). Although the scope of liability protection varies from state to state, partners of a registered LLP typically are not liable for debts arising from torts, but remain liable for other partnership obligations.

In many situations, investors can insulate their personal assets from business debts by operating as a limited partnership. In a partnership, all partners other than limited partners are jointly liable for partnership obligations, and are jointly and severally liable for obligations that arise from another partner's wrongful act or breach of trust. Under state law, limited partners are not liable for partnership obligations that exceed their capital contributions. This protection against personal liability is not available to limited partners who participate in managing the partnership's business affairs. A limited partnership must have at least one general partner whose individual assets may be reached by partnership creditors. Many ventures reduce the total amount of nonbusiness assets at risk in the enterprise by having a corporation act as the general partner. This arrangement limits the total liability of all investors to the amount of capital invested in the partnership, and the capital owned by the corporate general partner.

[b]　Management and Control

Business owners should consider how each business form affects the way they may operate and control their enterprise. Corporations are centrally managed by a board of directors that acts in a representative capacity for the shareholders who elect them. Thus, shareholders generally lack direct, immediate control over corporate operations and managerial decisions. Shareholders of closely held corporations, however, can directly control corporate operations by serving as directors and officers.

General partnerships usually allow more flexibility than corporations in structuring management and control arrangements, because partners can specify each party's managerial role through appropriate provisions in the partnership agreement. The agreement may grant any partner or group of partners control over all business affairs, or it may limit their discretion to particular kinds of decisions. For example, the partnership agreement can ensure a dominant role for minority partners by giving them control over certain key business decisions. In contrast, a similar corporate arrangement for minority shareholders would require complex voting agreements or voting trusts.

The control and management of a limited partnership is closer to the corporate structure than that of a general partnership, because the general partners provide central management for the limited partners. Management by general partners is required, because if a limited partner participates directly in partnership business affairs, he becomes personally liable for partnership obligations.

Limited partners may vote on, and thereby control, however, a number of important partnership business activities without losing their limited liability status. For example, limited partners may consult and advise the general partners about the partnership's business and may propose, approve, or disapprove of actions, such as making changes in the nature of the partnership's business and incurring debts outside the ordinary course of partnership business.

Unlike limited partners, all members of an LLC may participate directly in management without losing their limited liability protection. The governance of a member-managed LLC is similar to a general partnership. Alternatively, the LLC operating agreement may require governance by hired managers who are not members. Governance of a hired-manager LLC is similar to a corporation, and members exercise indirect control through their selection of the outside managers.

[c] Capital Structure

Investors should consider how the capital structure of each business form affects the way they share its income, profits, capital, and losses. Partnerships and limited liability companies generally provide the most flexibility in allocating these items among business owners, because partners and LLC members may contractually agree to share any item of partnership gain, loss, income, or expense to best meet the individual partners' financial and tax goals. For example, one partner may be given a greater share of the appreciation (and corresponding depreciation) of certain partnership assets, while another partner may obtain a larger share of the partnership's operating income or loss. The sharing arrangement the partners express in their partnership agreement ordinarily is respected under state law. An allocation in the partnership agreement is respected for tax purposes if it has substantial economic effect, that is, it substantially affects the values of the partners' interests independent of tax consequences.

[d] Transferability of Interests

Owners of business or investment interests should consider how the choice of business form affects their ability to sell or otherwise transfer their interests. Partnership interests, other than limited partnership interests, ordinarily are not readily transferable because all general partners must consent to the transfer. This feature protects the continuing partners against unwanted new partners whose actions can bind the partnership. Although a partner may assign his right to receive his share of partnership profits and capital, the assignee does not become a partner with rights to participate in partnership management unless all of the other partners consent.

Most constraints on transferability do not apply to limited partnership interests. Limited partners may freely assign their interests, and the assignee obtains the assignor's right to share in partnership profits. Because limited partners do not participate in partnership management, an assignment of a limited partner's interest in partnership profits is equivalent to a sale of the interest. Also, the partnership agreement may allow an assignee to become a substitute limited partner, with rights to inspect partnership books and to vote on certain matters, without the consent of the other partners.

Corporate stock theoretically is a more liquid form of investment than a partnership interest because shareholders may transfer their shares without anyone's consent, and the transferee obtains all the transferor's rights and interests. In a closely held corporation, however, shareholder's right to transfer his shares is likely to be subject to substantial contractual or statutory restrictions. These restrictions usually preclude stock transfers that affect control of corporate affairs; therefore, little difference exists between the liquidity of closely held corporate stock and partnership interests.

The limited liability company provides a great deal of flexibility in determining the transferability of members' interests. Generally, transfer rights are governed by the LLC operating agreement. The agreement can provide that a transferee of an interest automatically is admitted as a substitute member, or it may require the consent of some or all members for the transferee to be admitted. A member who cannot transfer his interest to a new member may freely assign it; the assignee obtains the assignor's right to share in profits but does not receive any other membership rights.

[e] Death or Other Withdrawal of Owner

Investors should consider the consequences of any member's death, disability, or retirement. In a partnership, a partner's withdrawal causes a dissolution that negates every partner's authority to act as the partnership's agent except in matters relating to the wind-up of its affairs. The dissolution generally protects the withdrawing partner, or his successor, from personal liability for future obligations incurred by the other partners.

A dissolution does not terminate the partnership's business, however; the remaining partners may continue its operations. The continuing partners' obligations to liquidate or to purchase the interest of a deceased or retiring partner are usually specified in a buy-sell agreement. The parties also may agree in advance that a deceased partner's successor may join the partnership in continuing its business.

The effect of a member's withdrawal from a limited liability company is similar to a partnership. Generally, a limited liability company dissolves under state law upon the death, retirement, resignation, expulsion, bankruptcy, or dissolution of a member, or whenever a member's interest in the LLC terminates. However, most states permit the remaining members to elect to continue the LLC's business. If only one member remains, the LLC will no longer be taxable as a partnership unless a new member is admitted.

A corporation does not dissolve or terminate when a shareholder dies or otherwise withdraws. In a closely held corporation, however, the lack of a ready market for the corporation's stock often means that the practical effect of a shareholder's withdrawal is the same as a partner's withdrawal from a partnership. Thus, the corporation's business will terminate unless the other owners are willing and able to continue its operations. As in a partnership, the obligation of the continuing shareholders to liquidate or to purchase the stock of a deceased or retired shareholder may be specified in a buy-sell agreement.

A limited partnership does not dissolve or terminate when a limited partner withdraws. The partnership agreement typically specifies the time when a withdrawing limited partner is entitled to receive a distribution of the value of his interest. If the agreement is silent, the limited partner must receive a distribution of his capital after six months' notice to the other partners. The partnership agreement may contain a provision allowing a limited partner to designate his estate or other successor as a substitute limited partner. Withdrawal of less than all of the general partners does not dissolve a limited partnership if the remaining general partners are authorized to continue partnership business operations.

[3]   The Multinational Enterprise (MNE)

A substantial and growing portion of global commerce is conducted through multinational enterprises (MNE) that have production and marketing operations in more than one country. A commonly accepted definition provides that MNEs:[23]

> . . . usually comprise companies or other entities established in more than one country and so linked that they may co-ordinate their operations in various ways. While one or more of these entities may be able to exercise a significant influence over the activities of others, their degree of autonomy within the enterprise may vary widely from one multinational enterprise to another. Ownership may be private, state or mixed.

Recent statistics indicate that MNEs produce more than ten percent of the world's gross domestic product, conduct nearly two-thirds of global trade and engage in more than three-fourths of worldwide research and development activities.[24] Much of this economic activity is concentrated in

---

[23] Guidelines for Multinational Enterprises, Organization for Economic Cooperation and Development (OECD), June 27, 2000.

[24] United Nations Conference on Trade and Development (UNCTAD), World Investment Report 2002: Transnational Corporations and Export Competitiveness 4, U.N. Doc. UNCTAD/WTR/2002 (2002).

relatively few corporate conglomerates, so that fewer than 500 companies conduct more than seventy percent of global trade.

Many developing nations pursue and welcome MNEs for the jobs, capital, technology, access to world markets and overall economic growth they provide. Frequently, countries offer significant tax incentives, subsidies, regulatory exemptions and other benefits to induce MNEs to invest and operate within their borders. Indeed, substantial evidence exists that MNEs have greatly contributed to the recent economic growth that has improved living standards in most parts of the world.

However, the scope and concentration of MNE economic operations and power has generated considerable concern and commentary about the necessity and means for regulating and governing their activities. One area of concern is that MNEs often degrade global labor, environmental, product safety and living standards. This occurs, for example, when an MNE moves its production facilities to a developing country with lax standards to avoid more stringent regulatory regimes found in more developed economies. A second charge is that MNE operations often are not compatible with the long-term social and economic development needs of the host country. MNEs, it is argued, can distance themselves from accountability for these operations by subcontracting work to exploitive or unscrupulous local firms.

In response to these concerns, various organizations have promulgated codes of conduct to provide guidelines for MNEs operating in developing nations. The earliest and most important code, entitled *Guidelines for Multinational Enterprises* was first issued by the Organization for Economic Cooperation and Development (OECD) in 1976 and reissued in revised form in 2000.[25] This code is most significant because the OECD represents the world's most economically-developed nations that are the home base for more than ninety percent of MNEs. The Guidelines are not legally enforceable and are not intended to substitute for, nor override local law and regulation. However, the OECD does monitor and report on how the Guidelines are implemented by its member nations.

The basic policy of the OECD Guidelines is that MNEs "should take fully into account established policies in the countries in which they operate and consider the views of other stakeholders." Specific MNE policies should:

1. Contribute to economic, social, and environmental progress that will achieve sustainable development;

2. Respect the human rights of those affected by their activities;

3. Encourage local capacity building through close cooperation with the local community and business interests;

4. Encourage human capital formation by creating employment and training opportunities;

---

[25] Guidelines for Multinational Enterprises, Organization for Economic Cooperation and Development (OECD), June 27, 2000.

5. Refrain from seeking exemption from local legislation and regulation;

6. Support and uphold good corporate governance principles and practices;

7. Establish practices that foster confidence and trust with local communities;

8. Promote employee awareness and compliance regarding company policies;

9. Refrain from disciplining or discriminating against bona fide whistleblowers;

10. Encourage business partners to apply principles of business conduct that are compatible with the Guidelines; and

11. Abstain from improper involvement in local political activities.

Going beyond these general principles, the *Guidelines* set forth specific measures that MNEs should adopt regarding Corporate Disclosure, Employment and Industrial Relations, Environment, Combating Bribery, Consumer Interests, Science and Technology, and Taxation.

Several other important OECD initiatives relate to corporate and MNE behavior. The *Principles of Corporate Governance*, address issues of shareholder rights, equitable treatment of shareholders, the role of stakeholders, disclosure and transparency, and board responsibility.[26] The Convention on Combating Bribery of Public Officials,[27] which is similar to the U.S. Foreign Corrupt Practices Act (discussed at §3.03[5]), requires signatory governments to criminalize the offer of bribes to foreign officials to obtain a business advantage.

[4] Incorporating Offshore — Corporate Inversions

In recent years, an increasing number of U.S. companies have reincorporated outside the U.S., citing substantial corporate tax reduction as a major reason for the action. This kind of transaction, referred to as an *inversion*, generally replaces the U.S.-based parent corporation of a multinational group with a newly created foreign corporation located in a low tax or no tax country. The corporate restructuring is usually designed to shift ownership of the group's foreign operations outside the U.S.

Most commonly, the new foreign-based parent company is located in a jurisdiction that imposes no corporate income tax (e.g., many Carribean island countries). In connection with the inversion, various transactions between group members are employed to shift income from the U.S. group members to the low-tax foreign parent. The tax benefits of the inversion may include:

---

[26] OECD Principles of Corporate Governance, (May 26, 1999).

[27] OECD Convention on Combating Bribery of Foreign Public Officials in International Business Transactions and Related Instruments.

- Shifting ownership of foreign subsidiaries from the U.S. parent to the new foreign parent or subsidiary eliminates U.S. corporate taxation on these foreign operations.

- The amount of income taxed in the United States may be reduced by restructuring foreign operations through payments of interest and royalties or through transfers of customers, good will or know-how to the foreign parent.

- Future growth, and corresponding taxation, of the multinational's foreign operations may be shifted to foreign subsidiaries owned by the foreign parent.

- U.S. group members may reduce income subject to U.S. tax by generating deductible payments to foreign group members in a lower tax country. For example, intercompany indebtedness may be created requiring deductible interest to be paid to the foreign parent or affiliate.[28] Typically, the interest income is received in a country having low or no taxation. The U.S. withholding tax on interest payments to a related party often is substantially reduced or eliminated by a U.S. income tax treaty.

- Insurance companies may create reinsurance arrangements between U.S. and foreign group members that shift insurance premiums to low-or no-tax jurisdictions.

The reincorporation of the U.S. parent company abroad may be accomplished through one of the following transactions:

- **Stock Transaction.** Many transactions have involved reincorporation through formation of a new holding company (foreign parent) in a low-tax jurisdiction which then acquires all the stock of the U.S. parent corporation (U.S. parent). The shareholders of the U.S. parent, now a subsidiary of the foreign parent, exchange their U.S. parent stock for the foreign parent stock. Generally, this transaction is taxable to the shareholders of the U.S. parent as if they sold their stock.[29] The amount of gain is the difference between the value of the stock on the date of the transaction over their basis for the stock. However, no loss may be recognized and the loss merely reduces the basis of their stock in the new company.

- **Foreign Reincorporation — Asset Transaction.** In this transaction the U.S. parent is directly reincorporated in a foreign jurisdiction. This is accomplished by merging the U.S. parent into a new foreign corporation, or by conversion and continuation procedures under state corporate law. The U.S. parent recognizes gain (but not loss), computed as if all of its assets were sold at the time of the transaction at fair market value. Ordinarily, no

---

[28] Although IRC § 163(j) limits interest deductions to related parties, its complex rules have not been effective with regard to many inversions.

[29] IRC §§ 368, 367.

tax is imposed on the shareholders of the corporation and they take the shares of the new foreign parent with the same tax basis they had for their stock of the former U.S. parent.

- **Foreign Reincorporation — Drop Down Transaction.** In this transaction, the U.S. parent transfers its assets to a new foreign parent corporation, which then contributes a portion of those assets to a U.S. subsidiary of the foreign parent. To the extent the assets are contributed to the U.S. corporation, the tax consequences of the transaction are similar to the stock transaction described above. To the extent the assets are held by the foreign corporation, the tax consequences are similar to the Asset Transaction described above.

Inversion transactions may provide significant tax benefits to a corporate group without any significant impact on corporate management, operations or shareholders. Although the country of incorporation changes, the location of corporate headquarters and operations remains the same. Similarly, the inversion does not affect a company's access to U.S. capital markets and its stock may continue to trade on U.S. stock exchanges. Inversions do not dilute shareholder ownership and they continue to own the same interest in assets as before the transaction, but through a foreign, rather than U.S. corporation.

Although the restructuring usually involves a transaction that is taxable to the corporation or its shareholders, the tax cost may be relatively low. In Stock Transactions, the most common type of inversion, little or no gain is recognized by shareholders of a company whose stock price has declined because the shareholders have a high cost basis for their stock. Similarly, a company that has lost money in recent years may offset any gain from the inversion with its net operating loss. The future tax benefits from the inversion are expected to greatly exceed any current tax liability.

Note that the tax benefits of incorporating abroad can be obtained through means other than inversion of an existing U.S. company. For example, a new venture can be incorporated abroad at its inception, thereby eliminating the need for a future inversion to achieve the desired tax benefits. Similarly, an existing U.S.-based multinational company may be acquired by a foreign corporation. In all situations, the result is a foreign based company replacing a U.S. based company. Thus, imposition of rules restricting inversions may not be effective because other means of achieving foreign ownership status are available. The Treasury Department is reviewing existing tax rules and is likely to recommend changes to ensure that the tax system does not create a competitive disadvantage for U.S.-based companies in global markets.[30]

---

[30] Office Of Tax Policy, Department Of The Treasury, *Corporate Inversion Transactions: Tax Policy Implications* (May 2002).

§ 5.04   International Competition Law

[1]   Comparing Competition Law Regimes

Competition law encompasses the various methods governments use to encourage and regulate competition among producers to maximize consumer and national economic welfare. The national laws and regulations used to achieve these goals differ significantly, both in substance and enforcement procedures. The material in this section provides a brief overview of some of the major policy and enforcement differences between selected national competition law regimes.

[a]   Selected Regimes

The U.S. antitrust rules focus on ensuring that markets remain competitive through stringent limitations on abusive business practices of large firms that are in a position to impede competition, and on price and market fixing arrangements, such as cartels. However, the U.S. generally does not attempt to prevent large companies from expanding or preserving their market shares through aggressive, but fair, business practices or technological innovation. Similarly, the U.S. does not tend to regulate vertical arrangements between big firms and their suppliers or distributors that do not prevent competitors from entering the market.

Relative to other countries, U.S. antitrust laws are aggressively enforced. The responsible Federal enforcement agencies, the Department of Justice and Federal Trade Commission, maintain regional offices throughout the country (and the world) and are vigilant in finding anticompetitive conduct. This conduct may be addressed through administrative proceedings, or by lawsuits brought by the Federal government, private companies, or individuals. Antitrust violators also may face state antitrust actions brought by local regulators in state courts. Moreover, particularly offensive conduct, such as price fixing, may be punished by criminal penalties.

The primary goal of European Union (EU) competition law policy is to eliminate practices that obstruct the economic integration of the member states into a unified common market. [31] Secondarily, the policy focuses on implementing a system to ensure that competition in the market "is not distorted." [32] This differs significantly from the U.S. focus on ensuring competitive markets through limitations on abusive business practices.

EU antitrust enforcement appears to be less aggressive than in the U.S. Although the EU regulators will accept and act on information received about anticompetitive practices, it lacks regional offices to pursue such information. As a result, many prohibited business practices are not stopped because local member-state regulators lack incentives to expose arrangements that only affect other member states. Similarly, actions by

---

[31] *See* EC Treaty Art. 2.

[32] EC Treaty Art. 3.

private firms and individuals are hindered by the complexity involved in bringing an action in a foreign court and collecting evidence about conduct in other member-states. The lack of criminal sanctions also precludes that deterrent to antitrust violations.

For a variety of historical reasons, Japanese law does not begin with the premise of U.S. law that private agreements to regulate trade are injurious. Until the end of the Second World War, cartels of the largest Japanese businesses were encouraged to stabilize the economy through practices that prevented unemployment and focused private economic activity on public goals. Indeed, even after the War, the antitrust statutes imposed by the U.S. government were largely not enforced, and numerous large cartels were operating openly.

Although Japanese regulators have begun more regular enforcement of the competition laws, the social significance of cooperative action remains an important factor in business conduct. Consequently, government regulators (the Japanese Fair Trade Commission) does not vigorously enforce the antitrust laws, and few remedies are available through lawsuits by private parties. The lack of enforcement and a forum for private action has created trade tensions between Japan and its major trading partners, particularly the U.S.

In response to the perceived lack of competition law enforcement in Japan, the U.S. has aggressively and extraterritorially applied its own antitrust laws to many Japanese firms.[33] These enforcement actions have created some stress between the U.S. and Japan. The Japanese perceive the actions as an infringement of Japanese sovereignty, while the U.S. is concerned that the anticompetitive conduct is closing Japanese markets to U.S. companies.[34]

[b] Extraterritorial Effect

In structuring arrangements for selling, producing or licensing products or services in a foreign country, the effect of U.S. *anti-trust* and foreign *competition* laws must be taken into account. While U.S counsel may be familiar with the U.S. rules, many other countries — including the European Union, Canada, Mexico, and Japan — approach competition law quite differently. A U.S. firms that enters a foreign market generally must comply with both the U.S. and foreign rules. Similar considerations apply to a foreign company entering the U.S. market.

A basic concern in applying antitrust laws to international transactions is the many companies that attempt to avoid their domestic laws by transferring headquarters and production facilities to foreign countries and then export their goods back to their former home country. The U.S., E.U. and

---

[33] Cooper, *The Role Of Positive Comity In U.S. Antitrust Enforcement Against Japanese Firms: A Mixed Review*, 10 Pac. Rim L. & Pol'y J. 383 (March 2001).

[34] *See* International Competitiveness Advisory Committee (ICPAC) final report to the Attorney General and Assistant Attorney General for Antitrust, February 28, 2000.

several other nations have addressed this issue by applying their antitrust rules *extraterritorially* to foreign firms that engage in competition practices that adversely affect their consumers. This approach cannot be enforced, however, without the cooperation of foreign antitrust agencies that must assist in providing evidence of the alleged violations. To this end, the U.S. Department of Justice has negotiated a number of *mutual cooperation agreements* with the antitrust authorities in other countries.

The extraterritorial effect of national competition laws may create significant problems for companies engaged in multinational enterprise. Because each country's competition laws and enforcement policies differ substantially, companies must contend with diverse antitrust laws in each country in which they transact business. For example, to avoid possible antitrust litigation, a merger of two corporations may have to be approved by the antitrust regulators of each country in which both companies do business. In addition to the time and expense involved, these regulatory reviews provide opportunities for countries to use antitrust considerations as a pretext for action that is really designed to protect domestic firms from foreign competition.

[2] U.S. Antitrust Laws

The U.S. antitrust laws are designed to prevent business activities that harm U.S. consumers by restricting competition. These rules are premised on the idea that vigorous competition ensures the most efficient allocation of economic resources, which benefits consumers through lower prices and greater choice. The anti-trust laws described below deter anti-competitive behavior by providing civil and criminal remedies against parties who engage in anti-competitive and monopolistic practices.

[a] Sherman Act

The Sherman Act, enacted in 1890, is the primary U.S. statute governing anti-competitive actions by domestic and foreign companies.[35] Section 1 of the Act prohibits contracts, combinations, and conspiracies in restraint of trade or commerce "among the several States, or with foreign nations."[36] This provision makes certain types of agreements among competitors illegal *per se,* including agreements to fix prices, refrain from selling competing lines of products, or allocate territories in which they will not compete against each other.

An agreement that is not *per se* illegal is subject to a factual inquiry to determine whether it is an *unreasonable* violation of the antitrust rules. The inquiry considers whether the action will have a significant adverse effect on competition, if it is economically justified, and if the justification

---

[35] *Hartford Fire Insurance Co. v. California,* 509 U.S. 764, 796 (1993), where the Supreme Court noted that "it is well established by now that the Sherman Act applies to foreign conduct that was meant to produce and did in fact produce some substantial effect in the U.S."

[36] 15 U.S.C. § 1.

for the arrangement can be achieved in a manner that does not restrict competition. This determination is made under the *rule of reason* test established by the U.S. Supreme Court,[37] which balances the aspects of the agreement that enhance competition against its anticompetitive effects in finding whether it is a reasonable or unreasonable violation.

Section 2 of the Sherman Act, prohibits monopolization, attempts to monopolize, and conspiracies to monopolize any part of trade or commerce. These actions may include imposition of unfair pricing or trading conditions, discriminating among customers in a manner that harms competitors, or limiting production. These violations may lead to civil penalties and also are punishable as felonies.[38] The Act's provisions may be enforced by the Department of Justice or by private party plaintiffs.

Either of these sections may be violated by a merger or acquisition that decreases competition in a particular market. Parties contemplating mergers may be required to submit information to the Department of Justice (DOJ) and Federal Trade Commission (FTC) that will allow these agencies to determine the impact of the proposed transaction. Mergers and acquisitions that will have a significant adverse effect on competition may be blocked.[39]

Violations may be punished by civil or criminal penalties, injunctive relief, or, for private plaintiffs, by treble damages. The DOJ conducts all criminal enforcement actions and ordinarily limits prosecutions to conduct such as price fixing, customer allocation, bid-rigging, or other cartel activities that are illegal in many countries. Corporate defendants may be fined up to $10 million, and other defendants may be fined up to $350,000. Individuals may be sentenced to up to 3 years imprisonment.

The Department of Justice may initiate a civil proceeding to obtain injunctive relief against prohibited practices or treble damages if the U.S. government purchased affected goods or services. A private plaintiff may also obtain injunctive and treble damages for violations of the Sherman Act.

[b] Clayton Act

The Clayton Act was enacted in 1914, and substantially amended in 1950.[40] The key provision of the Act is Section 7, which prohibits a merger or acquisition that may substantially lessen competition or tend to create a monopoly.[41] In contrast to the Sherman Act, which prohibits activities that actually restrain trade, Section 7 of the Clayton Act is designed to prevent incipient activities that will tend to restrain trade. Generally, whether a merger or acquisition will restrain trade is determined from the

---

[37] *Standard Oil v. U.S.*, 221 U.S. 1 (1911).

[38] 15 U.S.C. § 2.

[39] 15 U.S.C. § 2.

[40] 15 U.S.C. § 12 *et seq.*

[41] 15 U.S.C. § 18.

increase in market share or industry concentration that would result from the transaction.[42]

Section 7A of the Act sets forth *pre-merger notification* provisions that are enforced by the DOJ and FTC.[43] Generally, these rules apply to merger or acquisition transactions in which one party has net sales or assets of $100 million and the other party has net sales or assets of at least $10 million. The proposed transaction must be reviewed within 30 days of notification (15 days for tender offers), although that period may be extended if the reviewing agency seeks additional information.[44]

The Attorney General or the FTC[45] may ask a court to enjoin completion of a merger that would violate the provisions of the Act.[46] Similarly, private parties may seek injunctive relief.[47] The FTC also may initiate an administrative proceeding to obtain a cease and desist order. The Clayton Act's jurisdiction extends to foreign firms.[48]

Under the Clayton Act, any person engaged in commerce may not condition the lease or sale of goods on the purchaser's agreement not to use a competitor's products, if the effect may substantially lessen competition or to tend to create a monopoly.[49] In determining the impact of a transaction on competition under the Clayton Act, a rule of reason test is applied that is similar to the analysis used for purposes of the Sherman Act.

Robinson–Patman Act. The Robinson-Patman Act is an amendment to the Clayton Act that prohibits unjustified price discrimination.[50] Under this provision, purchasers of a commodity from the same seller must be charged identical prices. The law applies only to sales in interstate commerce, and to sales of "commodities of like grade and quality." It is limited to goods sold for use, consumption, or resale in the U.S., and not to goods destined for export.

[c] Federal Trade Commission Act

The *Federal Trade Commission Act* established the FTC and authorized it to investigate antitrust violations and enforce antitrust laws.[51] Pursuant to this authority, the FTC may investigate and take administrative action against any anti-competitive conduct, including violations of the Sherman

---

[42] *See U.S. v. General Dynamics Corp.*, 415 U.S. 486 (1974).

[43] 15 U.S.C. § 18a.

[44] 15 U.S.C. § 18a(e).

[45] This FTC authority is found in Section 13(b) of the FTC Act.

[46] 15 U.S.C. § 15.

[47] 15 U.S.C. § 26.

[48] *See* 15 U.S.C. § 12 (defining commerce as "trade or commerce among the several States and with foreign nations . . .").

[49] 15 U.S.C. § 3.

[50] 15 U.S.C. § 13.

[51] 15 U.S.C. § 41 *et seq.*

and Clayton Acts. The Commission also may seek injunctive relief against such conduct.[52]

Under Section 5 of the Act, it is unlawful to engage in "unfair methods of competition" and "unfair or deceptive acts" in commerce.[53] This provision applies to unfair competition involving commerce with foreign nations, other than imports, but only to the extent that the unfair conduct has a "direct, substantial, and reasonably foreseeable effect" on the foreign commerce.[54]

[d] Hart-Scott-Rodino Act

The *Hart-Scott-Rodino Antitrust Improvements Act of 1976* (HSR Act), gives the DOJ and FTC procedural methods to help these agencies enforce the antitrust rules relating to mergers and acquisitions.[55] Under the HSR Act, persons engaged in commercial activities must notify these agencies about proposed mergers, acquisitions, and joint ventures that exceed specific size-of-party and size-of transaction criteria.[56] These persons are required to provide specified information about the proposed transaction and are subject to a mandatory *waiting period* before completing it. Because the government can stop an anticompetitive acquisition before it occurs, it can avoid the complex task of unwinding a completed transaction involving commingled assets. Certain international transactions that have little connection with U.S. commerce are exempt from the premerger notice rules.[57]

Under recent amendments to the HSR Act, pre-merger notice is required for any transaction valued at greater than $200 million, regardless of the number or value of the acquiring company or investors.[58] For transactions valued at $200 million dollars or less, a size-of-transaction and size-of-person test must be satisfied. For smaller acquisitions, notice is required if:

- the value of the transaction exceeds $50 million, and;

- the *ultimate parent entity* (the company or person on top of the chain of ownership) of one of the parties has assets or revenues of at least $10 million, and;

- the other party has assets or revenues of at least $100 million.

Acquisitions made within 180 days involving the same ultimate parent entities or their subsidiaries are aggregated to determine the value of the

---

[52] FTC Act § 13(b).

[53] 15 U.S.C. § 45(a)(1).

[54] 15 U.S.C. § 45(a)(3).

[55] 15 U.S.C. § 18a.

[56] These criteria are set forth in the HSR Act and the corresponding FTC regulations at 16 C.F.R. § 801.

[57] 16 C.F.R. § 801.

[58] 15 U.S.C. § 18A, as amended by the 21st Century Acquisition Reform and Improvement Act of 2000, effective on February 1, 2001.

transaction. Acquisitions of stock are always aggregated at the fair market value of the stock when an additional acquisition is contemplated. In some situations, prior asset acquisitions are aggregated with stock purchases.

The basic information that must be provided before the merger or acquisition includes:

- a description of the transaction and the final or most recent versions of all documents that constitute the agreement;

- all studies, surveys, analyses, and reports prepared by or for officers or directors to evaluate or analyze the transaction with respect to market conditions, sales, sales growth, competitors, and other matters relevant to an antitrust analysis, and;

- revenue figures for each party to the transaction broken down by lines of commerce categorized in the Standard Industrial Classification Manual.

Generally, the waiting period is 30 days, extended to the next business day if the 30-day period would end on a weekend or public holiday. The DOJ or FTC may extend the waiting period another 30 days by issuing a formal *second request* for additional information. The waiting period begins when all parties to the transaction have submitted the required filings. For purchases of stock from persons other than the issuer, however, the waiting period commences when the purchaser files. The proposed transaction must be completed within one year of the end of the waiting period or the parties must submit new filings. It should be noted that the fact that the DOJ or FTC does not oppose a transaction during the waiting period does not bar a later challenge or exempt the parties from private antitrust actions.

A person that fails to comply with the HSR Act is subject to civil fines of up to $12,000 for each day that the violation continues. The penalty period begins on the day the HSR should have been filed and ends on the day the filing is made. A court may also grant the DOJ or FTC injunctive relief if a failure of compliance occurs.

[e]   Export Trading Company Act of 1982

The antitrust provisions of the *Export Trading Company Act of 1982* (ETC Act) are designed to reduce the uncertainty about the application of the U.S. antitrust laws to export activities. The Act creates a procedure by which persons engaged in export trade may obtain an *export trade certificate of review* (ETCR) that provides immunity from civil or criminal antitrust action arising from the conduct covered by the certificate.[59] The ETC Act also clarifies the jurisdictional rules for non-import cases under the Sherman and FTC Acts.

To obtain an ETCR, which is issued by the Secretary of Commerce with the concurrence of the Attorney General, an applicant must establish the following facts about its proposed export conduct:

---

[59] 15 U.S.C. §§ 4013, 4016.

(1) It will not result in a substantial lessening of competition or restraint of trade within the U.S., nor a substantial restraint of the export trade of any of the applicant's competitors.

(2) It will not unreasonably enhance, stabilize, or depress U.S. prices of the class of goods or services covered by the application.

(3) It will not constitute unfair methods of competition against competitors engaged in exporting the class of goods or services exported by the applicant.

(4) It will not include any act that may reasonably be expected to result in the sale for consumption or resale in the U.S. of such goods or services.

An ETCR does not provide protection from antitrust action if:

- The party's conduct is outside the scope of the certificate.

- The certificate was obtained by fraud.

- The conduct violates the statutory criteria for obtaining a certificate described above. In this situation, a person injured by conduct under the certificate may recover actual, but not treble, damages.

- An ETCR is not, explicitly or implicitly, an endorsement or opinion by the Secretary of Commerce or by the Attorney General about the legality of any actions under the laws of a foreign country.

An ECTR may be revoked or modified if the applicant's export activities cease to comply with the statutory criteria for obtaining a certificate.

[f] Wilson Tariff Act

The Wilson Tariff Act prohibits combinations, conspiracies, trusts, agreements, or contracts intended to restrain trade or increase the market price of imported goods in the U.S.[60] The statute applies to agreements by or between persons or corporations engaged in importing articles from a foreign country into the U.S. Violation of the Act is a misdemeanor, punishable by a maximum fine of $5,000, or one year in prison. The Act also permits the imported articles to be seized.

[g] National Cooperative Research and Production Act

The *National Cooperative Research and Production Act*[61] seeks to encourage research, development, and joint production activities by providing a special antitrust regime. The Act requires U.S. courts to determine the competitive effects of these activities by applying a rule-of-reason standard that takes account of all relevant factors affecting competition, including effects on competition in defined research, development, product,

---

[60] 15 U.S.C. §§ 8-11.

[61] 15 U.S.C. §§ 4301-06.

process, and service markets. This DOJ and FTC maintain that this approach is consistent with the government's general antitrust treatment of joint ventures.[62]

[h] Webb-Pomerene Act

The Webb-Pomerene Act[63] establishes a limited antitrust exemption for the formation and operation of associations of businesses to engage in collective export sales of "goods, wares or merchandise." The exemption does not apply to any conduct that has an anti-competitive effect in the US or that injures domestic competitors of the export association's members. The Act also does not grant immunity from prosecution under foreign antitrust laws. Associations seeking an exemption under the Act must file articles of agreement and annual reports with the FTC, although pre-formation approval is not required.

[3] U.S. International Antitrust Enforcement

Although the U.S. antitrust rules always have applied to foreign business activities that affect U.S. consumers, government policy about their extra-territorial application has changed in recent years. The basic issue has been whether restrictions on anti-competitive action should apply only to conduct that harms U.S. consumers, or if it should also extend to anti-competitive conduct that occurs abroad. A key issue in this regard is the extent to which U.S. antitrust laws apply extraterritorially to foreign business entities.

Prior to 1994, the U.S. had adopted a somewhat *laissez-faire* international antitrust policy designed to prevent U.S. law from applying to conduct that occurs in and affects foreign countries.[64] It was hoped that this policy would create a *level playing field* for U.S. firms to compete abroad against foreign rivals who were not subject to similar antitrust rules. The policy was articulated by the DOJ in its 1988 *Antitrust Enforcement Guidelines for International Operations,* which stated that the government was "concerned only with adverse effects on competition that would harm U.S. consumers by reducing output or raising prices."[65]

Trade conditions during the early 1990's indicated that a more extraterri-torial application of antitrust enforcement was required to deal with anti-competitive actions of private firms that were making it difficult for U.S. companies to compete in global markets. Consequently, the 1988 guidelines requiring direct harm to U.S. consumers were withdrawn in 1993, and replaced with a policy that allowed action where conduct abroad violates

---

[62] Antitrust Enforcement Guidelines for International Operations, April, 1995.

[63] 15 U.S.C. §§ 61-65.

[64] *See* Epstein, *The Other Side Of Harmony: Can Trade And Competition Laws Work Together In The International Marketplace?*, 17 Am. U. Int'l L. Rev. 343 (2002).

[65] *See* U.S. Dept. of Justice, Antitrust Enforcement Guidelines for International Operations (1988), footnote 159.

antitrust laws, and directly and foreseeably affects U.S. exports, goods, or services.[66]

The current U.S. policy emerged with the enactment of the *International Antitrust Enforcement Assistance Act of 1994*,[67] which gives the Department of Justice (DOJ) and Federal Trade Commission (FTC) substantial powers to pursue antitrust actions against foreign companies. This was followed by significant revisions to the DOJ and FTC *Antitrust Enforcement Guidelines for International Operations* (Guidelines) in 1995.[68] These Guidelines indicate that international antitrust enforcement and cooperation is now a high priority for the DOJ and FTC (the Agencies).

The Guidelines describe U.S. antitrust policies relating to:

- Subject matter jurisdiction over conduct and entities outside the U.S.

- Considerations, issues, policies, and processes relating to the government's decisions to exercise that jurisdiction.

- Considerations of international comity.

- Mutual assistance in international antitrust enforcement.

- The effects of foreign governmental involvement on private entity antitrust liability.

- The relationship between antitrust and international trade initiatives.

[a] Antitrust Jurisdiction Over Imports

Subject matter jurisdiction regarding U.S. antitrust laws is not limited to conduct within the country, but extends to anti-competitive practices that affect commerce in the U.S. regardless of where the conduct occurs or the nationalities of the parties.[69] This approach is consistent with the Supreme Court's view that "the Sherman Act applies to foreign conduct that was meant to produce and did in fact produce some substantial effect in the U.S."[70] Because imports directly influence the U.S. market, conduct related to imports usually satisfies this jurisdictional test. The Agencies apply the same jurisdictional principals to mergers and acquisitions under the Clayton Act, based on their view that the jurisdictional scope of the Clayton Act is the same as for the Sherman Act.[71]

The Guidelines illustrate this jurisdictional reach in an example that assumes that foreign producers of the same product organize a cartel to

---

[66] Press Release, U.S. Dep't of Justice, Foreign Business Conduct that Harms American Exports (April 2, 1993).

[67] Pub Law 103-438.

[68] The prior Guidelines issued in 1988 were withdrawn.

[69] Antitrust Enforcement Guidelines for International Operations, April 1995.

[70] *Hartford Fire Insurance Co. v. California*, 509 U.S. 764 (1993).

[71] Guidelines, § 3.14.

raise the price of the product, and that substantial sales of the product occur in the U.S. Under these facts showing actual and intended participation in U.S. commerce, the subject matter jurisdiction is quite clear.

[b] Non-Import Jurisdiction

U.S. subject matter jurisdiction over non-import transactions is governed by the *Foreign Trade Antitrust Improvements Act of 1982* (FTAIA), which amended the Sherman and FTC Acts.[72] The amendment to the Sherman Act (which is similar to the FTC Act amendment) provides that the Act may apply to non-import conduct involving trade or commerce with foreign nations if:

(1) The conduct has a direct, substantial, and reasonably foreseeable effect:

- on trade or commerce other than trade or commerce with foreign nations, or

- on export trade or commerce with foreign nations of a person engaged in such trade or commerce in the U.S.;

(2) The effect gives rise to a claim under the Sherman Act.

To illustrate the application of these standards, the Guidelines assume that a foreign price-fixing cartel produces a product in several foreign countries, and that no cartel members have U.S. production facilities or subsidiaries. The cartel sells its products to a non-member intermediary outside the U.S., knowing that the goods will be resold in the U.S. The Guidelines indicate that U.S. antitrust jurisdiction would apply, based upon a determination that the conduct had "direct, substantial and reasonably foreseeable effects" on U.S. domestic or import commerce.

Exports. The Agencies will apply the FTAIA's jurisdictional test to anti-competitive conduct that affects U.S. exports if the conduct would have violated U.S. antitrust laws if it occurred in the U.S.[73] This requires that:

- the conduct has a direct, substantial, and reasonably foreseeable effect on exports of goods or services from the U.S., and;

- the U.S. courts can obtain jurisdiction over persons or corporations engaged in such conduct.[74]

For conduct that is unlawful under the importing country's antitrust laws, the Agencies will work with that country's authorities if they can better remedy the conduct, and are prepared to take action to address the U.S. concerns. The Agencies also may act against U.S. exporters that engage in conduct that has a direct, substantial, and reasonably foreseeable effect on trade or U.S. domestic or import trade, or commerce. This may occur, for example, if U.S. supply and demand are not particularly elastic,

---

[72] 15 U.S.C. § 6a (1988) (Sherman Act) and 45(a)(3) (1988) (FTC Act).

[73] *See* U.S. Department of Justice Press Release dated April 3, 1992.

[74] Guidelines, § 3.122.

and U.S. firms enter into an agreement about export amounts that will reduce supply and raise prices in the U.S. Conduct that is ostensibly related to exports may be subject to antitrust action if it affects the price of products sold or resold in the U.S. This may occur if, for example, U.S. firms fix the price of an export item that is incorporated into a product produced abroad for resale in the U.S.

[c] Personal Jurisdiction

In determining the extraterritorial effect of a U.S. antitrust rule, the U.S. courts must consider *personal* and *subject matter* jurisdictional requirements. Personal jurisdiction requires that an alleged violator purposefully conducted business in the U.S. and reasonably could have anticipated that it would have to defend itself there. The Guidelines indicate that personal jurisdiction will be asserted only in conformance with the due process clause of the U.S. Constitution. That clause requires the defendant to have such minimum contacts with the U.S. that a proceeding comports with "fair play and substantial justice."[75]

Under the Clayton Act, an antitrust action against a corporation may be brought in the judicial district where it is an inhabitant, may be found, or transacts business.[76] For this purpose, the Agencies interpret *transacting business* to include a company that conducts business in a district directly through an agent, or through a related *alter ego* corporation.

[d] Foreign Government Involvement

Foreign Sovereign Immunities Act. A foreign government, agency, or instrumentality is not subject to U.S. jurisdiction for antitrust or other causes of action that are not specifically permitted under the *Foreign Sovereign Immunities Act of 1976* (FSIA).[77] The FSIA provides U.S. jurisdiction if the foreign government:[78]

- Explicitly or implicitly waived its immunity.

- Expropriated property in violation of international law.

- Acquired rights to U.S. property.

- Committed specified torts in the U.S.

- Agreed to arbitrate a dispute.

- Engaged in commercial activity. Under the commercial activities exception, a foreign government is not immune if the action:

---

[75] The Guidelines cite *Go-Video, Inc. v. Akai Elec. Co., Ltd.*, 885 F.2d 1406, 1414 (9th Cir. 1989); *Wells Fargo & Co. v. Wells Fargo Express Co.*, 556 F.2d 406, 418 (9th Cir. 1977). They also note that to establish jurisdiction, parties must be served in accordance with the Federal Rules of Civil Procedure or other relevant authority. Fed. R. Civ. P. 4(k).

[76] 15 U.S.C. § 22.

[77] 28 U.S.C. § 1602, *et seq.*

[78] *See* Guidelines, § 3.31.

- is based upon a commercial activity carried on in the U.S. by the foreign state, or;

- upon an act performed in the U.S. in connection with a commercial activity of the foreign state elsewhere, or;

- upon an act outside U.S. territory in connection with a commercial activity of the foreign state elsewhere and that act causes a direct effect in the U.S.[79]

Foreign Sovereign Compulsion. A person involved in international commercial activity may find itself subject to conflicting legal requirements in its home country and in the countries where it operates. Although the person may be able to comply with foreign and U.S. law in many situations, a direct conflict arises when the foreign country's law compels conduct that is prohibited by U.S. antitrust law. In this situation, the Agencies will recognize such foreign compulsion as a defense under U.S. antitrust law if:[80]

1. The foreign government compelled the anticompetitive conduct under circumstances in which a refusal to comply would result in penal or other severe sanctions.

2. The foreign government compelled conduct that can be accomplished entirely within its own territory. The defense is not recognized if the conduct occurs in the U.S.

3. The order comes from the foreign government acting in its governmental capacity and not from conduct pursuant to the government's commercial activities.

Acts of State. The act of state doctrine is a judicial rule that applies to sovereign public acts of a foreign government within its territorial jurisdiction.[81] The Guidelines indicate that U.S. antitrust action will not be taken with respect to restraints on competition that directly arise from a foreign government's noncommercial public acts.

[e] Comity

Under the international principle of *comity*, countries are obliged to cooperate in enforcing their respective laws, and to resolve international conflicts in a fair manner that is sensitive to the interests of other nations.[82] The Guidelines indicate that the Agencies will consider international comity in determining whether to assert jurisdiction over or act against a party where significant interests of a foreign nation would be affected.[83] In making this comity analysis, the Agencies will take into account factors that include:

---

[79] 28 U.S.C. § 1605(a)(2).

[80] Guidelines § 3.32. *See InterAmerican Refining Corp. v. Texaco Maracaibo, Inc.*, 307 F. Supp. 1291 (D. Del. 1970)

[81] Guidelines, § 3.33. *Banco Nacional de Cuba v. Sabbatino*, 376 U.S. 398 (1964).

[82] Enforcing Antitrust Against Foreign Enterprises 1 (Cornelis Canenbley ed., 1981).

[83] Guidelines, § 3.2.

- the relative significance to the conduct in the U.S., compared to conduct abroad;

- the nationality of the persons involved;

- the presence of a purpose to affect U.S. consumers, markets, or exporters;

- the relative significance and foreseeability of the effects in the U.S., compared to the effects abroad;

- the existence of reasonable expectations that would be furthered or defeated by the action;

- the degree of conflict with foreign law or foreign economic policies;

- the extent to which the enforcement activities of another country regarding the same persons may be affected, and;

- the effectiveness of foreign enforcement, compared to U.S. enforcement action.

In applying these factors, the Guidelines note that:

- No conflict with foreign law exists if the person subject to regulation by two states can comply with the laws of both.[84] Thus, the U.S. may assert jurisdiction if no conflict exists between the U.S. and foreign country's antitrust laws and policies, or if the foreign country's policies are neutral on the issue involved.

- In deciding whether or not to challenge an antitrust violation, the Agencies will consider whether the foreign country encourages certain conduct, leaves parties free to choose among different strategies, or prohibits some strategies.

- The Agencies will take into account the effect of their enforcement activities on related enforcement activities by the foreign nation's antitrust authority.

- The Agencies will consider whether the objectives of U.S. law will be attained through foreign enforcement. Thus, in lieu of an enforcement action, the Agencies may try to eliminate the anticompetitive effects in the U.S. through consultations with foreign governments.

- A decision to prosecute an antitrust action means that the U.S. has determined that the antitrust enforcement is more important than other relevant foreign policy concerns.

- The DOJ does not believe that the courts should "second-guess" its determinations about the role of comity in antitrust enforcement decisions.

---

[84] The Guidelines cite *Hartford Fire Insurance Co. v. California*, 509 U.S. 764 (1993).

[f] International Competition Policy Agreements

Although the Agencies are committed to vigorous antitrust enforcement when jurisdiction exists, the Guidelines indicate that they will consider international comity, and cooperation with foreign antitrust agencies and competition policy officials whenever possible.[85] Bilateral arrangements already exist between the U.S. and some countries, including Germany, Australia, and Canada. Another avenue for international antitrust cooperation is through the numerous mutual legal assistance treaties under which the U.S. and foreign nations have agreed to assist each other in criminal law enforcement issues.

With respect to countries that are members of the OECD, the Agencies have agreed to consider their legitimate interests in accordance with existing OECD recommendations. Under one such recommendation, the responsible U.S. agency will notify a member country when an antitrust enforcement action may affect the interests of that country or its nationals. Such actions may include requests for documents situated outside the U.S., questioning potential witnesses outside the U.S., and intervention in cases that involve foreign conduct of foreign persons.

[g] Restrictions on Foreign Investment — The Exon-Florio Amendment

The *Authority to Review Certain Mergers, Acquisitions and Takeovers Amendment* to the Defense Production Act of 1950 is commonly known by reference to its sponsors as the *Exon-Florio Amendment*.[86] Under the statute, the President may prohibit, suspend or reverse an acquisition of a company engaged in U.S. interstate commerce by foreign persons if he determines that the acquisition can threaten U.S. national security. The President may block a foreign acquisition of a U.S. corporation, without judicial review, if he finds:

1. credible evidence that the foreign entity exercising control might take action that threatens national security, and

2. the provisions of law, other than the International Emergency Economic Powers Act, do not provide adequate and appropriate authority to protect the national security.

The initial review of a transaction that may be subject to Presidential action is conducted by the *Committee on Foreign Investment in the U.S.* (CFIUS), an inter-agency committee, headed by the Secretary of the Treasury. Generally, the review begins after CFIUS has received a complete written notification about the proposed transaction. The notice must describe the nature of the transaction, the parties, any contracts the parties have with U.S. military or other government entities, and any export

---

[85] Guidelines, § 2.9.

[86] The Omnibus Trade and Competitiveness Act of 1988, adding § 721 to amend Title VII of the Defense Production Act of 1950, 50 U.S.C. § 2158 *et seq.*

licenses for specified goods or technology. If deemed necessary, CFIUS may then order an investigation that must begin within 30 days after the notice is received. The investigation must end within 45 days. Pursuant to the *Byrd Amendment* enacted in 1993, an investigation is required if:[87]

- the acquirer is controlled by or acting on behalf of a foreign government, and

- the acquisition may result in control of a person engaged in interstate commerce in the U.S. that could affect U.S. national security.

Although no rule requires parties to a transaction to provide notice of an acquisition that may be subject to Exon-Florio, failure to do so may allow CFIUS to begin an investigation at any time after the acquisition occurs. CFIUS may commence its own review after written notice to the parties to a transaction An investigation may be reopened if CFIUS subsequently finds that the notice received was materially deficient, false, or misleading.

The regulations under Exon-Florio do not define national security, but merely assert that products, services, and technologies important to U.S. defense requirements would be significant to national security.[88] In determining the impact of a foreign investment on U.S. national security, CFIUS and the President may consider the following factors:

(1)   the domestic production required for projected national defense requirements;

(2)   the capability and capacity of domestic industries to meet national defense needs, including available human resources, products, technology, materials, supplies, and services;

(3)   the control of domestic industries and commercial activity by foreign citizens that affects U.S. capability and capacity to meet national security requirements;

(4)   the potential effect on the sales of military goods, equipment, or technology to a country that supports terrorism, or proliferates missile technology or chemical and biological weapons, and;

(5)   the potential effect on U.S. technological leadership in areas affecting national security.

A variety of transactions are exempted from the statute, including investments by parties acting in the ordinary course of business that amount to no more than ten percent of an entity's stock. Whether a party is a foreign person for purposes of the statute is determined by a functional approach that focuses on the person's potential to be controlled by a foreign interest.

Notwithstanding the broad scope of Exon-Florio, relatively few transactions have been barred by Presidential action. There is some concern,

---

[87] Section 837(a) of the National Defense Authorization Act for Fiscal Year 1993.

[88] *See* Preamble to 31 CFR Part 800.

however, that future administrations will be tempted to adopt a broad definition of national security as a pretext for protecting domestic industries from foreign competition. A more current issue is the frequent use of the corporate defense against hostile takeovers by foreign controlled entities. Domestic companies engaged in some aspect of defense contracting have sought Congressional or administrative pressure to open CFIUS investigations as a means to delay a takeover or subject the proposed transaction to adverse publicity.

[4] EU Competition Law

Competition law in Europe is implemented at two levels; central European Union (EU) regulators enforce European competition law,[89] and the national authorities of each country enforce both the EU rules and their specific domestic competition laws. In applying competition law to mergers (above a certain size), however, the EU authorities have sole jurisdiction. If the EU and national rules are inconsistent, the EU law generally preempts. To the extent that EU and national rules are not inconsistent, actions may proceed at both levels and multiple judgments may be obtained. Like U.S. antitrust law, the EU competition rules often have an extraterritorial impact by applying to foreign firms whose activities affect trade or commerce within the EU.

Generally, the EU rules are comparable to the domestic laws of its members states. A member state's domestic antitrust law may apply to an agreement that has an effect that is solely national. In that situation, the issue will be determined under local law without reference to the EU rules. Where both the EU and domestic rules apply, the local law may differ significantly by imposing additional or more restrictive requirements. For example, Germany and France have implemented price control rules that are not found at the EU level.

The basic EU competition rules are set forth in *Articles 81* and *82* of the *Treaty of Amsterdam*.[90] Article 81 governs agreements or concerted practices that have an anti-competitive object or effect. Article 82 concerns abuses of dominant positions that may affect trade between member states. Both Articles apply to restrictive practices by public and private *undertakings*, natural or legal persons, and any combination of legal persons engaged in an independent commercial activity. An *undertaking* is broadly defined to include any legal or natural person without regard to its legal status or financial structure. It encompasses corporations, partnerships, trade associations, sole practitioners, and State entities. It also covers non-profit enterprises that are engaged in commercial activities.

---

[89] Treaty Establishing the European Economic Community, effective January 1, 1958.

[90] Treaty of Amsterdam Amending the Treaty on European Union, the Treaties Establishing the European Communities and Certain Related Acts, Oct. 2, 1997, O.J. (C 340) 1 (1997)(hereinafter, The EC Treaty).

[a] Anticompetitive Agreements (Article 81)

Article 81(1), prohibits and voids any agreement or concerted practice that has the object or effect to prevent, restrict, or distort competition in the Common Market, and that may affect trade between EU member states. These rules expressly apply to agreements or practices that fix prices or trading conditions, limit production or markets, share markets or sources of supply, discriminate against other trading parties, or impose tying arrangements regarding unrelated products.[91] The agreement may be written or unwritten, formal or informal, and its existence may be inferred from the surrounding circumstances. Article 81 may apply to practices initiated outside the EU if implemented within the Union.[92]

Generally, an agreement will be deemed anti-competitive if its participants directly or indirectly exclude others from a market. Examples of such agreements include:

- **Market allocations.** Agreements that create territorial divisions of the market or divide a product's market among the participants. For example, a agreement by two producers to stay out of each other's territory or to establish market quotas would be illegal.

- **Restrictive intellectual property right licenses.** Agreements relating to pooled patents, or cross licensing arrangements in which patent owners combine their patents and cross-license to each another and/or collectively grant licenses to third parties. The EU competition authorities have granted block exemptions to certain categories of patent licensing agreements. Under U.S. antitrust law, however, these arrangements are tested under the *rule of reason* to determine if they are anticompetitive

- **Boycotts and refusals to deal.** A method for enforcing an anticompetitive agreement is through collective boycott or a concerted refusal to deal with competitors. This conduct also may be illegal if it takes the form of an unjustified refusal to admit a new member to a commercial association or accord. This may be inferred if the rules for admitting new members are not clear, neutral, and objective.

- **Price setting.** Agreements are prohibited if they set prices, pricing methods, or require a reseller or distributor to maintain certain prices or sales conditions.

[b] Abuse of Dominant Position (Article 82)

Article 82 prohibits a company from abusing its dominant position so as to adversely affect trade between EU member states. The prohibition applies to an undertaking if it:

---

[91] EC Treaty, art. 81(1), (a)-(e).

[92] *See* Case 89/95, *Ahlstrom v. Commission*, [1988] 4 C.M.L.R. 901, 901 (1988) (Predecessor to Article 81, applied to U.S. and Canadian wood pulp manufacturers that competed and sold directly to customers in the EC).

- has a dominant position in the market, meaning that it can act independently from its' competitors and customers in the market;

- abuses the dominant position to impose unfair conditions, and;

- can adversely affect trade between EU members states as a result its conduct.

An undertaking's dominant position is determined by reference to relevant product and geographic markets.[93] Generally, a market share of 50 percent or more is presumed to be dominant, although dominance may be deemed to exist with market shares between 40 and 50 percent. A company whose products cannot be substituted for with other marketed products is likely to have a dominant position. This also is true of a company that possesses sufficient technical advantage to control product development.

Whether a dominant position is being abused is a determined by reference to normal industry practices and from the type and scale of the conduct in question. Generally, conduct is abusive behavior if it decreases the amount of competition in a market by methods that differ from normal competition in products or services. Examples of specific types of abusive conduct include:

- **Abusive pricing.** Generally, unfairly high prices or predatory low prices are deemed abusive because the benefit to the company could not be obtained in a competitive environment. Similarly, unjustifiably imposing different prices for the same product in different areas may be considered an anticompetitive abuse.

- **Rebates.** An abuse occurs when a dominant company grants rebates to secure customers.

- **Intellectual Property abuse.** Imposing unfair licensing terms or charging an excessive price for a product protected by intellectual property rights may be an abuse.

- **Tying clauses.** A service supplier may not obligate a customer to buy a product as a condition of selling another product to that customer.

- **Discriminating against trading partners.** A dominant company may act abusively by imposing discriminatory and unfair conditions on another company with which it has contractual relationships.

- **Mergers.** A dominant undertaking may act abusively by permanently reducing competition through a merger.

The G.E.-Honeywell Merger

The difference between the U.S. and EU approach to competition law is illustrated by the proposed merger between General Electric

---

[93] *See, e.g.,* Case 27/76, *United Brands v. Commission,* E.C.R. 207, par. 44 (1978).

and Honeywell International in 2001. That $42 billion transaction was approved by U.S. and Canadian antitrust regulators but was barred by the European Commission (EC) on the ground that it would reduce aerospace competition in the EU market. Although both companies are U.S.-based, the merger was impractical if the new company could not compete in the large EU aerospace market. The decision is the first time that the EC barred a merger that had been approved by U.S. authorities.

In the U.S., the focus of antitrust law is to protect consumers and promote competition. Accordingly, a merger is permitted if its likely effect will be price reduction or better quality or innovation that will benefit the consumer and not substantially decrease competition. In the G.E. case, competition would not have decreased because General Electric and Honeywell were not competitors. A merger is not barred simply because the merged firms will be large, more efficient, or have a wide scope of products even if competitors of the merged firm may be harmed or driven from the market. Essentially, the U.S. (and Canadian) authorities allowed the proposed merger because it would benefit consumers.

By contrast, EU antitrust law emphasizes promoting competition by protecting competitors, rather than consumers. Companies are barred from obtaining dominance to the detriment of competitors in the market. The EU regulations require a three step evaluation of a proposed merger: (1) define the product and geographic markets; (2) determine whether the company has a dominant position; and (3) consider whether the dominant position will significantly impede competition. In the GE case, the regulators concluded that the size and scope of the merged company could allow it to *bundle* its products and thereby *dominate* Europe's aerospace industry.

[c] Government Action

EU competition law provides rules govern that the relationship between member states and private economic activity. Treaty Article 86 prohibits member states from enacting measures that are contrary to EU competition rules relating to public undertakings, and undertakings that are granted special or exclusive rights by a member government. Under Article 87, with certain exceptions, member states may not grant or provide aid or resources that will distort competition within the EU market by favoring certain undertakings or the production of certain goods.[94]

[d] Enforcement

Under the competition law procedural rules, the European Commission (Commission), an administrative agency of the EU, is responsible for

---

[94] EC Treaty, art. 87(2), (3).

enforcement of Articles 81 and 82.[95] The Commission acts in this area through its staff in the Directorate General for Competition. The Commission is empowered to obtain information through written interrogatories, to inspect business premises, and may require EU member states to carry out inspections for the Commission.[96] Upon a determination that a competition law violation has occurred, the Commission may enjoin the prohibited activity and fine the responsible party.[97] In addition, national courts of the EU member states may hear claims for damages from competition law violations and make appropriate awards to the plaintiff.

Negative clearance. A party that is unsure about whether an agreement will be considered an illegal restraint of trade that violates Article 81, may seek an individual exemption, or a negative clearance (or both) from the Commission. A *negative clearance* is a certification from the Commission that no grounds exist under Articles 81 or 82 to initiate an enforcement action.[98] The clearance is likely to be issued if any potential violation will not act as an appreciable restraint on competition among EU member states. The Commission will not act on a clearance or exemption until it has been formally notified about the proposed or existing agreement, decision, or concerted practice involved.

Individual exemption. A request for an *individual exemption* acknowledges that the agreement in question may violate Articles 81 or 82, but requests a certification that the Commission will not institute enforcement proceedings. The exemption may be granted if the Commission determines that the agreement:[99]

- improves the production or distribution of goods, or promotes technical or economic progress;

- allocates a fair share of the benefit to consumers;

- contains restrictions of competition that are indispensable to obtaining the permissible results, and;

- does not allow the parties to eliminate competition in a "substantial part" of the market.

The Commission has sole authority to grant exemptions, but its decisions are subject to review by the European Court of Justice. Individual exemptions apply for a limited period of time and do not prevent the Commission from implementing actions to remedy abuses of prohibited market dominating positions. Individual exemptions are periodically reviewed, and may be revoked or altered by a subsequent decision.[100]

---

[95] EC Regulation 17/62 (Regulation 17) adopted March 1962. This regulation does not apply to certain coal and steel products, transportation, or agricultural products.

[96] Regulation 17/62, articles 11–14.

[97] Regulation 17/62, articles 3, 15.

[98] Regulation 17/62, article 2.

[99] Regulation 17/62, articles 9.

[100] Regulation 17/62, article 8(2).

Comfort letters. To expedite the negative clearance and individual exemption process, the Commission issues numerous *comfort letters* each year. A comfort letter is a written assurance from the Directorate General for Competition that the Commission will not initiate an enforcement action unless a substantial change in circumstances occurs.[101] National courts and regulators, however, are not bound by a comfort letter in determining whether an agreement violates the competition law, although the letters may be considered.

Block exemptions. The exemption process has been expedited through the issuance of *block exemptions* that apply to entire categories of agreements. Regulations granting block exemptions must be authorized by the European Council.[102] Examples of current block exemptions that have been allowed include agreements relating to exclusive distributorships, franchising, patent and know-how licensing, motor vehicle distribution, air transport, and insurance.

[5] Japan's Competition Law

Before the end of the Second World War in 1945, Japan's economy was dominated by major cartels that controlled competition in most industries. Formation of these cartels, referred to as *Zaibatsu*, was encouraged by the Japanese government as a means of controlling the industrialization required to enhance the nation's military power. For example, legislation enacted in 1933 merged the major government-owned steel producers with seven private steelmakers to create a single enterprise that produced over 95% of all Japanese steel.

After the war, the U.S. occupation authorities adopted a policy to dissolve the industrial and banking combinations that controlled most of Japan's economic life. The Zaibatsu were broken up and the controlling families ordered to relinquish their ownership interests. The occupation authorities also required the Japanese government to enact laws to bar monopoly and restraint of trade, interlocking directorates, inter-corporate security ownership, and take other measures to provide a competitive business environment.

The first such law, the *Anti Monopoly Act* (AMA) enacted in 1947, established most of Japan's substantive and procedural competition law.[103] The AMA prohibits three categories of business behavior:

- unreasonable restraints of trade through collusive practices,

- private monopolies through mergers, holding companies, inter-company shareholdings and interlocking directorships;

---

[101] European Commission, White Paper On Modernization Of The Rules Implementing Articles 85 And 86 Of The EU No. Treaty, Commission Program No.99/027, April 28, 1999.

[102] EC Treaty, art. 87.

[103] 1947 Act Concerning Prohibition of Private Monopolization and Maintenance of Fair Trade.

- unfair business practices, specifically including unfair prices, unfairly inducing or coercing customers from a competitor, dealing on restrictive terms, unreasonable use of bargaining power, and unfairly interfering with competitors in transactions with third parties, and interfering in a competitor's internal affairs.

The AMA also established the Japan Fair Trade Commission (JFTC) as the nation's primary competition law enforcement agency. The Prime Minister appoints the JFTC Commissioners, who are usually retired bureaucrats representing various ministries. The JFTC deals with anticompetitive practices in any of the following ways:

- preventive consultations,
- informal cautions and warnings,
- formal recommendations and complaints, and
- criminal proceedings.

For many years, U.S. companies have complained that Japan's competition laws have been enforced inconsistently.[104] During the 1960s, for example, a number of cartels were broken up but others were permitted to operate in order to maintain employment and production during economic recessions. U.S. trade officials have asserted that the AMA sanctions are inadequate and that regulatory staff at the JFTC is too small and underfunded. This lax enforcement, it has been argued, creates an unfair trade barrier against non-Japanese companies seeking to operate in the Japanese market.

Japan's lack of enforcement may be attributable to its historic industrial policy, which was designed to increase the ability of Japanese companies to compete in international markets. This industrial policy promoted creation of very large companies, with attendant economies of scale, by encouraging mergers and discouraging new entrants into certain industries. In general, the government's strategic decision to support large integrated companies was deemed to override the competition principles of the AMA.

In response to these complaints, as well as a perceived need to deregulate its domestic markets, Japan strengthened many AMA provisions and increased the enforcement powers of the JFTC. These changes included bringing criminal charges against cartels, bid riggers and other serious violaters that had a substantial impact on consumers. Prison terms and fines were increased and, in 2001, persons injured by unfair trade practices were allowed to institute law suits for injunctive relief. Further, Japanese ministries were ordered to consult with the JFTC before issuing administrative guidance to firms about their investment decisions.

Although Japan's competition law and its enforcement have improved, the system still lacks sufficient penalties to create disincentives to

---

[104] *See* Harris, *Competition Law And Patent Protection In Japan: A Half-Century Of Progress, A New Millennium Of Challenges*, 16 Colum. J. Asian L. 71 (Fall 2002).

companies engaging in anticompetitive practices. One problem is the relatively low fines that can be imposed. More important is the lack of private antitrust lawsuits and possible high damage awards for the parties harmed by unfair business practices. Although such lawsuits are possible, they are difficult to initiate and rarely successful.

[6] China's Competition Law

China did not have, nor need, a competition law or policy until it changed from a centrally planned to a market economy in the early 1980s. When this momentous change occurred, the government soon perceived the necessity for rules to govern competition between the private firms that soon began to emerge. However, enforcement of these rules is generally poor and violations are unlikely to be discovered or punished. Many Chinese executives and managers are unaware that such laws exist and do not understand the kinds of behavior they prohibit. Local governments intent upon protecting local businesses often resist enforcement of the competition laws.

The primary competition law enforcement agency is the State Administration for Industry and Commerce (SAIC). SAIC and its local branches can investigate business practices and issue corrective instructions, suspend business licenses, and impose fines. However, SAIC does not have authority over anticompetitive acts of other government departments and ministries and generally lacks the political clout required to override local governments actions to protect local businesses or discourage investigations of local firms. Ordinarily, competition law issues are not resolved through judicial proceedings.

The basic Chinese laws and regulations governing Competition in China are summarized as follows:

1. *Regulations on Development and Protection of Competition.*[105] These regulations prohibit monopolization or sole proprietary management of products. An exception is provided for products managed exclusively by departments and organizations designated by the state. The regulations state that:

    "Competition must be introduced by breaking down regional blockades and departmental barriers. No locality or department is allowed to block the market. No locality or department should impose any ban on the entry of goods made in other places. Localities should ensure that raw materials can be transferred out according to state plans and must not create any blockade. Departments in charge of industry, transport, finance and trade must revise any part or parts of their existing regulations and systems which impede competition so as to facilitate competition."[106]

---

[105] Regulations on Development and Protection of Competition (State Council, October 17, 1980).

[106] *Id.*, Article 6.

2. *The Unfair Competition Law.* This law, enacted in 1993, defines the objective of China's competition policy as:[107]

"to safeguard the healthy development of the socialist market economy, encourage and protect fair competition, stop acts of unfair competition and defend the lawful rights and interests of operators and consumers."

The law bans or limits the following business practices:[108]

- False or misleading advertising, including advertising by agencies that are aware or should be aware of a seller's misrepresentation.

- Use of prizes as a marketing strategy, limiting prizes to 5,000 RMB (approximately $60) subject to honest drawing arrangements.

- Bribes and kickbacks.

- Fabricating or spreading of false information to injure a competitor's reputation.

- Copying trademarks and certificates of quality or origin.

- Use of brand identification (e.g., brand names, packaging or design) that may confuse consumers.

- Obtaining trade secrets illegally or distribution of such secrets by persons who know or should know that the trade secrets were illegally obtained.

- Bid rigging.

- Predatory pricing, meaning selling a product below cost to drive out a competitor.

- Tie-in sales or other unreasonable sales conditions against the wish of the buyer.

- Compelling purchase of goods or services by operators of public utilities or monopolies to exclude others from competing.

- Abuse of local government administrative power to force others to buy the goods from designated operators in order to restrict the business activities of other operators.

- Abuse of local government administrative power to restrict the entry of goods from other parts of the country into the local market or the flow of local goods to markets in other parts of the country.

3. *The Price Law.* The Price Law, enacted in 1998, is designed to curb predatory pricing and price wars in the consumer market.

---

[107] 1993 Unfair Competition Law, Art 1.
[108] *Id.* Art. 9.

The statute prohibits price fixing, predatory pricing, discrimination against business operators, spreading rumors about price hikes, and deceptive pricing to attract business. Penalties include fines but no criminal sanctions.

4. *Draft Antimonopoly Law.* A comprehensive antimonopoly law has been drafted and is expected to be implemented in the near future. The existing draft of the law covers most typical unfair business practices as well as mergers, acquisitions and other organizational issues that may affect competition.

In addition to these national rules, a number of provinces and major cities have enacted local unfair competition laws and regulations.

§ 5.05   Specific National and Regional Markets

[1]   The European Union

The economic, political and social integration of Europe is not based upon a distinct constitution, but has evolved through a series of limited-scope, multi-national treaties enacted over 50 year period. Economic integration began shortly after World War II, when six nations — France, Germany, Italy, the Netherlands, Belgium, and Luxembourg — agreed to share sovereignty over their coal and steel production by forming a European Coal and Steel Community (ECSC).[109] By placing these basic industries under common authority, these nations hoped to accelerate Europe's economic recovery from the war and make future conflicts far less likely.

Encouraged by the ECSC's success, the six nations broadened their economic, social, and political integration, and created a framework for expansion of the community to include other European countries. The Treaty of Rome, signed in 1957, established the European Economic Community (EEC) that would work towards merging the members' separate national market into one supranational market that allowed free movement of goods, capital, and labor within the community. The Treaty also created an Atomic Energy Community (Euratom) to enhance the use and production of nuclear energy. Eventually, the separate economic communities were merged together and now form the European Union (EU), which is often referred to as the Common Market.[110]

The EEC's achievements persuaded other Western European nations to seek membership. Denmark, Ireland and the United Kingdom became members in 1973, Greece in 1981, Spain and Portugal in 1986, and Austria, Finland, and Sweden in 1995.[111] The former East Germany entered as part

---

[109] Treaty of Paris. Expires in 2002 and coal and steel subsumed into EU.

[110] The Merger Treaty of April 8, 1965, established a single executive for the ECSC, the EEC and Euratom. The term European Community (EC) comprises merger of these three organizations.

[111] Norway negotiated membership in 1994 but its voters rejected membership in a referendum.

of a united Germany in 1990. A number of eastern European countries, including the Czech Republic, Cyprus, Estonia, Hungary, Latvia, Lithuania, Malta, Poland, Slovenia, and Slovakia became EU members on May 1, 2004. Citizens of the newly admitted countries will be subject to some restrictions on travel and work during an initial phase-in period. Also, some countries have negotiated barriers against hiring citizens of new member states for a period of time. The newly expanded union of 25 countries has a combined population of 455 million people.

The next EU expansion will occur in 2007, when Bulgaria and Romania join. Croatia and Turkey will begin negotiation for membership in in the near future. Other countries, such as Norway and Switzerland are not formally members, but have special agreements and relationships with the EU. Membership generally is open to a country that has a stable democratic government, an appropriate human rights record, a functioning market economy, and the ability meet its economic and political obligations to the EU.[112]

The original treaties on European integration were substantially revised and expanded by the Maastricht Treaty on European Union that became effective in 1993. The Maastricht Treaty focuses on three basic areas ("pillars") of economic, political, and social integration:

- creating a European Monetary Union (EMU), including a detailed schedule for implementing a collective economic policy and common currency;

- establishing a common foreign and security policy allowing for joint action in foreign and security matters;

- creating shared judicial and police policies on issues such as asylum, immigration, civil and criminal trials, anti-terrorism, drug trafficking and fraud.

Recognizing the growing importance of the social and political factors, the Treaty renamed the organization as the European Union (EU).[113]

[a] Governing Institutions

Through a series of treaties, European member states have gradually ceded portions of their national sovereignty to various EU institutions. In theory, a "subsidiary" principle applies, granting the EU jurisdiction over policies that must be broadly applied, leaving other decisions to national, regional, and local governments. The five basic EU governing institutions are: Parliament, Commission, Council of Ministers, Court of Justice, and Court of Auditors. Overall political direction is provided through bi-annual European Council summit meetings attended by the heads of government and the Commission President.

---

[112] Maastrict Accord (1991).

[113] The latest EU agreement, the Treaty of Amsterdam (May, 1999), enhances the organization's ability to undertake joint foreign policy actions. Many decisions no longer require unanimity, but can be reached by a qualified majority.

- **European Commission.** The Commission generates most EU policy by proposing legislation, administering its bureaucracy and budget, implementing the rules enacted by other EU institutions, and representing the EU in international trade negotiations. The commission may investigate and take legal action for violations of EU rules. There are 20 Commissioners — two each from France, Germany, Italy, Spain and the United Kingdom, and one from each of other member state, appointed for five-year terms. The national governments appoint the Commission President by agreement with the Parliament's approval. The commission has a very large administrative staff based in Brussels.

- **European Council (Council of Ministers).** The Council, comprising Ministers from each member state, enacts EU laws based upon proposals from the Commission. The participating minister depends upon the legislative topic (*e.g.*, the energy minister works and votes on energy legislation). Voting in the council is weighted according to the size of the countries. The Council presidency rotates among the members-states every six months. A Committee of Permanent Representatives, and a large Secretariat provide advice and bureaucratic support to the Council.

- **European Parliament.** The European Parliament is not a legislature; it does not enact laws, but has "co-decision" and veto powers over most legislation proposed by the Council. Members of the European Parliament are directly elected for five-year terms. In effect, the Parliament is a forum for debate of public issues, but has limited influence on Commission and Council policy.

- **Court of Justice.** The EU's highest court construes treaties to ensure that they are correctly applied. Its decisions are binding on EU states and institutions, companies and individuals, and may overrule the national courts.

- **Court of Auditors.** This court examines the receipts, expenditures, and financial management of the EU budget.

[b] The Common Market

The 1957 Treaty of Rome began the long process toward a single, unified, European domestic market by establishing a Customs Union. In a Customs Union, the member states agree to eliminate internal tariffs and other trade barriers among themselves, coordinate their trade policies, and establish a common tariff on imports from non-members. Although the European Customs Union was not effective in increasing cross-border trade, it did provide a foundation for expansion to a common market. A common market encompasses the principles of a customs union, but also provides for free movement of goods, capital, and people within the market.

The movement to change the Customs Union into a common market began in the late 1970s, when it became apparent that market fragmentation was hindering European economic development. Europe's economy was performing poorly and its technological and industrial development was falling behind its trading partners — particularly the United States and Japan. These problems were addressed in a "white paper" issued by the European Commission in 1985, which recommended numerous steps to form an internal common market, and fixed 1992 as the target date for completing that market. The white paper recommendations were adopted by the European Council and later reflected in the Single European Act (SEA) of 1987.

The SEA implemented a number of measures that integrated the European nations' economies by allowing freer movement of goods and people. These measures included:

- eliminating many national health regulations and passport controls;

- eliminating national educational barriers by requiring members to recognize each other's educational qualifications;

- permitting citizens of a member state to work in another member state while maintaining legal and union rights;

- harmonizing tax rules and regulations;

- removing trade barriers, including physical barriers, such as internal borders, as well as impediments created by dissimilar documentary requirements and technical standards.

Although the SEA required more than 300 separate rules and directives, it has achieved the goal of a unified internal market in which goods, capital, people, and services move freely among the EU countries. Creation of such a large market has resulted in significant economies of scale that have greatly increased the competitiveness of European business.

[c] Economic and Monetary Union (EMU)

The basic plan for achieving European Economic and Monetary Union (EMU) was approved by the European Council in 1989 and adopted in The Maastricht Treaty of 1992. The Treaty required the EU to obtain economic and monetary union in seven years; that is, by 1999. To meet this goal, participating countries had to establish a permanent value for their currencies relative to other members' currencies, abide by a centralized monetary policy, and eventually adopt a uniform currency. Transition to the EMU was planned to occur in three stages:

- Stage One (1990) removed restrictions on movements of capital across EU borders and encouraged members to coordinate their economic policies.

- Stage Two (1994) required member countries to converge their policies on currencies, interest rates, inflation, budget deficits, etc., and established the European Monetary Institute as the precursor to the European Central Bank (ECB).

- Stage Three (1999) required participating members to irrevocably lock the exchange rates of their currencies and then adopt the Euro as a single currency managed by the ECB.

The Euro. Twelve EU members — Austria, Belgium, Finland, France, Germany, Greece, Italy, Ireland, Luxembourg, the Netherlands, Spain, and Portugal — have adopted the Euro as their national currencies.[114] Denmark, Sweden, and the United Kingdom have decided, for the present, to retain their national currencies. Since 1999, participants in the Euro zone have used that currency to account for transactions in financial and capital markets, public debt, private bank accounts, credit card transaction, and many other areas. In 2002, participating nations will retire all other national notes and coins, leaving the Euro as their sole circulating currency.

To ensure the Euro's stability, participating states must continue implementing their financial obligations under the Maastricht Treaty with respect to their policies on interest rates, inflation, and budget deficits. A state that fails to meet its obligations can be subject to economic sanctions.[115] Monetary policy over the euro is governed by the European System of Central Banks (ESCB), comprising the ECB and the Central Banks of the euro countries.

EU Countries that have not adopted the euro. As noted above, three EU countries have opted not to adopt the euro as their currency. Also, many of the eastern European nations expected to join the EU may not satisfy the fiscal requirements for adopting the euro. Accordingly, special agreements will be needed to avoid excessive fluctuations between the euro and the currencies of the non-euro EU countries. Guidelines for these agreements issued in 1997 indicate that they will parallel the European Monetary System (EMS) that governed all EU currency exchange rates before the euro was adopted (*i.e.*, a future EMS II).

The EMS was created in 1979 to maintain stable currency exchange rates between participating EU members.[116] To provide stability, participating central banks were required to intervene in currency markets to prevent the exchange rate of their national currency from moving higher or lower than a specified range relative to another currency. The central bank had to buy the weak currency and sell the stronger. Funds for these purposes could be borrowed from other members' central banks.

---

[114] Eleven members adopted the Euro in January, 1999 and Greece was permitted to use it in January 2001. The euro zone is economically comparable to the United States, having a population of about 290 million, and around 20% of world trade and GDP.

[115] Stability and Growth Pact, agreed by EU Heads of State and Government in July 1997.

[116] By April 1998, 13 of the 15 Member States of the European Union belonged to the EMS exchange rate mechanism, all except Sweden and the United Kingdom.

[b] The Chinese Economy

The Open Door policies implemented by Deng Xiaoping after Mao's death in 1976 have greatly changed and improved China's economic and social policies. Under Mao, the basic economic policies focused upon central economic planning (usually for periods called five-year plans), collectivization of agriculture, state control and ownership of industry, and Chinese self-sufficiency in all economic sectors. The result was significant negative economic growth during the periods of the Great Leap Forward and Cultural Revolutions.

In contrast, Deng emphasized the development of free market forces, attracting foreign trade and investment from the West, and rapid economic growth. The result of these policies has been an average annual growth rate of more than 8 percent since 1978. Although this astounding rate of growth offers foreign businesses many trade and investment opportunities, it is important to note the very low economic level from which the growth began. By some estimates, China's output will exceed that of the U.S. by 2020. However, its per capital income, a more important measure of economic well-being, still will be fairly low compared to the West. A great deal of catch-up is still required before China becomes a great economic power.

The post-Mao reforms eliminated most central production and trade planning, privatized large sectors of industry and agriculture, and established a free market pricing system. Currently, it is estimated that the non-state sector produces more than two thirds of industrial output, although the state-owned sector still employs a far higher percentage of workers. Many sectors of China's economy are still in the process of transition from central planning to a free market economy and additional reforms are required to develop the legal, administrative and regulatory infrastructure of a modern economy.

Economic growth in China has been geographically uneven, benefiting the provinces along the Pacific coast far more than the central and western areas of the country. The coastal regions produce more than 80 percent of China's exports and attract more than 90 percent of its foreign investment capital. Most of the production from the non-state owned sector originates in the coastal areas, while the rest of the nation is far more dependent upon the inefficient state-owned enterprises (SOE).

In agriculture, collectivization has been replaced by a *responsibility system* that is, in effect, a return to family farming. Under the system, families lease land from the government for up to thirty years in return for an agreement to provide a quota of specified crops at a fixed price. The family can sell its surplus to the state or on the open market at market prices. The system has substantially increased China's agricultural output, eliminated domestic food shortages, and provided a higher standard of living for China's large rural population. An emerging issue is the steady shift by Chinese farmers away from food staples, such as grain, to more profitable cash crops (*e.g.,* fruit, vegetables, and tea), and non-agricultural activities. This trend, along with the foreign agricultural competition arising from China's entry into the WTO, is likely to affect the country's self-sufficiency in grain and certain other food crops. Of course, this aspect of global free trade is inherent in the theory of Comparative Advantage.

The success of the family responsibility system in agriculture increased rural per capital incomes to the point that allowed a rapid increase in small, local private, and collectively owned businesses. Many of these rural businesses, called *town and village enterprises* (TVE), are unusual alliances between local entrepreneurs and local government officials. During the early 1990's, the TVEs played an important role in absorbing excess rural labor, and providing a tax base for poorer provinces. There are recent indications, however, that the number of successful TVEs has diminished, partly due to the tax burden imposed by local officials who lack other revenue sources. To the extent that economic prospects on farms and in rural areas diminishes, the populations may begin to move to already overcrowded Chinese cities, increasing the potential for social unrest.

The most significant problem in the economic development of China involves the many unproductive *state owned enterprises* (SOE) that were at the core of its economy before the shift from central planning to a market based system. Generally, SOEs are owned by various central, provincial, and local government agencies that initially invested funds in the enterprises. The typical SOE is far more than a business enterprise, providing housing, schools, hospitals, pensions, and other benefits for its employees as part of a package of lifetime benefits that has been referred to as the *iron rice bowl*.[117]

Clearly, many SOEs will not be viable enterprises in the global economy that China is now engaged with, while other SOEs cannot compete if they must continue to employ and provide benefits to unnecessary workers. This is evident in the decline of SOE output, which has not been accompanied by a similar reduction in the number of employees to which they must provide employee benefits. Although SOEs accounted for about 80 percent of industrial output during the mid 1970s, the rapid growth of the private sector reduced that amount to about 40 percent of total output only 20 years later.[118]

Although the Chinese government has introduced a number of measures to address the SOE issue, including forced sales of shares to profitable companies, the problem is still acute. The basic problem is the lack of any national, regional, or local funded social insurance system. Obsolete SOEs cannot be sold or declared bankrupt until a social welfare program is in place, as well as a viable tax system to support it.[119] The government's

---

[117] Bosworth and Burtles, *Emerging Social Security Issues in Western Economies*, Brookings Institute Review, Summer 1997 Vol. 15 No. 3.

[118] Sun Xiuping, Zhu Huayou & Yao Tiejun, *Theory and Reality of Transition to a Market Economy* (Foreign Language Press, Beijing 1995).

[119] Feldstein, *Social Security Pension Reform in China*, National Bureau of Economic Research Working Paper 6794.

policy to develop an efficient market economy is impeded by the necessity to maintain social equilibrium, and avoid instability among workers and retirees.

[3] East Asia

A number of East Asian countries, including Taiwan, South Korea, Hong Kong, Singapore, Malaysia and Thailand have experienced high rates of economic growth and development over the past few decades. These countries, often referred to as Asian Tigers or Dragons, strive to expand their economies through high levels of exports to industrialized nations such as the U.S. Although there have been significant setbacks, these Asian nations generally have succeeded in advancing from third world to developed economic status in a relatively short period.

Many of these countries have adopted similar economic policies to enhance their economic development. These policies pursue substantial trade surpluses through undervalued currencies to enhance exports to industrialized countries and high tariffs and saving rates that restrain imports. Typically, the countries are governed by non-democratic and authoritarian political systems during early stages of development.

The Asian Financial Crisis.

Despite this extraordinary economic growth, many Asian countries suffered a sudden and severe financial decline in the late 1990s, now referred to as the *Asian Financial Crisis*. The crisis began in Thailand in July, 1997, and affected currencies, stock markets, and asset values in numerous Asian countries. Thailand, Indonesia and South Korea and were most affected, with severe impacts in Hong Kong, Malaysia, Singapore and the Philipines and some effects in a dozen other countries. In addition to economic damage, the crisis caused political and social disruption, including the fall of governments in Indonesia and Thailand and increased anti-western and anti-globalization sentiment, particularly focused on the International Monetary Fund.

The initial event occurred when pressure from the international foreign exchange markets forced Thailand to devalue its currency, the baht, by about 20% against the US dollar. The pressure from the markets arose when currency speculators and Thai citizens began rapidly selling baths and buying dollars, believing that the Thai government lacked the ability to maintain the currency's value. As capital outflows increased, interest rates soared, the stock and real estate markets tumbled, unemployment rose and a severe recession took hold. The process that began in Thailand swiftly affected other Southeast Asian nations. Because the devalued baht made Thai exports less expensive on world markets, other exporting countries had to take similar actions.

Many attribute the crisis to the surge of capital flows into and out of the affected countries. Huge amounts of private capital had been invested in these developing countries with little regard for the risks associated with investment in countries having little or no financial regulatory structure. Thus, a principal cause was the global investors who freely made large, unwise loans that often wound up in the pockets of corrupt politicians and inept entrepreneurs.

Some critics have charged that the economic slump was exacerbated by the actions of the International Monetary Fund (IMF).[120] In most cases, it is charged, the assistance offered to the affected countries by the IMF was conditioned on the acceptance of flawed economic strategies. These conditions included steep rises in interest rates that affected not only the banks and investors that precipitated the crisis, but induced severe recessions and high unemployment that harmed small businesses and workers. It is also possible that financial *bailouts* by the IMF are counterproductive because they create *moral hazard* problems. Moral hazard is the risk that investors will not act prudently because they expect governments to bail them out. Such bailouts require larger sums from the IMF, which then imposes even more onerous conditions on borrowers.

Although the Asian Crisis was severe, it was short-lived and most economies in the region have made remarkable recoveries. Contributing to the recovery was a high degree of financial and trade integration among Asian countries. This has been accomplished through a number of Free Trade Areas (FTA), Trade Blocs and Bi-lateral Investment Treaties.

An important FTA is ASEAN (Association of Southeast Asian Nations), comprised of Myanmar, Laos, Thailand, Cambodia, Vietnam, Philippines, Malaysia, Brunei, Singapore and Indonesia. The ASEAN region has a population of about 500 million and combined gross domestic product of over $700 billion, making it one of the largest markets in the world. This market will greatly increase in size through the recent accord between ASEAN and China. Apparantly, China, Japan, Korea and ASEAN, referred to as ASEAN plus Three, are in the process of integrating the East Asian economies into a unit capable of matching the bargaining power of the EU and NAFTA.

APEC (Asia-Pacific Economic Cooperation) is a governmental forum that holds annual meetings of the economic leaders from member nations to promote economic growth and development in the Asia-Pacific region. Its members include Australia, Brunei Darussalam, Canada, Chile, China, Hong Kong, Indonesia, Japan, Korea, Malaysia, Mexico, New Zealand, Papua New Guinea, Peru, Philippines, Russia, Singapore, Taiwan, Thailand, United States, and Viet Nam. The organization promotes regional trade and investment and helps developing members address economic and corporate governance issues.

---

[120] *See generally*, Stiglietz, *Globalization and Its Discontents.*

APEC is not a rule-based organization with enforcement powers, but operates informally through consultation and consensus. Members voluntarily adopt the policies established at the annual Leader's and Minister's meeting. An important meeting in 1994, in Bogor, Indonesia proclaimed the *Bogor Goals*, of creating the world's largest free trade area by 2020. These goals would be reached by pursuing three central APEC principles: trade and investment liberalization and facilitation, business facilitation and economic and technical cooperation.

[4]　Africa

Generally, the countries in Africa have derived little economic benefit from the recent global expansion of trade and investment. The continent, which comprises 54 nations and more than 800 million people, is home to most of the world's poorest countries and suffers low life expectancies and high violence rates. The governments of many African nations are unstable, often caused by the harsh corrupt dictatorships that came to power during inadequate transitions from colonial rule.

Although generally poor, economic development varies greatly among the countries and regions of Africa. Some areas of North and West Africa whose economies are linked to Europe or the Middle East are not impoverished, nor are a few countries with substantial oil reserves. Similarly, South Africa, the continent's wealthiest nation, has aided the economic development of some neighboring countries. The poorest nations have been engaged in severe civil wars that have caused or exacerbated famines and epidemics for decades.

Africa experienced fairly good economic growth in the 1950s and 1960s as a result of strong demand for its natural resources in Europe, the U.S. and Asia. That growth, however, faltered during the global recession of the 1970s and many countries never recovered from the resulting high oil prices and lower prices for their products. Since that time, Africa has become much poorer compared the other areas of the world, both in absolute and relative terms.

Nearly two-thirds of Africa's economy is tied to agriculture. Most African farmers engage in subsistence farming on small plots of land that can barely feed their families, leaving only a small surplus to sell for cash or trade for other goods. However, many agricultural operations are owned by large corporations that employ laborers to raise cash crops such as coffee, cotton, cocoa, and rubber for export to richer, economically developed countries. The lack of surplus production of foodstuffs such as grain is sometimes attributed to the high subsidies that the EU and U.S. provide to their own farmers, which lowers the global price to the point that African farmers cannot compete. Thus, African agricultural surplus is limited to exportable products that do not grow in northern climates.

A few African countries have large deposits of natural resources, such as gold, diamonds copper, and oil. These deposits support substantial mining and drilling industries with most of the products being exported to industrialized countries. The industries are often owned by large foreign corporations or corrupt governments which do not generally share or reinvest profits locally.

With the exception of South Africa, the continent has only a small industrial and manufacturing infrastructure. Most of its natural resources are exported for refining, development and manufacture elsewhere. Although abundant low-cost labor exists, few Africans work in industrial jobs. For many multinational companies, the lack of political stability, local infrastructure and an educated workforce makes Africa is an undesirable location for a plant or factory. Overall, there is a low rate of foreign investment in Africa.

[5] Free Trade Agreements and Customs Unions

A *Free Trade Agreement* (FTA) is an arrangement between two or more countries to reciprocally reduce or eliminate tariffs and other trade restrictions. Ordinarily, the countries participating in an FTA negotiate the nature and scope of the trade preferences they will grant each other, establish schedules for reduction of specific trade barriers and establish special dispute settlement procedures. In addition to direct trade barriers, FTAs often address social and economic issues affected by trade policy, such as environmental and labor standards and investment and intellectual property rights. Generally, each member of an FTA independently establishes its trade policies with respect to non-member nations. A notable example of an FTA is the North American Free Trade Agreement (NAFTA).

A higher degree of economic integration is established through a *Customs Union*. Countries participating in a Customs Union adopt a common external trade policy and set common tariffs, quotas, and trade preferences for non-member nations. Thus, the same trade rules apply to all goods imported into the Customs Union regardless of which country within the Union they enter. An example of a Customs Union is the Common Market of the Southern Cone (MERCOSUR), comprising Argentina, Brazil, Paraguay and Uruguay.

It should be noted that FTAs and Customs Unions are exempt from the most-favored-nation (MFN) rule that ordinarily applies to trade between member nations of the World Trade Organization (WTO). Under the MFN rule, a WTO member that provides a trade advantage to another country must grant the same advantage to all WTO members. See §2.02[3]. The MFN exemption, set forth in Article XXIV of the General Agreement on Tariffs and Trade (GATT), recognizes that FTAs and Customs Union agreements can enhance free trade by developing closer economic integration between member nations. To ensure that these arrangements liberalize trade rather than create new barriers or allow discrimination between trading partners, specific conditions, must be satisfied before the Aritcle XXIV exemption will apply. The basic condition is that the FTA or Customs Union must eliminate all tariffs and other restrictions on substantially all the trade in goods between its member countries.

These agreements can substantially impact a companies that market and distribute goods and services to countries that are members of an FTA or Customs Union. As of 2004, the United States was party to five FTAs, involving Israel, Jordan, Chile, Singapore, Mexico and Canada and negotiations for additional agreements were being negotiated with Australia, El Salvador, Costa Rica, the Dominican Republic, Guatemala, Honduras, Nicaragua and Morocco. Numerous other agreements exist to which the U.S. is not a party. The sections below provide a brief description of selected FTAs and Customs Unions in various areas of the world.

Latin American Free Trade Areas. A number of important FTA and Customs Unions currently exist or are being negotiated in the Latin American area. Some regional groups are in the process of merging and it is likely that a single regional free trade area encompassing all of Latin America will emerge in the near future. A larger proposal, the Free Trade Area of the Americas, that will include most of the countries in North and South America, also is being negotiated.

Two of South America's largest trading blocs, The *Andean Community* and *Mercosur* recently completed the first stage of merger negotiations toward establishing a South American Community of Nations patterned on the European Union. The Andean Community comprises Bolivia, Colombia, Ecuador, Peruand Venezuela. *Mercosur* is a free trade area comprising Brazil, Argentina, Uruguay and Paraguay. Associate members are Bolivia, Chile, Colombia Ecuador, Peru and Venezuala.

The Free Trade Area of the Americas (FTAA) is a proposed agreement to progressively eliminate trade and investment barriers among all 34 Western Hemisphere democracies (thus excluding Cuba). In effect, it is a hemisphere-wide expansion of NAFTA. A goal of the negotiations is to harmonize the more than 20 existing trade agreement among various nations into a single agreement. The agreement would encompass more than 850 million people having a total economy of over $13 trillion.

Although the goal was to complete the FTAA by 2005, this is unlikely to occur. The biggest obstacle to formation of the FTAA is the perception of many countries that U.S. economic power will dominate their own interests. In addition, many nations are reluctant to lift protective tariffs because they compete in many industries and economic areas. A comprehensive agreement also is hampered by the varying levels of economic development, labor and environmental standards.

[6] NAFTA

The North American Free Trade Agreement (NAFTA) is a comprehensive trade agreement between the United States, Mexico and Canada that became effective in 1994. With respect to Canada, the agreement incorporates many provisions of the pre-existing CFTA between Canada and the

U.S. Under NAFTA, many tariffs were either eliminated immediately or required to be phased out over a fifteen year period. Trade restrictions were eliminated on a wide variety of goods, including automobiles and automotive parts, computers, textiles, and agricultural products. The treaty also enhanced protections for intellectual property rights and removed restrictions on investment among the three signatory countries. Supplemental provisions cover various aspects of worker rights and environmental protection.

Although generally supported by the governments and business groups, NAFTA has been quite controversial and opposed by various constituencies in all three member countries. NAFTA supporters maintain that the agreement provides access to markets for members' goods and services, enhances investment opportunities that facilitate trade among members and creates a predictable business environment that reduces many risks associated with international business planning. The agreement is also seen as an important step towards free trade throughout the western hemisphere.

The most pervasive criticism of NAFTA, often cited by U.S. and Canadian labor unions, is that jobs will be lost in their countries because of the lower worker wages and benefits prevailing in Mexico. Some Mexican farmers oppose the agreement because they feel that the agricultural subsidies available to U.S. farmers result in lower prices for their products. Opposition also comes from numerous non-governmental organizations that maintain that NAFTA degrades health, environmental, human rights and similar non-economic standards in all countries.

Key NAFTA provisions include:

- **Tariffs:** By 2004, all tariffs to be eliminated on industrial products traded between Canada, Mexico and the United States. Some tariffs on U.S. exports of agricultural products to Mexico phased out over 15 years. All U.S.–Canada trade to be duty-free by 1998.

- **Non-Tariff Barriers.** Elimination of non-tariff barriers such as local content, and local production requirements.

- **Rules of Origin.** NAFTA reduces tariffs only for goods made in North America. The rules of origin determine whether a product qualifies for NAFTA tariff treatment. To qualify, goods must contain substantial North American content and labor, with special rules applying to specific industrial sectors. The rules of origin prevent address to the free rider issue, so that goods that have only minimal local content and labor cannot be transshipped through a NAFTA country into the free trade area.

- **Customs Rules.** Uniform Customs procedures and regulations implemented to ensure predictability and transparency in the exporting process. Particularly important are the procedures governing documentation of rules of origin. Customs administrations in each country will issue advance rulings about whether a product qualifies for NAFTA tariff preference.

- **Safeguards.** Safeguard provisions allowed member countries to reimpose tariffs for a limited time if a sector in its economy required time to adjust higher levels of imports that were injurious. Under *snap-back* rules, a country could reset its tariff at its original level. Specific safeguards applied to certain agricultural products and textiles. Global safeguards rules allow imposition of tariffs or quotas as part of a multilateral safeguard action if imports from a country are a substantial share of total imports and contribute to or threaten serious economic injury. Procedures for implementing safeguards are established and the country taking the safeguard action must compensate the country whose imports are affected.

- **Investment.** Generally, NAFTA provides investment rules that require member countries to treat nationals of each country in the manner as domestic investors. Specific investor rights include: repatriation of profits and capital; fair compensation for expropriation; and international arbitration in disputes in investors-government disputes involving monetary damages. However, certain industries are exempted from these rules.

- **Services.** NAFTA applies to most services, except aviation transport, maritime, and basic telecommunications. Thus, free trade in services is available in areas such as accounting, architecture, transportation, publishing, consulting, education, environmental services, advertising, broadcasting, construction, tourism, engineering, health care, and legal services. Special rules apply to financial services, telecommunications and certain other areas. Although each country controls its own licensing and certification rules, licensing of professionals such as doctors, attorneys and accountants must be based on objective criteria focused on competence, not on nationality. Professionals of one country may not practice another unless they satisfy the host country's license and certification procedures. For example, a U.S. architect, may temporarily enter Mexico for business persons, but may not practice there unless licensed.

- **Intellectual Property.** NAFTA generally provides high standards of protection for intellectual property rights such as patents, trademarks, copyrights, trade secrets, semiconductor integrated circuits, plant breeder rights, geographical indications and industrial designs.

- **Government procurement.** Suppliers are given broad access to federal government procurement markets in all member nations. This includes goods and contracts for services and construction. Specified procedures are required to guarantee fair, open, transparent and predictable competition for procurement procedures.

- **Standards-related measures.** These measures apply to technical specifications governing product characteristics, such as quality, performance, and labeling. NAFTA prohibits using such standards as obstacles to trade and requires that they be applied in a nondiscriminatory manner to domestic and imported goods. Companies and other interested parties from each country may participate in developing new standards other nations on the same basis as domestic firms. Adequate notice must be provided before new regulations become effective and an opportunity provided for affected industries to make comments. Working groups will establish compatible standards for each nation so that companies need not adapt products to comply with three different standards. Certification of safety and health standards by a laboratory in one country will be acceptable in the other nations.

- **Entry for business persons.** Transparent and uniform procedures facilitate temporary entry of business persons to conduct trade in goods, services and investment activities. These procedures mostly affect U.S.–Mexico entry and pre-existing U.S.-Canada arrangements are basically unchanged. These rules benefit many service providers such as installation, repair and maintenance, managerial and training personnel. Also eligible for such entry are sales representatives and agents, buyers, market researchers, financial service personnel, company executives and managers and a wide variety of professionals such as engineers and pharmacists.

- **Dispute resolution.** NAFTA established a Free Trade Commission to review trade relations among the member countries. The Commission may create panels of experts to resolve disputes about the interpretations or application of NAFTA. A panel that finds a nation's action to be inconsistent with its NAFTA obligations will recommend a method for resolution. A country that decides that it does not accept the recommendations must offer acceptable compensation or the affected country may withdraw "equivalent trade concessions. Special rules apply environmental, safety, health-related or other science-related disputes. Generally, these rules require a country that complains about another's environmental or health standards to bear the burden of proving that a NAFTA violation exists. NAFTA also provides for independent panels to review antidumping and countervailing duty disputes.

- **Investment disputes.** Investors may require a host government to submit to international arbitration or settlement of disputes involving monetary damages for violations of NAFTA invesrtment rules. Awards may be enforced under both NAFTA and international treaties on enforcement of arbitral awards.

- **Specific industries.** NAFTA eliminated most restrictions on cross-border operation of banks, securities, insurance and other financial firms, telecommunications companies, land transportation (trucking) and railroads.

Chapter 6

TAXATION OF INTERNATIONAL TRANSACTIONS

§ 6.01   Basic Income Tax Rules

[1]   Policy Considerations

Tax considerations greatly influence the decisions of entrepreneurs and corporations about where, how, and when to invest, operate, or build. Business people who do not account for the tax consequences of their foreign investments and operations may find their expected returns greatly diminished. Similarly, a country that is not aware of or sensitive to the impact of its tax policies may find its economy distorted by too little productive foreign investment or too many speculative ventures.

The distorting effect of national tax rules on the world economy raises difficult economic policy issues. A major concern is how to harmonize national tax systems to create greater *tax efficiency*. A tax system is said to be efficient if tax considerations do not encourage capital to be invested differently than warranted by economic factors. For example, a tax system in which countries only tax business and investment income earned within their borders may be inefficient if it causes capital to be attracted to low tax countries, rather than to be invested where the greatest pre-tax profit can be earned. Conversely, a system in which nations tax the worldwide income of their residents may cause a business in a low-tax country to be more profitable after tax than a more efficient competitor in a higher tax nation. In both situations, capital is not invested most productively, and global efficiency and prosperity declines.

An efficient global tax system that encourages productive allocations of capital can be achieved by equalizing the tax rates in all countries. In that situation, capital investment decisions in all countries will be based on economic, not tax, considerations. Obviously, this is improbable in the near future, because of the diverse national priorities and economic conditions that exist in different nations. For the present, the goal of U.S. tax policy is to adopt tax rules that minimize distortions in international capital flows in and out of the country caused by disparate national tax rates on business and investment income.

[a] Capital Export Neutrality

The basic U.S. policy, referred to as *capital export neutrality*, taxes investment income at the U.S. rate regardless of where the investor resides, so that tax considerations are minimized in deciding where to invest.[1] Capital export neutrality usually operates by allowing a domestic tax credit for taxes paid to foreign governments. As an unlikely alternative, the country that is the source of the income may relinquish its jurisdiction and grant the right to tax investment income to the country where the investor resides. The U.S. has adopted the tax credit method, so that any taxes paid by a U.S. person to a foreign country are subtracted from the taxpayer's U.S. tax liability on its *worldwide* income. For example, a U.S. person that invests in Japan must include the Japanese source income on its U.S. tax return, but subtracts any tax paid to Japan from its U.S. tax liability for that income. This system is only concerned about the rate of tax on an investment, rather than how much tax revenue will be received by any particular country. Although the global economy may be more productive under this system, some countries may lose net investments and the corresponding tax revenues.

[b] Capital Import Neutrality

A second approach, called *capital import neutrality*, taxes all investment income earned in one country at the same rate, regardless of where the investor resides. This system operates by having the taxpayer's residence country exempt foreign income from domestic taxation. Thus, tax is paid only in the country that is the source of the income; tax jurisdiction is *territorial* rather than worldwide. For example, a U.S. taxpayer will pay the same tax to Japan on earnings from that country as any other domestic or foreign firm that operates in Japan. This system focuses on equal treatment of all competitors in the same market, regardless of their nationality. Although this system might improve the competitiveness of U.S. companies operating abroad, exempting foreign income from U.S. tax is considered likely to encourage foreign over domestic investment.

[c] National Neutrality

A third system, called *national neutrality*, disregards the effect of foreign taxes, except to the extent that they reduce the profitability of the foreign investment. This system would operate by allowing foreign taxes to be deducted from the taxpayer's income in the same manner as business expenses. The foreign tax is treated as an additional cost of doing business abroad that reduces a taxpayer's income. This approach is not truly neutral regarding capital allocation decisions because it usually results in a higher rate of tax on foreign than on domestic investments. The goal is to discourage residents from investing their capital in foreign countries by

---

[1] *See* The President's Tax Proposals to the Congress for Fairness, Growth, and Simplicity (May 1985), p. 383.

reducing the after-tax rate of return on such investments. National neutrality is generally perceived as a protectionist policy that associates business investment in foreign countries with lower domestic income and welfare. In effect, the policy inhibits investments abroad in order to encourage domestic investment.

[d] Illustrations

To illustrate the practical effect of these different systems, assume that the U.S. tax rate is 35 percent, the tax rate in Nolo is 30 percent and John, a U.S. citizen, earns $100 from an investment in Nolo:

- The capital export neutrality system would allow John a U.S. tax credit for taxes paid to Nolo. John must pay $30 to the Nolo government and include the entire $100 on his U.S. tax return. The U.S. tax on that income is $35, which is reduced by a $30 credit for the tax paid to Nolo. John pays $5 in tax to the U.S. John's total tax is $35 ($30 to Nolo and $5 to the U.S.), which reflects the U.S. tax rate of 35 percent.

- Under a capital import neutral system, only the source country Nolo would tax John's transaction and he would pay a total of $30 in tax. The rate of tax is 30 percent, which is lower than the 35 percent rate that would apply to income earned in the U.S.

- Under the national neutrality approach, the tax paid to Nolo would be allowed as a business deduction instead of a credit. In that case, John would still pay $30 to Nolo and include the entire $100 on his U.S. return. The deduction for foreign taxes would reduce his income subject to tax to $70 ($100 − $30), which would be taxed at a 35 percent rate. The U.S. tax would be $24.50. John's total tax is $54.50, resulting in a tax rate of over 54 percent on the transaction. Thus, the tax rate on foreign source income is considerably higher than for income earned in the U.S.

[2] Tax Havens

Many countries compete for international capital by making their tax systems attractive to foreign investors. A consequence of this tax competition has been a general decline in national tax rates and relaxation of tax laws throughout the world. In effect, governments are restrained from increasing national tax rates because taxpayers can transfer their economic activities to lower tax environments.

A nation that imposes low (or no tax on foreign investments is often referred to as a *tax haven*. One view is that tax havens are generally beneficial because they require other governments to adopt efficient tax policies that enhance domestic savings and investment. Tax competition also enhances international capital flows, resulting in more efficient allocation of global financial resources.

Many non-tax haven countries disagree, however, maintaining that tax havens merely shift tax burdens from wealthy sophisticated individuals and companies to poorer taxpayers who cannot benefit from the expensive tax advice and complex transactions involved in cross-border investments. Tax havens are believed to distort trade and investment decision-making and erode the tax base of other national tax systems. This is particularly true with respect to tax havens engaging in practices that encourage non-compliance with other national tax laws.

An individual or company need not actually become a resident of the tax haven country to obtain desired tax benefits. Ordinarily, it is only necessary to establish a separate or subsidiary legal entity (typically a corporation, partnership, or trust) in the tax haven. Income from the assets transferred to the new company or trust are earned and taxable in the low tax jurisdiction. Although many countries have laws that would eliminate many of the hoped-for tax benefits (including the U.S.), these statutes are difficult to enforce because of the lack of transparency and secrecy permitted in the tax havens.

Recently, the non-tax haven nations have worked through the Organisation for Economic Cooperation and Development (OECD) to eliminate certain tax haven practices.[2] In determining whether a country is a tax haven, the OECD examines the following factors:

1. **Nominal or no taxes.** Generally, tax havens impose only nominal taxes and promote themselves as places that can be used by non-residents to escape tax in their home countries. The fact that a country has nominal or no taxes is not sufficient, by itself, to characterize a country as a tax haven. This recognizes that every jurisdiction has a right to determine its appropriate tax system and rates.

2. **Lack of effective exchange of information.** Ordinarily, tax laws or administrative practices of a tax haven afford businesses and individuals secrecy rules and other protections against examination by tax authorities.

3. **Lack of transparency.** Tax havens generally lack of transparency in the operation of their legislative, legal or administrative provisions. Lack of transparency makes it difficult or impossible for other tax authorities to apply their laws effectively. Examples of such practices include secret rulings, privately negotiated tax rates, inadequate regulatory supervision and restricted legal access to financial records.

4. **No substantial activities associated with the financial capital investment.** The lack of activity suggests that a

---

[2] The OECD has published the following reports on harmful tax practices: Harmful Tax Competition: An Emerging Global Issue (1998); Towards Glopbal Tax Co-operation: Progress in Identifying and Eliminating Harmful Tax Practices (2000); The OECD's Project on Harmful Tax Practices: The 2001 Progress Report (2001); The OECD's Project on Harmful Tax Practices: The 2001 Progress Report (2004).

jurisdiction is attempting to attract tax driven investments and transactions. This criteria also applies to a country that insulates its core tax base from the effects of the tax preference (i.e., by denying the preference to domestic taxpayers or activities). This type of tax regime is said to be ring-fenced.

In its 2001 Progress Report on Harmful Tax Practices, the OECD identified 42 nations as tax havens and pressed them to commit to establish transparency and effective information exchange practices. The 2004 Progress Report, by contrast, indicates that nearly all of those tax regimes have been or are in the process of being eliminated. At this time it is difficult to determine whether the tax havens have truly changed their rules and practices or if the OECD has adopted a new view and policy regarding tax havens.

[3] U.S. Taxation of International Transactions — Basic Principles

Unlike the vast majority of countries, the U.S. taxes its citizens and residents on their *worldwide* income, without regard to whether it is derived from U.S. or foreign sources. This broad jurisdiction to tax based upon the *nationality* of the taxpayer, is justified by benefits that U.S. citizenship and residency bestows.[3] By contrast, most countries' jurisdiction to tax is *territorial*, meaning that a nation only taxes income that has a source within its territory. Indeed, the U.S. also applies territorial jurisdiction, and taxes foreigners on many kinds of income they earn from U.S. sources.

These different standards often mean that two countries may assert jurisdiction to tax the same income. If a U.S. company earns income in France, for example, France will assert its territorial jurisdiction to tax the income, and the U.S. will assert its national jurisdiction to tax the same amount. Such double taxation of foreign investment, however, would violate the preferred U.S. policy of capital export neutrality described above. U.S. tax law provides the following statutory mechanisms, discussed in more detail below, for avoiding multiple taxation of international income:

- **Outbound transactions.** Transactions involving U.S. investments and businesses in foreign countries are generally referred to as *outbound* transactions. Generally, U.S. persons engaged in outbound transactions must include their worldwide income from foreign and domestic sources on their U.S. tax return. The U.S. person may then apply a *foreign tax credit* to reduce its U.S. tax liability by the amount of tax it paid to foreign countries on its foreign source income.

- **Inbound transactions.** Transactions involving foreign investments or businesses in the U.S. are called *inbound* transactions.

---

[3] *Cook v. Tait*, 265 U.S. 47 (1924).

The U.S. taxes nonresident aliens and foreign corporations on their inbound transaction only if the income has a sufficient nexus to the U.S. Generally, these taxes are collected by withholding at the U.S. source. Foreign entities that do not do business in the United States and are not controlled by US persons, are not subject to US taxes.

- **Tax treaties**. The basic U.S. tax rules frequently are replaced by special rules in bi-lateral tax treaties. The treaties directly address the double tax issue by specifying the country that has priority to tax various types of income.

[4] Outbound Transactions — Taxation of U.S. Persons with Foreign Source Income

[a] The Foreign Tax Credit

United States persons, which includes citizens, residents, and corporations, are subject to U.S. taxation on all income derived in the U.S. and abroad (*i.e.*, their *worldwide* income). A U.S. person's non-U.S. source income is first taxable in the foreign country where it is derived, and then included on that person's U.S. tax return. To prevent the foreign income from being taxed twice — in the source country and in the U.S.— the U.S. taxpayer is allowed to credit the amount of foreign tax against its U.S. tax liability for the foreign income. The foreign tax credit rules are elective on a yearly basis, meaning that a U.S. person may choose to deduct foreign taxes rather than treat them as a credit.

The foreign tax credit is the method applied by the U.S. to achieve tax export neutrality. Including a U.S. person's worldwide income on its U.S. tax return ensures that foreign and domestic income are taxed at the same rate. Allowing a credit for the taxes paid to foreign countries eliminates the additional tax burden on foreign source income.[4] The foreign tax credit may only reduce U.S. tax by the amount of foreign tax paid on foreign source income; the credit may not be used to reduce taxes on U.S. source income.

A *direct* foreign tax credit is allowed for foreign taxes paid or accrued by a U.S. person. In some situations, a U.S. corporation may be allowed an *indirect* foreign tax credit for foreign taxes paid by a foreign corporation in which it owns stock, if the foreign corporation has paid a dividend to the U.S. company.[5]

The amount of the foreign tax credit is limited to the proportion of U.S. tax that the foreign source income bears to worldwide income.[6] This rule prevents foreign tax credits from being applied to reduce U.S. tax on U.S. source income. In applying this limitation, complex rules place different

---

[4] I.R.C. § 901.

[5] I.R.C. § 902(a).

[6] I.R.C. § 904(a).

types of foreign income into different categories, or *baskets*. Credits attributable to one basket of income often can only be used to offset U.S. tax liability for foreign-source income in the same basket. Detailed rules also govern how a taxpayer must allocate expenses attributable to domestic and foreign-source income among the various baskets. A foreign tax credit that cannot be used in the current year because of the basket limitations, or because the U.S. taxpayer's total tax liability is less than the allowable credit, may be carried back to the two preceding tax years and carried forward to the first five succeeding tax years.

[b] Taxation and Business Structure

U.S. and foreign tax considerations greatly influence how a foreign investment is structured and organized. Indeed, tax considerations usually govern the choice of the appropriate business or investment entities, their location, and the number of tiers or layers of ownership and operation. The tax consequences differ greatly for enterprises conducted directly through an unincorporated entity, such as a partnership, limited liability company (LLC), or a branch (or division) of a U.S. company, and those that are operated indirectly through separate foreign corporations.

Because a corporation is a separate, tax-paying entity, its profits are taxed at the corporate level when earned and subjected to a second tax when distributed to shareholders as dividends. Corporate losses may not be deducted by shareholders, but can only be applied against corporate income. By contrast, partnerships and LLCs are not a separate tax-paying entities. Each partner or member is separately and individually taxable on its share of partnership or LLC profits or losses. The *pass-through* of items to partners and LLC members means that income avoids the double tax imposed on corporate income, and that losses may offset income the partner or member has from other sources. The different treatment afforded corporations and unincorporated entities often determines whether a foreign operation is structured as a *branch* of a U.S. domestic business entity, or as a foreign corporation owned by U.S. shareholders.

A key tax factor in international operations is the time that foreign source income is taxed in the U.S. If the income is taxable in the year it is earned, the tax is paid immediately, and the taxpayer loses the *time value* of the tax dollars it could otherwise invest. If, however, the U.S. tax on the foreign source income is *deferred* until the earnings are actually received in the U.S. (*repatriated*), the taxpayer may invest the tax dollars and benefit considerably from the time value of those funds. This valuable ability to defer U.S. taxation depends upon the business structure used for the foreign investment.

When a foreign branch is used, no separate legal identity exists between the domestic company and its foreign branch, and the U.S. company directly owns the assets involved in the foreign operation. For U.S. tax purposes, the branch is disregarded, and its income and losses are considered to be earned directly by the domestic company as foreign source income. The U.S.

tax is imposed on that income in the year it is earned, although the tax may be reduced by the foreign tax credit for any taxes paid to the source country.

A foreign corporation owned by U.S. shareholders, however, is a separate legal entity from its domestic parent, and is a resident of the foreign country where it is incorporated or chartered. If the U.S. shareholder is a corporation that owns a controlling interest, the foreign corporation is referred to as a *subsidiary* and the domestic corporation is called the *parent*. The status of the domestic parent corporation is that of a shareholder in a foreign company, even if the parent owns all of the stock in the subsidiary. Because the foreign corporation is a resident of the country where it is incorporated, income from its operations is not subject to U.S. tax until it is distributed to the U.S. shareholders (*repatriated*), typically in the form of a dividend. The U.S. shareholders are taxable in the year the distribution occurs, and may reduce their U.S. tax liability by the foreign tax credit for taxes paid by the foreign corporation.

The difference in the time that income is taxed to a branch or to a subsidiary is critical to international tax planning. Income earned by a foreign branch of a U.S. company is taxed in the U.S. in the year it is earned, while U.S. taxation of income of a foreign subsidiary is *deferred* until it is repatriated by a dividend to the parent. Because the U.S. parent controls its subsidiary's dividend policy, the U.S. tax may be deferred indefinitely. The time value of the deferred tax dollars is substantial, and may exceed the amount of tax involved in just a few years. The deferral is particularly valuable if the foreign corporation is a resident of a low tax country. In that case, little tax is paid in the income source nation, and the U.S. tax in the nation of residence is indefinitely deferred.

Generally, the U.S. tax law permits tax deferral for U.S. shareholders if the foreign corporation they own conducts active business operations. Supporters of such a deferral policy maintain that imposing immediate tax on U.S.-owned foreign corporations would impair their ability to compete against other lower-taxed companies operating in the same country. The deferral is, in effect, a form of capital import neutrality that exempts U.S.-owned companies from current taxation on foreign source income if they continue to use the income in their foreign business operations.

The American Jobs Creation Act, enacted in October of 2004, provides a temporary opportunity for U.S. corporations to repatriate earnings attributable to foreign business operations at a greatly reduced tax rate. Under the Act, U.S. corporation that controls foreign corporations can make a one-time election during 2005 to deduct 85 percent of the qualifying cash dividends received from the foreign corporations. The effect of the election is to allow a U.S. parent company to obtain earnings from a foreign subsidiary at an effective tax rate of 5.25 percent instead of the 35 rate that would ordinarily apply.

The Act's purpose is to remove the tax disincentive that has induced many U.S.-based multinational corporations not to repatriate their foreign earnings. These earnings have been used to expand overseas corporate facilities or make foreign acquisitions. A temporary reduction in the U.S. tax on repatriated dividends, it is hoped, will stimulate the U.S. economy by encouraging repatriation of foreign earnings that otherwise remain abroad.

To qualify for this deduction, the dividends must be reinvested in the U.S. in specified permitted investments pursuant to an approved domestic reinvestment plan. The Treasury Department has issued guidance on the types of expenditures that will be permitted, which include expenditures for certain business acquisitions, debt reduction, capital investment and advertising or marketing.

It is estimated that hundreds of billions of dollars in undistributed earnings from foreign affiliates may be repatriated. Indeed, the International Business Machines Corporation will repatriate $8 billion of foreign profits pursuant to the tax holiday policy. Companies that lack sufficient cash to distribute during 2005 are likely to borrow against their assets to fund repatriated dividend payments.

[c] Anti-Deferral Rules

To prevent abusive situations, however, the U.S. tax law contains a number of complex provisions to prevent domestic taxpayers from using foreign corporations as a tax deferral device. These rules focus on arrangements that merely shift income from passive investment and from transactions with related companies out of the U.S. (or other high-tax countries), to corporations organized in low-tax or *tax haven* jurisdictions. These *anti-deferral* rules operate either by immediately taxing the U.S. shareholders on their share of the foreign corporation's income, or by eliminating the time value of the deferral by charging interest on the deferred tax liability.

[i] Foreign Personal Holding Companies

The first anti-deferral provision, enacted in 1937, relates to *foreign personal holding companies* (FPHCs), which are foreign companies owned and used by wealthy individuals to shift their investment income to low tax countries.[7] A FPHC is a foreign corporation, in which five or fewer U.S. individual citizens or residents directly or indirectly own more than 50 percent (by vote or value) of the corporation's stock, and at least 60 percent of the corporation's gross income consists of passive income, such as dividends, interest, royalties, and rents. The statutes eliminate deferral by providing that all U.S. shareholders of a FPHC are currently taxable on their pro rata shares of the corporation's undistributed income.

---

[7] I.R.C. §§ 551-558.

[ii]   Passive Foreign Investment Companies

Because the FPHC rule only affects foreign corporations controlled by U.S. persons, it can be avoided by U.S. persons who own smaller interests in foreign-controlled corporations located in tax haven (no or low tax) countries. To close this loophole, a second anti-deferral regime was adopted in 1986 to govern *passive foreign investment companies* (PFICs), which are companies that mainly generate passive income or hold passive investment assets. A FPIC is defined as any foreign corporation if: (1) 75 percent of its gross income for the tax year consists of passive income, or; (2) 50 percent of its assets produce, or are held to produce, passive income.[8] The U.S. shareholders in an FPIC are taxed in one of three ways, regardless of their percentage of ownership:

- For certain PFICs (qualified electing funds), the shareholders may elect to currently include their shares of the PFIC's earnings in their incomes.

- For PFICs that are not qualified electing funds, the U.S. shareholders are taxable on the income from a distribution or gain from a sale of their stock *and* are charged interest to extent that the U.S. tax on that income or gain has been deferred. Ordinarily, the interest charge more than eliminates the benefit of the deferral.

- Shareholders owning marketable PFIC stock can make a *mark to market* election to be currently taxable on the difference between the fair market value of their PFIC stock at the close of the tax year over their adjusted basis in the stock.

[iii]   Controlled Foreign Corporations

A third set of anti-deferral rules concerns the income of foreign *base companies* that are established in tax haven countries to conduct operations and generate profits that, absent tax considerations, would ordinarily occur in the U.S. In effect, a foreign base company is a device that shifts profits from a U.S. entity, to a U.S.-controlled foreign corporation in a low tax country, in order to defer U.S. taxation. To eliminate tax deferral in this situation, the *controlled foreign corporation* (CFC) rules were enacted in 1962.[9] Generally, a CFC is any foreign corporation in which certain U.S. persons directly or indirectly own more than 50 percent of the corporation's stock (by vote or value). For this purpose, the only U.S. shareholders taken into account are those owning at least 10 percent of the corporation's voting stock.

If a company is a CFC, the 10-percent U.S. shareholders are currently taxable on their pro rata shares of certain corporate income defined in *Subpart F* of the Internal Revenue Code (*Subpart F income*), regardless of

---

[8] I.R.C. § 1291.

[9] I.R.C. §§ 951-954.

whether the income is distributed to them.[10] Subpart F income includes passive income and business income from transactions that can be easily structured to move income to a tax haven jurisdiction. These items include:

- foreign base company income, which is foreign personal holding company income (such as dividends, interest, rents, and royalties), foreign base company sales income, foreign base company services income, foreign base company shipping income and foreign base company oil-related income;[11]

- insurance income,[12] and;

- certain income relating to international boycotts and other violations of public policy.[13]

Special rules coordinate the various anti-deferral statutes to prevent multiple taxation of the same items. For example, the PFIC rules generally do not apply to shareholders subject to the CFC rules.

[d]   Tax Classification of Business Entities

As indicated above, the U.S. tax treatment of income derived from a foreign source greatly depends upon the form of entity used for the business or investment. Profits of a corporation are taxed at the corporate level when earned and subjected to a second tax when distributed to shareholders as dividends, and corporate losses may not be deducted by shareholders, but can only be applied against corporate income. *Pass-through* entities such as partnerships and LLCs are not tax-paying entities; each partner is taxable on its current share of partnership or LLC profits and may deduct its share of partnership losses.

Because foreign countries use different business forms, it is not always clear whether a foreign business entity should be treated as a corporation or pass-through entity for U.S. tax purposes. The U.S. tax regulations provide detailed rules for *classifying* foreign entities when determining the proper tax treatment under U.S. law.[14] Although these rules provide a *default* classification for entities that meet certain criteria, taxpayers may elect a different classification. Because the election is easily made, the classification rules are referred to as the *check-the-box* regulations. These rules apply in classifying any foreign entity, meaning an entity that is not created or organized in the United States or under any federal or state law.

The classification rules are summarized as follows:

- ***Per Se* Corporations.** Certain foreign entities are *per se* corporations that are automatically classified as corporations for tax purposes. The regulations provide an extensive list of the entities

---

[10] *Id.*

[11] All of these items are defined in I.R.C. § 954.

[12] I.R.C. § 953.

[13] I.R.C. § 952(a)(3)-(5).

[14] Reg. § 301.7701-3.

that are subject to this automatic classification.[15] Apparently, the Treasury believes that the similarity between these entities and United States corporations warrants automatic classification. A *per se* corporation may have one member or multiple members.

- **Check the Box** **Classification.** A foreign business entity that is not a *per se* corporation may accept the default classification provided in the regulations or it may elect the alternative classification. The default classification of a foreign entity depends upon two factors: (a) whether it has a single member or more than one member, and; (b) whether any member lacks limited liability under local law. Generally, a member of a foreign entity has limited liability if, under the law of the jurisdiction and the organizational documents, it lacks personal liability for the debts of or claims against the entity.

  ○ If the sole member of a foreign entity has limited liability, the default classification is treatment as a corporation. However, the sole member may *elect* to have the entity disregarded for tax purposes (*i.e.*, elect pass-through treatment).

  ○ If the sole member of the foreign entity lacks limited liability, the default classification is to disregard the entity for tax purposes (pass-through treatment). However, the sole member may elect to have the venture treated as a corporation.

  ○ If the entity has two or more members and all members have limited liability, the default classification is association taxable as a corporation. The entity may elect to be treated as a partnership for tax purposes.

  ○ If the entity has two or more members and at least one member lacks limited liability, the default classification is taxation as a partnership. The entity may elect to be classified as an association taxable as a corporation.

[e] Hybrid Branches

A number of U.S. companies have created foreign entities that are considered a branch or division that is *fiscally transparent* (*i.e.*, not a separate taxable entity) for U.S. tax purposes, but is treated as a separate entity under the foreign country's law (*i.e.*, non-fiscally transparent). This kind of foreign entity, referred to as a *hybrid branch*, has often been used to avoid the anti-deferral provisions governing CFCs and Subpart F income (described above). The Treasury defines a hybrid branch as one that is considered part of the CFC for U.S. tax purposes (*i.e.*, it is fiscally transparent), but is considered a separate entity (*i.e.*, not fiscally transparent) in

---

[15] Reg. § 301.7701-2(b)(8)(i).

the country where the CFC is organized.[16] A foreign entity's ability to be fiscally transparent for U. S. tax purposes has been simplified by the "check-the-box" regulations (described above) that became effective in 1997.[17] In the Treasury's view, these arrangements are merely devices designed to avoid Subpart F by creating deductible payments (generally interest payments) that reduce the CFC's income in the country where it actually operates and increase the passive income of its hybrid branch organized in a different, lower-tax, jurisdiction.

Although the Treasury has issued proposed regulations[18] that represent its view of how current law should be enforced, they will not be implemented until completion of a comprehensive study of Subpart F that is now underway. The proposed regulations will apply only to payments made in tax years beginning five years after the date they are made final. Thus, it is probable that the Treasury Department or Congress will significantly change the Subpart F rules before the regulations become effective. The proposed regulations merely establish a backup rule that will apply in the unlikely event that Subpart F is not substantially restructured.

In general, the proposed regulations provide that certain payments (hybrid branch payments)[19] between a CFC and its hybrid branch (or between a CFC's hybrid branches) are recharacterized as Subpart F income if:

- the payment reduces the payor's foreign tax;
- the payment would have been foreign personal holding company income if made between separate CFCs, and;
- there is a disparity between the effective tax rate on the payment in the hands of the payee and the hypothetical tax rate that would have applied if the payment had been taxed in the payor's hands.

[5]   Inbound Transactions — Taxation of Foreign Persons Having U.S. Source Income

Nonresident alien individuals and foreign corporations (*foreign persons*) are subject to U.S. taxation only on their income derived from U.S. sources. Generally, the source of income is the geographic location where income-producing assets are located or where services are performed. Income from international sales usually is allocated between the country that produced the goods and the country where the sales activity occurs.

The tax rules that apply to a foreign person's U.S. source income depends upon the type of activity that generated the income. A foreign person whose

---

[16] *See* Notice 98-35, 1998-2 CB 34.

[17] Reg. § 301.7701-3.

[18] Prop. Reg. §§ 1.954-1 through 9.

[19] The amount recharacterized as Subpart F income is the gross amount of the hybrid branch payment up to the CFC's earnings and profits attributable to non-Subpart F income.

U.S.-source income is *effectively connected* with a U.S. trade or business is taxed at the same rates and in the same manner as U.S. persons.[20] Income that is not effectively connected with a U.S. trade or business, such as investment interest or dividend income, is generally taxed at a flat 30-percent rate.

[a] Trade or Business Income

Foreign persons generally are taxed at the same rates and manner as U.S. taxpayers on income that is *effectively connected* with a U.S. trade or business. Income may be effectively connected with a U.S. trade or business even if derived from a foreign-source. Tax treaties often apply a different standard that limits U.S. taxation of a foreign person's U.S. operations to situations involving business conducted through a *permanent establishment* in the U.S.

Effectively connected income is taxed on a net basis, meaning that appropriate expenses may be deducted in computing the amount subject to tax.[21] Other deductions are allowed for personal exemptions, contributions to U.S. charities, and casualty and theft losses. No standard deduction is allowed to nonresident aliens. An individual who is a nonresident alien at any time during the year must file as single or married filing separately; the joint return or head of household status is not permitted.

Whether a foreign person's income is derived from a U.S. *trade or business* is determined from the nature of the activities and the economic interests located in the U.S. Typically, business income includes:

- Compensation for personal services performed in the U.S. A *de minimus* exception applies for amounts less than $3,000 paid by a foreign employer to a nonresident alien in the U.S. for fewer than ninety days during the year. Tax treaties often extend the period to 183 days and change the $3,000 ceiling.

- Income from operating a business in the U.S.

- Income from the sale of U.S. business assets or real property.

- Income from business or investment real estate.

- Income from a partnership engaged in a U.S. trade or business.

Income may continue to be effectively connected if received by a foreign individual who was formerly active in that trade or business. Similarly, assets used in a trade or business generate effectively connected income if sold within ten years after the business ceases.

[b] The Branch Profits Tax

The branch profits tax is imposed on income earned by a foreign corporation that operates in the U.S. directly rather than through a domestic

---

[20] I.R.C. § 864.

[21] I.R.C. § 873.

subsidiary. The purpose for the tax is to ensure that foreign corporations operating in the U.S. bear the same tax burden as their U.S. competitors. Income of a U.S. corporation is subject to double taxation, first when earned at the corporate level, and again at the shareholder level when distributions are made. The branch profits tax imposes a similar burden on foreign corporations, by imposing a second tax on the foreign corporation's profits, as if they were paid as a dividend to its home office.

The branch profits tax applies a 30 percent tax on the profits of the foreign branch *as if* the profits were distributed to the foreign corporation's home office without regard to whether an actual funds transfer occurs.[22] This tax is imposed in addition to the regular U.S. corporate income tax. The branch profits tax is not imposed, however, if the corporation reinvests its after-tax profit in the U.S. In that case, the branch profits tax is postponed until the amount is subsequently withdrawn from the U.S.

To avoid the branch profits tax, most foreign corporations structure their activities in the U.S. through a U.S. subsidiary. The U.S. corporation, even though foreign-owned, is not subject to a branch profits tax. However, a tax will be imposed on the foreign parent when the U.S. subsidiary distributes its earnings as a dividend. Many U.S. income tax treaties do not apply the branch profits tax to foreign corporations engaged in U.S. business activities

[c] Investment Income

U.S. source income that is not effectively connected with a U.S. trade or business is generally taxed at a flat 30-percent rate.[23] The tax is imposed on gross income, so deductions for expenses are not permitted. This tax is collected through withholding at source.[24] The flat rate and withholding rules are designed make the tax very broad and easily administered. A tax treaty may reduce or eliminate the tax rate on investment income.

The 30 percent rate applies to U.S. source *fixed or determinable annual or periodical* (FDAP) income and specific other types of income set forth in the statute. FDAP includes items such as dividends, interest, and royalties. To attract foreign investment, however, Congress has exempted from tax certain kinds of interest earned by foreign persons, including portfolio interest, bank interest, and short-term original issue discount interest. Capital gains that are not effectively connected with a U.S. business generally are exempt from U.S. tax. However, a nonresident alien individual who is present in the U.S. for at least 183 days during the year pays a flat 30 percent tax on U.S.-source capital gains.

---

[22] I.R.C. § 884.

[23] I.R.C. §§ 871, 881.

[24] I.R.C. § 1441.

[d] Income from U.S. Real Property Interests

Rental real property. A real estate activity that constitutes a trade or business is subject to the general rules for taxing effectively connected income described above. In that case, the tax is based on net income, meaning that gross income from the property may be reduced by all allowable expense deductions. Rental activities usually are not considered a trade or business unless the activities and maintenance of the property are regular and continuous, and the owner is involved in advertising for renters, repairing, and similar activities. Merely holding rental property and collecting rent is not sufficient. Similarly, a net lease arrangement that requires the tenant to pay all expenses and pay net rent to the owner is not a U.S. trade or business.

If the real estate activity is not a trade or business, all rental income is taxed at a flat 30 percent rate on the gross income. Consequently, deductions for expenses incurred to maintain the property are not allowed. The tax on gross income is collected by withholding at source. Generally, treaties do not change the manner in which income from local real estate is taxed.

The inability to deduct expenses for maintaining the property creates a significant disadvantage for foreign owners of U.S. real property. To alleviate this problem, the tax law allows the foreign owner an election to treat income from the property as effectively connected with a trade or business. The election allows the foreign owner to determine its income from the property on a net basis, that is, after deducting appropriate expenses, including depreciation. These deductions usually significantly reduce or eliminate the U.S. tax. If a net loss is incurred, however, the excess loss cannot be carried back or carried forward to offset income in other years. The election is irrevocable, and remains in effect for the year of the election and all subsequent years.

[e] Disposition of Interests in Real Property

Dispositions of U.S. real property by non resident aliens are subject to special rules under the *Foreign Investment in Real Property Tax Act* (FIRPTA). Generally, the statute provides that gain or loss from a sale or other disposition of US real property interests (USRPI) by a nonresident alien is treated as effectively connected with a U.S. trade or business, regardless of the actual use of the property. This treatment applies to a sale by a:

- a non-resident alien individual;
- foreign corporation;
- foreign trust;
- domestic partnership which has a foreign partner.

Such treatment also applies to a distribution by a foreign corporation to a shareholder, or a distribution by a domestic or foreign partnership to a partner. Real property includes undeveloped land, buildings, residential dwellings, options on land, and real estate partnerships. It also includes interests in US real property through stock and other equity interests in US corporations that own real property.

A purchaser of a USRPI from a nonresident alien may be required to withhold 10 percent of the proceeds to be applied to the seller's tax on the gain. The IRS may agree to a lower withholding if the tax is expected to be less than 10 percent of the proceeds. A number of exceptions apply to the withholding requirement, including an exemption for a purchaser that acquires the property as a personal residence for a price that does not exceed $300,000.

§ 6.02   Taxation of International Electronic Commerce (E-commerce)

[1]   Determining the Source of Income

The term *electronic commerce* refers to transactions involving the exchange of goods or services between parties using electronic tools and techniques.[25] It includes the purchase of goods over the Internet from web sites all over the world that display wares as pictorial images similar to mail order catalogs. It also includes sales of information in electronic form from on-line data bases or portable CDs that provide access to international books, newspapers, magazines, and statistics, and research materials about a vast array of on topics. Services, such as accounting, consulting, and even health care can be purchased and provided electronically. Videoconferencing can be used for business meetings, medical diagnosis, job interviews, education, and training. Numerous financial services are now available online, including routine banking transactions, and stock market trades.

The growth of e-commerce means that an increasing number of transactions will occur without regard to the nationality or geographic location of the parties. A U.S. retailer can easily purchase inventory over the Internet from a Mexican exporter and then sell the product from its web site to a French end-user. Similarly, a U.S. consulting firm can provide its services to a British firm through electronic data transmissions and videoconferences without either party leaving its home office.

But where and how are these transactions taxable? Tax authorities in many countries are concerned about identifying the parties involved in e-commerce transactions and enforcing their tax laws with respect to parties outside their borders. Many countries worry that their tax bases will substantially decrease if an unregulated, unreported e-commerce network develops outside of the established institutions.

In addressing these issues, the U.S. Treasury suggests that existing tax principles must be adapted to electronic commerce, taking into account that

---

[25] *Selected Tax Policy Implications of Global Electronic Commerce,* November 1996.

it generally operates without regard to national borders. The traditional approaches to cross-border transactions are to tax income based either upon the *residence* of the taxpayer or upon the *source* of the income. The U.S. applies both methods, using residence as the basis for taxing its citizens and residents on their worldwide income, and using source as the basis for taxing non-residents on their income earned in the U.S. Many other jurisdictions, however, only tax income derived from a source within their borders.

In applying the source rules, foreign persons are subject to U.S. tax on income from personal services performed in the United States, and income effectively connected with a U.S. trade or business. The source rules apply a little differently if the foreign person is from a U.S. tax treaty partner. In that case, U.S. taxation occurs if business is conducted through a permanent establishment in the U.S. A permanent establishment usually requires a fixed place of business.

For many e-commerce transactions, however, it may be difficult to determine if a U.S. trade or business or permanent establishment exists. Much e-commerce does not have or require a specific location, but is transacted in electronic circuits called *cyberspace*. A foreign person may conduct numerous and repeated transactions with U.S. customers without physically entering the U.S. Although a trade or business exists, is the business in the U.S. for tax purposes? If the foreign person's activities are akin to soliciting orders in the U.S., it is unlikely that a trade or business is present in the U.S. However, more extensive activities may be considered a U.S. trade or business even if the foreign person is never physically present in the country.

Similar questions arise about whether maintaining or using telecommunications devices, computer servers, or similar equipment in the U.S. constitutes a U.S. business or permanent establishment. Because the location of such equipment usually does not affect the underlying e-commerce transaction, its site may be seen as relatively unimportant in determining whether a fixed place of business exists. Traditionally, a permanent establishment does not exist if U.S. facilities are used solely to store, display, or deliver goods or merchandise.[26] By analogy, electronic servers and transmission apparatus may be comparable to a warehouse or delivery equipment. If the site of electronic apparatus is considered significant, businesses will simply move their equipment to low tax jurisdictions.

A foreign person that does not maintain equipment in the U.S. may conduct transactions through a U.S. Internet or telecommunication service provider. It is possible, but unlikely, that this relationship constitutes an *agency* that will impute a U.S. trade or business, or permanent establishment to the foreign person. An agency typically will not arise when a U.S. company provides a telephone connection or access to a web site for a foreign person. By contrast, a foreign person that provides telecommunications

---

[26] *See* U.S. Model Tax Convention, Article 5, paragraph 4(a); OECD Model Convention, Article 5, paragraph 4(a).

services in the U.S. clearly has a U.S. business and permanent establishment regardless of where the electronic equipment is located.

An important e-commerce tax issue concerns sales of electronically transferred digitized information, such as computer programs, books, music, or pictures. For example, a U.S. person may purchase and download programs or other information from a computer located in a foreign country, perhaps with a right to reproduce additional copies. The issue raised is whether the transaction is comparable to the purchase of one or more copies of a book, or the payment of a royalty for the right to use copyrighted material. Absent a U.S. trade or business or permanent establishment, income a foreign person receives from selling a book in the U.S. is not subject to U.S. tax, while royalty income may be taxable. It is likely that the appropriate tax treatment must be determined on a case by case basis, by reference to how closely the transaction resembles a traditional sale or royalty arrangement that does not involve digitized information.

[2] Compliance Issues

The most difficult emerging e-commerce issues involve tax administration and compliance. The Treasury is particularly concerned about the potential consequences of new forms of *electronic money* that may replace cash, checks, debit cards, and credit cards as the primary form of payment. Electronic money may take the form of a simple *smart card* that can be loaded with a digital equivalent of cash backed by the card issuer. The card can be loaded with digital cash, for example, at an ATM or by downloading to a disk drive over the internet.

Unlike electronic debit or credit cards, which are payment mechanisms in transactions between identified parties, electronic money represents a new digital *token of value* similar to a prepaid telephone card. As such, it is potential method for storing large sums of unaccounted digital cash that can be easily transported and spent without an record of how, and by whom it was used. Unaccounted digital money poses the same compliance issues as the many unreported cash transactions that currently occur. Although a large underground cash economy exists, its potential for tax evasion is limited by the difficulty and danger of carrying large amounts of cash. By allowing large unaccounted amounts of money to move across borders on small cards, electronic money creates a great potential for tax avoidance.

Other compliance issues arise when internet sales occur that do not provide the identity or location of the buyer or seller. Source-based income taxation requires the location of the seller be known, and other forms of tax, such as sales tax or VAT, require knowledge of the buyer's location. In debit or credit card transactions, it is possible, albeit difficult, to trace the identity and location of the parties from the banking records. This may not be possible, however, if payment is in the form of unaccounted electronic money.

Future tax compliance measures may require parties to use *digital signatures* that provide information about the identity and location of parties to an electronic transaction. Similarly, standard *electronic documents* will be developed and required that are verifiable and not readily altered or erased. Other steps may involve electronic vendors that move their operations to countries that do not aggressively enforce tax compliance rules. In such cases, tax authorities may utilize tax treaties or tax information exchange agreements to access records about funds transmission from foreign banks or financial institutions.

§ 6.03 Tax Treaties

[1] General Provisions

In an international transaction, the tax systems of two or more countries may apply to the same income.[27] The tax systems may be based upon fundamentally different legal and economic principles, define terms inconsistently, and operate in very distinct fashions. The complexities and expense of being subject to taxation in multiple tax jurisdictions would obviously inhibit cross border business and investment transactions.

To eliminate the burden of double taxation and coordinate the application of their tax systems, nations frequently enter into formal *tax treaties*. These treaties prevent multiple taxation of the same income by reciprocally reducing the tax imposed on foreign investors. The U.S. agrees to reduce its taxation of income investors from the treaty partner earn in the U.S. (*inbound* transactions), and the treaty partner agrees to reduce its taxation of income U.S. investors earn in that country (*outbound* transactions). Tax treaties do not reduce U.S. taxes on U.S. persons, so that U.S. citizens, residents, and companies are taxed without regard to the treaty. This last treaty rule, called the *saving clause*, responds to the Constitutional provisions that require revenue bills to originate in the House of Representative, while treaties are signed by the President and ratified by the Senate.

[a] Residence Requirements

Generally, the benefits extended to a treaty partner only apply to *residents* of that country, as defined under its domestic law. U.S. law treats a person as a resident for tax purposes if he or she is a U.S. citizen or permanent resident or has a *substantial presence* in the U.S. An individual meets the substantial presence by being in the U.S. for more than 121 days during a year.[28] A company incorporated in the U.S. is considered a resident, although many other countries determine a corporation's residence by reference to where its owners or managers live. It is important to note that a U.S. resident is subject to U.S. tax on its worldwide income.

---

[27] For complete discussion of the tax treaty process, see Berman, *Tax Treaties — Fundamentals*, Practising Law Institute, Tax Law and Estate Planning Course Handbook, 516 PLI/Tax 399.

[28] I.R.C. § 7701(b).

The residency rules may result in a person being considered a resident of both treaty partners. In that case, tax treaties generally provide *tie-breaker* rules that establish residence by reference to specific criteria relating to the person's relationships with each country. For individuals, citizenship ordinarily is the dominant consideration. Corporations often are considered residents of both treaty partners and denied treaty benefits related to residence.

Under most treaties, residence in a treaty partner is not sufficient, by itself, to obtain treaty benefits. To prevent *treaty shopping,* treaties often contain *limitation of benefits* clauses designed to bar treaty benefits to companies that satisfy minimal residency requirements, such as local incorporation, primarily to obtain these benefits. These clauses require a significant nexus with the treaty partner, other than residence, such as domestic ownership and business activities, and local taxation of its income.

[b] Taxation of Income

Generally, a foreign company is subject to tax in a treaty partner if it has a *permanent establishment* in that country.[29] When a permanent establishment exists, the local country applies its regular tax rules and rates to the foreign business. In the absence of a treaty, U.S. tax rules and rates apply to any *trade or business* conducted in the U.S., which is a lower level of activity.

Special lower treaty tax rates apply to various types of income.

- Absent a treaty, the U.S. taxes portfolio income, such as royalties and dividends, at a fairly high rate by withholding 30 percent of gross income. Under most treaties, however, the withholding tax on royalties is eliminated and the tax on dividends reduced to 15 percent (five percent for amounts paid to 10 percent owners of the corporation).

- Real property income generally is taxed at the rate provided by domestic tax law.

- Income a foreign person earns by providing independent personal services is not taxable by a treaty partner unless the service provider maintains a *fixed base* in that country. A fixed base is similar to a permanent establishment. Thus, income from transient services is taxable in the home country. Independent personal services include, among others, services provided by lawyers, accountants, architects, and engineers.

- Employment income generally is taxed in the local jurisdiction, unless the employee is: (1) is present in the local country for no more than 183 days in a year; (2) the foreign employer pays the compensation, and; (3) the compensation is deducted as an expense by a permanent establishment or fixed base in the local country.

---

[29] This provision is generally found in Treaty Article 5.

- The treatment of other types of income not specifically addressed (such as from new kinds of financial transactions) differs from treaty to treaty. The U.S. Model Tax Treaty would tax this income in the residence country, although some recent treaties permit taxation in the source country.

[c] Treaty Foreign Tax Credit

To prevent double taxation of the same income, tax treaties allow U.S. persons a tax credit for income tax paid to the treaty partner. The credit allowed under the treaty is subject to the same basic rules as the foreign tax credit allowed under the Internal Revenue Code with respect to non-treaty foreign taxes. The priority of taxation and the treaty foreign tax credit is allowed under the *three bites at the apple* rule. Prioritization may be required, for example, if a U.S. citizen resides in the treaty partner country and has U.S. source income. That person may be subject to taxation and allowed treaty benefits on its income in the source country and on his or her worldwide income in both countries.

Under the three bites rule, the first jurisdiction allowed to tax (first bite at the apple) is the country that is the source of the income. The treaty partner has the second right to tax it (second bite at the apple) as worldwide income of a resident, less a tax credit for the tax imposed by the source country. The source country may then collect additional tax on its citizen's worldwide income (third bite) if that amount exceeds the treaty partner's second bite tax. No tax credit is required against the third bite tax because the treaty only requires a credit for taxes due under the source of income rules.

[d] Limitation on Treaty Benefits for *Hybrid* Entities

The withholding requirements for foreign investors often are reduced or eliminated by a treaty between the U.S. and a foreign country. Congress enacted I.R.C. Section 894(c) in 1997 to prevent abuse of the lower treaty rates through *hybrid entities*. Generally, a hybrid entity is one that is taxed as a partnership (*i.e.*, as "fiscally transparent") in the U.S. and is taxed as a corporation (*i.e.*, not fiscally transparent) in a foreign jurisdiction.[30] For example, a Canadian company may own a large interest in a U.S. limited liability company taxable as a partnership in the United States, but treated as a subsidiary corporation in Canada. In that case, the U.S. subsidiary of the Canadian company may claim a U.S. tax deduction for an interest payment from the U.S. limited liability company to the Canadian parent, even though the payment is treated as an excludible dividend by the foreign parent for Canadian tax purposes. The tax withheld on the interest payment to the Canadian company would be limited to the reduced U.S.-Canada treaty rate of 10 percent rather than the normal 30-percent rate.[31]

---

[30] Reg. § 1.894-1(d)(1).

[31] *See* HR Rep. No. 220, 105th Cong., 1st Sess. 573 (1997).

A foreign person is not allowed a reduced treaty withholding rate on income derived through an *entity* treated as a partnership in the U.S. if:[32]

(1)   the amount is not included in that person's income under the foreign country's tax law;

(2)   the treaty does not state that the treaty applies to income items derived through a partnership, and;

(3)   the foreign country does not tax the distribution of the income item from the entity to that person.

Regulations under I.R.C. Section 894 clarify how treaty benefits apply to U.S. source income (not effectively connected with the conduct of a U.S. trade or business) of a hybrid entity.[33] The regulations allow reduced treaty rates for U.S. source income only for income "derived by" foreign residents of the treaty jurisdiction. Income is considered derived by an entity[34] that is a resident of a treaty jurisdiction in the following situations:

(1)   The entity is not fiscally transparent with respect to the income under the laws of the entity's jurisdiction.[35] Generally, an entity's jurisdiction is the place where it is organized (although it may be where management and control exits).

(2)   An interest holder in an entity may derive an income item by establishing that the entity is fiscally transparent under the laws of his residence jurisdiction.[36] To claim this treaty benefit, the interest holder itself cannot be fiscally transparent under the laws of its jurisdiction.

(3)   Income paid to a type of entity specifically listed in a treaty as a resident of that treaty jurisdiction is considered derived by a resident of that jurisdiction.[37]

Generally, an entity is *fiscally transparent* only if (1) its interest holders must include income from the entity regardless of whether it is distributed to them, and (2) the character and source of an income item ordinarily is determined as if the interest holder realized the item directly from the same source as the entity.[38] An entity may be fiscally transparent, however, even if its interest holders do not separately account for an income item if that does not result in different tax treatment under the tax laws of the treaty jurisdiction. Fiscal transparency is determined on an item-by-item basis, so that an entity can be fiscally transparent for one type of income, but not for another type.

---

[32] I.R.C. § 894(c)(1).

[33] Reg. § 1.894-1(d)(1), issued in TD 8889 (July 2000). These final regulations apply to items of income paid on or after June 30, 2000. Reg. § 1.894-1(d)(6).

[34] An "entity" is defined as a person treated by the United States or the applicable treaty jurisdiction as other than an individual. Reg. § 1.894-1(d)(3)(i).

[35] Reg. § 1.894-1(d)(3)(ii).

[36] Reg. § 1.894-1(d)(3)(iii).

[37] Reg. § 1.894-1(d)(3)(iii)(B).

[38] Reg. § 1.894-1(d)(3)(ii), (iii).

Example 1:[39] LLCo is a business organization formed under the laws of Country X that has an income tax treaty with the United States. LLCo is treated as a partnership for U.S. tax purposes and also as a partnership under the laws of Country X. That is, LLCo is fiscally transparent under the laws of both jurisdictions. LLCo receives U.S. source royalty income.

Because LLCo is fiscally transparent in its resident jurisdiction, LLCo does not *derive* the royalty income for purposes of the income tax treaty and may not claim treaty tax benefits for the income.

Example 2: Use the same facts as Example (1). LLCo's partners are Apex Corporation, organized in Country Y and Beta Corporation, organized in Country Z. Neither Apex nor Beta are fiscally transparent in their countries of incorporation. Both countries Y and Z have tax treaties with the U.S.

Country Y treats LLCo as a partnership and requires Apex to currently account for its share of LLCo income. Country Z treats LLCo as a corporation and does not require Beta to include its share of LLCo income until actually distributed.

Apex derives its share of the U.S. source royalty income for purposes of the U.S.-Y income tax treaty because LLCo is fiscally transparent under the laws of Country Y. Since Apex itself is not fiscally transparent, it may claim treaty tax benefits for the royalty income.

Beta does not derive its share of the royalty income for treaty purposes because LLCo is not fiscally transparent under the laws of Country Z. Beta may not claim treaty tax benefits for the royalty income.

Domestic reverse hybrid entities. A *domestic reverse hybrid entity* is an entity that is not fiscally transparent under U.S. law but is fiscally transparent under the laws of the jurisdiction of a person claiming reduced withholding rates under a treaty.[40] The regulations provide that treaty benefits may not reduce the tax withheld on U.S. source payments received by a domestic reverse hybrid entity.[41] These benefits also are denied to foreign interest holders of a domestic reverse hybrid entity on income the entity receives from U.S. sources.

The existing regulations do not address the withholding treatment for payments paid by domestic reverse hybrid entities.[42] This issue has been addressed in recent proposed regulations that provide rules governing the character of such payments for treaty purposes and the extent to which the payments are eligible for a reduced rate of U.S. tax under a tax treaty. The proposed rules respond to the Treasury's concern about arrangements used by related parties to manipulate U.S. and foreign entity classification rules to reduce the tax on income paid from the U.S. to related foreign

---

[39] *See* Reg. § 1.894-1(d)(5).

[40] Reg. § 1.894-1(d)(2)(i).

[41] Reg. § 1.894-1(d)(2)(i).

[42] 66 FR 12445 (Feb 2001). This issue was specifically reserved by the regulations issued under I.R.C. § 894 in June 2000. Reg. § 1.894-1(d)(2)(ii).

interest holders.[43] Generally, these rules apply when a domestic entity makes a payment treated as a dividend to a related domestic reverse hybrid entity, and the domestic reverse hybrid entity makes a payment to a foreign interest holder that is both deductible in the U.S., and eligible for reduced treaty withholding rates.[44] The proposed regulations would recharacterize the latter payments as nondeductible dividends rather than deductible expenses and deny treaty withholding rates.

[e] Competent Authorities

Tax treaties are coordinated and implemented through direct communications between the treaty partners' tax officials (*competent authorities*). The competent authorities agree upon the interpretation of the treaty and negotiate on behalf of their residents to ensure that they receive the appropriate treaty benefits. The competent authorities may request and exchange tax information about taxpayers to monitor the treaty's operation and to prevent tax avoidance.

[f] Negotiations

Most U.S. tax treaty negotiations are based upon the terms of a model treaty published by the Treasury Department in 1997. That model is similar to the model treaty promulgated by the Organization for Economic Co-operation and Development (OECD), which is a common pattern for treaties between developed countries. The United Nations has developed a model treaty as a basis for negotiations between developed and developing countries. The UN model generally supports higher taxation by the source country than does the U.S. or OECD models.

U.S. tax treaties are negotiated by the Department of the Treasury under authority delegated by the Department of State. The factors considered in determining whether to negotiate a treaty include:

- Stability of the foreign tax system and government.
- Amount of investment or trade involved.
- Interest expressed by the business community.
- Problems or abuses experienced under other existing treaties.
- Existence of issues that can be resolved through a tax treaty.
- Likelihood of success in negotiations.
- Political or foreign policy reasons to enter into or avoid a treaty.

A completed treaty is signed by the Secretary of State or, as is usually the case, signing is delegated to the Secretary of the Treasury or the U.S. ambassador to the treaty partner. The treaty is then signed by the President, who then submits it to the Senate for its advice and consent to the ratification.

---

[43] Preamble to Proposed Regulations, 66 FR 12445 (Feb. 2001).
[44] Preamble to Proposed Regulations, 66 FR 12445 (Feb. 2001).

Because U.S. treaties must be ratified by the Senate, that body ordinarily participates in the negotiation process. This involves frequent consultations between the Treasury's Office of Tax Policy, which negotiate tax treaties, and Congress' professional tax staffs. After the President signs the treaty, the Congressional Joint Committee on Taxation staff reviews it and provides an explanation of its provisions and impact to the Senate Foreign Relations Committee. That Committee conducts a hearing after which the Senate may ratify, reject, or ask for a modification of the treaty. The Senate also may ratify the treaty with attached conditions, including a *reservation,* which has the effect of a modification, an *understanding*, which is an mandatory interpretation of the treaty text, or a *declaration*, which is a nonbonding comment.

§ 6.04 Transfer Pricing

[1] Transaction Between Related Entities

Transactions between different members of a multinational enterprise are not subject to the same market forces that exist between independent firms. Consequently, the price a member of the multinational group charges for goods or services it provides to another member may not reflect their actual market value. Transactions between group members that operate in different countries often involve price structures designed to take advantage of different tax rates and systems in each country. By using artificial transfer prices in transactions between members of a commonly controlled group, a multinational enterprise may reduce its overall international tax burden.

The goal of the multinational group is to allocate only minimal income to members in high tax jurisdictions and have most of its income realized by members in low tax countries. To illustrate, assume that P company produces widgets in Country X that imposes a 20 percent tax rate and that it sells that product to its subsidiary S in Country Y which has a 30 percent tax rate. If P charges a S $10 per widget and S sells the product for $12, the group realizes a $2 profit per item that is taxable at 30 percent in Country Y. However, if P charges S $12 per widget and S sells at that price, $2 of profit is shifted to Country X and taxed at 20 percent. Similar income shifting would occur if subsidiary S in low-tax country X provided services or licensed intellectual property to P at prices below their market value.

Obviously, many higher tax countries are concerned that such artificial transfer pricing erodes their tax bases. The issue is quite important, given that more than 25 percent of the world's trade in goods and services takes place within multinational groups of related parties. Many in the U.S. maintain that abusive transfer pricing is the reason that U.S. based members of foreign multinational enterprises typically report lower earnings than their U.S. counterparts. A recent U.S. Treasury study estimates that artificial prices for imports to the U.S. results in loss of U.S. tax revenue of nearly $3 billion each year.[45]

It should be noted that the lower U.S. profits reported by multinationals may result from factors other than artificial pricing arrangements. In many situations the price of goods imported to the U.S cannot be artificially raised without a consequent increase in import duties and tax in the exporter's home jurisdiction. Other economic factors may account for elevated prices for imports. For example, executives of the parent company may wish to maximize its profits in order to increase their own performance-based compensation. Executives also may prefer to generate income in their own country to make alternative investments, improve balance sheets, satisfy domestic regulatory requirements, reduce foreign exchange risks, or simply out of nationalistic motives.

Notwithstanding these alternate explanations, many countries, including the U.S., have implemented strong measures to discourage *transfer pricing* arrangements. These measures include complex rules and regulations for determining prices, and severe penalties for noncompliance. To avoid these hurdles, many companies are encouraged to enter into advance pricing agreements with taxing authorities that ensure against subsequent litigation or administrative action.

[2]   General Transfer Pricing Rules

Most transfer pricing rules are designed to assure that the income reported by international companies in a nation's jurisdiction is consistent with economic reality. Generally, these rules allow tax authorities to reallocate income purportedly earned by a member of a multinational group in another country to a member that resides in its own jurisdiction. Similarly, deductions claimed by the group member in their country may be reallocated to a member in another jurisdiction.

The standard applied in reallocating income and deductions between related companies is that inter-group prices should approximate the prices that would be negotiated between unrelated firms. This standard, referred to as the *arm's length principle*, is reflected in U.S. taw law by the provisions of I.R.C. Section 482. Similar provisions have been set forth in the Model Tax Convention of the Organization for Economic Co-operation and Development (OECD), an intergovernmental organization that includes most of the world's industrialized nations.[46]

[a]   Reallocation Under I.R.C. Section 482

I.R.C. Section 482 authorizes the IRS to allocate income, deductions, credits or allowances between commonly controlled organizations, trades,

---

[45] Report on the Application and Administration of Section 482, Office of the Assistants Commissioner (International), (Research & Statistics of Income) and Office of the Associate Chief Counsel (International), April 21, 1999, p. 1-13.

[46] Model Tax Convention, Article 9.

or businesses in order to prevent evasion of taxes or to *clearly reflect income*. The effect is to allow the IRS to re-determine an entity's income for U.S. tax purposes if there has been improper shifting of tax items between that entity and a related party. Although the statute also applies to domestic related entities, its most significant current application is to multinational enterprises. Most tax treaties between the U.S. and foreign countries contain similar provisions for reallocating income between companies residing in the treaty partners.[47]

The operative rules of I.R.C. Section 482 are found in the regulations, which generally provide that a transaction involving related parties clearly reflects income only if it would occur under the same terms between unrelated parties.[48] To ascertain these terms, the regulations allow the IRS to recast the transaction is if it occurred between an uncontrolled person dealing at *arm's length* with another uncontrolled person. To the extent that the income, deductions, or other tax items from the actual transaction differs from the arms' length standard, the IRS may reallocate the items among the parties.

The transfer pricing rules only apply to transactions involving parties that are directly or indirectly owned or *controlled* by the same interests. Obviously, control exists between a parent corporation and its subsidiary, even if exercised by a only by 51 percent ownership majority. However, control may be deemed to exist in many other cases, such as partnerships and joint ventures, where the parties jointly operate to shift income or deductions between tax jurisdictions.[49]

To apply the arm's length standard, the transaction between the commonly controlled parties is measured against a *comparable* transaction between uncontrolled persons. The factors considered to determine if the transactions are comparable include the functions, contractual terms, risks, economic conditions, and nature of the property or services involved.[50] Comparability need not be exact, but the transactions must be similar enough to reliably determine the arm's length standard.

Generally, the regulations indicate that the *best method* under the circumstances must be used to determine the results of a hypothetical arm's length transaction.[51] This means that the in situations where a variety of pricing methods can be used, the parties must apply the method that most reliably approximates an arm's length result.

---

[47] Model U.S. Income Tax Convention, Article 9(1).

[48] The regulations under § 482 were issued in July 1994. T. D. 8552, 1994-2 C.B. 93. *See e.g.*, Reg. § 1.482-1(a)(1).

[49] *See e.g.*, Rev. Rul. 65-142, 1965-1 C.B. 223; *B. Forman Co. v. Commissioner*, 453 F. 2d 1144 (2d Cir. 1972), *cert. denied*, 407 U.S. 934 (1972).

[50] Report on the Application and Administration of Section 482, Office of the Assistants Commissioner (International), (Research & Statistics of Income) and Office of the Associate Chief Counsel (International), April 21, 1999, pp. 2-8.

[51] Reg. § 1.482-1(c)(1).

A number of complex, special rules, methods, and safe harbors apply in calculating the arms' length result in a specific transactions. These include sales of tangible goods and transfers of intangible assets. The basic approach of these special rules is to use financial analysis, based upon sophisticated economic models, to compute the *net income* (rather than sales price) expected from a specific transaction or operation if conducted at arms' length.

[b] Transfers of Tangible Property

For transfers of *tangible property,* the regulations allow the result of an arm's length transfer to be determined under any of five specified methods:[52]

(1)   The **comparable uncontrolled price** (CUP) method. In determining whether the controlled and uncontrolled transactions are comparable factors such as volume, market, geography, trademarks, and most importantly, similarity of products, are taken into account. The IRS generally considers this the most reliable method, if reasonably comparable transactions are available.

(2)   The **resale price** method. This method compares the gross profit margins earned in the controlled and uncontrolled transactions. This method usually is not applied if the controlled taxpayer increases the value of the goods by adding its own intangibles, such as a trademark, to increase the value of the goods.

(3)   The **cost plus** method. This method compares the gross profit markup in the controlled and uncontrolled transactions. It focuses on the value of the production functions, so that comparability does not depend on the similarity of the products being produced.

(4)   The **comparable profits** method. This method compares the operating profit earned in the controlled and uncontrolled transactions. Comparable profit level indicators include the ratios of operating profit to operating assets, operating profit to sales, and gross profit to operating expenses. Generally, the analysis must be made over a three-year period.

(5)   The **profit split** method. This method is applied using one of two alternative approaches, both of which are designed to compare how combined operating profit or loss earned in the controlled transaction is allocated between the parties with the allocation that would occur if the transaction was uncontrolled.

[c] Transfers of Intangibles

The regulations governing intangibles reflect a 1986 amendment to I.R.C. Section 482, stating that income from the transfer of an intangible, by sale

---

[52] Reg. § 1.482-3. Any unspecified *best method* also may be used. Reg. § 1.482-3(e).

or license, must be "commensurate with the income attributable to the intangible." This language ensures that multinational groups in high technology industries, such as software or pharmaceuticals, do not transfer the results of their research to foreign subsidiaries in return for an artificially low royalty. The IRS has interpreted the amendment to authorize it to keep open licensing agreements and make periodic adjustments to the royalties in subsequent years, even if the initial royalty rate satisfied the arms' length standard. This interpretation has been criticized by many U.S. multinationals and trading partners.

For transfers of intangible property, the regulations allow the result of an arm's length transfer to be determined under the comparable profit method or the profit split methods described above and a special *comparable uncontrolled transaction* (CUT) method that is considered most reliable.[53] Factors considered in determining whether a transaction is comparable include the presence of exclusive or nonexclusive rights, the stage of development, the duration of the license and, most importantly, the similarity of the comparable intangible properties. Intangibles may be comparable if they are both used in similar products or processes and in the same general industry or market, and have similar profit potential.

[d] Penalties and Records

A *substantial valuation misstatement* penalty may be imposed on taxpayers that do not comply with the transfer pricing rules. The penalty is 20 percent of the understatement of tax attributable to the misstatement.[54] The penalty for a "gross" valuation misstatement, however, is 40 percent of the tax understatement. This penalty applies if the net transfer price adjustment for the tax year exceeds either $5 million or 10 percent of the taxpayer's gross receipts. These penalties may be avoided if the taxpayer shows that none of the methods in the regulations could be used and that the method applied was likely to be correct.[55]

Foreign records. An IRS audit relating to a U.S. company's transfer pricing issues is likely to require examination of records of a related company located in a foreign country. To ensure access to such records, I.R.C. Section 6038A imposes reporting, record-keeping, and document production requirements on foreign-based groups and their 25 percent or greater U.S. affiliates. I.R.C. Section 6038C imposes similar requirements on foreign corporations engaged in a U.S. trade or business without regard to the percentage of foreign ownership.

The statute also grants the IRS authority to issue summonses regarding related-party transactions. If the foreign company does not accept or comply with the summons, the IRS may unilaterally determine, without review,

---

[53] Reg. § 1.482-4. Any unspecified *best method* also may be used. Reg. § 1.482-4(d).

[54] I.R.C. § 6662.

[55] I.R.C. § 6662(e)(3)(B)(ii).

the proper allocation deductions and costs to the domestic corporation.[56] A similar provision under I.R.C. Section 982 allows the IRS to issue formal requests for foreign documents. A taxpayer that does not comply with the request, without reasonable cause, may be barred from introducing the document in subsequent tax litigation. Because extra time may be required to obtain foreign-based documents, a number of statutory provisions extend the statute of limitations in transfer pricing cases.

Customs value sets tax value. I.R.C. Section 1059A prevents related parties from asserting a low value for imported goods for tariff purposes and a higher value for tax purposes. The statute provides that the value of goods used for purposes of determining taxable income cannot exceed the value declared for customs purposes when the goods were imported.

[e] Advance Pricing Agreements (APA)

To simplify transfer pricing issues and prevent lengthy administrative, judicial, and treaty dispute proceedings, the IRS has created an Advance Pricing Agreement (APA) process.[57] An APA is an advance agreement between the taxpayer, IRS, and foreign tax authority to establish an approved transfer pricing method. The IRS will consider the transfer pricing method agreed to in the APA as satisfying the arm's length standard. Therefore, it will only audit a transactions covered by the APA to determine if: (1) the taxpayer's representations relating to the APA were accurate; (2) the assumptions underlying the APA remain valid; (3) the pricing methodology in the APA has been applied correctly; and, (4) the results contemplated in the APA are being achieved. An APA may be restricted to specified years, affiliates, and intercompany transactions.

The APA focuses on establishing an appropriate transfer pricing methodology, not on a specific tax result. The pricing method must be supported by an economic analysis, and information about the applicants transfer prices for current and prior years. The economic analysis usually describes the business and market covered by the agreement, and identifies comparable uncontrolled businesses similar to the taxpayer's. The APA process often involves experts such as economists, statisticians, and engineers.

[3] OECD Rules

The *Organization for Economic Co-operation and Development* (OECD), which comprises most of the world's principal industrialized nations, has established extensive transfer pricing guidelines that are quite similar to the U.S. rules under I.R.C. Section 482. Although the OECD guidelines do not have the force of law, they significantly influence the tax authorities of the OECD members as well as a number of non-members. Unlike the

---

[56] I.R.C. § 6038A(e)(3). *See ASAT, Inc. v. Commissioner*, 108 T.C. 147 (1997) (upholding an IRS penalty determination of claimed related party costs and deductions as the result of the taxpayer's noncompliance with I.R.C. § 6038A).

[57] The procedures for obtaining an APA are set forth in Rev. Proc. 96-53, 1996-2 C.B. 375

U.S., many countries lack their own transfer pricing rules and rely on the OECD guidelines. The activities of the OECD have encouraged communication and cooperation between national tax authorities, and thereby internationalized the transfer price review of many multinational enterprises.

Although the OECD guidelines adopt many of the principles expressed under the I.R.C. Section 482 rules, important differences exist. To the extent that the U.S. and OECD rules are inconsistent, taxpayers risk multiple taxation of the same income and substantial penalties. Thus, careful comparison of the U.S. statutory rules and OECD guidelines is imperative. With respect to U.S. treaty partner, the transfer pricing standards are typically set forth in the treaty.

The OECD guidelines use an arm's length standard that is quite similar to the I.R.C. Section 482 rule. This standard is expressed in the OECD Model Tax Convention as follows:

> *Where conditions are made or imposed between the two enterprises in their commercial or financial relations which differ from those which would be made between independent enterprises, then any profits which would, but for those conditions, have accrued to one of the enterprises, but, by reason of those conditions, have not so accrued, may be included in the profits of that enterprise and taxed accordingly.*

A similar provision is provided in nearly all U.S. bi-lateral tax treaties.[58]

---

[58] *See* Article 9 of Model U.S. Income Tax Treaty.

INDEX

[References are to page numbers.]

[References are to page numbers.]

[References are to page numbers.]

M

[References are to page numbers.]

[References are to page numbers.]

[References are to page numbers.]

W